D1064540

RELIGION, STATE, AND SOCIETY IN MODERN BRITAIN

A PWPA Book

RELIGION, STATE, AND SOCIETY
IN MODERN BRITAIN

Edited by
Paul Badham

Texts and Studies in Religion
Volume 43

The Edwin Mellen Press
Lewiston/Queenston/Lampeter

Library of Congress Cataloging-in-Publication Data

Religion, state, and society in modern Britain / edited by Paul
Badham.
   p. cm. -- (Texts and studies in religion ; v. 43)
   Includes bibliographical references.
   ISBN 0-88946-832-X
   1. Great Britain--Religion--20th century. I. Badham, Paul.
II. Series: Texts and studies in religion ; 43.
BR759.R46 1989
291'.0941--dc20   89-36710
                                         CIP

> This is volume 43 in the continuing series
> Texts and Studies in Religion
> Volume 43 ISBN 0-88946-832-X
> TSR Series ISBN 0-88946-976-8

A CIP catalog record for this book
is available from the British Library.

A Professors World Peace Academy Book
The Professors World Peace Academy (PWPA) is an international association
of professors, scholars and academics from diverse backgrounds, devoted to
issues concerning world peace. PWPA sustains a program of conferences and
publications on topics in peace studies, area and cultural studies, national and
international development, education, economics and international relations.

Copyright © 1989 The Edwin Mellen Press

The Edwin Mellen Press   The Edwin Mellen Press
Box 450   Box 67
Lewiston, New York   Queenston, Ontario
USA 14092   CANADA L0S 1L0

The Edwin Mellen Press, Ltd.
Lampeter, Dyfed, Wales
UNITED KINGDOM SA48 7DY

Printed in the United States of America

RELIGION, STATE, AND SOCIETY
IN MODERN BRITAIN

TABLE OF CONTENTS

ACKNOWLEDGEMENTS

This book would not have been possible but for a decision by the United Kingdom Branch of the Professors World Peace Academy to convene a conference on the role of religion in contemporary British society. This conference took place in Jersey in April 1986 and was a tremendously stimulating event for all concerned. Ten of the chapters of this book began life as papers presented on that occasion. We gratefully acknowledge the debt we owe to the PWPA for this initiative, to its secretary David Hanna for making all the practical arrangements for us, and to the International Cultural Foundation for providing the finances necessary to make the conference possible.

We are also grateful to the ten contributors approached subsequent to the Conference for agreeing to provide additional chapters so that the planned book could provide even wider coverage of Religion State and Society in Modern Britain.

Dr. Jorgen Nielsen wishes to thank the Association pour l'Avancement des Sciences Islamiques for an invitation to present an earlier draft of his chapter at a Colloquium on "Islam in Europe Today" held in the Collège de France in Paris. This earlier draft was published in *Research Papers : Muslims in Europe,* no. 21, March 1984.

Dr George Moyser wishes gratefully to acknowledge the financial support of the British Economic and Social Research Council under Grant No E0022003 to himself and Geraint Parry and the research assistance of Neil Day and Kurshida Mirza.

Dr. Eileen Barker would like to thank the Social Science Research Council of Great Britain and the Nuffield Foundation for the grants which made possible the research on which her chapter is based.

RELIGION STATE AND SOCIETY IN MODERN BRITAIN

INTRODUCTION

PAUL BADHAM

What is the condition of religion in contemporary Britain, and what part does it play modern society? This volume of essays seeks to find answers to these questions. It does so by looking at each of the religious groups in modern Britain and exploring some facets of their life and work. It then seeks to gain an overview of the role of religion in society.

The book opens with a chapter on the Church of England by Gerald Parsons. He argues that the traditional comprehensiveness and toleration of the Church of England has been broadened still further in the twentieth century so that within a single Church can be found a bewildering range of mutually incompatible opinions across the whole spectrum of belief and practice. He explores the difficulties the Church faces in coming to terms with its *de facto* pluralism and notes the consequential "re-fighting of old doctrinal controversies every generation or so." Parsons believes that the Church should be more open in its acknowledgement of the reality of pluralism, and he is not happy with the way successive doctrinal commissions have tended to gloss over the fundamental differences in worldview which can be found within this single Church.

Paul Badham goes further with this critique, and argues that some trends in the Church of England amount not simply to reinterpretation of historic beliefs, but their repudiation. He is thinking here not of peripheral issues, like belief in the Virgin Birth, but central beliefs about the reality of God or of a future life. He highlights this by an exploration of the theological priorities of the report *Faith in the City*. He notes that while much of the substance of the report is a commendable reaffirmation of the prophetic witness of Biblical Christianity, its explicit theological teaching represents an almost total secularisation of Christian thought.

Turning from England to Wales, William Price shows that the popular image of Wales as a land of chapels and song, dominated by the non-conformist conscience, no longer corresponds to reality. The twentieth century has witnessed a dramatic collapse in the influence of the Christian Churches in Welsh society, partly parallel to and partly brought about by, the relative collapse of the Welsh language, (now spoken by only 19% of the population of the Principality). Moreover, to the extent that a framework of religious life survives, it is now largely represented not by non-conformity, but by a continuing, though disestablished, Anglican presence and by the expansion of Roman Catholicism.

In Scotland, too, the Christian Churches are on the defensive. The Kirk, which once seemed the embodiment of the Scottish nation is now second to the Roman Catholic Church in terms of regularly worshipping members, though neither can claim the attendance of much more than 7% of the population. Peter Bisset believes that attendance figures do not give a full picture, in that the heritage of Scottish Presbyterianism continues to influence many who still identify with her though they no longer worship with her. Yet he wonders how long such influence will continue, and whether any way can be found to reverse the tendency towards decline.

Northern Ireland contrasts with all other areas of modern Britain in that it remains a staunchly Christian, God-fearing and worshipping country. But is that any advertisement for the claims of Christ when a "religious war" appears to be taking place between the two Christian communities there? Many scholars have argued that the terms "Catholic" and "Protestant" are only convenient "labels" for two very different communities. But

Bill McSweeney disputes such claims and argues that the religious dimension of the dispute cannot be interpreted away. For on both sides, but particularly on the ultra-Protestant one, there are good grounds for seeing religious conviction as an essential factor in the ongoing dispute.

The story of the Roman Catholic Church in England and Wales since the Second World War is one of change, but not decay. Until recently their experience was of significant advance, and though there has been some decline more recently, the Catholic Church is now the majority Church in Britain if attendance figures alone are considered. Michael Hornsby-Smith shows that since the fifties the Roman Catholics have shown significant upward social mobility and can no longer be regarded as a characteristically working-class community. He also argues that the formerly distinctive sub-culture of English Catholicism has waned, and that the Catholic community feels more integrated in the life of the wider society. Hornsby-Smith also details the impact of the Second Vatican Council, and of a new spirit of questioning on the ethos of English Catholicism, leading to a much greater level of lay involvement in worship and to a greater readiness for ordinary Catholic men and women to decide for themselves on issues of personal morality such as the practice of birth-control, or a readiness to marry outside the Catholic community.

The Free Churches have suffered the fastest and deepest decline of any Churches in modern Britain, but David Thompson does not dwell on this oft-told story. Instead he seeks to characterise some of the changes in the non-conformist ethos which have contributed to the present situation. One is the upward mobility of Free Church members which has sometimes been accompanied by "leakage" into Anglicanism through the ethos of Public Schools or Oxbridge. Another is the extent to which voluntary work initiated by the Free Churches has been taken over by the State or local authorities, and a third is the displacement by the Labour party of the old Liberal party with which traditional non-conformity so strongly identified. Other issues discussed by Thompson are the question of a Free, rather than a specifically denominational, identity in contexts where chaplaincy service, town planning, or media opportunity, presuppose a tripartite division of Christendom into Anglican, Roman and Free, and look for a Free Church presence. He also considers the rationale of a continuing emphasis on independence in a context where the Church of England has ceased, either to perceive itself or to be perceived, as an organ of the state.

But not all Free Churches are in decline. Iain MacRobert draws attention to the dramatic growth of new black-led Pentecostal Churches in Britain and speculates whether this will be the dominant form of Christianity in the next century. From his vivid and well-documented description of their life, one gains a picture of vibrant, experience-based living and expanding Churches, but with a fundamentalist and puritanical strain which may alarm a liberal reader.

The dynamism of Black Christianity stands in stark contrast with the institutionalised apathy of the folk-religion of the English people described by Edward Bailey. He writes of the believing but uninvolved "Christians" who ask the Churches for baptism, marriage and burial, but at other times generally keep their distance. Yet Bailey believes that it is wrong to dismiss such requests as of no account, for genuine conviction of the worthwhileness of "Christianity" and the need for a religious and ethical dimension to life often lie behind the wish for appropriate ritual to mark the great moments of human life. And the influence of the Churches and of the teaching of Christ owes much to the wider penumbra of interest and attachment so often looked down on as "folk-religion".

If folk-religion is at home in English society the sects are not. In the next chapter, Bryan Wilson probes the tensions which arise between sects and the wider society, especially in the many areas where particular sects diverge from the "accepted" values of the surrounding culture. Such disputes can focus on health as when a Christian Scientist spurns medicine, or a Jehovah's Witness forbids a blood transfusion to a dying child. Other problems can arise when sects discourage higher education, or do not permit their children to participate in school outings or parties, or when a sect forbids members to join trade-unions or serve in the armed forces. Concern often surfaces when sects make converts and the converts abandon long cherished career plans and embark on a new life of total commitment and dedication, often eschewing their former way of life and breaking with friends and relatives associated with that past. Yet Wilson shows that, in general, the sects encourage patterns of behaviour which our society professes to respect and he urges that they continue to be extended that toleration which history has won for the non-conforming groups of earlier ages.

This plea is taken up by Eileen Barker in a chapter explicitly concerned with the "New Religious Movements" which have entered Britain since the Second World War. Like other new religions before them they have been strongly criticised from many quarters, though as the author points out such verbal attacks are very different from the physical torture and martyrdom which would have been their fate in earlier less pluralist societies! This does not excuse the failure to treat these movements with the courtesies we extend to longer established groups but it does place such issues in context. Dr. Barker's chapter focuses on the Unification Church as the main subject of her detailed research, but she also considers the problems faced by other comparable groups.

Most books addressing the question of religious observance in contemporary Britain focus on the various Christian Churches. But this is to ignore the fact that for centuries Britain has hosted people of other faiths, and that in many areas of our major cities these are now the dominant religious presence. The longest established non-Christian religion in Britain is of course the Jewish faith. Rabbi Dan Cohn-Sherbok explores its place and role in our society. He gives a valuable overview of the 450,000 Jewish presence and the various organisations of the Jewish community. But the main thrust of his paper is to challenge his co-religionists to show more concern for other immigrant groups who have entered our society more recently. They could greatly benefit from a Jewish response which was faithful to the prophetic and rabbinic concern for the poor which ought to characterise a living Jewish community.

The Islamic faith, with over a million members in Britain, is clearly of great and growing significance to any appraisal of religion in contemporary society. Jorgen Nielsen describes how this community came into being and the steps it has taken in recent years to seek to safeguard and develop its religious life as Muslim immigrants came to understand themselves as permanent citizens of Britain. Hence the nine mosques of 1960 have become the 329 mosques of 1985, and this looks like just the beginning of steps to ensure adequate provision for nurture in their historic faith.

Hinduism also is now planting its roots deep in British society. One difficulty it faces however is that many who share this faith have diverse understandings of it, and also come from a variety of ethnic, cultural and linguistic backgrounds. Hence, separation on ethnic grounds is a common feature of Hindu society, and this is accentuated by distinctions made on the grounds of caste and kinship. Kim Knott points out further that Hinduism as a living religion often differs significantly from the literary Hindu philosophies described by western textbooks, and that to understand Hinduism one must first understand the pluralism and complexity of Hindu life and thought.

Sikhism presents a clearer picture and Owen Cole describes succinctly the history and thought of this movement which he estimates enjoys the allegiance of 400,000 British citizens. As with Hinduism and Islam there has been a notable revival of concern for religion within the community, as it came to psychological recognition of the permanency of its settlement, and the role of religion in its self-identity.

Buddhism differs from the other religions which have taken root in Britain this century in that Buddhism enjoys the support of relatively small immigrant communities. On the other hand, unlike the other religions, it appears to catch the imagination of many young western people and claims to be the fastest growing religion in Britain at the present time. Deirdre Green explores the reasons for this appeal, but voices a concern lest in adapting itself too readily to the thought-forms of the modern west some vital elements of Buddhist thinking might be being overlooked.

Looking at the overall religious scene in Britain we see therefore in the Christian churches a steady decline in membership and appeal as well as the danger of secularisation from within. This tendency is least pronounced in Roman Catholicism where decline is a more recent phenomenon, and we also note that Northern Ireland is quite unlike the rest of Britain in the continuing vitality of its traditional religious base. The decline in the mainstream churches in the rest of Britain, however, is contrasted with the vitality of the Pentecostal churches, as well as of some sects and New

Religious Movements, though in numerical terms these in no sense compensate for numerical loss in the traditional Churches. Among the other religions, Judaism faces many of the same problems as Christianity, but in Muslim, Hindu, and Sikh communities there is a strong movement to consolidate the religious identity of the immigrant communities. Buddhism is in a category of its own as a missionary non-Christian religion winning the allegiance of many western minds but perhaps in the process calling into question aspects of its own identity.

But despite the decline in Christianity it remains the religion with the greatest influence in the main-stream of British life. This will undoubtedly change as the immigrant communities increasingly participate in the corporate life of the wider community but it remains the situation at present. We therefore explore the impact of Christian teaching on three areas of modern life, starting with a discussion by Myrtle Langley on attitudes to women in the British churches. This discusses the picture of ideal womanhood portrayed in the Catholic tradition, and contrasts that with the growing emphasis on the equality of women in recent centuries, which she sees supported not only by enlightenment thought but also by the dissenting Christian tradition and by the experiences of women in the mission field. The central thrust of her paper however is the question of women in the ministry of the Christian churches where she surveys the current position in each of the major denominations and perceptively discusses the arguments for and against women's ordination.

The contribution of the churches to the development of the "permissive" society is considered by Christie Davies with reference to the legislation of the 1960's which liberalised the laws relating to abortion and divorce, legalised homosexuality and abolished capital punishment. He notes that in principle, though not always in detail, these reforms were supported by non-Roman Catholic Christian opinion and he exemplifies this by discussing the arguments used by spokesmen for the Established church in the debates abolishing capital punishment and legalising homosexuality.

This is followed by a chapter by George Moyser exploring the relationship between religion and political involvement in Britain. This provides a mass of valuable data on the present place of religion in British society and the impact this has on people's political stance. Ironically he shows that while church leadership often takes a radical line, this does not in any way represent the thinking of the ordinary member of the church for whom the leadership is speaking!

The book concludes with a chapter by Ninian Smart challenging the continuance of an Anglican or even of a Christian "establishment" in a society as religiously pluralist as modern Britain has become. He believes that establishment, even in the watered-down form in which it now exists, encourages a false consciousness in the Churches, and in numerous minor ways tends to deny a full sense of belonging to all those who do not participate in the Christian tradition.

CHAPTER I

THE RISE OF RELIGIOUS PLURALISM
IN THE CHURCH OF ENGLAND

GERALD PARSONS

"From the beginning the Church of England has tried to be *comprehensive*." So observed Stephen Neill in a famous, if now rather dated, review and exposition of the nature of Anglicanism. Neill went on to acknowledge that, especially since the nineteenth century, the comprehensiveness of Anglicanism has been one in which the differences in belief and practice have been so great that it has often seemed impossible that such divergent attitudes should be able to remain within a single communion. In explanation and defence of this phenomenon, and of the conflicts within Anglicanism which inevitably ensue from it, Neill offered the classic Anglican apology: "that tensions may be regarded not as a weakness, but as a price that has to be paid for the privilege of a particular vocation."[1] The particular vocation in question is that of holding together understandings of Christian truth which are only held separately in other churches, and thereby acting as a bridge between the separated parts of the whole church and an instrument for the restoration of Christian unity. Neill quotes with approval the judgement of the 1948 Lambeth Conference Report of the

Committee on the Unity of the Church: "If at the present time one view were to prevail to the exclusion of all others, we should be delivered from our tensions, but only at the price of missing our opportunity and our vocation."[2]

This is the characteristic self-justification of modern Anglicanism in general and of the modern Church of England in particular: the Church of England portrayed and justified as the *via media*, a church catholic yet reformed standing between the major divisions of western Christendom and in which apparent contradictions are held in often costly tension, thereby demonstrating the many-sided complexity of Christian experience and the complementary nature of many of the aspects of Christian belief elsewhere held in isolation. It is an interpretation of the nature of the Church of England which still commands wide support.

In recent years, however, an alternative interpretation of the variety within the modern Church of England has also become well established. In 1976, the then current Doctrine Commission of the Church of England published a report entitled *Christian Believing* and subtitled "The Nature of the Christian Faith and its Expression in Holy Scripture and Creeds." After identifying four main, and divergent, approaches to the use of creeds in the modern Church of England, the Report observed that,

> ...the issues here - on the one hand loyalty to the formulas of the church and obedience to received truth, on the other adventurous exploration and the Church's engagement with the contemporary world - appear to point in very different directions and to reflect different conceptions of the nature of religious truth. *It is, to say the least, very difficult to explain divergencies of this fundamental kind merely as complementary aspects of the many-sided wisdom of God.*[3]

The Report goes on to repeat the traditional Anglican argument that the tension of such divergence must be endured and that everything possible should be done to make the tension creative by facilitating dialogue and cross-fertilization of ideas and insight. To this extent the Report remains in continuity with the traditional position by acknowledging that the modern Church of England in fact presents a *choice of doctrines*, not merely a doctrinal comprehensiveness of such breadth that radical divergence can be accomodated within a single but multi-faceted position. Almost a decade later we find Anthony Dyson forcefully making the same point about the

Church of England but now also placing it within the wider context of the position of religion as a whole in contemporary Britain:

> It is imperative that we admit openly and unambiguously that there is a great diversity of belief in the churches. And the churches are themselves just one element in a religiously diverse society in Britain. No good will come of pretending that Christians are really one in belief, but just express their shared beliefs a little differently. In particular, in the Church of England there is, as a matter of fact, a wide scale of types of biblical and doctrinal interpretation, ranging from the very literal to the very symbolic.[4]

One can hardly argue with Dyson's statement. As Paul Avis has observed recently, "Since *Essays and Reviews*, (1860) which first signalled the fact that the methods of German biblical criticism had penetrated the Church of England, there has been a steady broadening of permitted theological opinion until we have reached the point where there exists a diversity of fundamental Christian worldviews within a single church."[5] In 1976 *Christian Believing* characterized the four main approaches to the creeds as: the view that creeds are a norm and adherence to them essential; the desire to identify with the general faith of the Church, expressed in creeds, whilst maintaining reservations about specific clauses; an allegiance to the ongoing Church rather than to past beliefs which are inevitably relative to the culture of their own times and hence cannot be either affirmed or denied; and a commitment to God and to Jesus which was above any provisional assent to credal propositions.[6]

It was a good summary, but as Avis' remark above suggests, the actual "choice of doctrines" is in practice even wider, running from a biblically based conservative evangelicalism (which often verges on fundamentalism) or a credal conservatism of a catholic variety (which is often scarcely less fundamentalist than its evangelical counterpart), through a spectrum of moderately conservative and moderately critical theological positions, to a further variety of liberal and radical theologies which themselves range from a self-conscious development of the old Broad Church-Modernist tradition (seeking to reform and reinterpret the understanding of traditional belief whilst retaining its substance) to a radicalism which frankly rejects much of the received tradition as no longer intellectually credible. In addition to such a spectrum of theologies, there is a powerful charismatic movement which cuts across conventional conservative positions (both forging new alliances and causing new divisions as it does so) and an increasingly influential movement advocating a more contextual, grass roots theology, rooted in local experience and setting little store by the traditional intellectual theological tradition. It is stretching credulity beyond reasonable limits to maintain that such a diversity is an expression of comprehensiveness understood in terms of complementarity. Such diversity is not an expression of multi-faceted complementarity. It is an example of pluralism. The contemporary Church of England contains a number of different Anglicanisms each of them derived from one or other (or several) of the overall bundle of traditions and ways of life which constitute the historical legacy of the Church of England. These Anglicanisms cross-relate and cross-fertilize, often in surprising ways, but they are simply not susceptible to arrangement in a unified, uncontradictory structure. Even a critic of the current diversity within the Church of England such as Stephen Sykes recognises the reality of the pluralism and, for example, welcomes the clarity with which *Christian Believing* set out the "choice of doctrines" available in the contemporary Church of England because it thereby exposed, in Sykes' view, a "bogus theory of comprehensiveness" which had for too long obscured the parlous state of Anglican doctrine and thereby compromised the very integrity of the Church of England.[7]

As Sykes' polemic against a "bogus" theory of comprehensiveness implies, the doctrinal pluralism of the Church of England is not a new development. Its origins lie at least as far back as the mid-nineteenth-century and, arguably, by the beginning of the twentieth century doctrinal pluralism was already a reality within the Church of England. The new feature of the last quarter of a century is that both the reality and the extent of pluralism have become obvious and inescapable. Nor, moreover, is the pluralism of the contemporary Church of England merely a matter of doctrine and theology, although in common with virtually every major Christian denomination doctrinal diversity occupies a prominent place on the Church of England's agenda of concerns precisely because of the emergence in modern Christianity of a fundamental division between theological liberals and theological conservatives.

Beyond doctrine alone, however, the pluralism of the contemporary Church of England is also manifested in other ways. In worship and liturgy for example the long process of liturgical revision finally issued, in 1980, in the publication of the *Alternative Service Book*. The ASB is, in some ways, an excellent example of the pluralism of the modern Church of England, for it embodies, not a single eucharistic rite, but a set of alternatives, and at many points in the liturgy offers a choice of wordings and expressions. Moreover the ASB does not simply replace the 1662 Prayer Book. The Prayer Book remains available for use, although, of course, there are many who insist that without greater "protection" it will in time simply disappear from the church's worship.

The variety and pluralism of worship in the contemporary Church of England is not, however, merely (perhaps not even primarily) a matter of the licensed pluralism of the ASB and the Prayer Book. There continues in the contemporary Church of England to be available a remarkable range of styles and patterns of worship. It is true that the impact of the Liturgical Movement in general, and of the Parish and People Movement in particular, have resulted in a Church of England in which the Sunday morning Parish Communion is probably the most common act of worship. But the variety of particular styles and patterns persists: the Church of England remains a church in which, according to one's taste, inclination and convictions, one may choose to attend Holy Communion or Mass; make the Parish Communion or Matins or Evensong the focus of one's personal devotional life; attend Benediction and go to Confession; and worship amidst incense, elaborate vestments, processions and ceremony or amidst moderate and modern catholic ceremony or in a church using patently protestant surplice and stole alone. Whilst doctrine and the limits of doctrinal pluralism continue to be sources of sharp controversy in the contemporary Church of England, liturgy and worship - in general - now excite less bitter and certainly less protracted confrontations (the ongoing arguments over the Prayer Book notwithstanding). The less bitter and sustained controversies are, however,

6

evidence of a well-established liturgical and devotional pluralism, not a uniformity of worship.

Last but not least, the contemporary Church of England is pluralist in its approaches to ethics and to social and political issues. The attention of this essay will focus predominantly upon doctrinal, theological and liturgical issues because the aim of the essay is to demonstrate the rise of a specifically *religious* pluralism in the Church of England. The precise relationship (or relationships) between the rise of *religious* pluralism in the Church of England and the parallel emergence of a moral, social and political pluralism is without doubt one worthy of careful examination, but it lies beyond the scope of the present essay. What must be noted here, however, is the fact that the modern Church of England has also become increasingly pluralist in its approach to moral, ethical, social and political issues.

In matters of personal morality - questions of sexual morality for example such as contraception, sex before marriage, homosexuality, or the possibility of abortion, the contemporary Church of England displays an openness of options barely thinkable a quarter of a century ago and unthinkable half a century ago. There has been a shift in the moral and ethical thinking of the Church in general (parallel to similar shifts in other churches over the same period) from a traditional and static approach based upon moral certainties derived from the bible, tradition and revelation, to a more dynamic, relative and situational approach. But it is important to note that the shift is not an exclusive one. The more traditional and conservative moral and ethical attitudes still have their supporters, who are frequently active and vocal in their championing of a "traditional" morality - both within the Church and in public debate. The characteristic stance of the Church of England has tended to be that outlined by Giles Ecclestone in a recent essay on "The General Synod and Politics." The Synod, he suggests, has shown wisdom in identifying issues where the Church of England should contribute to public debate but not press the issues to a conclusion. He takes as his example the 1981 debate on homosexual rights in which the Synod refused to recognise homosexual relationships as of equal validity with heterosexual ones, but also refused to condemn homosexual relationships. To the critic of the Church of England this will appear simply as evasion and fence-sitting.

To the more sympathetic observer it will appear - as Ecclestone suggests - as an example of an increasingly prevalent stance on the part of the Church of England in respect of social ethics whereby the issue is left open and a *de facto* pluralistic position adopted, not on grounds of indifference but out of respect for the diversity of relevant testimonies and experience.[8]

Something similar, but certainly not identical, has occurred in respect of the political stance(s) and role(s) of the Church of England. In the collection of essays on *The Church and Politics Today*, of which Ecclestone's essay is a part, it becomes abundantly clear that, whilst there is much that we simply do not yet know about the subtleties of the political orientations and configurations of the membership, lay and clerical, of the Church of England, confident generalizations about the politics of the established church are likely to prove untenable - whether the generalization is of the old-fashioned "the Church of England is the Tory party at prayer" type, or of the newer type which envisages either a steady drift left-wards by a church leadership and bureaucracy infatuated with fashionable and progressive secular opinions, or a soft-centered drift into the middle-of-the-road C of E as the equally middle-of-the-road SDP at prayer. The reality is a good deal more complex than the customary stereotypes allow,[9] and is further complicated by the fact that *political* liberalism and conservatism are by no means automatic concomitants of *theological* liberalism and conservatism. From whichever direction one approaches the contemporary Church of England, doctrinal, liturgical, moral or political, the characteristic most likely to strike one is the plurality, the choice of options, available within the institution. The rest of this essay will examine the ways in which the specifically religious aspects of this pluralism arose.

The Church of England has indeed, from the beginning, tried to be comprehensive. It has never been a monolithic institution and has always encompassed variation and shades of opinion. The Elizabethan Settlement was certainly intended to establish a framework in which both catholic and protestant theological convictions could co-exist. The Act of Uniformity of 1662 - not to mention the penal legislation which followed it - must present difficulties for even the most committed apologist for the Church of England, but nevertheless, the Church of England of the late seventeenth and eighteenth centuries also continued to encompass both catholic and reformed theological convictions and in addition included within its scope the mediating rational theology of the Cambridge Platonists and their latitudinarian successors.

Despite such theological variations, however, the Church of England which entered the nineteenth century possessed a unity which the Church of England that entered the twentieth century did not. Even until 1830 the Church of England remained essentially settled and possessed a doctrinal consensus which rested upon clear acceptance of the reformed aspects of the Church of England, the supreme authority of scripture, and the ideal of an established religion in which church and state in England were seen as one society. It was a consensus in which scripture was held to be inerrant, and in which scripture and the "evidences" of design in creation and of prophecy fulfilled sustained a strictly conservative scheme of Christian doctrine. Although there were "High" and "Low" church "parties", evangelicals and liberals, there was an essential evenness of temper - some would say a scandalous complacency - about the Church of England at the end of the third decade of the nineteenth century.

By contrast, the Church of England of the decade and a half before the outbreak of the First World War was a church of readily identifiable and often bitterly opposed parties, radically differing styles of worship, and sharply divergent doctrinal standpoints. It was a church which, both in theology and worship, was more catholic than it had been eighty years earlier. It was also a church which was more theologically and doctrinally diverse and variegated, much less theologically settled and certain. It was a church in which Evangelicals and Anglo-Catholics confronted each other concerning the acceptable limits of ritual in worship and the theological implications of such limits and such ritual. The Evangelicals opposed the catholicism and "popery" of the Anglo-Catholics from the basis of a fiercely evangelical protestant theology centred on the atonement and a highly conservative, near fundamentalist, biblicism. The conservative Anglo-Catholics opposed the protestantism of the Evangelicals and stressed the catholic claims of the Church of England, an incarnational theology, and a view of doctrine and the Bible often scarcely less conservative than that of the Evangelicals. Both Evangelicals and Anglo-Catholics found themselves united in opposition to the third of the major parties, however, namely the Modernists for whom the priority was "to unite Churchmen who consider that dogma is capable of re-interpretation and re-statement in accordance with the clearer perception of truth attained by discovery and research," as the foundation document of their Union proclaimed.[10] Last but not least, between the conservatism of the Evangelicals and Anglo-Catholics and the outright liberalism of the Modernists were to be found the exponents of a Liberal Catholicism which sought to move beyond traditional versions of orthodoxy whilst stopping short of the views of the Modernists.

Between the Church of England of 1830 and the Church of England of 1914 there lay three momentous movements. The first was the emergence in the Victorian era of an acknowledged religious pluralism within English life as a whole. Even in 1820 the ideal of established church and state as one society was at variance with the facts of English religious and political life: there were already large numbers of Dissenters and Roman Catholics. The Repeal of the Test and Corporation Acts in 1828 and the passing of Catholic Emancipation in 1829 began a process of reform over the next fifty odd years by which England became pluralist in law as well as in fact. The civil disabilities of Nonconformists and other nonmembers of the Church of England were progressively removed and the Church of England, despite its continuing established status, became increasingly in practice more like one religious denomination among others in English life. The other two movements occurred *within* the religious and theological life of the Church of England. The first was the emergence and development of the Oxford Movement and its successors in the form of the Anglo-Catholic and Ritualist movements. The second may equally well be described as the Victorian crisis of faith or as the rise of a modern, historically and scientifically conscious, critical theology. The latter process was not, of course, peculiar to the Church of England, but in the present context it is the occurrence of it within the Church of England with which we shall be concerned.

The origins of the Oxford Movement lay in the fear aroused among some High Churchmen by the development of a more secular, pluralist state. It was the attempt in 1833 of the civil government to reform and rationalize the position of the established church in Ireland which caused John Keble to preach a sermon on "National Apostasy" and set in motion a movement to re-emphasise the specifically catholic heritage of the Church of England. Between 1833 and 1845 (when Newman converted to Roman Catholicism) the leaders and members of the Oxford Movement set out to challenge in their writings - and especially in a series of *Tracts for the Times* - the degree to which, in practice, the Church of England had become predominantly protestant in ethos, theology and sensibilities. They advocated a rediscovery and reacceptance of the catholic and apostolic nature of the Church of England. One of the important effects of this process was the breaking of the tacit doctrinal consensus of the era prior to the Oxford Movement. Catholics and Evangelicals now actively opposed one another within the theological life of the Church of England and the controversies inevitably heightened the self-consciousness and honed the identity of both wings of the church.[11]

The consensus-ending role of the Oxford Movement was continued by its second generation in the Ritualist and Anglo-Catholic movements of the second half of the nineteenth century. The Ritualist and Anglo-Catholic clergy of the period from 1850 to 1900 self-consciously set out to catholicise the worship of the Church of England and introduce to the Church of England ritual, liturgical and devotional practices of an explicitly catholic kind. The use of vestments, altar candles, the mixed chalice, using the sign of the cross, incense, genuflections, holy water, crucifixes, processions, the cults of Mary and the saints and the reservation of the sacrament and the practice of confession were examples of the changes they sought to introduce. The result was a period of intensely bitter controversies. At the popular level there were riots and much of the popular anti-catholic feeling previously directed at Roman Catholics was redirected against Anglo-Catholicism. At the official level the bishops sought to restrain Ritualist and Anglo-Catholic clergy. When persuasion and local ecclesiastical discipline failed, recourse was had to the church courts and to a Royal Commission. When these also proved inadequate to curb Ritualist practice recourse was finally had in 1874 to a Public Worship Regulation Act. This too proved ineffective. The Church of England and the civil government were faced with the profoundly unedifying spectacle of priests being imprisoned for their conscientiously held convictions. They became martyrs and public opinion turned against the 1874 Act which in due course became a dead letter. In the end, a further Royal Commission was set up.

When the Royal Commission on Ecclesiastical Discipline reported in 1906, it presented two main conclusions. The first was that the current law of public worship in the Church of England was too narrow, needlessly condemning much that many loyal members of the Church of England found valuable in worship. The second was that since existing machinery for adjusting or controlling ecclesiastical discipline had proved inadequate, new procedures should be established and the Church should be authorised to consider changes, specifically in the law of worship.[12]

In this way the Royal Commission recognised and supported the *de facto* reality of a diversity of styles of worship in the Church of England and recommended that the state and the church make appropriate adjustments to cope with this situation. The Church of England did duly seek to amend its law of worship, presenting a revised prayer book for the approval of Parliament in 1927 and 1928. It was twice rejected, not least because of an alliance between extreme evangelicals and extreme catholics for whom the book was either too catholic or not catholic enough - an excellent, if frustrating, example of the degree of liturgical and theological pluralism by then established in the Church of England. There followed, in due course, the long process of liturgical revision which finally led to the publication of the *Alternative Service Book* and a contemporary situation in respect of liturgical diversity in the Church of England which has led the present Archbishop of York to reflect on the possible virtues of a "planned pluralism" in worship in the Church of England rather than the "haphazard variety" which currently prevails.[13]

If the emergence of the Oxford Movement in the 1830's was, in retrospect, a decisive moment for the development of liturgical and devotional pluralism and for the sharpening of the identities of both the Catholic and Evangelical wings of the Church of England, the 1850's and 1860's were equally crucial for the eventual emergence of doctrinal and theological pluralism in the established church. For members of the Church of England who were concerned that their Christian belief should be both consistent with modern knowledge and in harmony with the highest moral standards, the 1840's and 1850's presented a number of difficulties. Of these, two were particularly pressing. Developments in astronomy, geology and natural history, together with the development of critical and historical methods rendered a literal interpretation of the Bible untenable. Equally pressing however was the moral challenge of those who maintained that the traditional scheme of salvation (complete with substitutionary atonement, a wrathful God in need of appeasement and eternal punishment for those not believing in this God and his scheme of salvation) was in fact profoundly immoral. In the middle decades of the nineteenth-century a number of Church of England theologians set out to respond to these challenges by demonstrating not only that Christian belief could be modified and reinterpreted so as to avoid conflict with such insights, but that a Christian belief so modified was in fact more faithful to the best aspects and highest insights of its own tradition. Thus, in 1853, F.D. Maurice, Anglican Professor of Theology at King's College London, published a collection of *Theological Essays* within which he challenged the morality of both the standard substitutionary view of the atonement and the notion of eternal punishment, in each case presenting theological alternatives which he argued were morally and theologically more sound. Then, in 1860, a group of seven Anglican scholars and clergy published an anthology entitled *Essays and Reviews*. Taken as a whole (though in fact the seven essays in it were intended as individual pieces) *Essays and Reviews* proposed that it was both possible and desirable that Christian belief should take account of modern scientific and historical methods and knowledge, that the Bible should be treated critically (thereby revealing how significant its message really was), and that eternal punishment was a less morally and theologically sound notion than that of universal salvation.

The official response to these two books was significant. Maurice was dismissed from his professorship. (He has subsequently become a theologian much favoured by apologists for modern Anglicanism, partly because of his theories of comprehensiveness, partly, one suspects, because his style is obscure and complex and can thus be made to appeal to many groups and to function in many contexts.) *Essays and Reviews*, meanwhile, became the centre of the greatest theological furor and controversy of the Victorian era. The book was synodically condemned and made the subject of a declaration by 11,000 clergy and 137,000 laity affirming their belief in the "whole Canonical Scriptures" as "being the Word of God" and their belief that those scriptures taught the doctrine of everlasting punishment. Two of the authors were also prosecuted for heresy - Rowland Williams for denying the inspiration of scripture and Henry Wilson for denying both the inspiration of scripture and the doctrine of everlasting punishment. They were found guilty by the ecclesiastical courts but were acquitted on appeal to the Privy Council. Thus, although the mid-nineteenth-century Church of England's own verdict on the theological liberalism of *Essays and Reviews* was a resounding rejection and condemnation, the use of the courts actually established the right of the clergy to hold such views. The controversy damaged both sides involved in it. The conservatives discovered that the law would not support their narrower conception of the boundaries of legitimate theological opinion in the Church of England. The Broad Church authors of *Essays and Reviews* won the right to hold their views and remain clergymen but the debate was so bitter and the victory so legally and technically based that the mid-Victorian Broad Church party never again produced a major work. When theological liberalism did establish itself more securely within the Church of England it was in a rather different form and the insights of the Broad Church tradition were never fully worked out.

With the legality of liberal theological opinion established there was a steady development of liberal theology within the Church of England between 1865 and 1914. Conservative opposition did not stop, but it was not subsequently able to gain official support as it had over *Essays and Reviews*. In 1869, Frederick Temple, who had been one of the contributors to *Essays and Reviews*, became Bishop of Exeter. Subsequently, he went on to become Bishop of London and then Archbishop of Canterbury. In the 1870's and 1880's, B. F. Westcott, R. H. Lightfoot and F. J. A. Hort at Cambridge embarked on a series of New Testament commentaries which sought to embody a moderate biblical criticism. The series was not completed but the commentaries that were published secured an accepted and recognized place for at least a moderate critical stance within the Church of England. In 1889

14

a more momentous landmark occurred with the publication of a collection of essays entitled *Lux Mundi*. The essays were by a group of Oxford-based theologians, led by Charles Gore, who were on the Anglo-Catholic wing of the Church of England. Gore set out their aims in the preface to *Lux Mundi* where he asserted that the authors wrote as servants of the Catholic Creed and Church, aiming only at interpreting the faith they had received, but recognising that the profound intellectual and social changes of the age made some restatement of the claims and meaning of the faith necessary. In seeking to fulfill those aims, the authors embraced a theory of progressive revelation which allowed an acceptance of evolutionary science and moderate biblical criticism. There was again an outcry from conservative churchmen, especially from conservative Anglo-Catholics who saw *Lux Mundi* as a betrayal of the legacy of the Oxford Movement. There was no official condemnation however, rather the book was widely welcomed and marked the emergence of a distinctively Liberal Catholicism. Several of its contributors went on to become bishops. Thus far had theological liberalism progressed in the almost thirty years since the publication of *Essays and Reviews*.

In 1898 the existence of a substantial body of liberal theological opinion within the Church of England was given formal public expression in the formation of "The Churchmen's Union for the Advancement of Liberal Thought" (in 1928 the society changed its name to The Modern Churchmen's Union) and in 1897 a theological college, Ripon Hall, had also been founded at which a specifically liberal or modernist style of theology was taught. In 1912 another group of Oxford theologians produced a further collection of essays entitled *Foundations: a Statement of Christian Belief in Terms of Modern Thought*. This collection pressed decisively beyond the position of *Lux Mundi* in 1889. Two essays were especially significant. That by B. H. Streeter on "The Historic Christ" affirmed the resurrection appearances of Jesus as "objective visions" and did not accept the idea of a bodily resurrection and also interpreted the life of Jesus in the light of the current German emphasis upon the eschatological context of the Gospels and their essentially devotional and practical, not historical, purpose. The essay by A. E. J. Rawlinson, meanwhile, presented the case for a more flexible and empirical approach to credal statements. *Lux Mundi* had drawn a line at the acceptance of criticism of the Old Testament and a rapprochement with evolutionary science: the New Testament and the creeds were not to be subjected to such criticism. *Foundations* pressed on logically to include the creeds and the New Testament within the critical approach.

By 1914 the boundaries of acceptable theological opinion within the Church of England had thus become impressively wider than they had been in 1860 or even 1889. But they were not unchallenged in their breadth. The successive volumes of essays, and works by individual theologians of liberal views, regularly brought forth conservative protests. By 1914 even Gore, the "liberal" of 1889, was challenging the right of clergymen to deny the clauses of the creed concerning the virgin birth or the bodily resurrection of Jesus. Gore, indeed, gradually emerged as the champion of the conservative opposition to the increasing Modernist influence: an example, as Paul Avis has pointed out, of the way in which - and the speed at which - the permitted limits of theological opinion had steadily broadened.[14] The conservative protests were not without force however. In 1914 resolutions were passed in Convocation affirming that the historical facts stated in the creeds were an essential part of the Faith of the Church. The resolutions also included a qualifying statement, however, that it was also recognized that there were new problems raised by historical criticism and that the freedom of thought and inquiry of clergy and laity should not be unduly limited. There should be considerateness in dealing with that which is tentative and provisional in the thought and work of earnest and reverent students. Such resolutions, together with such qualifying statements, are not only a characteristic feature of the modern Church of England, they are also a sure indication of the fact that, by 1914, the Church of England had become, *de facto*, doctrinally pluralist.[15]

The reality of that pluralism was formally recognized, albeit still in the language of "comprehensiveness" and "complementarity" in the report, published in 1938, entitled *Doctrine in the Church of England*. The report was the result of some sixteen years of work by a Commission set up in 1922 after a particulary controversial conference of the Modern Churchmen's Union at Girton College, Cambridge in 1921. The conference had presented particularly radical proposals concerning Christology and conservative protests had been so severe that the Archbishop of Canterbury, Randall Davidson, had accepted that a doctrine commission was the most positive way forward.

Doctrine in the Church of England is something of a neglected classic.[16] A fine statement of the position of theology and doctrine in the Church of England between the World Wars, it fell victim itself to the crisis of the Second World War and the post-war era of biblical theology and the preoccupation of the Church of England with the liturgical movement and the revision of canon law. The report was a milestone because of the way in which it actually addressed the *content* of Anglican belief and achieved unanimity not merely by the use of studied ambiguity and vague, undefined notions of consensus, (although the report certainly does contain passages of studied ambiguity), but by a courageous acceptance and acknowledgement of the fact that on certain issues it was possible to believe quite different things and still be an Anglican. The approach was both simple and bold. It conceded that there is a diversity, a pluralism, about what Anglicans believe. As the late Geoffrey Lampe observed, the 1938 report recorded a remarkable degree of agreement whilst also acknowledging agreement to differ without disrupting common fellowship within the Church of England: moreover that agreement was secured not by bogus unanimity but by including "frequent and important expressions of differences within the body of the document."[17]

The era of biblical theology which continued through the 1950's was itself brought to an abrupt halt by the theological radicalism of the 1960's. Rather as Charles Gore, the liberal of 1889, had become, as the limits of opinion broadened, the conservative of 1914, so the "modernists" of the early and mid-twentieth-century Church of England found themselves out-flanked by a theological radicalism which pressed beyond their earlier versions of doctrinal liberalism. The classic document of the 1960's was *Honest to God*, published in 1963 by the then Bishop of Woolwich, John Robinson.[18] It was a frank personal statement of Robinson's own dissatisfaction with traditional ideas about God, Jesus, prayer, the miraculous, and the church and offered, in place of traditional teachings on such matters, a radical theology owing much to the thought of Rudolf Bultmann, Paul Tillich and Dietrich Bohnhoeffer. The immense impact of the short book was in part a result of the neglect of liberal theological ideas in the 1940's and 1950's, in part the result of its being the work of a bishop, but most of all the result of its intentionally popular style. It ushered in a decade of theological ferment in which radicals urged the merits of "secular Christianity," "man come of age" and "a new Reformation." In 1968 the Archbishops' Commission on Doctrine issued a report on *Subscription and Assent to the 39 Articles* which proposed that assent to them by those about to be ordained should be replaced by a more general form of assent to the formulations of the Church of England placed in the context of scripture and creeds.[19] The tradition of questioning and exploratory collections of essays was continued in *Soundings* published in 1966 and in a collection focusing on Christology, *Christ, Faith and History* published in 1972.[20] In 1975 the recommendation to replace assent to the 39 Articles by a more general assent was accepted by the General Synod. The culmination of the period of liberal and radical theological thought begun by *Honest to God* was the 1976 report of the then Doctrine Commission, *Christian Believing*. As we noted at the beginning of this essay, *Christian Believing* was forthright in its recognition of doctrinal pluralism in the Church of England. In its advocacy of the coexistence - in creative tension, not mere complementarity - of different ways of believing, *Christian Believing* was the most bold and frank acknowledgement of the doctrinal pluralism of the Church of England yet to have emerged from an official report.

During the 1970's, however, there was a steady resurgence of conservative evangelicalism in the Church of England and a steady growth in the influence of the charismatic movement. The 1976 doctrine report was seen by many as too much a product of the theological radicalism of the 1960's. It was, accordingly, never passed to the General Synod for formal discussion or officially commended to the Church of England. Instead a new doctrine commission was appointed. It included only one member of the previous commission and presented its report in 1981.

The title of the 1981 report, *Believing in the Church*, sets out the message of the report in the word-play of its title, and, lest its meaning should be missed, is clarified in its sub-title, "The Corporate Nature of Belief."[21] In the report, the essentially corporate nature of belief and the notion of "the mind of the church" are expressly and insistently placed over against the "exaggerated individualism" of much recent Anglican theological thought.

Believing in the Church cannot plausibly be described as a conservative document. It has much to say, in the traditional modern Anglican manner, of the need for theological exploration and respect for the conclusions of those engaged in it. But in its emphasis upon corporate believing and the mind of the church, and its criticism of "exaggerated individualism," it is a distinctly more conservative document than *Christian Believing*. There is a retreat from the acknowledgement and acceptance of pluralism.

How, then, are we to conclude this survey of the rise of religious pluralism in the Church of England? Without question the contemporary Church of England is pluralistic, not merely diverse or comprehensive. To that extent, the 1976 doctrine report was simply correct: whatever the nature of belief or the state of doctrine *ought* to be in the Church of England, the *de facto* situation of the Church of England in the last quarter of the twentieth century is one of doctrinal pluralism. Nor is the pluralism one limited to doctrine. The contemporary Church of England is also pluralistic in worship and devotional life and in the range of moral and political opinions and allegiances held by its members.

For some, both members of the Church of England and observers from without, such pluralism as now prevails is an admirable outworking of the historical tradition of comprehensiveness which is found in the very beginnings of the Church of England. To others, the current state of affairs is adequate, so far as it goes, but could be improved by an outright acceptance and exploration of the pluralism expressed in the 1976 doctrine report. To others, again, the current state of affairs is - and has long been - shambolic and chaotic, a cause for regret and a situation in need of correction by a return to a narrower and more traditional conservative theological position. For yet others, there is a need for a more moderate re-trenchment, a tolerance (but not an advocacy) of a degree of pluralism, but one centred around a more clearly defined and corporate core of beliefs, attitudes and policies. There are some signs (but only as yet signs) that the current leadership of the Church of England may (but only may) favour an approach along the latter lines. The 1981 doctrine commission report is one such sign. The statement by the House of Bishops of June 1986 on *The Nature of Christian Belief* is another, especially in its discussion of the individual and collegial responsibility of bishops for the faith of the Church.[22] (The *Times* recognized the essential conservatism of the statement, observing in a neat turn of phrase that the Bishop of Durham, whose remarks concerning the virgin birth, the resurrection and the nature of providence had prompted the statement, was deemed by it to be "deviant, but not so deviant as to be damned.")[23] The notion of collegiality has also emerged in the attempts of the present Archbishop of Canterbury to develop a more coherent and unified response by the Church of England to political and social issues.[24] Last but not least there are those who would see in the *Alternative Service Book* an attempt to impose gradually a new and more uniform style of worship.

Whatever route the Church of England takes, however, it would do well to pay greater attention to its modern history than it often does. One of the most remarkable aspects of the recurrent doctrinal controversies of the modern Church of England is the extent to which the controversies are replays of previous ones. Very few of the controversies of the post-1960 era are truly novel or innovatory. Most of the issues have been raised and debated (often several times) before - the present controversy surrounding the Bishop of Durham is an excellent example. A greater awareness of past controversies, an assimilation of the resolutions passed and the compromises reached, the diversities tolerated and the truths affirmed would go far to easing the distress and removing the shock of the current pluralism of the Church of England. But, alas, the modern Church of England not only espouses corporate belief but also suffers from corporate amnesia, and hence repeatedly condemns itself to the refighting of old doctrinal controversies every generation or so.

A greater attention to its modern history would also serve the contemporary Church of England well in its attempts to explore further internal religious pluralism or to draw back from it. If the Church of

England goes forward into greater pluralism then an understanding of the degree of pluralism which it has already enjoyed since the nineteenth century, and of how that pluralism came to be, will be of great value in the further exploration that lies ahead. And if the Church of England is to draw back and seek greater uniformity and a less pluralistic style, then it would do well to understand that in so doing it will be seeking to reverse a trend which has been in progress - sometimes more swiftly, sometimes more slowly - for some one hundred and fifty years. To reverse or modify such a trend would be a momentous undertaking. To attempt to do so without at least attending to its history would be not only momentous but foolhardy.

REFERENCES

[1] S. Neill, *Anglicanism*, Penguin Books, 1958, p. 246.

[2] Quoted in Neill, *op. cit.*, p. 247.

[3] *Christian Believing: The Nature of the Christian Faith and its Expression in Holy Scripture and Creeds*, S.P.C.K., 1976, p. 38.

[4] A. Dyson, "The Bishop of Durham and All That," *The Modern Churchman*, n. s. 27, 1985, pp. 1-2.

[5] P. Avis, "The Church's One Foundation," *Theology* 89, 1986, p. 259.

[6] *Op. cit.*, pp. 35-38.

[7] S. Sykes, *The Integrity of Anglicanism*, Mowbrays, 1978 p. 34.

[8] G. Ecclestone, "The General Synod and Politics," in *Church and Politics Today: The Role of the Church of England in Contemporary Politics*, ed. G. Moyser, T. and T. Clark, 1985, pp. 126-127.

[9] Moyser, *op. cit., passim*. See also G. Moyser and K. Medhurst, "Political Participation and Attitudes in the Church of England," *Government and Opposition*, 13, 1978, *passim*, but especially pp. 94-95.

[10] Quoted in A. M. G. Stephenson, *The Rise and Decline of English Modernism*, S.P.C.K., 1984, p. 243. On pages 7-9 Stephenson offers an excellent thumbnail sketch of a Modernist.

[11] P. Toon, *Evangelical Theology 1833-1856: A Response to Tractarianism*, Marshall, Morgan and Scott 1979, demonstrates this development whilst also showing the common ground between Evangelicals and Tractarians.

[12] For a fuller account of ritualism and the response to it, see J. Bentley, *Ritualism and Politics in Victorian Britain: The Attempt to Legislate for Belief*, Oxford U.P., 1978.

[13] J. Habgood, *Church and Nation in a Secular Age*, Darton, Longman and Todd, 1983, p. 143.

[14] Avis, *op. cit.*, p. 260.

[15] For fuller accounts of the history of theology in the Church of England between 1830 and 1940 see B. M. G. Reardon, *Religious Thought in the Victorian Age: A Survey from Coleridge to Gore*, Longman, 1980; and A.M. Ramsey, *From Gore to Temple: The Development of Anglican Theology between Lux Mundi and the Second World War*, Longman, 1960. For a more detailed analysis of the theological and liturgical diversification of the

Victorian Church of England see my essay, 'Reform, Revival and Re-alignment: The Experience of Victorian Anglicanism', in *Religion in Victorian Britain: Volume 1 Traditions*, ed. G. Parsons, MUP, 1988.

[16]Although it has recently been re-issued with an excellent introduction locating the report within the context of modern Anglican theology, *Doctrine in the Church of England: The 1938 Report with a new introduction by G. W. H. Lampe*, S. P. C. K., 1982.

[17]New introduction to the 1938 Report, *op. cit.*, pp. l and liii.

[18]J. A. T. Robinson, *Honest to God*, SCM, 1963.

[19]*Subscription and Assent to the Articles*, S. P. C. K., 1968.

[20]*Soundings: Essays Concerning Christian Understanding*, ed . A. R. Vidler, Cambridge U. P., 1966. *Christ Faith and History*, ed. S. W. Sykes and J. P. Clayton, Cambridge U. P., 1972.

[21]*Believing in the Church: The Corporate Nature of Belief*, S. P. C. K., 1981.

[22]*The Nature of Christian Belief: A Statement and Exposition By the House of Bishops of the General Synod of the Church of England*, Church House Publishing, 1986.

[23]*The Times*, editorial, June 6th, 1986.

[24]See for example the essay by G. Moyser and K. Medhurst, "Lambeth Palace, the Bishops and Politics" in ed. Moyser, *Church and Politics Today*.

CHAPTER II

SOME SECULAR TRENDS
IN THE CHURCH OF ENGLAND TODAY

PAUL BADHAM

The external signs of secularisation in England today have been well documented. Whatever statistics are chosen: baptism, confirmation, marriage, ordination, Sunday school membership, electoral roll membership, or Church attendance; all show a fairly steady downward drift for the past seventy years.[1] But what appears to be less often noticed is the internal secularisation of the Church of England, by which I mean the steady erosion of the distinctive characteristics of Christian thought and life among many clergy and laity who yet remain "faithful" in terms of belonging and participation.

This "erosion of faith" should not be confused with that necessary and continual reformation and reinterpretation of Christian doctrine which has been so characteristic of Anglican theology in the past century and a half. Any religion which is alive rather than fossilised will change and develop in the light of new learning and social change. This is true even of the Church of Rome for as the Second Vatican Council put it: "Christ summons the Church, as she goes her pilgrim way, to that continual reformation of which she always has need."[2]   And if this is true of Rome, how much more of a Church which owes its separate existence to its insistence on reformation. Moreover it is possible to claim, as I have argued elsewhere,[3] that secular learning - as instanced by the development of autonomous historical, literary and scientific judgement - played an important role in that reformation and purification of Christian belief which took place in England during the Victorian crisis of faith and which has continued in the liberal, "modernist," or broad-church tradition in the Church of England.   But the struggle to reform, restate, and reinterpret the central themes of Christian faith must be distinguished from translating that faith into an entirely secular frame of reference.   Naturally it is impossible to draw any sharp dividing line between these two activities, and there will be many a controversy where scholars legitimately differ in their evaluation of whether or not a particular reinterpretation of an article of faith represents an authentic development of Christian doctrine.   Nevertheless, while there are many shades of grey it remains the case that there is a difference between black and white, and I wish to argue that any revision of Christian doctrine which entails the abandonment of belief in a transcendent God, or which reduces Christianity wholly to a this-wordly dimension, represents so great a secularisation of Christian thought and life that it cannot truly be regarded as continuous with the main stream of the historic Christian tradition.   I shall apply a similar verdict to proposals for Church reform which discount the value of passing on the Christian tradition to the next generation, or which so emphasise the desirability of social reform that they discount the need to help the individual to encounter and relate to a transcendent God.

The most striking instance of the secularisation of Christian thought is the widespread collapse of confidence in the rationality of belief in God among the clergy. This very rarely leads to an explicit atheism. Don Cupitt's rejection of belief in an objective God is unusual,[4] nor do many follow Michael Goulder into a public acknowledgement of loss of faith.[5] But what is very common is an assertive "Fideism" in which faith is seen as an act of will independent of all rational considerations. Tertullian and Kierkegaard would be two ancestors of this position,[6] though of greater impact in Britain would be the "Biblical theology" movement which represents an English response to the Neo-orthodoxy of Karl Barth.[7] Features of this movement are a distrust of human reason, or of any appeal to religious experience, and a conscious focusing on revelation as the sole source of Christian knowledge.

This had the consequence that it is relatively rare to find any systematic or reasoned preaching about God in the Church of England today. When I myself preached on such a theme recently, a very distinguished lay Churchman remarked to me afterwards that it was the first time for many years that he had heard such a sermon. And I suspect this is general, partly because the many books of sermon guidelines recently published so rarely focus on God,[8] but more significantly because preaching has become increasingly liturgically based and the lectionary of the *Alternative Service Book* reflects the principles of the "Biblical theology" movement. Hence, for example, if one looks through the recommended themes for Sunday preaching in that lectionary, it is hard to see where a sermon arguing for the reasonableness of belief in God could actually be fitted in. This is the consequence of the view shared both by the exponents of "Biblical theology" and by much secular thought that arguments for God's existence based on nature or religious experience are extremely problematical. Hence the clergy tend to ignore the question of the foundations for faith in God today, and concentrate instead on providing little talks about the life and work of Jesus Christ, in the context of which God can be referred to. In fact if one analyses the themes of the *Alternative Service Book* lectionary it at once becomes apparent that the compilers assume that an exclusive concentration on the life and person of Christ will fully meet the needs of the contemporary worshipper. This is even true of the 9th Sunday before Christmas where "Creation" is listed as the topic for the day. One might feel that this at least could provide the basis for a sermon about God, but if one looks at the choice of New Testament readings, it at once becomes apparent that it is assumed that the preacher will wish to speak of creation solely in relation to Christ, a concern which might be of interest in a course on Christology, but which does nothing whatever to help contemporary puzzlement about the concept of creation. I do not deny the importance of the Person of Christ to Christianity. It is what gives Christianity its distinctive message and appeal. But, in the end. teaching about Jesus Christ is only of any *religious* importance if it is supposed that God was revealed by, or incarnate in, Christ and for this to be intelligible, some prior concept of God is essential.

If all metaphysical claims about God really are discounted, then to say that Jesus is God incarnate would mean no more than to say that Jesus' life and example is of importance. Yet not even this is true without the back-up of a more general belief in the reality of God. And where clergymen are unwilling to talk of God except as part of the picture of a first- century life, then for all practical purposes God has existentially dropped out of contemporary life even within the Church's own life. For unless it can be supposed that there are grounds today, either in nature, or in religious experience, for affirming the reality of God then the everyday expectations of the regular Church-goer may be in practice as secularised as the expectations of the conscious atheist. The weakness of an apologetic which avoids the challenge of making and defending propositional claims about the nature of reality is that faith ceases to have any significant content by which it can be differentiated from non-faith, except in the willingness of Christians to attend Church, listen to stories from the distant past, and modify their behaviour in accordance with the ethical teaching contained therein.

A second aspect of secularisation in contemporary Christianity is the quiet dropping of belief in a future life. Historically, this belief was the life-blood of dynamic Christianity. The early Christians thought of themselves as "aliens and exiles on earth" and as persons whose true citizenship was in heaven.[9] And throughout the Christian centuries, belief in a future life was at the heart of all living faith. Now however, this faith, though rarely denied, is equally rarely affirmed. I myself acquired two degrees in Christian theology and completed all the requirements for ordination to the anglican ministry without receiving any instruction in this doctrine, or even being exposed to sermons about it. And the overwhelming weight of evidence in a recent *Credo* inquiry showed that my experience was only too typical.[10] Investigation of recent works ostensibly on the Christian hope reveal that the most many contemporary Christians feel able to hope for is that God will remember them after they are no more[11] while a more general ploy is to reinterpret the language of resurrection, immortality and eternal life so that it is perceived as simply a way of talking about present experience within this life.[12]   There could be no greater instance of the *secularisation* of contemporary Christianity than in its being confined to this world only. Yet this is in practice what has happened.   And if one turns to contemporary worship one can see clear evidence of this.   Consider, for example, the latest two supplements of *Hymns for Today*; one cannot help noting that they contribute no hymns for singing at funeral and commemoration services, or on either of the themes: "the Church triumphant" (in heaven), or "the Communion of Saints."[13]   This suggests strongly that in its offer of comfort to the bereaved the Church has to rely on the faith of earlier ages rather than on the actual expectations of contemporary Christians.   Moreover, if we turn to the eucharistic heart of Christian worship, we notice once more the process of secularisation at work.   For while earlier generations received the sacrament with the promise of being brought to everlasting life, the contemporary Christian is offered the sacred elements with the words "keep you in eternal life," with the suggestion that "eternal life" is something which is essentially part of present experience rather than the outcome of an immortal hope.

The loss of the transcendent other-worldly dimension in Christianity affects the life of the Church in a number of ways. First its worship is often transformed so that the focus of its thought is not a transcendent and holy deity to be approached in awe, wonder, and solemnity, but rather the focus is an experience of "God" believed to come about in and through the encounter with the neighbour. This has had the consequence that religious experience which in the past was generated by religious institutions is no longer typically associated with Christian worship.[14]   Indeed David Hay's survey of contemporary religious experience shows that only 7% of profound religious experiences reported today are associated with worship.   But this is not particularly surprising for he also found that so far from contemporary Churches being vehicles for the sense of the holy, it is often the case that "modern Church services have about as much feeling for the numinous as the average bus station."[15]

According to the Oxford English Dictionary, "secular" means "concerned with the affairs of this world." The secularisation of Christian thought can best be exemplified therefore by seeing how much of its activity and interest is now focused almost exclusively on the problems of the world. This can perhaps be seen at its clearest in the enthusiastic reception given by the General Synod of the Church of England to the report *Faith in the City*. For this report, though ostensibly concerned with "faith," is in fact almost entirely devoted to an analysis of the appalling material conditions prevalent in urban priority areas and the need for constructive and socially just measures to be undertaken to rectify these ills. I have no wish to dispute the appropriateness of Christian concern in these matters. Love for one's neighbour is a manifest Christian priority, and the prophetic appeal for righteousness, justice and care for the poor is a central theme of the whole Bible. And the Church of England has a right to be proud of its record of social concern, from the achievements of its Evangelical statesmen, to the labours of its Anglo-catholic slum priests, and the continuing witness of its Christian Socialist tradition. Yet what marks out this Archbishop of Canterbury's Commission from earlier Anglican examples of social concern is the lack of any other dimension in the Report's findings.

The chapter on *Theological Priorities* takes as its text the remark of an Advice Worker that, "the Church seems to offer very little to people in the inner city but surely Christianity has a lot to say."[16] The endorsement of this quotation is most extraordinary for, implicit in it, is the assumption that the ministry of the word and sacraments, the life of prayer and worship, the good news of God's loving search for humanity, and the message of life eternal "offer very little," and that the only way Chrisitianity can contribute to human well-being is to add its "say" to the case for inner city renewal. The Commission explicitly states that the Gospel cannot be presented to people suffering physical hardship: "We have seen areas where unemployment, poor housing, and the threat of criminal violence...so dominate people's thinking and feeling that no presentation of the Gospel is possible that does not relate to these material deprivations."[17] If we compare this with the point of view of the New Testament or of historic Christianity we notice at once how utterly different the perspective is. The first Christians had no hesitation in proclaiming their faith to slaves and outcasts whose material lot was infinitely worse than that of the inhabitants of our inner cities. For the early Christians believed that they had good news about God's eternal love which "far outweighed" all the sufferings life might bring.[18] Indeed St. Paul explicitly proclaimed his conviction that "nothing in all creation can separate us from the love of God in Christ Jesus," and certainly not "affliction or hardship, persecution, hunger, nakedness, peril, or the sword."[19] According to William Barclay, the whole point of the "blessedness" taught by Jesus in the Sermon on the Mount was that it was "independent of outward circumstances" for "Christian bliss is the life of God, and is therefore a joy no man can take from us."[20] And this is overwhelmingly true of Christian experience throughout the ages: to feel at one with God is to know a peace and fulfilment worth more than any conceivable material improvement in the conditions of life and work. It was this "blessed assurance" that drove Wesley to preach in the unimaginable squalor of the towns of the industrial revolution and that led the devoted slum priests of the nineteenth-century to devote their lives to awakening a sense of God and of "the immeasurable riches of his grace."[21]

But it is precisely this sense of the immediate presence of God to the human soul that the Commission repudiates. According to their report "few philosophers now allow for a separate component or 'soul,' with which religion can be uniquely concerned, and modern philosophy encourages us to return to the idiom of the Bible, according to which God addresses our whole person along with the social relationships amid which we live....The suggestion that religion is an entirely personal matter of the relationship of an individual with God should now be...unacceptable."[22] The Commission is of course right that many philosophers today reject the concept of the soul, but what it overlooks is the fact that for the very same reasons they also reject belief in God. As Anthony Kenny points out,"most contemporary philosophers find immateriality problematic"[23] and if anything the difficulties are greater with belief in God "a non-embodied mind active throughout the universe" than with the soul. If one is going to make majority secular opinion determinative for faith one cannot pick and choose thus, and certainly not between two concepts of the same logical status. Moreover it is not true that God according to the Bible *addresses* the whole person. For we do not see God with our eyes, or hear him with our ears, rather as St. Paul claims "spiritual things are...spiritually discerned."[24] And the entire mystical tradition of Christendom insists that the immediate awareness of God which is at the heart of all religious experience is neither mediated nor assisted by the senses. If secular analysis has convinced the Archbishop's Commission that such experiences are delusory or unintelligible then it is indeed right to reject them, but let it be clear on what it is doing, and not evade the issue by cheap gibes at a caricature of cartesianism which ignores Descartes' main contribution to philosophy which was his insistence on the total interaction between mind and body. The commission is of course right to insist that religion is more than a personal matter between God and the individual, but it is most misleading to present this in such a way as to imply that the personal encounter is therefore of no real significance.

What permeates the whole report on *Faith in the City* is a sense that the insights of the Bible and the Christian tradition are no longer of any real help to people grappling with the problems of life in Urban Priority Areas. Thus the report is quite explicit that, with regard to the training of the clergy, "what matters is whether they have developed habits of reflection and social awareness such that they can draw creatively on their resources of theology and spirituality in the face of new realities."[25] This is explicitly contrasted with the old (1944) approach which stipulated that the minister "must know what the gospel is. He must believe it. He must have studied it in itself in the historical form it appeared, in its workings in the Biblical history and the history of the Church."[26] Indeed the Report notes with amazement that "as recently as 1983" the purpose of the General Ordination Examination was stated to be "to test so far as it can the candidates' grasp of the faith they will be authorised to teach."[27] The futility of this kind of training is apparently its total irrelevance to the life of the minister today, for it seems that all "the knowledge thus painfully acquired was left behind as soon as the active ministry began."[28]

The report recommends a radically different approach to theology for all Christians in the inner cities. This should not take for granted the education or reading habits of the upper and middle classes, nor assume that truth is only received through sets of logically related propositions, nor should there be an over "preoccupation with intellectual consistency."[29] On the other hand, the Church could take seriously the example of Liberation Theology and note that, in that context, "theological reasoning has seemed relevant, and in a certain sense 'true' only if it results in a determination and a strategy to liberate the poor from oppression."[30] Hence a wholly new way of "doing theology" could be devised for inner cities. Such a theology would start "not from a conventional academic syllabus of Christian knowledge or biblical study, but from the personal experience, the modes of perception and the daily concerns of local people themselves...this will lead to the growth of theologies that are authentic expressions of local culture."[31]

The proposals outlined here only make sense on the assumption that the historic Christian faith has really nothing to say to the people of the inner city. For it will be noted that the issue is not phrased in the form of how the insights of the Christian tradition can be renewed and applied to the people of the urban priority areas today but rather it is assumed that a relevant theology must be determined by contemporary experience and that the wisdom of the past is of little real help in the world of the present. This is secularisation in a very extreme form in that it is the secular in its narrowest meaning of "the present age" which is to be all determinative. God, eternal life, and the heritage of Christianity, must all be deemed of secondary importance compared with the need to utter a prophetic witness against the manifest evils of urban deprivation. It would be hard to conceive of a more thorough-going betrayal of the Christian Gospel than this account. Except, and this is the real irony of the situation, that the motivation of the writers of the report is so clearly derived from the social teaching of the prophets, and the moral witness of Christianity through the ages. Faithfulness to the insights of the social Gospel *does* require a sense of indignation at what is going on in our urban priority areas. Yet the assumption that effective action requires a widespread secularisation of the Church's role needs to be called into question. Historically, one great motive for prophetic ministry has been the conviction that God's will must be done on earth as it is already being done in Heaven, and it is possible that there is no greater dynamic for radical social change than a firm belief in transcendent and eternal values that provide a perspective from which to gain a truer evaluation of our contemporary society.

REFERENCES

[1]David Perman, *Change and the Churches* (London: Bodley Head, 1977), ch. 2.

[2]"Decree on Ecumenism" para. 6 in Anthony Flannery (ed.) *Vatican Council 2, The Conciliar and Post-Conciliar Documents* (Dublin": Dominican Publications, 1975) p. 459.

[3]Paul Badham, "Secularisation and the Need for a New Reformation of Christianity," Assembly of World Religions, New Jersey 1985, *Faith and Freedom*, volume 39. number 116. Summer 1986.

[4]Don Cupitt, *Taking Leave of God* (London: SCM, 1980).

[5]Michael Goulder and John Hick, *Why Believe in God?* (London: SCM, 1983), ch. 1.

[6]Cf. Tertullian's classic statements, "I believe because it is absurd....It is certain because it is impossible". (de Carn. Chr. 5,4.) cited with discussion in Hans Von Campenhausen, *The Fathers of the Latin Church* (London: A. & C. Black, 1964), p. 23. These may be compared with Soren Kierkegaard, "Faith Begins Precisely where Thinking Leaves Off" *Fear and Trembling* (New York: Anchor, 1954), p. 64 See also Kierkegaard, *Philosophical Fragments* (Princeton, 1967), passim.

[7]For discussion on Barth cf. Heinz Zahrnt, *The Question of God* (London: Collins. 1969). ch. 1. For Biblical Theology see J. Leslie Houlden's article on the topic in John Bowden (ed.) *A New Dictionary of Christian Theology* (London: SCM, 1983) p. 69.

[8]E.g., Douglas W. Cleverley Ford, *The Ministry of the Word* (London: Hodder, 1979); Geoffrey Cuming, *The Ministry of the Word* (Oxford: University Press, 1979), John Gunstone, *Commentary on the New Lectionary* (London: SPCK, 1973).

[9]1 Peter 2:11, Hebrews 11:13.

[10]"Life after Death", a *Credo* Documentary (broadcast on London Weekend Television April 26th, 1986).

[11]E.g,. Norman Pittenger, *After Death, Life in God* (London: SCM, 1980); Hubert J. Richards, *Death and After* (London: Fount, 1980); Hans Küng, *Eternal Life?* (London: Collins 1984), and David L. Edwards, *The Last Things Now* (London: SCM, 1969).

[12]Rudolf Bultmann, "New Testament and Mythology", in Hans Werner Bartsch, *Kerygma and Myth* (New York: Harper, 1961), Peter Selby, *Look for*

the Living (London: SCM, 1976); and Harry A. Williams, *True Resurrection* (London: Beazley, 1972).

[13]*Hymns Ancient and Modern: New Standard* (London: Clowes, 1983), pp. XLIV ff.

[14]David Hay, *Exploring Inner Space* (Harmondsworth,:Penguin, 1982).

[15]*Ibid.*, p. 203.

[16]Report of the Archbishop of Canterbury's Commission on Urban Priority Areas, *Faith in the City* (London: Church House, 1985) p. 47.

[17]*Faith in the City*, p. 51.

[18]2 Corinthians 4:17.

[19]Romans 8:35-39.

[20]William Barclay, *The Plain Man Looks at the Beatitudes* (London: Collins, 1963), p. 13.

[21]Ephesians 2:7.

[22]*Faith in the City*, p. 50.

[23]Anthony Kenny, *The God of the Philosophers* (Oxford: Clarendon, 1979), p. 127.

[24]1 Corinthians 2:14.

[25]*Faith in the City*, p. 119.

[26]*Ibid.*, p. 120.

[27]*Ibid.*, p. 120.

[28]*Ibid.*, p. 120.

[29]*Ibid.*, pp. 62-63.

[30]*Ibid.*, p. 64.

[31]*Ibid.*, p.65.

CHAPTER III

CHURCH AND SOCIETY IN WALES SINCE DISESTABLISHMENT

WILLIAM PRICE

Since 1920, Wales, unlike England and Scotland, has had no Established Church. This paper seeks to examine the condition of the Anglican or Episcopal Church in Wales sixty-six years after its disestablishment, and also to assess the influence of organized religion in contemporary Wales.

The possibility of the disestablishment of the Church of England has recently become a matter of considerable discussion. Some see a glorious future for an Anglican Church in England liberated from state control; others see catastrophe, if not extinction, for a Church of England released from such control. The example of Anglicanism in Wales may be instructive in some respects, for Wales shares the same political, legal and economic system as England, and even its formerly distinctive cultural and social peculiarities are apparently becoming blurred within the context of modern Britain.

The following discussion is divided into four sections - a brief account of disestablishment in Wales; the position of the Anglican Church in Wales in the 1980's; possible parallels if the Church of England were disestablished; and a general account of the place of the churches in modern Wales.

Disestablishment in Wales[1]

By the middle of the nineteenth century Anglicans had become a small minority in Wales, although the Church of England remained the privileged Established Church throughout England and Wales. The four Welsh dioceses were an integral part of the Province of Canterbury. In the religious census of 1851 about 77 per cent of worshippers in Wales were Protestant nonconformists, the great majority of them belonging to the four large denominations, the Calvinistic Methodists, the Independents, the Baptists and the Wesleyan Methodists. The Anglican Church could not claim more than about 20 per cent of worshippers. It should also be noted that almost half the population of Wales attended no place of worship on the Sunday when the census was taken.[2] Nonetheless, the later nineteenth century witnessed the domination of urban and rural Wales by Protestant nonconformity. "Below the veneer of upper-class ascendancy maintained by the (Anglican) landed gentry at so many levels in the (eighteen) eighties, the Welsh democracy was a thriving and creative one. It was nonconformist leadership and ideology that largely made it so."[3] All the social, economic and political grievances, real or imaginary, of the majority of the Welsh, and increasingly from the 1860's their nationalist aspirations as well, were focussed in the call for the disestablishment of the minority Anglican Church.

The striving for disestablishment became more clamant with the growth of the Liberal party, especially as the franchise was widened. The first attempt at legislation came in 1870, following the disestablishment of the Anglican Church of Ireland, and it was to be a long struggle. The Act received the Royal Assent in September 1914. During these years the Anglican Church greatly improved its organization and effectiveness,[4] and more significantly there were clear signs that nonconformity was losing its dominant place in Welsh life, in spite of the remarkable revival of 1904 and 1905. By the time of the passing of the Disestablishment Act all the main nonconformist denominations were experiencing losses in membership.[5]

The 1914 Act, dissolved every cathedral and ecclesiastical corporation in the Anglican Church in Wales, removed its bishops from the House of Lords, abolished the legal status of the courts of the Church in Wales, with its ecclesiastical law, and diverted tithes from the Church to local authorities.

The Act was to become operative at the end of the war. This delay in implementation made possible the Church Temporalities Act (commonly known as the Amending Act) of 1919, by which the Church in Wales received a grant of 1 million pounds from the Treasury to enable it to survive the loss of its endowments.[6] On 31 March, Maundy Thursday, 1920, the Church in Wales unwillingly became disestablished, an autonomous province within the Anglican Communion. All denominations in Wales were legally equal in status, except in a few parishes on the English border which remain within the Church of England to this day.[7]

The Church in Wales in the 1980's

Two new dioceses were created soon after disestablishment, and the Church has been made up of six dioceses ever since.[8] Each diocese has a bishop, elected by an electoral college representative of the whole Church. One bishop is elected archbishop. He retains his diocese, so that the archbishopric is not permanently associated with one particular area. The absence of a fixed primatial see is an interesting reflection of the intense localism of the Welsh and of the tensions between various parts of the country, which would make one immovable archiepiscopal see unacceptable to members of the Church in other parts of Wales. Each bishop has his chair in a cathedral, and each cathedral is served by a dean and chapter, the chapter consisting of senior clergymen within the diocese, nominated by the bishop and not resident at the cathedral. The cathedrals have preserved the distinctive character of the cathedrals of the Church of England. A visitor would find little apparent difference in atmosphere between, say, Llandaff Cathedral in Wales and Hereford Cathedral in England.

Moreover, it seems to be the practice on royal visits to Wales that any religious observances are held in a cathedral, when the presence of Lord Lieutenant presenting bishop to monarch recalls all the pomp of Establishment. When the Queen distributed the Royal Maundy in St. David's Cathedral, Dyfed, in 1982 she was present as Sovereign of the United Kingdom, not as Supreme Governor of the Church in Wales, although uniquely in St. David's she is also, as Sovereign, a member of the cathedral chapter as first cursal canon, in a cathedral the legal status of which had been dissolved by the assent of her grandfather, also, of course, first cursal canon. One doubts whether the Queen has ever been inside a nonconformist church in a country where all denominations are legally on a par. Disestablishment transformed the legal position of the cathedrals but not their important place in local life. They serve as naturally impressive settings for many social and cultural, especially musical, occasions.

The Church in Wales preserves a parochial system which covers every square inch of the country, except for such extraparochial areas as the environs of those cathedrals which are not also parish churches. In this respect the Church in Wales differs from some other Anglican churches, notably the American Episcopal Church in which there are no parish boundaries within dioceses. One senior American churchman has written that he would "find it an encumbrance" on his pastoral care if he felt "the responsibility for every household in a given city, simply because we were the established church."[9] An English visitor to Colorado has contrasted the territorial parochial system with that in America, with the comment that "certainly if we were disestablished...we would lose this sacred geography, this ideal of universal care."[10] Disestablishment in Wales has not affected this aspiration of universal care. Ecclesiastical parishes in Wales have no legal status, except in marriage law, but the Church in Wales has laid stress in its Constitution[11] on its parochial system. The parish priest is styled the incumbent, the office of churchwarden is maintained, and so is the ancient Easter Vestry, although voting rights are confined to members of the Church, not to all inhabitants of the parish. Every parish also has a Parochial Church Council. Ecclesiastical courts continue to exist, their authority no longer derived from law but from the concept of a compact made between all members of the Church to be bound by their decisions.

Most members of the Church in Wales would in general agree with the observation of the Bishop of Monmouth, and later also Archbishop of Wales, to his clergy in 1946: "as incumbents you have a ministry to all the souls in your parishes. This includes Roman Catholics and Nonconformists as well as the unbaptized." The scholarly bishop's further references to Roman Catholic clergy and nonconformist ministers being "strictly speaking, intruders" because the Church in Wales was the "Catholic Church in this land" raised a storm of protest, and Anglicans today might not express themselves in such uncompromising terms, but Bishop Morris's sentiments would still be approved in principle.[12] The Anglican incumbent can be more than the pastor of a congregation. The actual status of an incumbent within a community naturally varies with the individual and with the circumstances of his ministry - and spiritual leadership is probably more practicable in rural areas than in urban contexts - but it appears that, however contentious the theory of the "Catholic Church in this land" may be, the parochial system is as effective in Wales as it is in England, in spite of disestablishment. Many parishioners in Wales, especially retired immigrants from England in coastal resorts, may actually be unaware that the Church in Wales is disestablished. The Roman Catholic Church in Wales also has territorial parishes, but it seems that Roman Catholic priests do in effect restrict their pastoral care to members, or would-be members, of their Church. Nonconformist ministers serve members, active or nominal, of their congregations, in the tradition of the gathered church.[13]

Disestablishment had profound legal consequences for the Church in Wales, but the daily life of the parishes was little changed. Disendowment, however, was a serious and real problem.[14] The Church in Wales was impoverished, and it has always been unable, and perhaps unwilling also, to provide many specialist posts outside the parochial system, not even full-time residentiary canons in the cathedrals. For decades the clergymen of the Church in Wales were paid lower stipends than those of the Church of England. Many priests felt called to move to England, causing the wry comment in Crockford's preface that "not a few parsons seem to prefer the shackles of an Established Church to the 'freedom' which some within it seem to desire."[15] Until the 1950's the Church in Wales could, to some degree, afford to lose many young clergymen for it was perhaps over-staffed, particularly in rural areas which contained many small "one-church" benefices, but more recently a critical shortage of clergy in Wales has occurred, as the number of candidates for ordination has decreased and as the movement of clergymen to England has continued.[16] The shortage of clergymen has, however, allowed the Church in Wales to increase clerical stipends to a level above those in the Church of England, which indicates that the emigration of priests to England is not solely the consequence of financial pressures.

The ministry of the nonconformist churches in Wales has declined in numbers even more sharply than that of the Anglican Church, so that in many communities the Anglican priest is the only resident stipendiary minister. Some years ago in the village of Beddgelert, Gwynedd, the Anglican incumbent was given pastoral charge of two nonconformist churches without ministers, a significant comment on Wales sixty years after disestablishment, and undoubtedly likely to be emulated elsewhere.[17]

The Church in Wales was disestablished against its will, and in some respects it has been deliberately slow to take advantage of the freedom from Parliamentary control forced upon it since 1920. In liturgical use it was content to use the *Book of Common Prayer* of the Church of England until 1966, and after a protracted period of cautious experiment, the *Book of Common Prayer* of the Church in Wales is the most conservative recent revision in the Anglican Communion.[18] This conservatism, which extends beyond liturgy, may explain the continuing movement of younger priests to England. Positions of influence in the Church in Wales have very often been occupied by rather elderly and traditional bishops, priests and laymen.[19]

The contribution of the Anglican Church to Welsh culture has been considerable for centuries. In the nineteenth century, for example, there were "very many able Welsh scholars, antiquaries, publishers and literary figures within the Church," and clergymen, not all of them Welsh speaking, gave great support "to the resuscitated Eisteddfod, the learned societies and the learned journals of the day."[20] After a bizarre century and a half when no native Welsh-speaking bishops were appointed to Welsh sees, many Welsh-speaking bishops since 1870, and especially after 1920, have displayed a deep commitment to Welsh traditions. This is indubitably true of all six bishops in 1986, and also of many parish priests. Welsh speakers form a minority in the population of Wales - 19 per cent in 1981 - but the Church in Wales has striven deliberately to implement a bilingual policy,[21] although there is hostility to the Welsh language in some anglicised areas, reflecting a wider tension in Welsh society. In recent years the Church in Wales has shown much concern for economic and social issues in Wales, especially in the work of the Advisory Commission on Church and Society, established in 1972. Reports on, for example, "Rights" in 1984 and "Work in Contemporary Society" in 1985 have been impressive in quality of analysis, although their impact on society in general may be limited. Some priests have, as individuals, taken leading roles in local politics, with perhaps a majority being in left-wing and nationalist parties.[22]

Wales may be easily defined in geographical terms, but it is not easy to discover what is distinctive in contemporary Welshness. There are many linguistic attitudes - the natural Welsh speaker, the committed Welsh zealot (often a learner of the language), the non-Welsh speaker who feels himself to be Welsh and who regrets his inability to speak the language, the unconcerned non-Welsh speaker (who prefers to have his television tuned to transmitters in England), and the non-Welsh speaker who is hostile to the Welsh language. And many people in Wales are natives of England, with little or no understanding of the distinctiveness of Wales. Further, ancient suspicions still divide inhabitants of North Wales and South Wales. To all these groups the Church in Wales seeks to minister, and to a considerable extent it is the only denomination in Wales which does seek thus to do so, for many nonconformist denominations are still heavily committed to the Welsh-speaking population, while the Roman Catholic Church has limited impact on Welsh speakers, especially in rural society.

The Church in Wales has sometimes been termed "a disestablished church with an Establishment mentality." The description has usually been intended as derogatory, implying a seeking after lost privilege and status, but it may also be interpreted in a positive sense of a church which seeks to preach and serve throughout the country.

Parallels with England

If the Church of England were to be disestablished in, say, 1990, seventy years after the Church in Wales, would its position thereafter be like that of the Church in Wales after 1920, legally disestablished and disendowed, but in outward appearance, in diocese and parish, largely seemingly unchanged? The proportion of Protestant nonconformists in England in the 1980's is much lower than that in Wales in 1920, but the contemporary Roman Catholic Church in England is much more in evidence, with a larger active membership than the Church of England itself. The non-Christian proportion of the population is, of course, much higher. The presence of the Church of England in the larger cities is weak, as is that of the Church in Wales in the smaller cities of Wales. Disestablishment would not strengthen the Church of England in urban areas, but it might not actually weaken it further. In prosperous suburbs, smaller towns and villages, disestablishment would have little visible effect on the Church of England, if we may judge from the experience of Wales, where Anglicanism was, even in a nominal sense, the denomination of a minority, unlike in England where the majority of Christians are baptized members of the Church of England.

The loss of an episcopal presence in the House of Lords would scarcely cripple the Church of England, while even the secularization of historic endowments would be less seriously felt as endowments form a diminishing proportion of the income of the Church of England.[23] Disestablishment in England would not be a panacea for all ills, but neither would it signal the extinction of the Church of England. England would not become a "churchless nation."[24] The ingrained tradition of centuries, and the diocesan and parochial framework, which need not be abandoned at disestablishment, as we have seen, would maintain a recognisable Anglican presence in England. The Welsh Church has, it must be added, probably preserved its national character in part because of the continuing example of establishment in England, and a disestablished Church of England would not have the benefit of surviving establishment in an influential larger neighbour, but its position as the Church of England does not derive solely from legal establishment.

The Churches and Welsh Society

The twentieth century has witnessed a dramatic collapse in the influence of the Christian churches in Welsh society. "It became clear, in the aftermath of the armistice (of 1918), that the chapels were no longer the social or spiritual forces that they had been in Victorian or even in Edwardian Wales."[25] Nonconformity suffered from the decline of the Welsh language and from its failure to adapt to new intellectual, cultural and social outlooks. The dominant influence of religion in Wales at the beginning of the century, much stronger than in England, made its decline appear even more drastic. "Over the country as a whole the decline was so rapid and so widespread as to amount to a cultural change of major proportions which would inevitably have profound effects on moral and political, as on religious, attitudes and behaviour."[26] By 1950 Wyn Griffith could write that "it may be that we are now in the presence of the last generation of men and women to regulate their lives by it (the Welsh nonconformist tradition), whose acceptance of it is not mere habit."[27] The disestablishment of the Anglican church did not lead to any increase in the number of nonconformists, and indeed the membership of nonconformist denominations has decreased consistently since 1920, especially after 1945. "It was nonconformity which was to suffer more from increasing secularisation, general anglicisation and an increasing emphasis on social Christianity. Politically, it was to suffer from the gradual erosion of Liberal influence."[28] Membership of the Anglican Church has remained fairly constant, within an almost static total population, while the Roman Catholic Church has increased its membership greatly, from a low initial total, without noticeably expanding in influence in Welsh society.[29]

Ecumenism has made less progress in Wales than in England, partly no doubt because of lingering animosities after disestablishment. A Council of Churches for Wales has existed since 1956, without making much impact on Welsh life. A Covenant to work for unity between the Church in Wales, the Presbyterian Church in Wales (formerly the Calvinistic Methodist Connexion), the Methodist Church in Wales, the United Reformed Church in Wales and some Baptist congregations was signed in 1975, but its consequences have been limited, little more than the appearance of a general, if not yet universal, spirit of benevolent good will, which embraces also denominations outside the Covenanted churches. Discussions between the Church in Wales and the Roman Catholic Church in Wales have enabled leaders of these churches to become more closely acquainted, although there is less evidence of cooperation at a parochial level. The impact of *all* the churches in Wales is marginal and decreasing. Since there is no legislative assembly in Wales, there is no single forum for the discussion of Welsh affairs, while the pronounced localism within the Principality makes it difficult to convert initiatives into achievements in Wales as a whole. Is Wales a nation?

The land of chapels - although only half the population attended worship on census Sunday in 1851 - has become "as secular as anywhere else."[30] The decline of nonconformist membership and influence, including that of its once important press, has been a key factor in changing the identity of Wales. "To visit those parts of the country where the chapels are most deeply embedded in the landscape and local history, to live in Methodist Yorkshire, or Baptist Wales, or Independent East Anglia, or Unitarian Lancashire is to recognise the real plight of Nonconformity in the (nineteen) sixties. Anyone can point to shining exceptions in particular places, but over large tracts of country, behind the peeling facades and plaintive wayside pulpits, there is nothing left but a faithful ingrown remnant, whiling away its Pleasant Sunday Afternoons and its Women's Bright Hours in dingy rooms from which whole generations and classes and intelligence levels have long since fled."[31] Or, as an Anglican bishop in industrial Wales wrote in 1961: "The Welsh language and Nonconformity have declined together; the Club has replaced the Chapel; Bingo or its equivalents provide the social opportunities once found in the Literary Society or the Preaching or Singing Festival; Pop music has ousted the Oratorio; and the dynamic leadership of the minister has vanished, to be replaced, if at all, by more secular and humanist figures."[32]

The "nonconformist way of life" survived longer in the rural and Welsh speaking areas, but even in these the old values have been challenged in the twentieth century, most obviously in the matter of the Sunday opening of public houses. In a referendum in 1960 most of urban, industrial, anglicised Wales voted for Sunday opening. In 1968 most of English speaking rural Wales followed. And in the most recent referendum only Cardiganshire and Dwyfor - the two areas in which the Welsh language and nonconformity remained strongest - voted to keep public houses closed on Sundays, notwithstanding the marked dependence of these districts on tourism. By the 1970's it was clear that "the young, the industrial worker, and their wives, and perhaps the languid middle class as well" no longer took seriously the traditional, or at least Victorian, values of Welsh nonconformity.[33]

Prospects for Wales, the report of the 1982 census of the churches, provided a wealth of statistical material on religion in Wales in the early 1980's.[34] The report indicated that there were over 5,750 churches in Wales, served by over 2,300 ministers. Church members amounted to 24 per cent of the adult population, while the number of adults attending church services was only 13 per cent of the population, little more than half the church membership. Most congregations in Wales were small, three quarters of the churches having fewer than fifty members. The average membership of a church in Wales was 46 persons, compared with 76 in England. Membership had declined since 1978, and doubtless the decline has continued since 1982.[35] It seems unlikely that the majority of congregations will survive, on existing trends, long into the next century.[36] The decrease in numbers is most striking in Welsh-speaking congregations.[37] Growing congregations are to be found, however, especially in English-speaking urban areas. Some are Anglican and Roman Catholic, although the majority may be of newer denominations, often evangelical and charismatic, often perceived by their members as arks of salvation in a sinful world, rather than as centres of service to the world.

Attendance at worship has become the activity of a small minority.[38] The churches within society seem to be, to borrow Tolstoy's phrase, like deaf men answering questions which no one has asked them. They have lost their old authority without discovering a new role. Some ministers have taken leading positions in the Welsh Language Society, the Eisteddfod and the Peace Movement, but the churches as institutions exist on the fringe of society. According to the most distinguished contemporary Welsh historian "Wales has become not much more than nominally a Christian country."[39] The decline of the Welsh language, changes in population structure and distribution, and the emergence of secularism and indifference have combined to weaken the sense of tradition. "To many outsiders Wales and the Christian religion are tightly woven together, from the hymns sung at International Rugby Matches to small Nonconformist Chapels in dark mining valleys. Those, however, who have closely observed church life in the principality over the last few decades have seen a general decline in church membership and attendance, coupled with the closure of many chapels, especially in those valleys. To many it seems that Max Boyce's song, 'Ten thousand instant Christians,' has a poignant reality."[40]

A paper which has largely been devoted to the fortunes of the disestablished Anglican Church may fittingly conclude by quoting from a leading Welsh historian who is "committed to neither the Anglican nor the nonconformist point of view":[41] "The final irony remains that, while few churchmen would now wish to return to the old days before 1914,[42] nonconformists look back nostalgically at the dynamic years half a century ago when they were chafing under the burdens and restraints of the state establishment."[43]

REFERENCES

[1] General accounts of disestablishment may be found in P. M. H. Bell, *Disestablishment in Ireland and Wales* (London, 1969), and W. B. George, "The Disestablishment of the Anglican Church in Wales" (Ph.D. thesis, Columbia University, 1963). See also R. Tudur Jones, "The Origins of the Nonconformist Disestablishment Campaign," *Journal of the Historical Society of the Church in Wales* (1970) pp. 39-76, and W. B. George, "Welsh Disestablishment and Welsh Nationalism," *Journal of the Historical Society of the Church in Wales*, (1970), pp. 77-91. For a general account of the development of the Church in Wales see D. Walker (ed.), *A History of the Church in Wales* (Penarth, 1976). And see P. Morgan and D. Thomas, *Wales: The Shaping of a Nation* (Newton Abbot, 1984), pp. 155-177.

[2] For the census see K. O. Morgan, *Rebirth of a Nation: Wales 1880 - 1980* (Oxford, 1981), pp. 14-15. Morgan's authoritative work is essential for an understanding of recent Welsh history.

[3] Morgan, op. cit., p. 18.

[4] Bell, op. cit., p. 238; Morgan and Thomas, op. cit., pp. 167-168.

[5] Morgan, op. cit., pp. 134-135.

[6] Bell, op. cit. pp. 258-259, 308-318; Morgan, op. cit., p. 183-185.

[7] Bell, op. cit. p. 305.

[8] A useful discussion of the Church in Wales since 1920, by David Walker, may be found in David Walker, op. cit., pp. 164-187. A proposal to increase the number of bishoprics was defeated at a meeting of the Governing Body (General Synod) of the Church in Wales in 1980.

[9] Canon J. R. Gundrum to the present writer, 22 Jan. 1986.

[10] "The American Way of Life," *Church Times*, 8 Nov. 1985.

[11] The Constitution of the Church in Wales is reprinted from time to time, and available from Church in Wales Publications, Woodland Place, Penarth, South Glamorgan.

[12] The Bishop of Monmouth (A. E. Morris), *The Church in Wales and Nonconformity* (Newport, 1949), *passim*. I am grateful to Mr. J. S. Peart-Binns, whose biography of Archbishop Morris is soon to be published, for assistance in this reference.

[13] Congregations were formerly larger than the numbers of their paidup members because of the presence of "adherents" : D. B. Rees, *Wales : The Cultural Heritage* (Ormskirk, 1981), p. 17.

[14]Bell, op. cit., pp. 311-312. £722, 522 was raised by a special appeal to members of the Church in Wales during the economic depression, 1920-1934, to make up financial resources: Bell, op. cit., p. 325. Archbishop Green felt in 1935 that the end of tithe had been a great blessing: C. A. H. Green, "Disestablishment and Disendowment in Wales," reprinted in the *Official Handbook of the Church in Wales* (Cardiff, 1936), pp. 12-19.

[15]*Crockford's Clerical Directory* (1953-54), p. xx.

[16]Although in 1985 the movement of the clergy into Wales showed a sudden increase, possibly because of the increased stipends in Wales: *Report of the Central Committee for the Training of Ordinands* (Cardiff, 1986), p. 9.

[17]In parochial terms, antagonism between Anglicans and nonconformists was doubtless mitigated by mixed marriages, so that most families contained members of several denominations, seldom deeply versed in doctrinal matters and increasingly aware of their common Christian profession as society became more secular. Religious education in Wales has not been impressive in this century.

[18]*The Book of Common Prayer for use in the Church in Wales* (Penarth, 1984).

[19]Archbishop Glyn Simon called in 1970 for a reduction in the average age of members of key committees of the Governing Body from 65 to 50 or younger, but one sees little evidence of his words being heeded: *Highlights,* Oct. 1970, p. 3.

[20]H. I. Davies in the *Handbook of the Welsh Church Congress* (Cardiff, 1953), p. 62.

[21]Walker, *History of the Church in Wales,* p. 186.

[22]For example, the Labour Chairman of South Glamorgan County Council, the Independent Chairman of Gwynedd County Council, the Labour Chairman of Merthyr Tydfil District Council and the leader of Plaid Cymru (Welsh Nationalist) on Merthyr Tydfil District Council have all been Anglican priests. Clergymen of the Church in Wales may stand for election to the House of Commons, unlike clergymen of the Church of England. None has even been elected, to the present writer's knowledge, although one at least has stood for the Labour party, in Worcester, England, in Feb. and Oct. 1974, and one for Plaid Cymru in Feb. 1974.

[23]*A Sharing Church* (The Finances of the Church of England 1983-86) (London, 1985), p. 1.

[24]See Mrs. Alexander's hymn, quoted in Bell, op. cit.. p. 158:
"Look down, Lord of heaven, on our desolation!
Fallen, fallen, fallen is now our Country's crown,
Dimly dawns the New Year on a churchless nation,
Ammon and Amalek tread our borders down."

[25]Morgan, *Rebirth of a Nation*, p. 197. See pp. 197-201 for an account of nonconformity between 1918 and 1945. For an argument that the nonconformist churches lost support as a result of concentrating too much on disestablishment and not sufficiently on economic and social problems, see I. G. Jones, "Language and Community in Nineteenth Century Wales," in D. Smith (ed.) *A People and a Proletariat* (London, 1980), p. 68.

[26]D. Williams, *A History of Modern Wales* (London, 1977), p. 300.

[27]W. Griffith, *The Welsh* (Harmondsworth, 1950), p. 32.

[28]G. E. Jones, *Modern Wales* (Cambridge, 1984), p. 276.

[29]For statistics and interpretation, see P. Brierley and B. Evans, *Prospects for Wales* (London, 1983), *passim*.

[30]D. Smith, *Wales! Wales?* (London, 1984), p. 155.

[31]C. Driver, *The Future of the Free Churches* (London, 1962), pp. 16-17. The few sociological studies of religion in modern Wales include V. Jones (ed.), *The Church in a Mobile Society* (Llandybie, 1969) and D. B. Rees, *Chapels in the Valley* (Upton, Wirral, 1975). See also J. G. James, "Disestablishment and After", in E.T. Davies (ed.), *The Story of the Church in Glamorgan* (London, 1962), pp. 88-107.

[32]The Bishop of Llandaff (W. G. H. Simon), *Then and Now* (Penarth, 1961), p. 27.

[33]Morgan, *Rebirth of a Nation*, p. 355.

[34]Brierley and Evans, *Prospects for Wales*. The statistical material has been generally accepted as a fair reflection, although not all details are precisely accurate.

[35]Brierley and Evans, op. cit., p. 5.

[36]*Ibid* p. 6.

[37]*Ibid* p. 5.

[38]Attendance at worship in 1982 according to *Prospects* was Roman Catholic 20 per cent; Church in Wales 29 per cent; nonconformist 51 per cent. The Church in Wales was the largest single denomination: Brierley and Evans, op. cit., p. 20.

[39]Glanmor Williams, *Religion, Language and Nationality in Wales* (Cardiff, 1979), p. 108.

[40]Brierley and Evans, op. cit., p. 20.

50

[41]K. O. Morgan, *Freedom or Sacrilege? A History of the Campaign for Welsh Disestablishment* (Penarth, 1966), p. 1.

[42]I am by no means convinced of the truth of this statement.

[43]Morgan, op. cit., p. 31.

CHAPTER IV

KIRK AND SOCIETY IN MODERN SCOTLAND

PETER BISSET

The trends in Scotland's church life have followed with seeming inevitability those apparent in other parts of the United Kingdom. The land where the Kirk holds sway has not escaped the process of secularisation.

In the early 1900's the voices of churchmen were raised in concern that faithfulness in church attendance was lessening. It is difficult to judge whether statistically that assessment was well founded. What was apparent to many, however, was that religion was no longer so profoundly the motivating influence in people's lives as once it had been.

For Scotland that was a critical observation. Traditionally the Scots had been regarded as a god-fearing people. The Kirk played a central role in the ordering of their lives. The Reformation which had transformed the face of the Church in Scotland had been in great measure a People's Reformation. The Presbyterian government of the Scottish Kirk, with its emphasis upon the key place of the ruling elders, effectively expressed the spiritual and social aspirations of a nation. Scotland, in the Act of Union, denied any separate political identity, found such identity within its Kirk. Presbyterianism provided a congenial ethos in which the independent Scottish spirit could be expressed.

In every parish in Scotland the Kirk Session ruled. In its supreme court, the General Assembly, the Kirk spoke with independent mind to assert the sovereign rule of Christ Jesus within the nation's life. The distinctive character of Scottish Church life can be clearly seen in any comparison of membership statistics.

	Episcopal	Presbyterian	Roman Catholic	Other
England	39%	3%	32%	26%
Wales	23%	17%	29%	31%
Scotland	3%	69%	22%	6%
N.Ireland	19%	33%	42%	7%

(U.K. Christian Handbook 1986/7)

For Scotland, Presbyterianism stands supreme. In no other part of the United Kingdom does the membership of one denomination so evidently dominate church allegiance. The Kirk's influence may be on the wane, but Presbyterianism still places its clear stamp upon the life of the land.

It was an aggrieved Episcopalian, disappointed by the failure of the 1959 bid for closer Anglican and Presbyterian relations, who opined "It is nothing new for Scottish church life to be at variance with the trends prevailing generally throughout Christendom, it is nothing new for the Scots to consider themselves a peculiar people who have received something akin to a special revelation!"

Such a judgement would probably be received with pride by the average Scot. "Here's tae us, wha's like us!" might be the instinctive and immediate response. Where else in the United Kingdom could a daily paper have heralded the proposals of Anglican-Presbyterian unity with headlines which sounded a call to national vigilance, and warned its readers of near national betrayal. "SECRET PLOT. BISHOPS IN THE KIRK," proclaimed the Daily Express, and at that point, meaningful discussion ceased. A nation's identity was at stake, and the integrity of Presbyterian Scotland was too precious to be entrusted to the ecclesiastics!

So, it had been through the years. The Kirk was symbol of a nation's identity, guarantor of her liberties, and if, indeed, the Kirk was found wanting there was never lack of contender to maintain the true face of Scotland's Kirk. Hence the contentions and schisms of the years. Hence the energetic resistance of power and privilege. Hence the stubborn insistence upon the right of a true Scot to choose his "own man" to be the pastor of his soul.

The Kirk was Scotland's Kirk. It moulded the nation's life. It guided its affairs. It cared for its poor, and guarded its young. None escaped its pervasive presence. Ministers of the Kirk figured notably in the life of the land, adorning its scholarship, informing its public life, contributing notably to its affairs.

In a real sense the pulpits of Scotland provided the backdrop against which the life of Scotland was acted out. It was the Kirk which gave meaning and significance to the common life. So much was this so, that a Roman Catholic writer, Moray McLaren, could aver that there was no one in Scotland, agnostic, atheist, or even comfortably indifferent who could escape the impress of the Scottish Reformation which had "contributed to the making of his mind in the deepest places."

It is against that background that the process of secularisation must be understood in its effect upon the Scottish churches. We cannot escape from our history. It is part of our heritage even when we renounce it. So it was that while church leaders at the turn of the century questioned disturbing trends in Scottish Church life, it did not appear that these trends were so deeply disturbing as those apparent in the English scene.

In Scotland, there were, indeed, reasons for hopefulness. If the ecclesiastical divisions of the nineteenth-century had been evidence of the passionate vitality of Scottish church life, there were those who looked at the splintered church, and saw the wastefulness of divisions which had robbed Scotland of a Kirk which was evidently the church of the land. Churches which were united in evangelical conviction and Presbyterian principle, churches which purported to care for the Christian good of Scotland, could not in good conscience continue separate identities which weakened their witness and enfeebled their service. The history they shared was greater than the issues which divided.

So it was that with two great Church unions in 1900 and 1929 the Scottish Presbyterian family was largely reunited, and Scotland once again had a Kirk which could in great measure claim to be Scotland's Kirk. True, in the Highlands, the Free Church maintained an independent witness and marked out a separate identity which in many areas still prevails, but by and large Scotland once more had a Kirk, holding fast to principles dearly won and proudly prized. It was a Church national and free, a church which saw clearly its role to stand for the values of Christ's Kingdom at the heart of the nation's life, and not be bound by any requirement of State to violate its conscience or restrict its witness. Its constitution as a National Church would be the envy of many State Churches the world over.

The reunited church had a membership of 1.27 million, representing 40% of the adult population. It applied itself with energy to the task of bringing new vigour to the parish system with the combined resources of the uniting churches. There was a mood of euphoria abroad. "The reunited church," maintained one writer, "is a national symbol. One may even doubt whether there could be a Scotland without it!" "... with a re-united church," wrote the Secretary of the Kirk's Home Board, "setting out on her labours at the beginning of a new century a Christian Scotland is something more than a vision, it is a promise waiting acceptance by a divinely inspired Church."

Whatever the hopes, dreams, or convictions which had attended the birth of the reunited Kirk in 1929, it was certain that churches which had rivalled each other over the years now required a period of peace during which the inevitable problems of the union could be resolved and the merger of the various agencies of the uniting churches be effectively accomplished. Such opportunity was not to be granted. It was only ten years until the nation was plunged into war. At the end of the conflict the Kirk's membership had declined by 2%. This in itself was not surprising. It has been noted that times of war, far from leading to a mass return to religion, tend to unsettle and disturb the patterns of church allegiance. But, on the whole. the Kirk could be well content. A union had been forged that gave new hope for the future, and over the period when the Kirk's membership had plateaued and slightly declined, membership rolls in the Church of England had fallen by 18%.

It was the end of the Second World War, however, which appeared to bring all of the promise of 1929 to fulfilment. In the shaping of a new society, Scotland's Kirk would come into its own. That was certainly the conviction of a distinguished Commission of the General Assembly which during the years of war had sought to discern God's will for Church and Nation. It was the Church through these dark days that had resisted the powers of tyranny and oppression. It would be the lay people of the Church who would be the leaders in the dawning of a new day. "On nothing does the future health of our society more depend," they asserted, "than on the initiative of our Christian laity." It was the laity who would face the difficulty and grasp the opportunity. It was they who in a new enterprise of mission would carry the Gospel into every area of the nation's life. And if the call was specially to the laity, there was also an urgent call to youth. It was the young people of the Church who particularly could provide the leadership required by the changing times.

It was certainly a Kirk with a youthful zest which faced the post war years. George McLeod, the Kirk's disturbingly prophetic pioneer, summed up the aspirations of many when he called for the renewal of Church and Society - "We shall rebuild."

The General Assembly itself gave the signal to advance. A report to the Assembly "Into All The World" summoned the church to new ventures in evangelism. The call was heeded. Evangelism became the agenda for Presbyteries throughout the land.

It was the beginning of a period of high adventure in the story of the Kirk. The evangelistic initiatives of D. P. Thomson, Evangelist of the Kirk, the pioneering work of Church Extension planting new churches in the burgeoning new housing areas, the creative initiatives of Religious Programmes Organiser, Ronnie Falconer at the B.B.C., all pointed towards a national programme which would give full expression to the concern to plant the Church and the Gospel at the heart of the nation's life.

So was born "Tell Scotland", a movement in mission which was to carry the Kirk forward to a new height in its membership and a new vitality in its life. At the centre of it all was the Rev. Tom Allan whose book "The Face of my Parish" was to become a classic in the literature of evangelism. Tom

Allan had already proved himself in the realms of scholarship when the wars took him into active service. It was those years which also brought him to personal encounter with his Lord, and a call to ministry which found remarkable fulfilment in a Glasgow parish. In that parish, Allan saw the church of Jesus Christ reborn, lives remade and the call to mission rediscovered. He also found the great and hurtful problem of a kirk which in large measure did not wish to be disturbed from its contented complacency, a church which effectively resisted the intrusion upon its settled life which outgoing mission necessarily entailed.

Much of all that Tom Allan had learned in a Glasgow parish found expression in the programme of "Tell Scotland," It had been the congregational group at the heart of the church's life which he had seen giving new authenticity to the meaning of the Church. It would be such groups throughout Scotland committed, convinced, and caring, who would make the Gospel count once more within the life of the land. It was they who would bridge the dichotomy between those who saw the essential expression of the Gospel either in caring deed or saving word. Throughout Scotland the Gospel would be incarnated in the lives of men and women who in word and deed would make Jesus known.

The vision was marvellous; its fulfilment throughout Scotland as congregations embarked upon mission was wonderfully exciting. It seemed that the Kingdom could not be long delayed as the membership figures of the Kirk soared to new heights! In 1956 the Kirk could boast a membership roll of 1.3 million. Unhappily, in the previous year. "Tell Scotland" embarked upon a course which signalled its imminent demise. At the instigation of Tom Allan, whose leadership had inspired and shaped "Tell Scotland," Billy Graham was invited to conduct the "All Scotland Crusade." The invitation was resisted by those who had committed themselves to "Tell Scotland" but who were deeply suspicious of American Revivalism. Such was Allan's leadership, however, that hesitations and reservations were set aside, and, in the event, it seemed that they had been groundless. The Graham Organisation had never met with such overwhelming response. It appeared that throughout Scotland there were those who had been simply waiting for this opportunity to make commitment, and certainly there were parishes where the encouragement of the Crusade brought new heart to congregational endeavour. But it was the end of an era. After, the peak of 1956 membership toppled, and within a few short years all that had been gained was lost.

There were, of course, the inevitable recriminations. Understandably Billy Graham became the scapegoat for those who had never hailed his coming with joy. In fairness, it was not simply those who had had fundamental reservations about the Crusade who reviewed their experience with regret. Among those who voiced concern was the Kirk's veteran evangelist, D. P. Thomson, who surveying the Scottish scene, discovered how few of the converts of the Crusade had found their way into the Church's life. Sadly he concluded that the less spectacular years of "Tell Scotland" had been a sounder investment in Christian work and witness than the costly apparatus of the "All Scotland Crusade."

Graham himself was not the essential target of such criticisms. There were few who doubted his integrity. What was suspect was the "organisation," the "circus," the personality focus, and the "Americanisation" of something that had grown out of the soil of Scotland. The fundamental concepts of "Tell Scotland" had been impaired, if not damaged by the Crusade. The central significance of lay witness, and the creative alliance between contending aspects of Christian witness appeared to be destroyed by the high focus upon Crusade evangelism.

There were those, of course, who found their scapegoat elsewhere. If there had been any "failure" during the high days of the Crusade then the blame could be laid at the door of the National Church. It was understandable that converts would fall away if there were no welcoming fellowship into which they could be introduced. In the light of Tom Allan's confessed experience in pastoral charge, such allegation could not be lightly set aside. Unfortunately for those who saw the failure of the Kirk, there is little evidence that the more warmly evangelical denominations fared any better during these critical days. Indeed, there is evidence that some who saw no increase in membership until the stirring days of the Crusade experienced a falling away more disastrous than that which affected the Kirk.

Whatever the verdict, it is beyond argument that the mid-fifties were a significant period in the life of the Scottish Church. If the outcome was disappointing, this does not itself detract from the dedication of those who sought to further the mission of the Church during these days. There are, indeed, clear indications that their endeavour was a response to a sensed "readiness for religion." D. P. Thomson witnessed to that fact wherever he travelled in his campaigns. He found a responsiveness unprecedented in his experience. Such had been the experience of Ronnie Falconer at the B.B.C. Such was the experience of ministers in many parts of the land whose congregations were relatively untouched by the larger movements of mission.

It is difficult not to conclude that the "revival" of the post-war decade was a response to the longing of many to see a new society arising out of the debris and devastation of war. And it is a significant tribute to Scotland's Kirk that in such an hour the people turned to the church as the essential heart of such an enterprise. "The Church in the Midst" had been the call of National Church Extension as it sought to plant the Kirk in the new communities. Such had been the church's place in Scotland's story. It was the post-war dream that it should be so.

1956 was the end of a dream. From that point onwards Scottish experience mirrored that of the Church of England, although there are aspects of the Kirk's decline which curiously reflect the Scottish ethos.

The first signal of decline came from the children of the Kirk. The baby boom of the post-war years resulted in large Sunday Schools which regularly overflowed church premises into local schools. It was all part of the dream of the new society in which the stabilities of home and family life were held dear. It is, therefore, all the more strange that 1955 should herald the beginnings of a falling away. The pattern was clear. From the age of 10 onwards, young people increasingly disappeared from church and Sunday School. A special survey undertaken in 1958 identified the trends and marked the deficiencies of the Kirk's educational programme. There was complacency abroad which accepted that "children went to Sunday School" irrespective of the quality or effectiveness of the church's provision for their Christian education. But more serious was the suspicion that parental example did not appear to be of such character as to provide a model for the growing child.

Perhaps the analysis was simplistic. The patterns of a child's behaviour will be formed within the parameters set by home, church, and society, and within that complex the patterns established by family life will have to be vitally strong if they are to survive the erosion of an unbelieving world and an ineffective church.

Since the formative years of these children lay within the boom years of church growth in Scotland, the question must inevitably be posed as to how deep that religious revival went within the nation's life. If church membership collapsed within a climate of radical questioning, how differed the Kirk from other pillars of the establishment which found their foundations shaken.

Radical questioning was the order of the day within as without the Kirk. It was the urgent concern of successive Committees and Commissions to help the Church rediscover its identity, and learn what it meant to be Christ's Kirk for Scotland in vastly changing times. Regretfully, they frequently concluded that the only changes palatable to congregations were those which made no difference!

Strangely, one of the problems still remaining stemmed from the union of 1929. The schisms of the years had provided most communities in Scotland with a variety of churches each with its own separate history and dearly won identity. The union decreed that all, as congregations of the National Church, were now "parish churches" with territorial responsibilities. Unhappily, the requirements of Church procedure have commonly been understandable only to congregations jealous of their "rights," and seldom by the communities subjected to ecclesiastical surgery! It was, of course, envisaged that the years would bring an increasing uniting of congregational resources. The reality is that union and readjustment are more often dictated by financial stringency than any desire to be united in Christ's cause, and a Kirk which sees its role in national terms is frequently frustrated by the narrow perspectives of congregational loyalties.

So the Kirk toils on, facing an age of radical change, and finding difficulty in encouraging congregations to respond positively to new situations and conditions. But significantly the dream lingers on.

There are those who wonder at Scotland's story and particularly question the claim to distinctive nationhood of a country which so easily, it appears, surrendered its identity at the Union of the Crowns. There is reason to question, but there is also reason to believe that Scotland clung to its identity by prizing those symbols of nationhood which marked out the distinctive character of its life. Scotland's law, its education, and its Kirk established the Scottish difference.

There is a strange reflection of it in the Kirk's membership statistics. Superimpose upon the graph of declining membership, the graph of Communion Attendance (perhaps a more realistic measure of the Kirk's practising membership), and it will be seen that in contrast to the steady line of declining membership the graph of Communion Attendance is interrupted by occasional peaks. The peaks correspond to those moments in the life of Scotland when devolution has become an issue, and Scottish nationhood is most apparent. A direct relationship between faithful churchmanship and political awareness would be hard to establish, but it appears that within the nation's life, there are times of national aspiration or discontent when a mood expressed politically in Scottish Nationalism is also expressed in a quickening of the Church's life. The notion of mood is further emphasised by the fact that each time a peak in Communion Attendance appears, it introduces a new gradient in the graph of membership decline. So, in 1967 a spectacular leap in Communion Attendance was followed by a steeper gradient of decline - a rebellion against the Swinging Sixties followed by an acceptance of sad inevitability? Likewise, a peak in 1975 is followed by a lessened gradient of decline, which perhaps mirrors the inconclusiveness of the abortive Devolution Campaign but signals some awakening of nationhood not dependent upon political institutions. Strangely, there appears at this very time a growth in Adult Baptisms into membership of the Kirk, indicating an increase in conversion growth within a church which has traditionally depended upon Infant Baptism and the Christian nurture of its children as the main entry to membership.

It is apparent that there is change in the church life of Scotland, even if for the Kirk it comes slowly and reluctantly. A survey carried out in 1984 gives tantalising glimpses of it. Church membership continues its decline, but church attendance to a lesser degree. There are signs that membership may at last owe more to conviction than convention. With one in four Scottish churches registering growth, and these markedly the larger congregations, it is claimed that most Scottish worshippers now belong to growing churches. Does this give hint of the shape of things to come? Will it be those churches which most successfully respond to the challenge of a new age which will mark out the shape of Scotland's kirk for tomorrow?

However this may be, the Roman Catholic community now dominates the west of Scotland in those very areas where the invasion of Irish Roman Catholic labourers in the last century was most resented and resisted. Indeed, in Scotland as a whole, the Roman Catholic Church can now claim a greater attendance of worshippers than can the Kirk. But overall, the picture has changed little. Both the Kirk and the Roman Catholic Church can claim 7% of the population attending Sunday worship with all of the other denominations registering 2%.

But in the end statistics matter little. Someone has cynically remarked that there is little difference between the Kirk alive and dead! With only 29% of its membership in church on Sunday there remains in Scotland a vast mass for whom the Kirk is still their church. That mass is not just the mass of non-attending members, it is the even greater battalion of those who "used to be members," a regiment which now outnumbers any official membership roll. It is tempting to think that the strength of the Kirk lies in its traditional loyalty rather than its record of faithfulness, but it may uneasily be questioned how long the Kirk can continue to maintain its place in the life of the land with a lapsing membership and disappearing youth.

There are those who have hoped that decline would only be a temporary phase in the church's story. Professor T. C. Smout in a recent book, acknowledges that the decline in the Scottish Church did not set in so early as in other European countries, but judges that the change which has now come is fundamental, and the Kirk's endeavours to halt it unavailing. "The Church of Scotland," he claims, "never did find a solution to the other and more fundamental problems posed by the death of hell, the rise of class, and the spread of other entertainment."

That judgement cannot be treated lightly. It sets the agenda if Scotland's kirk is to have any future credibility. The questions raised, however, do not invite a despairing answer.

Sociologists suggest that there are two courses open to the Church in a secular society. The choice is to separate or accommodate. The charge against the Kirk is that it has effectively accommodated itself to its environment until the Christian community has lost its distinctiveness. The charge can scarcely be denied when only a minority of the Kirk's membership show any great degree of Christian faithfulness, and the thrust of its mission is blunted by the outsider's inability to discern any Christian "difference." The charge is most energetically made by those who have spurned the way of accommodation, and taken the way of separation. It is the Conservative Presbyterian Churches in the Highlands and Islands who have most determinedly declared the Christian "difference," and have seen themselves as guardians of a Calvinistic heritage betrayed by an accommodating Kirk. Hell for them was not dead! Unhappily it is these churches which are now experiencing most drastic decline abandoned by a generation which cannot relate the categories of fundamentalist belief to the thought forms of their society.

C. S. Lewis once remarked that Christian faith had little to do with either with the furniture of Heaven or the temperature of Hell! Such healthy agnosticism is urgently required in a society where the bankruptcy of secular thought is becoming apparent. It is precisely at this time that the Church has opportunity to interpret the Faith relevantly for a new generation, and it is a sign of Scotland's searching for its soul that, increasingly, candidates for the ministry are men and women drawn from other vocations and professions who, in the maturity of life and experience, have chosen to devote their gifts to Christian ministry. Recently a leading Q.C. at the Scottish Bar and a senior Secretary at the Scottish Office have taken that step, although perhaps more noteworthy in the popular mind was the fact that the Kirk accepted and trained for the Christian ministry two men who had served prison sentences for murder and embezzlement. Such "signs" cannot be easily disregarded. They spell out simply and decisively the limits of secularisation.

The question of class the Kirk cannot avoid. Its strength has ever been that it is a kirk of the people. It was amidst the cheering masses that one of Scotland's finest hours was acted out, when in 1843 forty per cent of the Kirk's ministers walked out of the General Assembly to found the Free Kirk. Their act was protest against the principle and practice of patronage. For them the freedom of the Kirk was dear - to be a kirk for the people. And yet that great act of protest had implications for the Kirk far beyond the schism which sundered its life. The supporters of the new Church denied State funding were the emerging middle classes prospering in the Industrial Revolution. Subtly, another form of patronage was appearing! New boundaries were being established. The new church might have won the plaudits of the throng but it would never be "their" kirk, as was the parish kirk. Strangely, through the years the tradition has lingered, and in many communities throughout Scotland ordinary folk will recognise the church which is theirs by right! It will unfailingly be the "old" parish church. But it was in the cities that the Industrial Revolution produced most clearly the territorial divisions of class, and it is in the cities that the estrangements are most evident. "Church-going" areas, and "non church-going" areas distinguish the "winners" and the "losers."

As boundaries of class are established so are corresponding role expectations. In Scotland the church-going male is a rare species, especially within the Kirk, and particularly among the working population. Not uncommonly a working man will explain to a minister that he must not take his absence from the kirk as evidence of irreligion. It is a matter of role. The church has to do with home and family life. It is, therefore, by clear definition the business of his wife. He does not spurn the church. It just does not belong to his world. Indeed, it is part of his confusion that the Kirk no longer seems to fulfill its expected role as it is deserted by the children to whom it should be teaching Christian values.

The Kirk has a proud record in Industrial Mission, but the respect it meets in the work place is only with difficulty related to the life of the local church. It is not wondered at that it is in the cities, the home of Industrial

Man, that the Kirk faces its greatest challenge and suffers its severest losses. Nor can it be wondered that the Kirk lacks credibility when churches are seen in abundance in the affluent suburbs and abandoned in the drearily decaying inner city.

Does the parish kirk have a future? Much of the argument of the past years has focussed upon that question. Many believe that Scotland needs new and varied forms of parish ministry to meet the needs of the hour. Too often congregations refuse to see new possibilities. They cling to the shadows of the past rather than respond to the challenge of a new day. The question with all its ramifications is decisive.

And, as for the counter attractions, any survey will reveal that an ordinary Scottish congregation longs for a worship that is simple and homely. The mental exercises of the minister in the pulpit no longer provide the intellectual stimulus of the parish. There is far more to exercise and centre the thinking of the common man than the delights of theological discourse. John Knox spoke admiringly of Calvin's reformed kirk in Geneva as the most perfect school of Christ. Scotland's inheritance could thus be defined. The problem is that, Scotsman come of age repudiates such religion. He looks rather for a centre of belonging. It was so that the parish kirk once figured in his life. It is still so in Scotland's growing churches. Enter their fellowships and you will find a sphere in which people have discovered what it means to belong.

A church's health and growth depend not only upon the environment it enjoys but the way in which it relates to that environment. So, through the years Scotland's kirk gave focus to the nation's life. But what of today? Can the proud eminence of the Kirk remain? The Roman Catholic Church, its identity clearly preserved by its separate schooling, threatens to outdo the Kirk in the faithfulness of its membership. The Scottish Episcopal Church with its own distinctive cultural identity shows signs of advance, and Scottish Baptists are proclaiming the turn of the tide. But within the Kirk a varied pattern appears. In the cities, drastic decline, in the Border regions, signs of recovery, but in the north growth. It might be claimed that this is simply the last ditch stand of traditional religion. The evidence is not quite so clear. It is not (e.g.) all churches on the island of Lewis which are experiencing growth. And it is not the conservative Presbyterian churches which are seeing their faithfulness rewarded. No, the growth will be found most strikingly in the town of Stornoway where young people with a history of vital religion in their community are being encouraged to translate that living faith into the categories of their own world. In a land of the psalms they strum their guitars and sing popular choruses. With the armoury of NATO around them they argue the cause of justice and peace. During the past five years when the Kirk has declined in membership by 12% the Kirk in Lewis has increased by 12%. Must secularisation triumph here, or can another island reclaim Scotland to her Christian heritage.

CHAPTER V

THE RELIGIOUS DIMENSION OF THE "TROUBLES" IN NORTHERN IRELAND

BILL McSWEENEY

Is the conflict in Northern Ireland really about religion? The question is frequently raised by inhabitants of the secularized world, astonished that, in this day and age, people could still fight and kill for their theological beliefs. If the respondent is a Roman Catholic bishop, a liberal academic or, above all, a sociologist, the questioner will be left in no doubt that the truth is not as obvious as it appears. Northern Ireland, while it may be peculiar in other ways, is in this respect no different from any other place where a dispute over power and money is organized around other labels of convenience, such as language or colour. To emphasize the fact, it will be pointed out that the paramilitaries who spearhead the armies on both sides may be "Catholics" and "Protestants" but, for the most part, they are also atheists. Religious language and symbols may be much in evidence, but the real factors which activate the conflict are the commonplace ones of the distribution of power and resources. Northern Ireland is not as medieval as it appears.

Since I do not wholly subscribe to this view and since I feel that the case for taking the religious factor seriously is at least as strong as the case for ignoring it entirely and has the advantage of being a more interesting case to argue, I shall try to defend the obvious in this paper. Northern Ireland is not medieval, but it is peculiar in the sense that religious beliefs are not merely a reflection of socio-economic conditions, but are a factor in their own right in stimulating violent conflict.

Before attempting to defend that view, it is useful first to look briefly at the range of explanations of conflict in Northern Ireland currently on offer, all of which share a common disregard for the content of religious belief as a real factor. There has been a sizeable publishing industry at work on Northern Ireland since the outbreak of the present troubles in 1969 and a rough classification of the theoretical explanations given indicates the diversity of opinion and the complexity of the situation.[1] To reduce the list to four, we can speak of economic, political, racial and psychological accounts, many of them drawing on the same historical and survey material, but interpreting the data according to their preferred theoretical models. Within each of these categories, several subdivisions add to the variety and confusion; there are ethnic, race-theory and cultural explanations under the heading of "racial"; nationalist, imperialist and comparative fall into the "political" category and the diversity of the "economic" is as great for Northern Ireland as it is for the Third World.

What these explanations have in common is that they all relegate religious belief to the area of rationalization or redundancy. The fact that in Northern Ireland, more than in other conflict areas where religious labels are in evidence, many people insist that they are fighting for religious priniciples, is either ignored or it is theorized away as a form of false consciousness. It just could not be true. Northern Ireland must be like other areas of the world where conflict is organized around some convenient cultural agent and it would be simplistic to take seriously the actors' view of the significance of culture. Just as the struggle in South Africa is patently not about colour and the war in the Lebanon is not about creed, so it would be absurd to take at face value the claim that conflict in Northern Ireland is about religious beliefs.

So we read that "in Northern Ireland, Catholics are Blacks who happen to have white skins....Racial distinction between the colonists and the natives is expressed in terms of religion." Or "The religious conflict in Ulster is an artificial conflict in the sense that the relationship between two communities is no longer a necessarily antagonistic one, but only the social institutions make it remain so."[2] This view that religious language diverts attention from the real issues at stake has been repeatedly emphasized by the leadership of the Roman Catholic church and occasionally echoed in ecumenical statements of the four major churches.[3] Why do so many and such disparate observers refuse to take seriously the claim that religious belief is a real factor in the conflict?

Superficially, one can guess why the mainstream churches are anxious to reject the religious explanation. Mainstream churches, after all, are by definition in the mainstream of modern theological opinion and it is not easy to square a positive commitment to ecumenism with a recognition that the churches in Ireland are replaying the quarrels of the Reformation. Furthermore, by embracing a quasi-Marxist perspective on the conflict, the churches can disclaim responsibility for it and evade the challenge that undesirable social consequences follow from holding strong religious beliefs. If the apparently religious elements can be reduced to socioeconomic factors, then the scandal of violence can be placed at the doors of the various political institutions, even if this means that the churches, on this occasion, are affirming the validity of a broadly Marxist perspective.

But not all churches reject the religious argument and, of those that do, it is the Roman church which most emphatically and consistently takes the reductionist lead. (It is the conservative Presbyterian church - above all the Free Presbyterians led by Ian Paisley - which insists that the conflict is primarily about religious beliefs.) A number of reasons can be suggested to account for the Catholic preference for the reductionist or functionalist explanation.

Firstly, it is difficult for the Roman church to acknowledge that Roman faith and practices are a stimulus to violence against Protestants when this is manifestly not the case in other parts of the world, and Roman Catholicism is self-defined as a universal belief system. Secondly, because the historic identification of Catholicism with Irish nationalism inclines the church towards the political and economic argument of the nationalists, and this is a more popular case to advance. Thirdly, because, while the case against the Roman church is partly true, its validity does not rest on the Roman *creed*, but rather on certain political implications of that creed. The theological dimension of conflict in Northern Ireland lies essentially in the belief system of Presbyterian Fundamentalism, not in the creed to which it is opposed.

The dismissal of religion as a factor in the conflict has become a commonsense assumption of observers throughout the world, adding to the international isolation of Northern Protestants and reinforcing the attachment to reductionism of the Roman church. Socialist commentators in the USSR and their anti-socialist rivals in the US, if they agree on little else, share a common view that conflict in Northern Ireland is not about religion and a common distaste for Ulster Protestantism as the agency of imperialism.

Reductionism has long been an easy temptation for sociologists. Confronted with a complex social phenomenon and endowed by their founding fathers with a functionalist theory to match - a functionalism, moreover, of the Marxist left and of the Durkheimian right - they easily ignore the complexities and reduce everything to the components of their preferred theoretical model. There is understandable irritation on the part of theologians and the religiously-motivated at this apparent refusal to take seriously their own understanding of the meaning of their actions. When sociologists dismiss the theologians' view of ecumenism or fundamentalism, for instance, and insist that it is the latent, not the manifest, function which is significant in stimulating these religious movements, they seem to be making the claim that the actors are little more than ideological dupes. When the reductionism is supported only by the evidence of theory and not of empirical data, the irritation is justifiably increased. Such sociology appears to theologians to be more like a form of methodological imperialism than a branch of the social sciences.

Reductionism of the Marxist kind seems at once more extreme and less defensible than the Durkheimian variety because of the weight given by Marxism to the concept of false consciousness. In addressing religious phenomena in general, the imputation of false consciousness to believers appears to be at once indiscriminate and dogmatic. It has all the defects which the secular observer ascribes to the religious dogmatist, with the additional one of purporting to be a scientific statement.

It is not intended, in this criticism of reductionism, to claim that all action must be understood only in terms of the actor's interpretation. That would be to deny the role of ideology in shaping beliefs and behaviour and to deny the possibility that actors may be unaware of the underlying function of their actions. It is clear that religious beliefs do have a social function: things could not be otherwise since religion is inescapably bound up with the social and political order. It is clear also that some explicitly religious perceptions of a situation may be so much a rationalization of other more mundane factors as to justify the description of false consciousness. One could mention here the Christian interpretation of anti-Communism as a case in point, or the religious justification of slavery in the nineteenth century or apartheid in more recent times. But in these cases, there is concrete evidence to support the view that religion is not the real factor, or at least not the primary factor. The refusal to take the actor's view seriously follows on some evidence that the actor is inconsistent in some way, though it is usually only with hindsight that such inconsistency is revealed. In each of the three cases mentioned, as in the famous case of the rain ceremonials of the Hopi Indians, the observer is relating empirical evidence to a body of theoretical knowledge in order that there is a significant gap between what the actors claim and the persistence of the activity.

What is wrong with dogmatic reductionism - of the Marxist or of any other kind - is, firstly, its refusal to respect the subjective interpretation of meaning; secondly, its reliance on untestable evidence of the kind exemplified in the Marxist concept of false consciousness; and, thirdly, its failure to recognize that even where latent functionality is demonstrated it does not necessarily exhaust the meaning of the action. This last point has some relevance to the case of Northern Ireland and to the popular notion that the conflict is not about religion on grounds which can only justify the assertion that it is not only about religion. As John Kent writes:

> Much religious behaviour is neurotic, but that is not to say that religion is no more than an illness; religious institutions may identify themselves so completely with an existing social order that they seem to have no other identity, but such social statements are generalizations which fail to account for all the ideas and behaviour of the individual members of the institutions.[4]

As a methodological principle deriving from Max Weber, the first claim on the observer of social phenomena must be the actors' own perception of the meaning of their action. In the area of religion, this means taking seriously the content of belief, not just the social fact. In Weber's terms:

> However incisive the social influences, economically and politically determined, may have been upon a religious ethic in a particular case, it receives its stamp primarily from religious sources and, first of all, from the content of its annunciation and its promise.[5]

If we can show that social consequences necessarily flow from the religious beliefs or practices of a particular group and that these consequences are at the core of a conflict, then religion is a factor in that conflict.

In what way and to what extent does the political struggle in Northern Ireland represent a conflict of religious interests? We need to recognize from the outset that the terms "Protestant" and "Catholic" are labels for complex groups, not for monolithic communities. If we exclude the self-perceived atheists or agnostics among them, we are left with two religious groups of different political persuasions but with significant subdivisions of religious belief within each. As regards Protestants in particular, the lesson of countless surveys and research is clear: even within the different non-Catholic churches there is a diversity of belief and practice similar to, but not as extensive as among practising Protestants in the rest of the UK. Most Protestants in Northern Ireland are Presbyterians and it is within their Calvinist tradition that we find clearest evidence of the religious factor in the Northern Ireland conflict.

Northern Ireland Protestantism achieved its political domination over the province through the alliance of Unionism and the Orange Order - a network of socioreligious communities which linked the Church of Ireland with the Presbyterians and other free churches and functioned as the major channel for achieving political power. There are many countries where lip-service to religious belief is an important part of realizing one's political aspirations. There are scarcely any - outside Iran - where there is such a rigorous religious test as exists for Protestants in Northern Ireland. The link between politics and religion runs through the entire social system, eliminating at times of general elections all the issues which are normally contended between the political parties in other countries and in other regions of the UK. What matters in Northern Ireland is where the candidate stands on the constitutional question, and what determines that is whether the candidate is a Catholic or a Protestant. This capacity to identify political opinions with religious belief has been a constant feature of the province not only since Ireland was partitioned in 1921 but ever since the plantation of Ulster in the seventeenth-century. Then the Scottish settlers were put there by an English government which itself linked politics with religion in a similar way, regarding Roman Catholics in England as owing allegiance to a foreign power in a way not dissimilar to the Unionist perception of Roman Catholics today. This identification of religion and politics soon evaporated with the establishment of political stability in England and with the gradual relaxation of religious tension with the realization that Roman Catholics were not out to overthrow the state. In Northern Ireland, however, the experience of Protestants was different. They were not dealing with a weak minority whose allegiance to Rome required careful monitoring, but with an enemy throughout the country which was in the majority and which denied the rights of the Protestants to occupy the land which was now their home. As the tension receded in England, the battles only began in Ulster and the most powerful myths which nourish the collective identities of the rival groups are still drawn from the events of 1641 and 1690 and 1798. No graffiti in the world are as resonant of history as the writings on the walls and gables of Belfast and Derry.

There is little doubt that religion was a major factor in the conflict of the seventeenth-century. The antagonism to Roman Catholicism which was a common feature of Protestant denominations was particularly emphasized in the Calvinist tradition of the "Presbyterial Discipline" at the time of the

Civil War in England. Presbyterial government was opposed to the exercise of control over spiritual matters by bishops, ecclesiastical courts and magistrates on the grounds that scripture alone should be the guide to government. Presbyterian doctrine reflects this principle of government in its emphasis on the inherent sinfulness of man and on the Reformation belief in justification by grace alone. This doctrine separated Protestantism from Roman Catholicism clearly after the Reformation and the tension between rival understandings of salvation continued until the end of the nineteenth-century, with the advent of liberal theology and the first stirrings of the ecumenical movement. It is now confidently asserted by ecumenists that there is no substantive difference whatever between the Protestant and Catholic positions on justification.

The belief in the Calvinist tradition of justification by grace alone is particularly strong among those fundamentalists whose theological forebears resisted compromise during the various schisms which split the church in the seventeenth and eighteenth-century and who include fundamentalist evangelicals in the southern states of America and in Scotland. It is from this fundamentalist tradition that the Free Presbyterian Church of Ian Paisley derives its inspiration. The central doctrines of the main Presbyterian church in Northern Ireland differ from those of Paisleyism only in the intensity with which they are held, not in substance. For them, as also for Paisley, justification by grace alone has the major political implication that it guarantees the freedom of the individual - freedom primarily in the religious sphere of protecting the sacredness of the individual's relationship to God, but freedom also in the political sense of guaranteeing their liberty to exercise their beliefs without hindrance. Calvinism teaches that the political sphere must be subordinated to the religious. The proper task of government is "to cherish and support the external worship of God, to preserve the pure doctrine of religion, to defend the constitutions of the church...."[6] True religion could only survive if the political institutions were there to protect it. For Calvin, as for most Christians of his time, religion and politics were inextricably interwoven, though some had more theocratic ideas than others.

Throughout the nineteenth century, Presbyterians in Northern Ireland echoed the religio-political teachings of Calvin as their forefathers had done and as now they deemed even more mandatory in the context of the Home Rule movement for repeal of the Act of Union of 1801. At almost any period in the century, a glance through the Protestant journals of Northern Ireland would reveal the ceaseless and repetitious appeal to the idea of liberty as the fundamental reason for resisting Home Rule and for clinging to the union with mainland Britain. Liberty is above all the liberty of the saved, the elect, the individual justified by grace alone. In the Presbyterian understanding, the primacy of the individual conscience is the basic right from which all other liberties flow. This emphasis on the liberty of the individual as a consequence of grace alone is a classical theme of Calvinism and a core belief of the Presbyterian tradition everywhere. Theoretically, it lends to Presbyterianism a religious orientation which stands in some tension with the hierarchical churches, above all, with the Roman variant. In practice, however, the doctrine in most parts of the world has drifted apart from the political context in which it had originally been formulated and the commitment to ecumenical dialogue has discouraged Presbyterians from interpreting it in an anti-catholic way. (For their part, Catholics too have softened the edges of beliefs which were once defined in opposition to other denominations, such as the doctrine that outside the church there is no salvation.)

But in Northern Ireland since the 1830's, the political situation only served to heighten the sense of the theological significance of politics. The awareness that it could be blasphemous to identify a particular state system with the will of God was not lost on Presbyterian ministers during the Home Rule crisis at the beginning of this century.[7] Their need publicly to deny the charge of blasphemy or idolatry in advocating the rejection of Home Rule underlines the extraordinary extent to which - in their view at least - the word of God and a Protestant parliament were closely identified. This fundamentalist position was encouraged by the apparently similar fundamentalism of their Roman Catholic enemies in the South who, it appeared, had themselves quite openly demonstrated the political character of Catholicism by linking the nationalist cause with the Catholic, and who seemed to be under no pressure to defend themselves against the charge of idolatry in so doing.

After 1886, with a Home Rule Bill already prepared for Westminster, a massive protest movement explicitly linking theology and politics was organized in opposition to any attempt to tamper with the constitutional status of Northern Ireland. This movement to preserve "a Protestant government for a Protestant people" was classical Calvinism, with its primary emphasis on the religious ideal. The stress on religious services and prayer to support the resistance campaign and to ask God's help for violence, if necessary, was an indicator of the extraordinary bond between the religious and the political. But it was a bond forged not only out of faithfulness to a fundamentalist view of Calvin's teaching but out of a perception of the enemy which had emerged with increasing clarity since the 1830's. For it was then that the Home Rule campaign began under the leadership of Daniel O'Connell, and if it was not sufficiently clear to Protestants at first that Home Rule meant Rome Rule, that point was unambiguously made when O'Connell took the fateful step of linking the campaign for political goals with a campaign for Catholic emancipation.

As noted above, Presbyterianism in general in Northern Ireland differs from the fundamentalist evangelical Presbyterianism of Ian Paisley only in the fervour and intensity of belief. But one important part of that belief which most Presbyterians share for reasons of their Calvinist origin and of their Ulster experience, but which is particularly emphasized by the Free Presbyterian Church, is the idea that the Roman Church is a monolithic system which is both political and religious. In the extreme version held and widely popularized by Paisley, this church has worldwide imperialistic designs which it is intent on and capable of realizing in Northern Ireland. While such extremism would not be common outside Paisley's community, nonetheless many would share with him his view of the nature of the Roman church. For Paisley, Protestantism is to Catholicism as liberty is to tyranny.

Ian Paisley emerged to political prominence in the mid-sixties, when he led the protest against the conciliatory moves of the then Prime Minister Terence O'Neill towards the Republic of Ireland. He was later prominent in fuelling the Protestant opposition to the campaign for Civil Rights in

Northern Ireland and he is by far the most popular politician in Ulster in terms of electoral support. An important part of his influence in the polarized community of Northern Ireland lies in the threat he poses to other Unionist politicians not to stray too far from rigid adherence to the traditional Protestant position expressed in the slogan inherited from the Siege of Derry in 1689: "No Surrender!" In the climate of opinion which has prevailed since 1969, no Unionist politician can afford to appear to compromise on the main question which has dominated politics since the Plantation: a Protestant majority is the only guarantee of Protestant liberty because the only alternative is a province ruled effectively by Rome.

Since the main characteristic of Roman Catholicism, as perceived by Presbyterians in Northern Ireland, is its rejection of the doctrine of justification by grace alone, and since that is seen as having as its necessary political consequence a government controlled by the Roman Church, it seems clear that there is a strong religious dimension to the conflict on the part of Presbyterians in general - a factor which cannot be dismissed as a rationalization of social or economic needs.[8] These are Christians fighting for their beliefs, whatever else they may also be doing, and however quaint or repugnant their beliefs may seem to others around the world.

Since their perception of Roman Catholicism is a crucial element in the Protestant grasp of the situation, without which they would presumably be as willing to be governed by Catholics in Northern Ireland as Protestants are elsewhere in the world, we must ask if that perception is correct. There are two aspects of that perception which must concern us. One is the view derived from Protestant - but particularly Presbyterian - tradition, that the Roman Church is essentially a political as well as a religious movement and that its political aspirations lead it to employ any means necessary to expand its influence and its domination over secular and religious bodies alike. In addition, there is the related view that Catholicism is always and everywhere like that - "monolithic" is the popular epithet which every staunch Presbyterian learns to define and spell at Sunday School.

The second aspect of Catholicism as seen by Presbyterians is clearly absurd. Since the Second Vatican Council, diversity within Catholicism has increased to the point that it is now not clear whether it is meaningful to speak of Roman Catholic beliefs and practices. There exist today divisions on beliefs and morals within the Catholic Church as sharp and problematic as any between the different churches.[9] These divisions do not extend to the college of bishops which forms the leadership of the church, it is true, but there is sufficient evidence of differences between national churches and even within national churches - even in Ireland - to rule out any question that the church is monolithic.

That the Roman church seeks political power and that its exercise of that power will destroy the conditions favourable to Protestantism would seem equally absurd in most countries of the world today, but not quite so incredible from the perspective of Northern Ireland. The Catholic Church in Ireland has been intimately linked with nationalist aspirations for the past century and a half. Since O'Connell's merging of religion and politics, the church has gradually extended its influence over politicians to the point reached with the foundation of the state in 1921 that Catholicism was more powerfully placed in Ireland than the established church in Britain. To the Northern Protestant, it seemed that the majority church in Southern Ireland exemplified the worst aspects of ultramontanism in the nineteenth-century with all the implications for the liberty of the Protestant which that movement had. Irish Catholicism showed the Roman church in its true character, it seemed, and the twentieth-century has provided many specific instances of Roman authoritarianism which prove the point for the believing Presbyterian - the *Ne Temere* decree of 1908, establishing intolerable regulations to govern mixed marriages and to ensure a Catholic upbringing for all the children; the repeated interference by the church in political affairs in the Republic, particularly in the areas of education and family morality; the failure of the state in the Republic to protect the religious minorities.[10]

The history of Roman Catholicism in Ireland is not one that promises security for their liberties to any Protestant, liberal or fundamentalist. In effect, the majority church in the South has sought a Catholic parliament for a Catholic people in much the same way as the majority Protestant church has tried to monopolize the political process in the North. The major difference between them lies in the fact that Catholic intransigence arises from the need to protect institutional power and privileges, not from any necessary implication of doctrine. From the Catholic side, then, the confrontational impulse is rooted in religion in the institutional sense, not in theological doctrine. Catholic intransigence is based, not on the beliefs of Protestants but on the threat posed to the power of the church by pluralism and by the legislation which pluralism would require for the rights and liberties of all minorities: Protestant, Muslim, atheist. On the Protestant side, a pluralistic system would pose no threat to their beliefs and to their religious liberty. The real threat lies in the existence of a numerically-dominant Roman church. No avowal of a change of heart and a new tolerance on the part of Catholic leaders would encourage Northern Presbyterians to lower their defences against a church which Calvin and Irish history have taught them is by nature monolithic and politically monopolistic. In Presbyterian eyes, this judgement has been vindicated by the recent expressions of popular support for the traditional Catholic position on divorce, indicating that the determination not to concede certain liberties to religious minorities is not restricted to bishops and clergy.

The view that the Northern Ireland conflict is not religious is mistaken, therefore, whether one considers either the Protestant or the Catholic share of responsibility for that conflict. Both sides are implicated in different ways and both can contribute to the reconciliation process, though at some risk. Given the current commitment to change on the part of the secular political institutions involved in Northern Ireland, time is running out for the churches to be seen voluntarily to make the concessions and sacrifices required before reconciliation is forced on them in the short term by governments, in the longer term by secularization.

In the aftermath of action taken to force the issue by the Westminster and Dublin governments, what signs are there that the churches are prepared to change? The official views have not altered. For the Presbyterians, there can be no surrender where doctrine is at stake; for the Catholics, the problem is not religious in any sense, so they have no responsibility for its solution. However, some shifts away from these positions can be detected. Among the many submissions by interested parties to the New Ireland Forum - an all-party attempt to formulate a political and cultural context which would reconcile the divided communities in Ireland - was a lengthy document from the Irish Episcopal Conference, the body of Catholic bishops which constitutes the leadership of the church throughout the whole of Ireland, North and South. Their written submission offered no hope that Irish Catholicism would bend to the needs of reconciliation. On pluralism they wrote:

> A Catholic country or its government, where there is a very substantial Catholic ethos and consensus, should not feel it necessary to apologise that its legal system, constitutional or statutory, reflects Catholic values....the rights of a minority are not more sacred than the rights of the majority.[11]

When the bishops agreed to discuss their submission before a public session of the Forum, a different attitude emerged. In a prepared statement, they denied that they sought "a Catholic state for a Catholic people". On the contrary:

> What we do here and now declare, and declare with emphasis, is that we would raise our voices to resist any constitutional purposes which might infringe or might imperil the civil and religious rights and liberties cherished by Northern Protestants.[12]

But a year later, in the June 1986 referendum to remove the constitutional ban on divorce, the bishops launched a pulpit attack on the proposed constitutional change which undoubtedly played a large part in its defeat by the electorate. Clearly the bishops' concern for the civil and religious liberties of Northern Protestants was not to be extended to Protestants in the South.

If there is no indication as yet of voluntary concessions on the part of the Roman Catholic hierarchy, there is nonetheless a real sign of change in church-state relations. Since the mid-seventies, clear evidence has emerged of the secularization of Southern Irish society of a kind which will strengthen the hand of the Dublin government and weaken the capacity of the church to control the process - begun with the New Ireland Forum - of harmonizing the cultures, North and South. Already the first manifestations of this change have appeared in the fact of open antagonism between church and state and in the fact that, for the first time in history, the Catholic hierarchy has been forced to exercise its political influence openly and publicly - as one among many pressure groups, even if still the most powerful of them all. No longer are church-state disputes settled by private memo and telephone call.

For reasons which are more structural than moral, change is harder for the Presbyterian community than for the Catholic. There is no hierarchical leadership which can speak and act for the church with the same assurance of consensus that obtains within Roman Catholicism. This limitation on Presbyterian leadership, imposed by its subscription to democratic values and by its theologically-based rejection of hierarchy, may be a positive good in checking dictatorial tendencies among leaders but it also functions to imprison them in the ultra-conservative mould which popular opinion demands. Unlike their Roman counterparts, Presbyterian ministers risk office and career if they overstep the boundaries of safety drawn by their constituents, whether these be parishoners or the electorate. New ideas are dangerous, particularly if they point in the direction of compromise with the ancient enemy, the church of Rome.

It was not surprising, therefore, that the signing of the Anglo-Irish Agreement in November 1985, giving the Dublin government a consultative role in the affairs of Northern Ireland, was denounced by the Presbyterian Assembly and by Presbyterian ministers throughout the province. They saw themselves being cast, yet again, in the role of dissenters which they had played in the defence of their religion in the seventeenth-century. Now they were trapped, not by the sacramental test, but by a conspiracy between a treacherous Westminster and a cunning government of Catholics in Dublin. As Ian Paisley tried to unite the Northern Protestants around his call for a Protestant state, a remarkable statement was issued by a group of twenty-four Presbyterian ministers, distancing themselves from any such blasphemy and from the obdurate opposition to the Agreement expressed by their own Assembly. In language resonant of the Barmen Declaration of 1934, in which German Christians denounced the idolatry of identifying the kingdom of God with the Nazi state, the ministers set out four propositions about the Christian faith as a basis for prayer and discussion which implicitly denounced the uncompromising position of Protestant and Catholic fundamentalists in the following statement:

> The identification of the kingdom of God with any one
> political ideology is idolatry and an affront to Almighty God. It
> undermines Christian witness. It is a perversion of the Gospel
> of our Lord and Saviour, Jesus Christ. [13]

As the Irish Times leader noted on the day of publication, "Twenty-four Presbyterian swallows do not make a political summer." Given the structure of Presbyterianism and its significant role in the polarization of Irish society, however, these particular Protestant birds are more likely to come home to nest than if they had been Roman Catholics. At the time of writing, Northern Ireland is still in the throes of a complex quarrel in which God is invoked as referee. After seventeen years of the present "troubles," there is some hope in the fact that an influential group on one side of the religious divide has performed an act of unprecedented personal and political courage in the cause of reconciliation. It remains to be seen whether their unilateral decision to break ranks with the hallowed consensus on the Protestant side will elicit a similarly creative response on the part of the Catholic leadership.

REFERENCES

[1] Useful surveys of the literature can be found in John Hickey, *Religion and the Northern Ireland Problem*, Gill and Macmillan, Dublin, 1984; J. H. Whyte "Interpretation of the Northern Ireland Problem," in *Economic and Social Review*, No 4, 1978; John Darby: *Conflict in Northern Ireland*, Gill and Macmillan, Dublin, 1976.

[2] Liam de Paor, *Divided Ulster*, Penguin, 1970, p. 1. and Anders Poserup, "Power in a Post-Colonial Setting," in *Peace Research Society Papers*, vol 13, 1969. For an explicitly Marxist position, see also M. Farrell: *Northern Ireland: The Orange State*, Pluto Press, London, 1976, and P. Bew *et al The State in Northern Ireland 1921-1972*, Manchester UP, 1972.

[3] See Bishop Edward Daly *Violence in Ireland* (pamphlet), 1973, and Joint Letter of Religious Leaders, 1973, quoted in John Darby. *op. cit.*, p. 114.

[4] John Kent, "Reductionism," in Alan Richardson and John Bowden, eds. *A New Dictionary of Christian Theology*, SCM, London, 1983.

[5] Max Weber, "The Social Psychology of the World Religions," in Hans Gerth and C. Wright Mills, *From Max Weber*, OUP, New York, 1968.

[6] Calvin, *The Institutes of Christian Religion*, in John T. McNeill, ed, *God and Political Duty*, 1950, p. 46.

[7] For an account of Protestant resistance to Home Rule in the period after 1886, see R. F. G. Holmes, "Ulster Will Fight and Ulster Will Be Right," in W. J. Sheils, ed, *The Church and War*, 1984.

[8] The point is confirmed in Richard Rose, *Governing Without Consensus*, Faber and Faber, London, 1971, and in John Hickey, *op. cit., passim*.

[9] See Bill McSweeney, *Roman Catholicism: The Search For Relevance*, Blackwells, Oxford, 1980, chs. 8 and 9.

[10] An excellent account of church-state relations in Southern Ireland is given in J.H. Whyte: *Church and State in Modern Ireland*, Gill and Macmillan, Dublin, 1980 (2nd edition).

[11] The Irish Episcopal Conference, *"Submission to the New Ireland Forum,"* Veritas Publ., Dublin, 1984, p. 19.

[12] The New Ireland Forum, Report of Proceedings 9 Feb 1984, Government Publications, Dublin, 1984.

[13] *The Irish Times*, 29 November 1985.

CHAPTER VI

THE ROMAN CATHOLIC CHURCH IN BRITAIN SINCE THE SECOND WORLD WAR

MICHAEL P. HORNSBY-SMITH

I

In the early 1980's the Roman Catholic Church estimated its membership at around 4.3 million in England and Wales and a further 0.8 million in Scotland. These figures are based on returns made by parish priests and are lower than estimates derived from opinion surveys which suggest that the proportion of self-defined, but not necessarily "practising" Roman Catholics may be around 11% (5.4 million) in England and Wales and 16% (0.8 million) in Scotland. In spite of declining Mass attendance rates in recent years it seems that the Roman Catholic Church in England is now the largest in terms of church attendance.

It is necessary to note the fact that for the purposes of ecclesiastical administration there are two separate hierarchies of bishops for England and Wales, on the one hand, and Scotland on the other. This reflects their different historical, legal and religious traditions and, in particular, the different forms taken by the Protestant Reformation and subsequent emergence of Roman Catholicism after centuries of persecution and hostility to political emancipation in the nineteenth century and gradual social and religious acceptance in the second half of the twentieth century. While in

England and Wales the hierarchy of bishops was restored in 1850, it was not until 1878 that it was restored in Scotland (Beck, 1950; McRoberts, 1979).

The bulk of the subsequent growth in both communities must be attributed to the impact of successive waves of largely Roman Catholic immigrants from Ireland. In both communities up to the Second World War, Catholics were typically concentrated in largely Irish, inner-city, working class parishes. With post-war affluence and the expansion of educational provision, Catholics from both communities benefitted from the opportunities for both upward occupational mobility and outward geographical mobility. Thus there was the emergence of a "new Catholic middle-class" and new forms of suburban Catholicism in both communities. In both cases a traditional, pietistic, authoritarian form of Catholicism, tinged with an "ultramontanist" deference to Roman authorities, especially on the part of the bishops, gradually, if reluctantly, accommodated to the challenges of renewal implicit in the teachings of the Second Vatican Council which was held in Rome from 1962 to 1965 (Abbott, 1966). However, while the processes of change taking place were largely similar in the two communities, the pace and timing of them was different. Generally new religious ideas and forms of Catholicism were adopted more slowly in Scotland which retained a more defensive "ghetto mentality" for a longer period in the face of higher, albeit declining, levels of anti-Catholicism. These differences need to be borne in mind in the subsequent discussion which will largely focus on the Roman Catholic Church in England where there is a stronger research base from which to interpret recent changes.

Before considering recent changes it is necessary to emphasise the heterogeneity of the Roman Catholic community. At least four distinct groups can be identified (Hornsby-Smith, 1987). It is estimated that there are around 650,000 "recusant" Catholics in England and Wales who can trace their Catholicism to pre-Reformation days. Secondly, about 460,000 English Catholics are converts. Thirdly, it appears that there were some 590,000 first-generation and 700,000 second-generation Irish immigrant Catholics living in England and Wales in the late 1970's. Fourthly, apart from the Irish immigrants, around 670,000 Catholics in England and Wales were born in countries outside the British Isles. Of these, the largest groups came from

Italy and Poland but there are also over 100,000 black Catholics from African, West Indian and Asian countries. It has been estimated that there are about 460,000 second-generation immigrants with origins outside the British Isles (Hornsby-Smith, 1986). The balance of around one-third of English Catholics has a variety of other and mixed backgrounds but it is likely that the bulk of them will have an Irish ancestry which originated three or more generations ago.

II

In order to evaluate recent changes in English Catholicism it is necessary to context them in the changing social and religious climate of the post-war years. In the first place, the largely working-class Catholic community benefitted enormously from the universal provision of secondary education which followed the 1944 Education Act and the expansion of tertiary education which was signalled by the Robbins Report in 1963. Survey evidence indicates that Catholic men who had been born in Great Britain experienced slightly higher rates of upward social mobility than men generally (Hornsby-Smith, 1987). Catholics were appearing in the universities in noticeable numbers for the first time and it is clear that Catholics were growing a "new middle-class," upwardly mobile as a result of educational achievement and occupational advancement. In the affluent years up to the early 1970's one could interpret these changes as a process of "economic embourgeoisement." By the late 1970's the social class background of English Catholics was little different from that of the population as a whole (Hornsby-Smith and Lee, 1979).

Parallel with this social mobility there was evidence also of considerable shifts in the geographical location of Catholics. In general the occupational mobility of Catholics was accompanied by a decided movement out of the old, traditional, working-class, largely Irish, inner-city parishes into the new suburban estates in all major conurbations. An enormous building programme of new schools and churches in the suburbs mapped this emergence from the near-ghetto areas of pre-war Britain.

In the boom years of the 1950's, the Catholic population was swollen by a huge transfusion of Irish migrant workers and the Newman Demographic Survey estimated the ratio of Catholic infant baptisms to total live births to be over 16% in the early 1960's (Spencer, 1966:72). However, Irish immigration tailed off in the 1960's and practically dried up with the entry of the Irish Republic into the E.E.C. and the expansion of the Irish economy. What Irish immigration there was in the post-war years followed new routes of entry to Britain and the new employment opportunities in the Birmingham-London corridor rather than the traditional areas around Merseyside and the North. Thus the national survey of 1978 indicated that "while the proportion of Catholics in the general population (in England and Wales) is still the greatest in the North-West, two-fifths of Catholics are now to be found in London and the South-East" (Hornsby-Smith and Lee, 1979:36).

Apart from the social changes in the post-war years there was also a religious ferment in the Roman Catholic Church which emerged in the teachings of the Second Vatican Council (Abbott, 1966), and its call for renewal, new pastoral emphases, and its greater concern with the transformation of the contemporary world in the light of the gospel message. That there were shifts of theological emphasis can hardly be doubted. In the post-Vatican rhetoric greater stress was placed on the concept of the "people of God" and the encouragement of lay participation at all (well most, for men at least) levels in the Church and also the collegiality of the bishops. Though the reality fluctuated between what Berger called accommodation and intransigence (Berger, 1973) and has often fallen far short of the rhetoric, the formal teaching of Vatican II has provided a continuing ideological legitimation for progressive elements in the Church. In England and Wales these elements dominated the National Pastoral Congress in 1980 (Anon, 1981; Hornsby-Smith and Cordingley, 1983). Other writers have interpreted the changes as "the search for relevance" (McSweeney, 1980), the shift from an institutional to community, sacrament, herald and servant models of the Church (Dulles, 1976), or from a "mechanistic" to an "organic" organisational structure (Hornsby-Smith and Lee, 1979).

In Britain the ordinary "Catholic in the pew" first experienced these changes in the Sunday liturgies. The Latin of the Mass was replaced by English. The priest no longer said Mass with his back to the laity in a way which had emphasised his key mediatory role and his "apartness" from lay people. Now he faced the congregation in order to stress the community dimension of worship. Lay people read from scripture and led the new bidding prayers, brought up the gifts at the Offertory, and, more recently, have served as special ministers in the distribution of Holy Communion. The attempt has been made to shift the emphasis away from rules almost as ends-in-themselves which had led to casuistical concerns such as "how far can you go?" (Lodge, 1980). Thus, the penitential regulations concerning Friday fasting and abstaining from meat have been modified in the attempt to encourage greater personal decision-making and commitment. Not surprisingly, though, these changes have been traumatic for some and have been interpreted as a denial of a distinctive Catholic identity. As Mary Douglas bemoaned in her essay on the tenacious ritualism of the "Bog Irish":"now the English Catholics are like everyone else" (1973: 67). All the same, there is no doubt that the overwhelming majority of British Catholics have favoured the post-Vatican liturgical changes, though whether on ideological grounds or because of the sheer convenience remains a moot point. Similarly the almost universal delight among Catholics at the easing of religious conflict and the more favourable ecumenical climate is shrouded in the ambiguities of the meaning to be accorded to Christian Unity and the uncertainties about the extent to which a traditional Catholic identity should be retained.

In a recent review of research on English Catholicism (Hornsby-Smith, 1987), I concluded that the sort of distinctive Catholic subculture which could be identified at least up to the 1950's had largely dissolved by the mid-1980's. The process was not cataclysmic, the dramatic collapsing of the fortress walls as a result of a single explosive attack from without. Rather it was a gradual change which had taken place over several decades as a result of the steady dissolving of the walls surrounding the English Catholic community in the solvent of rapid external social change after the global trauma of the Second World War, and the internal religious *aggiornamento* encouraged in the 1960's by Pope John XXIII.

This conclusion appears to be clearly indicated by the evidence reviewed of the structural and cultural convergence towards the norms of British society generally. This is particularly apparent when considering the changing marital norms of English Catholics. Whereas under one-third of Catholics married before 1960 were in religiously mixed marriages and around one in eight in canonically invalid marriages, by the 1970's these proportions had increased dramatically to two-thirds in religiously exogamous unions and well over one-third in invalid marriages which had not been performed by a priest. These figures are eloquent testimony to the fact that by the 1980's there had been a major dissolution of the boundaries which for centuries had safeguarded the religious identity of Catholics and ensured the distinctiveness of their separate subculture by the enforcement of religious and social sanctions against out-marriage.

The religious consequences of post-war social change for the Catholic community were first explored by Joan Brothers (1964) in her study of the growing strains between the traditional inner-city parishes in Liverpool and the extraparochial grammar schools and universities attended by educational achievers. The evidence from the 1978 national survey also pointed to the tendency for the institutional Church to be disproportionately attractive to the professional middle-classes who were to be the main representatives at the National Pastoral Congress in 1980. The attempts to encourage lay participation in the church after Vatican II have tended to favour the articulate, educated middle-classes who in their occupational lives are more likely to develop the skills of public speaking, committee procedures and discussion group leadership, and decision-making. The consequence is that with the ending of mass Irish immigration, it has become increasingly apparent that the Roman Catholic Church is no more immune to the alienation of the working-classes than other mainline religious traditions in Britain (Archer, 1986).

Secondly, the evidence suggests overwhelmingly that in the areas of personal morality, particularly in the matter of contraception, Catholics are "making up their own minds" over an expanding area of issues. There seems little doubt that a major transformation of religious authority is under way. Whereas up to the 1950's Catholics, whatever their actual practice, might generally have been prepared to accept the legitimacy of the clerical authorities, particularly the pope, to provide rules for both religious and moral conduct, it seems clear that this is increasingly contested over a wide range of issues from contraception to intercommunion. A process of "normative convergence" to the population norms is particularly noticeable among young Catholics who seem to be increasingly alienated from institutional religion. Meanwhile, for the great mass of British Catholics, in spite of several attempts in recent years to involve them in processes of consultation, the recent changes are of no great consequence and are either largely uncritically accepted as "the way things are done in the Church" or approved of for their greater convenience or attractiveness. While there are honorable exceptions, particularly in the growing justice and peace movement, the bulk of older British Catholics, two decades after the end of the Second Vatican Council, still retain the mark of their earlier socialisation into a passive, deferential, and undemanding lay role.

III

One consequence of the dissolution of the defensive walls surrounding the Catholic community in the post-war years is likely to have been a decline in its political importance. Two issues, in particular, provide some evidence for this conclusion: Catholic education policy and abortion legislation.

In a useful review of the suspicious and sometimes downright hostile Catholic responses towards the post-war creation of the Welfare State, Peter Coman has recorded that part of the explanation was "a pervading fear that the distinctive Catholic subculture would be undermined by the wider society with a different normative system, operating through its political expression in the very powerful twentieth-century state" (Coman, 1977: 67). In the early post-war years there was little dissent among Catholics in defense of the justice of their claim to a separate school system and control over the religious curriculum and moral teaching. In the event it was the financial implications of the 1944 Education Act which led to the mobilisation of the

Catholic community. Thousands had participated in country-wide demonstrations and the lobbying of M. P. s. The net cost to the Catholic community of the school building programmes in the 1960's and 1970's in a period of unprecedented inflation and high interest rates was felt to be crippling. In order to ease this burden the government grant available for school building programmes was raised from 50% to 85% in a number of stages as the bitter religious antagonisms of the years up to 1944 gradually declined and there was an "end of 'passionate intensity'" over the issue (Murphy, 1971:121-9).

To the extent that the Catholic community won the right to a segregated school system substantially paid for out of public funds and that the dual system is now an established and uncontroversial political fact in England and Wales, it could be argued that it had demonstrated a considerable ability to mobilise its membership for a protracted struggle. On the other hand it is very doubtful if such an exercise of mobilisation could be repeated in the different circumstances of the 1980's. For one thing, the Catholic community no longer feels so defensive as the barriers separating it from the wider society have steadily dissolved. Within the Catholic community itself doubts have been expressed about the validity and effectiveness of Catholic schools, from the point of view of subsequent adult religious commitment, and about the priority it has hitherto been accorded in pastoral planning. If ever there was clear evidence that new ethnic schools, especially for the Moslem community, were seriously divisive (in a way which Catholic schools have not been in England and Wales), then it is extremely doubtful that the Catholic community could be successfully mobilised on behalf of the dual system.

The second test of the political power of Catholics concerns recent abortion legislation. Abortion is regarded with particular abhorrence by official Catholicism. Any claim that Catholics constitute a politically powerful interest group in British society must therefore address the issue of their failure to prevent the passage of the 1967 Abortion Act or of the several attempts subsequently to amend it. According to one non-Catholic commentator "the fact is that in Britain the Catholic Church is astonishingly unorganised for political action or the applying of public pressure" (Scott, 1967: 79).

All the same the Roman Catholic Church has been regarded as a major opponent of the Act and the hierarchies of both Scotland and of England and Wales issued joint statements at the time of the Corrie Bill to amend it in 1979/80 (Marsh and Chambers, 1981: 131, 144). This was the ninth parliamentary attempt to amend it and Roman Catholic M.P.s were prominent in all of them. Roman Catholics have also comprised a large part of the memberships of the two main groups in the anti-abortion lobby: the *Society for the Protection of the Unborn Child* (S.P.U.C.) and *Life*. Marsh and Chambers analyse in detail the failure of the attempts to amend the 1967 Act and point to the strategic and tactical weaknesses among the Corrie supporters. For our purposes here it is of interest to note that a major reason "was the divisions which existed on the anti-abortion side" (Marsh and Chambers, 1981: 162). In particular the "fundamentalist" stance of the extra-parliamentary lobby resulted in the failure to determine priorities and seek appropriate political compromises which might pragmatically have resulted in more restrictive legislation. It might tentatively be suggested that the conflict between a fundamentalist stance on principle and a pragmatic need to compromise in pluralist democratic societies is likely to result in practice in a weak Catholic contribution to political decision-making.

Both issues of educational policy and abortion legislation suggest, therefore, that Roman Catholics are not a powerful force in British politics and this is perhaps reflected in the fact that the proportion of Catholic M.P.s is only about half their proportion in the population generally, a situation which has remained unchanged for decades. A predominantly "other-worldly" religious stance, at least until the last few years, can be said to have reinforced this weakness. Archbishop (then Bishop) Beck attributed this to the loss of the large Irish constituency at Westminster, and at the centenary of the restoration of the hierarchy, observed that:

> ...it seems to be generally admitted that the influence of the Catholic community in England and public life is by no means commensurate with its size, and there seems to be a good case for arguing that, at least until very recent years, this influence has been throughout the greater part of this century declining.

It has been said that the height of Catholic influence was
reached about the period when the Liberal Government of
1906 took office. The Irish influence in the House of
Commons was then at its strongest and was later to die away
almost entirely. Nothing in Catholic public life has replaced
it....Politically, since the withdrawal of the Irish members, the
Catholic influence has, on the whole, been negligible (Beck,
1950: 602-603).

There seem to be no strong grounds for believing that the situation has
changed significantly in recent decades.

The gradual realisation that international Catholicism poses no threat
to the Protestant British State is reflected in the ending of the long-standing
imbalance in the nature of the diplomatic relationships with the Holy See.
Whereas there had been British diplomatic representation at the Vatican
since the First World War, it was not until 1938 that there was an Apostolic
Delegate (i.e., without diplomatic status) in London.   While diplomatic
privileges to the Pope's representative here were gradually extended in the
post-war years, it was not until 1982, shortly before the highly successful visit
of Pope John-Paul II to Britain, that he was accorded ambassadorial status as
Apostolic Pro-Nuncio.

IV

Paradoxically, though, the political impotence of the Roman Catholic
Church in Britain goes hand-in-hand with the emergence of an unassuming
and charismatic leader in Cardinal Hume who genuinely commands wide
respect among the population as a whole. His leadership style represents a
sharp break with the princely primates from Wiseman to Heenan. Whereas
the dominating Cardinal Heenan is reported to have boasted how easily he
could lift the telephone to speak directly to the prime minister, Cardinal
Hume's "enabling" leadership style is characterised by sensitivity and an
ability to listen and "make space for others" (Longley, 1986). The eased
ecumenical climate which manifested itself especially at Canterbury during
the pope's visit and continues to be expressed in the remarkable
collaboration between Archbishop Worlock and Bishop Sheppard in the

stricken city of Liverpool, has meant that Roman Catholics no longer feel it necessary to defend their vital interests with the pugnacity of earlier decades.

One unanticipated consequence of recent reforms has been the tendency to concentrate primarily on institutional renewal and "churchy" matters such as liturgical change and lay participation in new advisory structures at both diocesan and national level. Thus the Church can be characterised as a "greedy institution" (Coser, 1974), consuming a disproportionate amount of the time and energies of lay people for what Michael Winter (1973) characterised as the tasks of maintenance rather than mission. Paradoxically, therefore, in the two decades since the Second Vatican Council, in spite of its call to lay people to transform the social world in which they live, it is unlikely that Roman Catholics are making as big an impact in the search for social justice as they were in the days when "Catholic Action" was much more explicitly under the control of the ecclesiastical authorities. It seems that nothing has replaced the single-minded "anti-communist" ideology which served to motivate many Catholic trade unionists in the Cold War years and nothing has yet emerged to replace the Catholic Social Guild which attempted to offer Christian answers to many of the great social issues up to the 1950's.

However, a second tendency seems more promising from the point of view of mission or the search for social justice in the world. With a steady decline of traditional Catholic organisations, formerly the focal point for the mobilisation of Catholic Action in defence of Catholic interests, such as the schools system, or of a moral position, such as opposition to abortion legislation, there has been the emergence of organisations which are primarily lay-run and increasingly ecumenical in their orientation, such as the Catholic Institute for International Relations. These are offering an influential Catholic critique of the powerful institutions of global capitalism, such as the trading relations with developing nations, the arms trade, the role of the multinational corporations, and so on. In their openness to the influence of the methodology of liberation theologians in the Third World and to the substantive implications of a theology of struggle, they may have an important prophetic contribution to make.

In sum, there can be no doubt that there have been major transformations in the Roman Catholic Church in Britain since the Second World War. Post-war social change which has led to the "economic embourgeoisement" of Catholics, on the one hand, and the much more friendly ecumenical climate, especially since the Second Vatican Council, on the other hand, have together resulted in the gradual but steady dissolution of the defensive walls which had previously been erected to defend a "fortress Church." Cardinal Hume has called instead for a "pilgrim Church on the move" but it could be argued that the bulk of British Catholics were too successfully socialised into a passive and rather deferential and subordinate lay role in the decades up to Vatican II to have yet heeded that call.

A realistic judgement, therefore, would be that British Catholics can be regarded as a "domesticated denomination," unlikely to rock the boat of British complacency to any marked extent, content rather with the status quo and marginal social engineering to file down the most pointed injustices. There is no evidence that British Catholics are likely to mount a sustained attack on the weaknesses and injustices of the British form of mixed economy and representative democracy. The powerful in Britain can sleep safely, confident that there will be no prophetic uprising of six million Catholics determined to bring the "Good News to the Poor" (Hornsby-Smith, 1987). All the same, perhaps the powerful should beware, for in the emerging justice and peace movement with its growing ecumenical linkages, there may well be the seeds of a major political challenge to the bastions of power and privilege in our country.

REFERENCES

ABBOTT, W. M. (ed.), (1966) *The Documents of Vatican II*. London: Geoffrey Chapman.

ANON. (1981). *Liverpool 1980: Official Report of the National Pastoral Congress*. Slough: St. Paul Publications.

ARCHER, A. (1986). *The Two Catholic Churches: A Study in Oppression*. London: S. C. M.

BECK, G. A. (ed). (1950). *The English Catholics: 1850-1950*, London: Burns Oates.

BERGER, P. L. (1973). *The Social Reality of Religion*, Harmondsworth: Penguin.

BROTHERS, J. (1964) *Church and School: A Study of the Impact of Education on Religion*. Liverpool: Liverpool University Press.

COMAN, P. (1977). *Catholics and the Welfare State*, London: Longman.

COSER, L. A. (1974). *Greedy Institutions: Patterns of Undivided Commitment*. London: Collier Macmillan.

DOUGLAS, M. (1973). *Natural Symbols: Explorations in Cosmology*, Harmondsworth: Penguin.

DULLES, A. (1976). *Models of the Church: A Critical Assessment of the Church in All Its Aspects*. Dublin: Gill and Macmillan.

HORNSBY-SMITH, M. P. (1986). "The Immigrant Background of Roman Catholics in England and Wales: A Research Note," *New Community*, 13, No. 1, Spring-Summer, 79-85.

HORNSBY-SMITH, M. P. (1987). *Roman Catholics in England: Studies in Social Structure Since the Second World War*. Cambridge: Cambridge University Press.

HORNSBY-SMITH, M. P. and LEE, R. M. (1979). *Roman Catholic Opinion: A Study of Roman Catholics in England and Wales in the 1970s*. Guildford: University of Surrey.

HORNSBY-SMITH, M. P. and CORDINGLEY, E. S. (1983). *Catholic Elites: A Study of the Delegates to the National Pastoral Congress*, Occasional Paper No. 3. Guildford: University of Surrey.

LODGE, D. (1980). *How Far Can You Go?* London: Secker and Warburg.

LONGLEY, C. (1986). "Ten Years at Westminster," in CASTLE, T. (ed.), *Basil Hume: A Portrait*, London: Collins, pp. 134-147.

MARSH, D. and CHAMBERS, J. (1981). *Abortion Politics*, London: Junction Books.

McROBERTS, D. (ed.). (1979). *Modern Scottish Catholicism: 1878-1978*. Glasgow: Burns.

McSWEENEY, B. (1980). *Roman Catholicism: The Search for Relevance*. Oxford: Blackwell.

MURPHY, J. (1971). *Church, State and Schools in Britain: 1800-1970*. London: Routledge.

SCOTT, G. (1967). *The R. C.s: Report on Roman Catholics in Britain Today*. London: Hutchinson.

SPENCER, A. E. C. W. (1966). "The Demography and Sociography of the Roman Catholic Community of England and Wales" In BRIGHT, L. and CLEMENTS, S. (eds.). (1966). *The Committed Church*. London: Darton, Longman and Todd, pp. 60-85.

WINTER, M. M. (1973) *Mission or Maintenance: A Study in New Pastoral Structures*, London: Darton, Longman and Todd.

CHAPTER VII

THE FREE CHURCHES IN MODERN BRITAIN

DAVID M. THOMPSON

In the 1880s a number of Free Church leaders expected that the coming century would be "their century." They had witnessed the advance of democracy in their own lifetimes, particularly with the extension of the franchise in town and countryside by the Reform Acts of 1867 and 1884. They thought they saw a decline in the political power of the aristocracy. They were confident that the privileges of the Established Church had been significantly weakened; and they looked forward to disestablishment in the belief that, once the churches stood on equal terms, the superiority of the Free Church position would be clear beyond dispute. All this crystallized in the tendency to look across the Atlantic to the example of the United States, where the massive numerical strength of Methodists, Baptists, Presbyterians and Congregationalists by comparison with the relatively small size of the Episcopal Church seemed to be positive proof of the shape of things to come. It is fascinating to reflect on why these leaders proved to be mistaken. Had they missed a crucial difference between Great Britain and the U.S.A. which they should have noticed? Or were they affected by developments in twentieth-century Britain which could not have been foreseen?

The twentieth century has, in fact, seen a remarkable erosion of the position of the Free Churches in modern Britain. The main Free Churches in England and Wales - Methodists, Congregationalists, Baptists and Presbyterians - reached their maximum membership in the years just before the First World War: the actual year is different for each denomination. Between 1914 and 1970 their total membership dropped by about one third. Again there are differences between the denominations: the Congregationalists declined by well over 40%, more in England than in Wales, whilst the Methodists declined by around 26%. This decline has been much sharper since the Second World War than it was before it: in the period between 1914 and 1939 the average decline in England and Wales was 6% (in England alone it was slightly higher), but between 1939 and 1970 the average decline in England and Wales was 30% (in England alone it was slightly less). Moreover, the position is worse than even these figures suggest, for whereas in the years up to the First World War nonconformist church attendance was generally reckoned to be larger than the official membership - perhaps even twice as large - in the later twentieth century, nonconformist church attendance is definitely less than the official membership.[1]

It is tempting to write a whole essay on the reasons for this numerical decline. But apart from the fact that this has already been done,[2] it should be noted that some nonconformist groups have not declined - the Society of Friends has been more or less static, and actually had a thousand more members in 1970 than in 1914 - whilst some heterodox groups like the Jehovah's Witnesses and the Mormons have increased dramatically. The position of the Church of England has also been eroded since the Second World War. Before the specific reasons for the decline of the Free Churches can be discussed therefore, it is necessary to establish their homogeneity. The point deserves emphasis because it has become so normal to speak of the Church of England, the Roman Catholic Church and the Free Churches as the main religious groupings in England and Wales, that the collective nature of the Free Church category is often overlooked. Is it possible to regard the different Christian churches which make up nonconformity, dissent or the Free Churches (each of those words having a subtly different nuance) as a single category?

Certainly the Free Churches entered the twentieth century with a strong sense of corporate identity, and this survived at least until the Second World War. The form of this identity was threefold - ecclesiastical, political and social.

Ecclesiastically, the Free Churches were those excluded from the established Church of England. Classically, dissent had been defined in terms of those who were not prepared to subscribe to the Act of Uniformity of 1662, with the substantial addition in the eighteenth century of those products of the Evangelical revival which the Church of England was unable to contain, principally (but not exclusively) the Wesleyan Methodists and their offshoots. Originally there were differences of polity (independency or connexionalism) and theology (Calvinism or Arminianism), but these differences were lessened by the evangelical consensus and the considerable difficulties which any kind of central authority had in exercising effective control over the localities in nineteenth-century England. Nevertheless, these differences never disappeared completely and in the twentieth century they were exposed once more by historical reflection on the traditions from which the Free Churches had sprung. The Roman Catholics too were excluded from the Church of England by their refusal to subscribe to the Act of Uniformity, and had made common cause with Dissenters on civil liberties in the eighteenth century. In some important respects also they absorbed something of a nonconformist ethos,[3] but the nineteenth century saw a widening of the gap. "No popery" counted for more after the Evangelical Revival, and it was strengthened by the development of the Anglo-Catholic party in the Church of England. The Irish immigration with a different devotional style, the development of ultramontanism and the dogmas of the Immaculate Conception and Papal Infallibility all combined to destroy much of the former sense of a common cause. This was highlighted by and focussed in the education question, which strengthened nonconformist solidarity in the first decade of the twentieth century in the resistance to the 1902 Education Act.

Politically, the Free Churches were united by a common Liberalism in the early twentieth century. Perhaps this has sometimes been exaggerated. There always were solid nonconformist Tories, particularly in Methodism, and their numbers increased after the Liberal split over Irish home rule in 1886. On the other hand, some of those Free Churchmen who lost their Liberal enthusiasm because of this either relapsed into a rather passive Liberal Unionism or became non-political. Part of the significance of the Education Act of 1902 was the way in which it revived Liberal political solidarity.[4] At the other end of the political spectrum a number of nonconformists were moving in a Progressive or Labour direction.[5] The significance of this in fracturing the Liberal party before 1914, however, should probably not be exaggerated. What is more striking in some ways is the way in which between the wars the Free Churches became even more identified as the constituency of the Liberal party - though this is as much a sign of Liberal weakness as of nonconformist strength.

Socially, too, the Free Churches still had much in common in 1900. Here generalisation is fraught with hazard. It does not make much sense to fit particular denominations to particular social classes. This is partly because the terminology of social class is insufficiently precise; and it is partly because social differences between denominations make more sense in the local context than the national. A Wesleyan chapel might be the natural meeting place for agricultural labourers if the other chapel in the village were Congregational; but if the other chapel was Primitive Methodist it might be the natural meeting place for farmers; and if there was only one chapel in the village anyway such fine distinctions would have little point. There is limited value in trying to gross up these local situations into a national average. More often, however, it is the predominantly middle-class nature of nonconformity that is emphasized; and the point of such a comment is to draw attention to the relative lack of representation among the Free Churches of the aristocracy and the working classes. The former lack is more significant than the latter. None of the Churches did well among the working classes, though the Roman Catholics did better than many. But this should not obscure the significance of nonconformity in the upward social mobility of a number of working-class people, particularly those who reached positions of leadership in trade unions or political parties.

The social homogeneity of nonconformity is seen most clearly in the virtual absence from their ranks of those in the aristocracy and the great professions. This is linked to the Anglican monopoly of the public schools or Oxbridge. Although the two ancient universities were opened to nonconformists in the 1850s, and College Fellowships were opened in 1871, there was a generational lag before nonconformists took advantage of this in significant numbers. Nonconformist theological colleges were moved to Oxford and Cambridge: Mansfield College, Oxford (Congregational, 1886); Westminster College, Cambridge (Presbyterian, 1889); Cheshunt College, Cambridge (Congregational, 1905); Wesley House, Cambridge (Methodist, 1921); and Regent's Park College, Oxford (Baptist, 1926). But the date from which change began should not be confused with the time it took the change to happen. Until the Second World War it was the great provincial universities which were patronised by nonconformist benevolence; and after 1945 the social base of Oxford and Cambridge broadened for other reasons to the benefit of nonconformists but not of them alone. In the later nineteenth century the nonconformists had also founded public schools of their own, because it was difficult for a boy's nonconformity to survive education in an Anglican school. However, it was in professions like the Army, Navy and the Law where the Anglican monopoly remained least affected for so long. It is probably not surprising that nonconformists were not eager to enter the armed forces; but the Law, or at least the Bar, was never the object of a concerted agitation in the way that the universities were. Hence nonconformist MPs were generally businessmen: thus they tended to be older than average, because they needed to make their fortunes before embarking on a political career, and therefore they were less likely to achieve Cabinet office. In an age when aristocratic titles were still linked to the land and politics, this also restricted the opportunities for nonconformist entry into the aristocracy. In an important sense the world of nonconformity was that of the city or market town rather than the village or nation. In a city or market town a nonconformist minister could enjoy considerable prestige and nonconformist families could exercise considerable influence after the political changes of the 1830s. But on the national level, and indeed in London, such influence was more difficult to come by; whilst in the villages nonconformists were usually a perpetual minority. The new county and parish councils which were introduced in the 1880s and 1890s created opportunities for nonconformist influence in rural political life that had been very limited whilst local government remained in the hands of the county bench of magistrates.

The Free Church solidarity at the turn of the century is aptly expressed by the Free Church Unity movement, which had led to the formation of the National Council of the Evangelical Free Churches in 1896. The Liberal General Election victory of 1906, for which the National Council under its secretary, the Rev'd Thomas Law, took some credit, also seemed to herald new opportunities for the Free Churches: and men from rather different nonconformist backgrounds like Asquith and Lloyd George occupied positions of influence in the new administration.

Nevertheless, Free Church homogeneity should not be exaggerated. The relationship of Methodism to the other Free Churches had always been ambiguous, particularly for Wesleyans who cherished a special relationship with the Church of England. But the 1890s were probably a period when Wesleyan Methodism felt most decidedly "Free Church," as exemplified by Hugh Price Hughes's prominent position in the Free Church Unity movement. It was also a period when Anglican ritualism had a high profile and this always tended to accentuate Wesleyan free churchmanship.

Another question mark concerns the Quakers and the Unitarians. These had been the virtual elite of nonconformity from a social point of view in the early nineteenth century. But although not unaffected by the evangelical revival, they did not share in the numerical increase of nonconformity. The Quakers lost members until the mid-1860s, and then began a slow recovery. In the First World War the traditional peace testimony seems to have been a source of strength rather than weakness, and in the early 1920s the trend towards establishing a separated ministry was arrested. If anything, therefore, the Quakers were becoming more nonconformist rather than less. The Unitarians were much more static, and in some ways illustrate what might have happened to the rest of dissent without the evangelical revival. As it was, their liberal theology, whilst attractive to some, did not lead to conversionist zeal. Another rather different group is the Salvation Army. It can only be understood against its nonconformist background, but it is not likely to be confused with any of the other Free Churches. The Army's unique achievement was to win the respect of others for a ministry and witness which did not encroach upon but rather complemented that of the more traditional churches. The sense that "I could not be one but it is important that some people should be" was significantly different from more conventional forms of denominational rivalry.

A third question mark concerns the so-called "sects" - Christadelphians, Jehovah's Witnesses, Seventh Day Adventists, Spiritualists, Christian Scientists, etc. A conventional amnesia eliminates such groups from the consciousness when the Free Churches are discussed, which can be justified on grounds of relative size and significance, or their non-involvement in such collective activities as the Free Church Council. Yet there is a spectrum here: the Christian Brethren or the new Pentecostal groups of the early twentieth century are closer to the well-established Free Churches than, say, the Jehovah's Witnesses. And even where there are peculiar or heterodox doctrines, it is far from clear that they dominate what might be called the routine spirituality of the groups. In the period since the Second World War, however, such groups have increased, sometimes dramatically: Jehovah's Witnesses doubled in the 1950s, and the Mormons increased sixfold between 1957 and 1967. It may or may not be significant that a number of these groups have been able to draw on money and personnel from North America.

The various qualifications to Free Church homogeneity mentioned so far are relatively timeless in their implications. Since the Second World War, however, the homogeneity described at the beginning of the century has begun to break up in a number of ways. These changes are as much concerned with the relationships of nonconformity to the wider society as they are with internal developments in the Free Churches.

The first change, and in some ways the most fundamental, has been a social one. The Act of Uniformity of 1662 succeeded in its objective of excluding religious nonconformists from positions of social and political influence. From this point of view the Toleration Act of 1689 which guaranteed the right of nonconformists to exist was a minor concession by those who wanted to exclude them from political power. Only in the nineteenth century was civil equality established, and in the intervening period nonconformist identity had become closely associated with a sense of social exclusion. Even the relatively prestigious Quakers and Unitarians could not easily ignore the invisible cords which separated them from full social acceptability; and if they did forget them, they usually acknowledged this by renouncing their former religious allegiance.

Thus nonconformist upward social mobility in the nineteenth century did not mean automatic absorption into the governing class. It was quite a long time before the liberalizing measures of nineteenth-century governments had their effect in this area. The point may be illustrated by looking at the Lloyd George family. David Lloyd George's father was a teacher, and his uncle, who brought him up, was a shoemaker and an elder of the Church of Christ at Criccieth. David went to a local school, became a solicitor and then went into politics, eventually becoming Prime Minister. His son, Richard, was also educated at a local school, but went to Christ's College, Cambridge and then joined the Royal Engineers. The present Earl Lloyd George was educated at Oundle and served in the Welsh Guards. Most nonconformists did not travel so far or so fast, but the pattern could be repeated many times. Perhaps most interesting of all is the way so many Anglican clergy and even bishops have come from nonconformist backgrounds. Michael Ramsey, Archbishop of York and Canterbury, was brought up in the Sunday School at Emmanuel Congregational Church, Cambridge (as it was then), where his father was deacon. The warm embrace of the public schools and of Oxford and Cambridge have been especially important here. This is why the Free Churches established student societies in the universities from the 1930s onwards in order to stem the leakage of nonconformist students to the Church of England or to unbelief. These changes are as much inter-generational as intra-generational, and it may be a mistake to explain them in terms of twentieth-century secularization, when their roots lie in a nineteenth-century process of liberalization. From this point of view the difference between the British and the American religious experience in the twentieth century may be related to the continuing social prestige of particular types of religious affiliation in Britain, in a way which has never affected the U.S.A.

Penetration of the "social establishment" was in a sense willed by nonconformists themselves: alongside that development was another which only in a more ambiguous sense was the result of an act of will - what might be called the way in which nonconformity has been "captured" by the state. The development of state power is one of the primary themes of twentieth century history, and it has affected liberal democracies as much as the totalitarian regimes which normally receive most attention. It may be seen most clearly in education. In the early nineteenth century nonconformists established primary schools of their own, either through the inter-denominational British and Foreign Schools Society, or through denominational bodies such as the Congregational Board of Education. After the 1870 Education Act established locally-elected School Boards, many nonconformist schools were handed over to the new boards because they represented the whole community and were not dominated by the established Church. This was also in line with the strength of nonconformity in urban local government. By the time of the 1902 Act when the Anglican voluntary schools were absorbed into the system on rather different terms, the majority of nonconformist schools had ceased to exist as voluntary schools, apart from a small number of Wesleyan ones. Thus nonconformist efforts over the nature of Religious Education in schools, which did not become compulsory until 1944, were directed towards securing a syllabus acceptable to all, rather than time for denominational instruction. These efforts, expressed in the L.E.A. Agreed Syllabuses from the 1920s, left effective decision-making in the hands of Local Education Authorities rather than the Churches. So long as the Authorities were convinced of the need for and value of Religious Education this solution posed no problems; but since the 1960s, with a greater urging of humanist values and the problems of a multi-faith society, this solution has seemed more fragile. Moreover, since 1944 the state's willingness to meet the capital costs of voluntary schools has risen as they have become a smaller proportion of the total: thus Anglican, and particularly Roman Catholic, voluntary schools now receive up to 80% support from the state, and in such schools Religious Education remains denominational. So the early nonconformist support for the post-1870 system looks, in retrospect, like surrender to the secular state.

There are other examples of voluntary work begun by the Churches being entrusted to local authorities in the early twentieth century. Jeffrey Cox's study of Lambeth has shown how this happened in the fields of adult education, libraries, school meals, district visiting (which was taken over by social workers), benefit societies, district nursing and infant welfare.[6] Lambeth was probably more advanced than many local authorities before the First World War, but in the 1920s this development became more widespread. It is noteworthy that most of these activities, which became part of the general provision of the welfare state after 1945, were originally handed over to local authorities. Given the strength of nonconformity in provincial politics such a step did not originally seem to mean very much more than access to more professional administration and greater financial resources: there was no sense that the Churches were abdicating a role. Since 1945, however, these activities have come to depend on various kinds of subvention from central government; and in recent years when levels of support have been cut or have failed to increase in line with expectations, there has been a tendency within and outside the Churches to say that "the Church should be doing more," apparently forgetful of the original initiatives of the Churches in these areas.

The development of Free Church chaplaincy work is a further example of the same trend. In the armed forces Free Church chaplains first began in the First World War, probably due to the influence of Lloyd George at the War Office. In hospitals, the introduction of Free Church Chaplains was assisted by the Free Church Council. Subsequently, provision for Free Church chaplains has been made in many prisons, and also many educational institutions, especially the new universities and technical colleges established since the 1960s. This kind of chaplaincy is significantly different from the traditional role of the nonconformist minister as the pastor of a gathered congregation or group of congregations. It also implies a more positive recognition of the role of the civil authorities than was characteristic of the extreme disestablishment phase of nonconformist life in the nineteenth century. This shift is reflected in a significant statement published by the Free Church Federal Council in 1953 on *The Free Churches and the State*, which considered the possibility of some national recognition of religion as an alternative to disestablishment.

The third major change affecting nonconformity has been political. After the First World War the Liberals were replaced as the main opposition party by Labour. In retrospect this change seems more rapid and more final than it did to contemporaries. In 1929 and in 1945 there were high expectations among nonconformists that the General Election would bring a Liberal victory; but these hopes were disappointed. The result has been to expose a spectrum of political allegiance among nonconformists which was wider than before. Some moved easily from progressive Liberalism to Labour, but others found it equally natural to identify with the Conservative party. Again Lloyd George's family might be regarded as paradigmatic: his son, Gwilym, was Minister of Food under Churchill (1951-54) and Home Secretary under Eden (1954-57); his daughter, Lady Megan, became a Labour MP in 1957 after being a Liberal from 1929 to 1951. Despite Morgan Phillips's oft-quoted remark the "the Labour party owes more to Methodism than to Marx," Labour has never been the natural party for nonconformists to support in the way that the Liberals once were. Even more interesting have been the political changes at the end of the 1970s when the progressive consensus that had dominated British politics since 1945 was successfully challenged by Mrs Thatcher's brand of Conservatism. This owed little to traditional Tory ideas but drew heavily on the principles of Gladstonian Liberalism - sound finance and a minimum of state intervention. This might be expected to have some appeal for nonconformists, and Mrs Thatcher has from time to time evoked the ideals of her Methodist shopkeeper parents in Grantham, though not to the same political effect as Stanley Baldwin's evocation of a nonconformist background in the 1920s. In their Assemblies and Conferences the main Free Churches have been more critical than supportive of Mrs Thatcher's policies. But such resolutions and statements have often provoked vehement reactions from some nonconformist Conservatives in the pew, though they have not attracted the same press attention as the reaction of Anglican Conservatives to similar positions taken up by the General Synod of the Church of England. What it shows is that nonconformist solidarity is increasingly confined to the religious sphere.

In late twentieth-century Britain, however, churchly solidarity now includes more than the Free Churches. The ecumenical movement has significantly changed the Free Churches' perceptions of themselves. Before 1914 ecumenical contacts between the Church of England and the Free Churches were slight, despite the occasional meetings organised by the indefatigable Sir Henry Lunn at Grindelwald in the 1890s. Some historians have even interpreted the Free Church Unity movement as essentially anti-Anglican in posture. The National Free Church Council of 1896 drew together local Free Church Councils, and reflected the provincial base of nonconformity. In 1919 the Federal Council of the Free Churches was formed on the initiative of J.H. Shakespeare, General Secretary of the Baptist Union, to draw the Free Churches together as national bodies; and it was the Federal Council which provided the team which responded to the *Letter to all Christian People* issued by the Lambeth Conference of 1920. These conversations were the first serious ecumenical discussions involving the Church of England and the Free Churches since the seventeenth century.

The two Free Church Councils combined in 1940 to form the Free Church Federal Council; and two years later the formation of the British Council of Churches created a permanent forum in which Anglicans and Free Churchmen could meet together. Archbishop Fisher's Cambridge sermon of 1946, which was designed to divert Free Church attention from the kind of union scheme canvassed in the 1930s and about to be realised in South India, provoked different reactions among the Free Churches. Most found the Archbishop's suggestion that they should "take episcopacy into their system" an unacceptable starting point: but the Methodist Church, itself newly reunited in 1933, expressed its willingness to discuss the matter. So began the Anglican-Methodist conversations which, after interim reports in 1958 and 1963, led to proposals for a two-stage union of the two Churches. Though approved by the Methodist Conference, the plan failed to gain sufficient support either in the Convocations of Canterbury and York in 1969 or in the newly formed General Synod of the Church of England in 1972. It would be exaggerated to say that this episode dented Free Church unity; in some ways the negative voices on each side were saying that the leopard could not change his spots. But it illustrated the way in which ecumenical developments produced new alignments. When the Churches' Council for Covenanting was formed in 1978 to follow up the work of the Churches' Unity Commission (1947-78), it included from the Free Churches the Methodists, the Moravians, the United Reformed Church (formed in 1972 from the Presbyterian Church of England and the majority of the Congregational Church) and the Churches of Christ (most of whom joined the United Reformed Church in 1981). But it did not include the Baptists; so again the larger Free Churches were not all following the same path.

The Free Church Federal Council also began to reflect on its role in relation to the British Council of Churches. Some Free Churchmen thought there was no longer a need for a separate Free Church Council. But without it, how would the specifically Free Church cooperative activities, such as chaplaincies, be managed? Ironically, the new ecumenical interest of the Roman Catholic Church after the Second Vatican Council tended to reinforce the Free Church Federal Council's role. The Roman Catholic hierarchies in England and Wales and in Scotland did not join the national Council of Churches as some Roman Catholic hierarchies did in other parts of the world. Instead they looked for relations with the leaders of other Churches. Thus it has become more usual for the Archbishop of Canterbury, the Archbishop of Westminster and the Moderator of the Free Church Federal Council to assume a joint role as spokesmen for the English Churches when the need arises. The Moderator of the Free Church Federal Council therefore finds himself thrust into a leadership role which is somewhat strange to Free Church assumptions. This in turn is another aspect of the way in which ecumenism has begun to challenge Free Church assumptions about themselves.

A final change since the Second World War, therefore, might be termed the appearance of more sharply divergent views about the function of the Free Churches today. This interacts with the numerical decline of the larger Free Churches. In some ways it is not an exclusively Free Church problem, and it may be misleading to discuss it as though it were; but the collective nature of the Free Churches as a category, and their diversity, makes it more apparent. Put rather crudely it might be described as a tension between world-affirming and world-denying views of the Church. In one perspective the history of the Free Churches might be described as the story of those who, because of their open structure, were free to move with the religious mood of the times, adopt new ideas, leave behind hierarchical structures and superstitious religious practices characteristic of the mediaeval world - in short to be a "modernizing" force in society. From another point of view, however, the Free Churches may be seen as bastions of the world-denying religious mentality, preaching a stern moral ethic, rejecting many of the traditional religious practices of the community - in short as a community distinctly set apart, accepting cheerfully the social isolation this brought. In analysing the reasons for the growth of nonconformity in the nineteenth century it is possible to draw on either picture as an explanation, and indeed to relate them to middle class and working class attitudes respectively. In the twentieth century, however, the two pictures tug in opposite directions. It is possible to argue that the world-affirming view is an aspect of the secularization of the Churches. Lacking the institutional structure and the power of tradition possessed by the Anglican and Roman Catholic Churches, the larger Free Churches thus find themselves without a distinctive religious *raison d'être* since it is no longer necessary to be religious in order to be modern, and it may indeed be a disadvantage. Thus the Free Churches have declined faster than the other Churches. On the other hand, where a world-denying ethic has survived, for example, in evangelicalism or in sectarian positions, the Churches holding those views have been able to draw on the forces of resistance to modern culture and have held their own or even increased in numbers. In such a way one might be able to explain why the Congregationalists, whose nineteenth-century theology seems to have been the most eclectic, have declined more rapidly than any other Free Church this century; and one might also be able to explain the relatively better performance of the Baptists, the most obviously evangelical of the contemporary Free Churches, as well as the striking growth of the Jehovah's Witnesses and the Mormons.

The danger of such an approach, apart from the very high degree of generalization involved, is that too hasty a link is made between a particular religious attitude and the position of a whole denomination. Just as one cannot equate a whole denomination with a particular social class, so one cannot say that all Baptists are evangelical and no Congregationalists are. In any case, national statistics do not have a reality of their own, except as the aggregate of a series of local situations. Thus it was apparent that village nonconformity was in trouble by the 1890s, but since the denominations were near evenly spread geographically, some may have suffered from this disproportionately, not for denominational reasons, but because they happened to have more chapels in the most distressed areas. In the twentieth century there has been a swing away from the large city-centre congregation centred on a preaching ministry towards community-orientated suburban congregations. Some denominations in some places shifted their emphasis earlier than others. Hitler's bombers were sometimes a blessing in disguise by destroying old chapels and indirectly making available compensation money which could be used to build elsewhere, whilst the chapels that survived in 1939-45 may have encountered greater problems later. New planning legislation after 1947 and varying ecumenical hopes and fears affected church extension strategy. A determination to implement the "Lund dictum" of 1952 to do all things together except those which conscience compelled to be done separately might make a denomination less inclined to put money into what might seem like a competitive church extension venture than would be the case if there was a burning conviction of the need for a strong evangelical witness. This point is another way into the question of why a continuing Free Church witness is necessary, and whether it is understood as Free Church before it is understood as Methodist, Baptist etc., or only after.

Another element in this discussion has been exposed by a further important post-war development - the emergence of the black-led Churches. One of the biggest reproaches to the lifestyle of the English Churches since the arrival of the first boatload of West Indian immigrants in 1948 has been the extreme difficulty which Caribbean immigrants have experienced in integrating themselves into English Christianity, notwithstanding their high level of church attachment. This situation is quite different from the problems of integration experienced by Asian immigrants from India, Pakistan and East Asia who were not usually Christians. Time and time again one hears stories of how West Indian immigrants who did go to English churches were discouraged from coming again. In the end, several black-led churches were established in England, and these are now loosely grouped in the Afro-Caribbean Council of Churches. This development has also overlapped and interlocked with the development of Pentecostal Churches since the 1960s. What is most interesting for the present purpose is the historical similarity between such congregations (colour alone excepted) and those of the Churches of the Evangelical Revival established in new towns among groups of migrants in the early nineteenth century. Could there be a more striking illustration of the way in which denominational continuity can obscure social and functional change or discontinuity?

The issue facing the Free Churches at the end of the twentieth century may be put something like this. English nonconformity was born out of a mixture of religious convictions and social and political exclusion. As it became more acceptable socially and politically, its continued existence depended more on the sustaining of the religious convictions, which were massively reinforced by the Evangelical Revival. Even so the Free Church ethos which resulted depended quite heavily on its being an alternative to that of the established Church. In the twentieth century, as all Churches have come under external pressure with an erosion of the role of religion in public and private life, and as the ecumenical movement has emphasized that which unites all Christians, the maintenance of a specifically Free Church ethos has often seemed of less importance than the maintenance of a Christian ethos. Moreover, in the Free Churches, apart from the ministers and the more heavily committed laity, the level of commitment to a particular denomination has never been high, as is indicated by the ease with which many Free Church folk move readily from one denomination to another if they move house. From this point of view the formal denominational structures may provide an illusory guide to the nature of nonconformity. In such a situation the weakening or loss of conviction about the necessity of separate Free Church identity can produce a quite rapid decline. The Roman Catholic Church in Holland underwent a similar internal crisis after the Second Vatican Council when almost overnight a whole series of symbols of their difference from Protestants was swept away.

The fundamental question for nonconformists, therefore, is whether a continuing separate identity is necessary. If they see their congregations as serving the local community rather than drawing the committed out from it, how do they differ from the local parish church? Above all there is the question of the confidence required for new ventures and new projects. Nonconformist expansion has historically been associated with the planting of new congregations: periods where the emphasis has been on the maintenance of those which already exist have tended to be periods of decline. What may require explanation is not so much twentieth-century decline as early nineteenth-century expansion. In a situation where the Church of England itself has shed many, though not all, of the features which made it an established church, and particularly where a gap threatens to open up between the Church of England and the state, a continuing role for the nonconformist churches seems very much open to question. Also, in the present century the institutional prerequisites for success have subtly changed the internal roles and relationships within the Free Churches themselves, so that the older ethos of a separated group of covenanting free spirits seems to be found more in groupings other than the mainstream Free Churches. The scene could be set for a change in the basic structure of English Christianity more radical than at any point since the seventeenth century.

116

REFERENCES

[1] R. Currie, A. Gilbert and L. Horsley, *Churches and Churchgoers*, Oxford, 1970, give the following membership figures:

England and Wales

	1914	1939	1970
Methodists	818,617	788,683	605,597
Congregationalists	454,071	416,442	256,734
Baptists	389,718	358,728	245,447
Presbyterians	273,009	255,807	167,537
Total	1,935,415	1,819,660	1,275,315

The following figures are also available for smaller groups:

Great Britain

	1914	1939	1970
Quakers	19,942	19,673	20,752
Mormons	6,885	6,393*	68,217
Jehovah's Witnesses	-	5,945	59,705
Seventh Day Adventists	2,671	5,966	12,145

I have included more recent statistics on the non-Methodist Free Churches in my essay on "The Older Free Churches" in Rupert Davies (ed), *The Testing of the Churches, 1932-1982*, London, 1982.

[2] Currie, Gilbert and Horsley, *Churches and Churchgoers*; A. D. Gilbert, *The Making of Post-Christian Britain*, London, 1980, pp. 75-98.

[3] J. Bossy, *The English Catholic Community, 1570-1950*, London, 1975, pp. 391-401.

[4] D. W. Bebbington, *The Nonconformist Conscience*, London, 1982, especially pp. 8-17, 88-97, 127-52; J. M. Turner, "Methodism in England 1900-1932," in R. Davies, A. R. George, and G. Rupp, *A History of the Methodist Church in Great Britain*, iii, London, 1983, pp. 349-353.

[5]Robert Moore, *Pit-men, Preachers & Politics*, Cambridge, 1974, pp. 178-190; Stephen Koss, *Nonconformity in Modern British Politics*, London, 1975, pp. 145-176.

[6]Jeffrey Cox, *The English Churches in a Secular Society*, New York, 1982, pp. 196-206.

CHAPTER VIII

THE NEW BLACK-LED PENTECOSTAL CHURCHES IN BRITAIN

IAIN MacROBERT

According to one estimate, by the year 2000, Christianity's centre of gravity will have shifted from the Northern to the Southern hemisphere and the majority of Christians will belong, not to the historic denominations, but to the "Third Force in Christendom." They will be members of the indigenised, oral narrative Pentecostal-type churches.[1] What could not be achieved by almost two millenia of European missionary enterprise is being brought about within a century of the birth of the Pentecostal movement.

Pentecostal-type churches have outgrown Protestantism in many South American nations and are the fastest developing religious groups in parts of Africa, Asia and the Soviet Union. Furthermore, their emphasis on the Holy Spirit has influenced many people in the historic denominations and stimulated the development of the Charismatic movement. Glossolalia is now heard, not only in the proletarian Pentecostal meeting, but in St Peter's Basilica, Rome, Canterbury Cathedral and hundreds of non-conformist chapels throughout the land.[2]

There have been Pentecostal congregations in Britain since 1907, and one of these early groups was led by a West African - Thomas Kwow Brem-Wilson.[3] However, this was exceptional; most congregations were white working-class with some middle-class leadership. It was not until the early 1950's that the immigration of people from the Caribbean into the urban conurbations of England resulted in the establishment and rapid growth of significant numbers of black independent churches.[4] Not all such black-led congregations are Pentecostal and those which are do not always describe themselves as such. With about 250 different organisations represented in Britain, there is considerable theological diversity in the black Christian traditions, even if there are also some common elements. Among the non-Pentecostal groups which have been transplanted to Britain since the 1950's are the African Methodist Episcopal Church and the African Methodist Episcopal Zion Church which both came into existence as a reaction against the racism of white Methodism in the United States at the end of the eighteenth and the beginning of the nineteenth century.[5] Similarly, the Wesleyan Holiness Churches, which also originated in the United States of the nineteenth century, had the abolition of slavery as a major reason for their separate existence.[6] The Seventh Day Baptist Church, which was established in Britain in the seventeenth century, was *resurrected* as a result of the influx of members from the West Indies, as was the Seventh Day Adventist Church.

Since the 1960's there have also been independent West African churches in Britain. Groups such as the Church of the Cherubim and Seraphim, the Aladura International Church, the Divine Prayer Society and the Musama Disco Christo Church (Army of the Church of Christ) are very different from the independent American groups and often reflect the African indigenisation of high Anglicanism or Methodism.

The most numerically significant black groups in Britain are, however, the Pentecostals who comprise over 80% of the people attending independent black-led churches.[7] It is upon these groups that the rest of this chapter will concentrate. Furthermore, although there are people from most of the Caribbean Islands and Africa to be found in Pentecostal congregations, the overwhelming majority are from Jamaica or are of

Jamaican parentage. Thus it is upon this island that we will focus some attention. To understand the nature of black Pentecostalism in Britain requires some consideration of the origins of the Pentecostal movement in the United States, the cultural and religious heritage of those who brought it to birth in 1906, and the dynamics of its transplantation and indigenisation in the Caribbean.

William J. Seymour and the Black Roots of Pentecostalism

The most significant figure in the genesis of the Pentecostal movement was William Joseph Seymour. Born in 1870, the son of emancipated slaves, Seymour grew up in the Southern States where the lynching of black people by the Ku Klux Klan and the White League was still common. He became literate largely as a result of his own efforts and set himself to study the Christian scriptures. Foremost in his socialisation was the distinctively black understanding and practise of Christianity which had developed in the bi-cultural crucible of slavery. Seymour imbibed from his community both those West African elements which had survived the Middle Passage and the brutality of slavery, and been reinterpreted in terms of the Christian faith, and other themes which had developed largely as a response to the dehumanising conditions black people were forced to endure.[8]

From West African primal religion the black Christian community inherited a perception of the world which integrated the sacred and profane; the spiritual and material into a holistic system in which individuals were in constant interaction with the supernatural, with each other and with their ancestors. Black religion was communitarian rather than individualistic - not so concerned with a person's relationship to God as with the interrelationships between members of the worshipping community and the powers of the supernatural realm. Central to this world view was belief in the availability of the power of the spirits or Spirit, without which man is impotent. Healing, the transformation of society or any other major undertaking in the material world could only be successfully achieved by utilising this spiritual power. Thus, the primal religions of West African and the syncretised Christianity of the African diaspora were concerned with a pragmatic spirituality which sought to tap the *Force Vitale*. Religion was primarily experiential. God, Christ, the Spirit or the spirits were to be felt, experienced and demonstrated within the worshipping community, and this was usually achieved with the extensive use of rhythm: in music, singing, drumming, swaying, stamping, clapping, dancing and other motor behaviour which was associated with spirit possession in West Africa and with "getting the Spirit" in the United States.[9]

Some continuity of black Christianity with the beliefs and perceptions of primal religion was ensured by the oral narrative tradition of those brought from West Africa. It was in myths, legends, folk tales, riddles, songs, proverbs and other aphorisms that African theology was enshrined, codified and transmitted from generation to generation. In the New World, these oral narrative methods continued to preserve and communicate many African leitmotive which were now reorchestrated in an ostensibly Christian form.[10]

In addition to those West African perceptions and beliefs which were reinterpreted in terms of Christianity, were other powerful themes which grew out of black people's experiences of slavery and oppression. Foremost among them was the desire for freedom, dignity and equality. Freedom in the songs of the slaves meant - when the white overseer or missionary was listening - the evangelical idea of freedom from sin, but when they would "steal away to Jesus" in their clandestine meetings, it meant freedom to be oneself; freedom to let one's mind, body and emotions be overwhelmed by the experience of the presence and power of the Spirit; and - most importantly - freedom from "Pharaoh's" bondage in the "Egypt" of the Southern States. The God who delivered Israel would, they believed, one day deliver them. They also found hope in those passages of the Bible which speak of the cataclysmic eschatological revolution to be inaugurated by the Second Advent of Christ with the overthrow of the present order and establishment of a kingdom where the oppressed are set free, the poor and humble exalted, and the rich and the oppressor put down and punished. Furthermore, if one day they were to "walk and talk with Jesus in the New Jerusalem" it was because they were on their way to the "Promised Land" now; they were God's children now in spite of the daily reality of their bondage and suffering. This inaugurated eschatology transformed the self- concept of the Christian slave and brought human dignity, pride and hope into the humiliation of his servitude.[11] These leitmotive recur again and again in black American Christianity and were part of the cultural heritage which Seymour grew up with.

By the close of the nineteenth century most of the churches in the United States, both white and black, had undergone a process of embourgeoisement which resulted in the alienation of many proletarian Christians. Blacks in particular were concerned that emancipation had not brought about equality either outside or inside the churches, and there was an expectation among both black and white Holiness people that a great revival was about to break out as the harbinger of the imminent Second Advent of Christ.[12]

Such was the situation when in December 1905, Seymour enrolled at the Bible School of Charles Fox Parham in Houston, Texas. He was particularly attracted to Parham's school after hearing reports that glossolalia was occurring there as evidence of the presence and power of the Holy Spirit. However, when Seymour attended classes he was segregated from the white students and had to sit outside the classroom door which had been left ajar for his benefit. Parham was a racist who wrote in support of the Ku Klux Klan.[13]

Early in 1906 Seymour accepted an invitation to serve a small black Holiness congregation in Los Angeles. Upon his arrival he began to preach on - among other things - divine healing, the imminent Second Advent and glossolalia as an evidence that a person had received the "baptism of the Holy Spirit"; and this inspite of the fact that he had not yet spoken in tongues himself. Originally greeted with scepticism and hostility, Seymour's message of Spirit possession bore fruit on the 9th of April, 1906 when seven or more black people in a "cottage prayer meeting" burst forth in "other tongues." Three days later Seymour received his glossolalic Pentecostal experience, and within six months the now interracial movement was meeting at a run-down wooden chapel at 312 Azusa Street with around seven hundred and fifty in attendance and a further four or five hundred, for whom there was no

124

room, standing outside. Within two years the movement had spread to over fifty nations.[14]

For Seymour and the early black Pentecostals, glossolalia was important as the initial evidence of Spirit baptism but, like their fathers in slavery and their ancestors in West Africa, they perceived the Spirit as the power which could bring about radical changes in the social world. The importance of being possessed by the Holy Spirit was not merely a glossolalic experience but an infusion of the love and power which could transform the inequalities, animosities and divisions of a racist society and a segregated church, and prepare the world for the end of history when the social order would be reversed. These early Pentecostals also regarded glossolalia as foreign languages which would enable them to preach the gospel in all the world, and they perceived themselves as the agents of God who would hasten the imminent parousia of Christ with its revolutionary effects.[15]

Three Streams Diverge: Three Stage, Two Stage and Oneness Pentecostalism

In October 1906 Parham arrived at the interracial Azusa Mission to find a Christian community which worshipped on the basis of complete equality. He was horrified by the mixing of the races and by the behaviour of the whites, who, like their black co-religionists, were shaking, jerking, dancing, falling down and speaking in tongues "under the power" of the Holy Spirit. In spite of Parham's racism and criticisms of West African type motor behaviour, the Azusa Mission remained an interracial fellowship.[16]

In 1911, while Seymour was away on a preaching tour, the white Pentecostal, William H. Durham, took over the Azusa Mission in order to propagate a view of sanctification which differed from the Wesleyan ideas of the original Pentecostals. Seymour and the first Pentecostals, both black and white, were substantially from a Wesleyan-Holiness background and believed in a "second work of grace" following conversion whereby a Christian is "entirely sanctified." To the two experiences of conversion and sanctification they added the baptism of (or in) the Holy Spirit. Hollenweger has designated them "three-stage Pentecostals" because they emphasise the three crises experiences of conversion, sanctification and Spirit baptism.[17]

Durham taught that sanctification was complete at conversion - a tenet which he called the "Finished work of Calvary." His contentious doctrine split the movement and led in 1914 to the formation of the white dominated "two-stage" Assemblies of God. However, these two-stage Pentecostals who rejected the Wesleyan-Holiness view of sanctification also reinterpreted Durham's teaching in terms of sanctification as an ongoing process rather than the instant eradication of sin at conversion. The majority of white Pentecostal churches in Britain (Assemblies of God and Elim) are part of this two-stage tradition.[18]

In 1916, a second major schism occurred in the Pentecostal movement, although this only affected the two-stage wing. Prior to 1913 it was quite common for some Pentecostals to use the simple formula - "in the name of Jesus" - rather than the more common triadic formula of Matthew 28:19 when baptising converts. However, from April 1913 this became increasingly linked to a modalistic understanding of the Godhead (which Pentecostals called "Oneness") and ultimately to a view of baptismal regeneration which made "full salvation" dependent on the "three steps" of repentence, water baptism "in the name of Jesus" and Spirit baptism with the evidence of glossolalia. On the other side of the debate, the Trinitarians became increasingly tritheistic as the belligerents polarised in mutual antagonism.[19]

In 1914, the split between the three-stage and two-stage Pentecostals had led to the formation of the overwhelmingly white and white-dominated Assemblies of God which withdrew from the wider interracial fellowship. Two years later, the Oneness Pentecostals were expelled for *heresy* and with them went most of the few remaining blacks. Anderson questions:

> Was the emergence of the Assemblies as a de facto 'lily white' denomination a wholly unanticipated or unwelcome consequence of the doctrinal struggle? Since 1916, except for a few black faces here and there in urban congregations in the Northeast, the Assemblies (of God) has remained a white man's church.[20]

Thus, in the first ten years of the Pentecostal movement we have the degeneration of a united interracial body into one which mirrors the racial divisions of the older denominations in the United States and which has split into three streams: three-stage, two-stage and Oneness.

Pentecostalism in Jamaica

Although the Pentecostal movement spread to Jamaica within four years of its birth in Los Angeles, it was not until after the Second World War that it became the fastest growing religious movement on the island. Between 1943 and 1970 the number of people who identified themselves with the major Protestant denominations fell from 82% to 55% while the Pentecostals grew from 4% to 20% during the same period. This expansion has occurred within an era of transformation from a rural agrarian to an urban industrial society. Pentecostalism both reflects the values of modernity and provides a sense of community and stability in an increasingly fragmented and anomic society.[21]

While white Pentecostal missionaries from the United States and Britain have had some influence on the island, the movement's phenomenal growth since the early 1950s has been largely under the leadership of indigenous ministers, many of whom were introduced to Pentecostalism while migrant workers in the United States. Furthermore, Jamaican Pentecostalism is an indigenised and syncretised religious movement in the same tradition as the proletarian Afro-Christian sects (Convince, Cumina, Revival Zion, Pocomania and Native Baptist) which, like slave religion and early Pentecostalism in the United States, resonated with the black leitmotive. Oral narrative theology, community, spirit possession, glossolalia, prophecy, dreams, simultaneous individual praying, repetitive chorus singing, call and response, testifying, dancing, percussive emphasis, polyrhythms, fasting, prayer for healing by the power of the Spirit, water baptism (immersion) adventism and millenarianism all preceded the coming of Pentecostalism in the syncretised ancestral and revivalist sects. While Pentecostalism differs both in doctrine and pneumatology from the Afro-Christian sects, its indigenisation in Jamaica has meant that the leitmotive of black folk belief reinvigorated the movement, which had been largely *de-Africanised* by white Pentecostals, and thus restored many of the perceptions and themes which had been present at the birth of the Pentecostalism in Los Angeles.[22]

Migration to Britain

Beginning in June 1948, workers from Jamaica migrated to the urban conurbations of England. Escaping from the grinding poverty in their homeland, they came to the nation they had been taught to look upon as their "mother country." In London some 54% of the 92% who claimed religious affiliation were church attenders and 16% members of Christian denominations.[23] On their arrival Jamaicans were shocked to discover that the white population were both extremely racist and largely a-religious or anti-religious. Christian migrants were also confronted with the same prejudice and discrimination inside the churches as they were outside. The majority of black Christians who visited white churches were stared at but otherwise ignored, a few were greeted with extreme hostility and a few were actually made to feel welcome. Some endured in the white-led denominations, many left - their faith undermined by the heresy of racism - while others established or joined their own black-led congregations.

While both personal and institutionalised racism and prejudice were the major reasons for the failure of the white congregations to welcome their black brethren, there were also other factors such as the unrealistically high expectations of Christians from the Caribbean, the cultural temperament of white Christians - "Traditional English Conservatism" - and the diverse interests of black and white Christians which sprang from their different stages in the life cycle. Most migrants in the 1950s were young, while white inner city congregations were often elderly.[24] Most white congregations also lacked characteristics which black Christians considered concomitants of authentic faith and spirituality: demonstrable love, life and spiritual power; a high degree of visible Christian commitment; a strong sense of community and full opportunity to participate at every level.

128

Some Functions of the Black Pentecostal Congregations

To say that the formation of independent black-led congregations was a reaction to the "coldness, deadness" and rejection black Christians experienced in the white denominations is only partly true, and to explain their growth simply in terms of status frustration or perceived deprivation is also a gross oversimplification.

Many migrants to Britain were already Pentecostals and a few were ministers who had received their ordination in the United States or Caribbean. Furthermore, many of the black Christians who had attended non-Pentecostal churches in Jamaica, nevertheless came to Britain with a distinctively *black* liturgy and understanding of the Christian faith. While the black Pentecostal congregation was - and still is - a haven of *warmth, life* and cultural familiarity in the midst of a white Christianity which the first generation often perceived as unloving, powerless and paternalistic, there is also a constellation of other sociological and psychological functions. Sydney A. Dunn, leader of the First United Church of Jesus Christ (Apostolic) in England, writes that,

> ...the Church over the years has been a sanctuary for the black community in the face of many dangers and prejudices and has served as a succourer for the physically uprooted, the emotionally displaced, the socially and culturally bereaved, and the spiritually bankrupt.[25]

For the first generation, the black Pentecostal congregation does provide a focus for ingroup solidarity as a protection against the disdain and rejection of white society and the white churches, but for both generations it is also a participative community which draws all its members together - both adults and children - into active involvement, creates a sense of belonging and worth, and affirms black personhood and dignity. In a racist society which constantly assaults the self image of black people with negative evaluations and responses, the Pentecostal congregation provides a source of positive self image and ego gratification, the redefinition of the values upon which status is based and the hope of an eschatological status reversal. In the black congregation people can function in valuable and prestigious roles as Bishop, Overseer, Elder, Pastor, Minister, Evangelist, Missionary, Deacon,

Assembly Band Leader, Sunday School Teacher, Saint and so on. The values of the wider society, though internalised by the Pentecostal, can be cast aside (at least temporarily) and replaced with those abilities and characteristics which are perceived as being of value to God and the congregation: testifying, singing, playing music, talking in tongues, exhorting, preaching, experiencing the Spirit, holiness of life, tithing obeying the rules and taboos and so on.

The Pentecostal community is also a sympathetic milieu for the development and expression of creativity, artistry and leadership in the black liturgical tradition. The Bishops, Pastors and Elders are the authentic leaders and representatives of a substantial proportion of the black community, and their lack of formal academic training is offset by a commitment to ministry which is based on vocation (the call of God) rather than professionalism (a career for financial reward).

The black Pentecostal congregation is also a pneumatic community which perceives itself as interacting with the supernatural in such a way as to bring the power of the divine to bear on problems which are often beyond the capability of the Pentecostal to deal with, and to overcome feelings of powerlessness which in a fundamentally racist society are confirmed by the economic, social and political limitations placed on most black people. The congregation forms a mutual support network which provides spiritual, practical, financial and psychological aid for its members, particularly in times of hardship and crisis. However, such support is generally denied to those who deviate from the norms and question or break the rules and taboos of the church.

Like their liturgy, the black encounter with God is holistic: emotions, body and mind are all committed to worship and the celebration of life. The immanence of God is felt and demonstrated physically; known and confessed orally; in a way which integrates both the total personality, and the individual into the gestalt of the worshipping community. Even the sermon is often a communitarian and participative drama in which the congregation become totally involved as they respond to the preacher with ejaculations of praise: Hallelujah! Amen! Glory! Praise the Lord!

Doctrine and Practice: White Fundamentalism and the Black Leitmotive

While most of the black Pentecostal organisations in Britain have "articles of faith" which they have inherited from their white (and occasionally black) parent bodies in the United States, there are varying degrees of disjunction between their apparent cognitive allegiance to such fundamentalistic statements, and the affective and behavioural manifestations which indicate their continuing sensitivity and commitment to the black leitmotive.

The two major black Pentecostal traditions in England are the three-stage and Oneness types. The former most commonly use the name "Church of God" with additional words to designate their particular faction. For example: the All Nations Church of God, Beulah United Church of God, Bible Church of God, Bible Truth Church of God, Calvary Church of God, Church of God Fellowship, Church of God Ground of the Truth, Church of God Independent, Church of God Universal, and the oldest of the black American Pentecostal churches, the Church of God in Christ.

The Oneness Pentecostals often include the word "Apostolic" in their name. Thus there are the Church of Our Lord Jesus Christ (Apostolic), First United Church of Jesus Christ (Apostolic), Mt. Zion Pentecostal Church (Apostolic), Pentecostal First Glorious Temple Church of God in Christ (Apostolic), Rehoboth Emmanuel Church of Jesus Christ (Apostolic), Shiloh United Church of Christ (Apostolic) Worldwide, to name but a few. The oldest Oneness organisation is however called the Pentecostal Assemblies of the World, and other Oneness groups use the terms "Bibleway" or "Shiloh."

The following list of "Church of God Teachings" is fairly typical of all the three-stage Pentecostals in Britain, although there are many subtle differences which are beyond the scope of this brief chapter.

1. Repentance. Mark 1:15; Luke 13:3; Acts 3:19.
2. Justification. Romans 5:1; Titus 3:7.
3. Regeneration. Titus 3:5.
4. New Birth. John 3:3; 1 Peter 1:23; 1 John 3:9.

5. Sanctification subsequent to justification. Romans 5:2; 1 Corinthians 1:30; 1 Thessalonians 4:3; Hebrews 13:12.

6. Holiness. Luke 1:75; 1 Thessalonians 4:7; Hebrews 12:14.

7. Water baptism. Matthew 28:19; Mark 1:9, 10; John 3:22, 23; Acts 8:36, 38. (That water baptism be administered by ordained or licensed male ministers, and that it be in accordance with the commission given by Jesus in Matthew 28:19, "Baptizing them in the name of the Father, and of the Son, and of the Holy Ghost.")

8. Baptism with the Holy Ghost subsequent to cleansing; the enduement of power for service. Matthew 3:11; Luke 24:49, 53; Acts 1:4-8.

9. The speaking in tongues as the Spirit gives utterance as the initial evidence of the baptism of the Holy Ghost. John 15:26; Acts 2:4; 10:44-46; 19:1-7.

10. Spiritual Gifts. 1 Corinthians 12:1, 7, 10, 28, 31; 1 Corinthians 14:1.

11. Signs following believers. Mark 16:17-20; Romans 15:18,19; Hebrews 2:4.

12. Fruit of the Spirit. Romans 6:22; Galatians 5:22, 23; Ephesians 5:9; Philippians 1:11.

13. Divine healing provided for all in the atonement. Psalm 103:3; Isaiah 53:4, 5; Matthew 8:17; James 5:14-16; 1 Peter 2:24.

14. The Lord's Supper. Luke 22:17-20; 1 Corinthians 11:23-26.

15. Washing the saints' feet. John 13:4-17; 1 Timothy 5:9, 10.

16. Tithing and giving. Genesis 14:18-20; 28:20-22; Malachi 3:10; Luke 11:42; 1 Corinthians 9:6-9; 16:2; Hebrews 7:1-21.

17. Restitution where possible. Matthew 3:8; Luke 19:8, 9.

18. Premillennial second coming of Jesus. First, to resurrect the dead saints and to catch away the living saints to Him in the air. 1 Corinthians 15:52; 1 Thessalonians 4:15-17; 2 Thessalonians 2:1. Second, to reign on the earth a thousand years. Zechariah 14:4; 1 Thessalonians 4:14; 2 Thessalonians 2:1. 2 Thessalonians 1:7-10; Jude 14, 15; Revelation 5:10; 19:11-21; 20:4-6.

19. Resurrection. John 5:28, 29; Acts 24:15; Revelation 20:5, 6.

20. Eternal life for the righteous. Matthew 25:46; Luke 18:30; John 10:28; Romans 6:22; 1 John 5:11-13.

21. Eternal punishment for the wicked. No liberation or annihilation. Matthew 25:41-46; Mark 3:29; 2 Thessalonians 1:8, 9; Revelation 20:10-15; Revelation 21:8.

22. Total abstinence from all liquor or strong drinks. Proverbs 20:1; 23:29-32; Isaiah 28:7; 1 Corinthians 5:11; 6:10; Galatians 5:21.

23. Against the use of tobacco in any form, opium, morphine, etc. Isaiah 55:2; 1 Corinthians 10:31, 32; 2 Corinthians 7:1; Ephesians 5:3-8; James 1:21.

24. A New Testament interpretation of the use of meats and drinks in accordance with the following scriptures: Romans 14:2, 3, 17; 1 Corinthians 8:8; 1 Timothy 4:1-5.

25. Christian day of worship. Romans 14:5, 6; Colossians 2:16, 17; Matthew 28:1; Acts 20:7; 1 Corinthians 16:2.

26. That our members dress according to the teachings of the New Testament. 1 John 2:15,16; 1 Timothy 2:9; 1 Peter 3:1-6.

27. That our members conform to the Scripture relative to outward adornment and to the use of cosmetics, etc., that create an unnatural appearance. 1 Peter 3:3-5; 1 Timothy 2:9, 10; Romans 12:1, 2.

28. That our members adhere to the scriptural admonition that our women have long hair and our men have short hair as stated in 1 Corinthians 11:14, 15.

29. Against members wearing jewelry for adornment or decoration, such as finger rings (this does not apply to wedding bands), bracelets, earrings, lockets, etc. 1 Timothy 2:9; 1 Peter 3:3.

30. Against members attending movies, dances and other ungodly amusements; further, that extreme caution be exercised in viewing and in the selectivity of television programmes. 1 John 2:15, 16; Romans 13:14; 1 Thessalonians 5:22; Phillipians 4:8; 2 Corinthians 6:14-7:1.

31. Against members going swimming with opposite sex other than immediate family. 1 John 2:15, 16; 1 Timothy 2:9; 1 Corinthians 6:19, 20; Romans 6:13; 2 Peter 1:4; Galatians 5:19.

32. Against members belonging to Lodges. John 18:20; 2 Corinthians 6:14-17.

33. Against members swearing. Matthew 5:34; James 5:12.

34. Divorce and remarriage. Matthew 19:7-9; Mark 10:11, 12; Luke 16:18; 1 Corinthians 7:2, 10, 11. (All parties who have put their companions away for the cause of fornication, having been divorced and remarried, provided they are otherwise qualified, are eligible for membership in the Church of God.)[26]

While most Oneness Pentecostals adhere to the majority of the same tenets as their three-stage co-religionists, items 5, 7 and 8 above are interpreted differently. Sanctification is generally understood as an ongoing process, "believers' baptism" is administered "in the name of Jesus" and, like Spirit baptism, is perceived as having soteriological significance. Thus the "Doctrine" of the Pentecostal Assemblies of the World - the oldest Oneness organisation - itemises:

a. The one baptism, as recorded in Acts 2:4; 10:44-48; 19:1-6, is evidenced by the speaking of other tongues as the Spirit gives utterance as the initial evidence thereof.

b. The New Birth ("being born again") includes a genuine repentance, water baptism in Jesus' Name, and Baptism of the Holy Ghost, evidenced by the speaking in other tongues as the Spirit gives utterance.[27]

The Oneness Pentecostals, unlike the Trinitarian three-stage Pentecostals, are also modalistic (rather than unitarian as is so often erroneously claimed). Their doctrine states:

We fully believe in the mystery of the Godhead. We fully believe that Jesus was both human and divine, and further, that the Godhead be understood to mean all the fullness of God. We believe that Jesus was Mary's son and Mary's God, Creator and creature, God manifest in the flesh; that the flesh of Jesus was the same as ours with the exception that it had no sin; that Jesus was the Eternal Father made visible, apart from whom there is no God. We believe that at the final consumation of all things there will be only one God, and that will be our Lord Jesus Christ.[28]

However, any understanding of black Pentecostalism which is solely based on such written statements is utterly inadequate, for beneath this *white* fundamentalistic overlay, black Pentecostalism continues to reverberate with the leitmotive of black folk religion. The *real theology* of the black Pentecostals is not generally found in what is written but in what is said, sung and done. It is in the oral narrative forms of the dramatic sermon, the testimony, the story, the proverb, the chorus, simultaneous individual praying and even the account of the dream or vision: methods of communication which are available to all and understood by all.

Furthermore, this communication operates at two levels. While there is an overt *conscious* message which superficially often carries a meaning which conforms to white Pentecostal fundamentalism, there may also be a parallel subconscious theme which sets up a kind of *sympathetic resonance* in the rest of the congregation whenever the black leitmotive are touched upon. What is *felt* is generally of far greater importance than what is simply heard. Jamaican Pentecostal, Yvonne McFarlane expressed it thus:

> What a thrill we feel when we get together with God's wonderful people! How we love the thrill! The singing of this song brought us great joys and the shouts of praises and hallelujahs could be heard and felt all over the place....Praise the Lord! It is better felt than told....Nothing can express the thrill as he (the preacher) spoke through the power of the Holy Ghost.[29]

This *sympathetic resonance* responds to those *deeper levels of meaning* which express the heartfelt beliefs, longings and hopes which are profoundly significant to black Christians. In the black Pentecostal service it is often demonstrated by a crescendo of antiphonal responses, motor behaviour or dancing which, once again, expresses the behavioural as well as the ideational continuity between *black* religion in West Africa, the Americas and Britain.

The balance between white fundamentalism and the black leitmotive, and the degree of black cultural expression generally varies according to the amount of white influence and black autonomy in each Pentecostal organisation. The three-stage Church of God congregations are either tied to white dominated parent bodies in the United States or have severed their connection to set up their own autonomous black-led organisations or, in a few instances, are branches of black American churches. The first tends to be culturally, liturgically and ideationally ambivalent while the latter two are free from white control or influence to be culturally, liturgically and ideationally *black*. This is also particularly true of the Oneness organisations which - with the exception of the United Pentecostal Church which is white-dominated in the United States but multi-racial in Britain - are linked to black bodies in the United States and the Caribbean and represent the section of the movement with the most well developed sense of cultural and ecclesiastical identity. This is not to suggest, however, that black Pentecostals perceive themselves as ethnic churches. On the contrary, almost without exception, they declare themselves to be open to all races and cultures.[30]

Division and Multiplication

The black Pentecostal churches in Britain began in September 1953 with a meeting of 17 people at the YMCA in Wolverhampton.[31] Today they number some sixty-seven and a half thousand in more than a thousand congregations. They have been extremely prone to internal dissentions which have split them into a multiplicity of groups which are often doctrinally very similar if not identical to each other. Although these schisms may have been detrimental to individual congregations, the overall effect has been to stimulate further evangelism, proselytisation and the growth of the black Pentecostal movement as a whole.

The two largest organisations are the three-stage groups linked to white parent bodies in the United States: the New Testament Church of God and the Church of God of Prophecy. The former has 6,790 members in 112 congregations and the latter 5,658 members in 105 congregations.[32] Most of the other three-stage organisations are either autonomous or have black parent bodies in the United States or the Caribbean. They number around a hundred and ninety seven with forty and a half thousand adherents in some six hundred and eighty congregations.

Of the Oneness organisations, only one has a white parent body in the United States: The United Pentecostal Church. The others all have black leadership. The total number of black Oneness Pentecostals is around thirteen and a half thousand in some two hundred and thirty congregations representing around forty-seven organisations.[33] There are also perhaps over a thousand sabbatarian Pentecostals in Britain.[34]

The total number of black-led Pentecostal organisations is around two hundred and thirty, some with only one branch, others with over a hundred. Concentrated mainly in the industrial conurbations of England are a total of about 1,150 congregations with 67,600 adherents meeting regularly. If we add to these the members of non-Pentecostal black-led congregations, the number exceeds 84,500.[35]

Social and Political Involvement

While the black-led Pentecostal churches have always been concerned for the material and social welfare of their people, the degree of involvement in social issues and action in the secular world has tended to be related to the size and resources of each organisation and their freedom from white influence and control. Although there are recent exceptions (particularly among the New Testament Church of God congregations), the larger organisations which are answerable to white American overseers have generally demonstrated the least involvement, while those which have been exposed to the black American Christian tradition of social and political action have become increasingly engaged in providing occupational training for their young people (often with MSC funding), accommodation for their families, centres for their elderly and disabled, bursaries for their potential academics and advice centres for the black community.[36]

While the second generation of black British Pentecostals are generally far more politically aware than most of the first generation (among whom there are notable exceptions) the influence of the anti-politics taboo inherited from white Pentecostalism in the United States, is still very strong. The church/world dichotomy of white American fundamentalism is in direct conflict with the authentic tradition of black American political Christianity. This tension is resolved by many young Pentecostals who, while vehemently maintaining that they are a-political, are nevertheless vociferous in their enthusiastic support for those who seek to overthrow apartheid in South Africa and racism in Britain.

As yet, black Pentecostals have seldom taken corporate stands on social or political issues but this will probably change within the next decade as the fragmented black-led organisations begin to cooperate with each other. In 1976 the Afro-Westindian United Council of Churches (AWUCOC) came into existence as "a Federation of Black-led Churches established to promote a sense of 'Unity without conformity'" and to "work together on tackling social and educational issues."[37] The majority of the churches which joined AWUCOC are Pentecostal and the 1984 edition of their handbook included an article by Robinson Milwood entitled "How is Theology Political." In a footnote Milwood states:

> The Pentecostal churches are attracting not only black youngsters but young people as a whole, not only because of the nature of identification there of religious worship and culture, but also because the Pentecostal churches are now beginning to break out into the world of political consciousness, economical consciousness, educational consciousness: and thus I would say that it does attract the majority of black people...[38]

While Milwood may have overstated the involvement of white youth, in other respects he is perfectly correct. The black Pentecostals in England are beginning to rediscover their Christian heritage of *Exodus* theology where spiritual and political liberation meet, and where, as for William Seymour and Martin Luther King, the Holy Spirit is available to empower the Church to change the world.

REFERENCES

[1]Barrett, David B. 1970, "AD 2000: 350 Million Christians in Africa," *International Review of Mission* 59:233, pp. 39-54. Barrett, David B., (ed.), 1982, *World Christian Encyclopaedia*, Oxford: Oxford University Press. Van Dusen, Henry Pitt, 1958, "The Third force in Christendom," *Life* 9th June, 1958, p. 13. Walls, A. F. 1976, "Africa's Place in Christian History," Pobee, John S. (ed.) *Religion in a Pluralistic Society*. Leiden: E. J. Brill, p. 182. I am using the term "Pentecostal" to designate those sects which comply with the rather narrow self-definition of white Pentecostalism in the United States. That is to say, those groups which stress that glossolalia is the initial evidence of Spirit baptism. By "Pentecostal-type" I refer to those sects and movements which comply with a much broader definition. Walter Hollenweger's summary is a good example of this broader definition:

1. orality of liturgy;

2. narrativity of theology and witness;

3. maximum participation at the levels of reflection, prayer, decision-making and therefore a form of community which is reconciliatory;

4. inclusion of dreams and visions into personal and public forms of worship; they function as kinds of icons for the individual and the community;

5. an understanding of the body/mind relationship which is informed by experience of correspondence between body and mind; the most striking application of this insight is healing by prayer.

Although I deal only with those groups which are Pentecostal in terms of the former definition, all of the black-led independent churches in Britain have characteristics which conform to the second. Hollenweger, Walter J., (ed.), 1986, *Pentecostal Research in Europe: Problems, Promises and People*, Studies in the Inter-cultural History of Christianity. Frankfurt/Bern: Peter Lang Gmbh. Chapter reproduced in *Bulletin of the European Pentecostal Theological Association* 4:4, pp. 129, 130.

[2]In 1975 more than ten thousand Pentecostal Roman Catholics gathered at St Peter's in Rome to receive the endorsement of Pope Paul VI, and in 1978 some two thousand Pentecostal Anglicans gathered in Canterbury Cathedral to be addressed by Archbishop Donald Coggan.

[3]Brem-Wilson, the son of a wealthy African Chief, was born in Dixcove, Gold Coast (Ghana) in 1855 and came to London in 1901. From 1909 until his death in 1929 he was pastor of "London's Oldest Pentecostal Assembly" on Sumner Road, Peckham.

[4]Although, to use B. R. Wilson's (1963) typology, the black Pentecostals form sects of the conversionist type, there are also elements of the revolutionary type evidenced by their eschatological orientation; of the pietist type shown in their concern for personal holiness; and the thaumaturgical type in their insistence that it is possible for people to experience the supernatural in their lives. However, use of the term "sect" is perceived by black Pentecostals to be derogatory, demeaning and offensive. For this reason, and because I have not found the term particularly useful in the context of this chapter, I have preferred to use the expression "church" in its generic sense and the designation "congregation" as a neutral category. The latter is particularly appropriate as some black groups do not yet possess their own church buildings and continue to meet as congregations in rented halls. Wilson, B. R. 1969, "A Typology of Sects," Robertson, Ronald, *Sociology of Religion*, Middlesex: Penguin Books, pp. 361-83.

[5]MacRobert, Iain, 1988, *The Black Roots and White Racism of Early Pentecostalism in the USA*. London: Macmillan, pp. 23-27.

[6]For an account of the establishment and growth of the Wesleyan Holiness Church in Britain see Pemberton, Pemberton and Maxwell-Hughes, 1983, *Pilgrims in Progress*, Birmingham: Wesleyan Holiness Church.

[7]Statistics are primarily based on personal research which was largely carried out by means of telephone conversations with black Church leaders around the country. See also Brierley, Peter, (ed.), 1984, *UK Christian Handbook*, 1985/86 Edition, London : MARC Europe, p. 111.

[8]The most comprehensive work on Seymour is Douglas J. Nelson's (1981) unpublished doctoral dissertation: *For Such a Time As This: The Story of Bishop William J. Seymour and the Azusa Street Revival*, University of Birmingham. MacRobert, *Early Pentecostalism*, pp. 34-36.

[9]MacRobert, *Early Pentecostalism*, pp. 11-18; 29-36.

[10]MacRobert, *Early Pentecostalism*, Ibid.

[11]Cone, James H. 1972, *The Spirituals and the Blues: An Interpretation*, New York: The Seabury Press. MacRobert, *Early Pentecostalism*, pp. 31-36.

[12]MacRobert, *Early Pentecostalism*, pp. 41-42.

[13]Nelson, *For Such A Time*, pp. 32-35.

[14]Nelson, *For Such A Time*, pp. 188-214.

[15]Matthew 24:14. Seymour was primarily responsible for the view that the power of the Holy Spirit could transform a segregated church in a racist society, while Parham emphasised glossolalia (or more correctly xenoglossia) as a means of evangelism. Parham, Charles Fox, 1902, *A Voice Crying in the Wilderness*, Joplin: Joplin Printing Co., p. 28. All early Pentecostals, both

140

black and white, also believed glossolalia to be an eschatological sign (cf Joel 2:28-32 and Acts 2:14-21).

Parham, *Voice*, pp. 83, 91-100. Parham, Charles Fox, 1911, *The Everlasting Gospel*, Baxter Springs: np, pp. 71, 72, 168-70. Parham, Sarah E., (comp.), 1930, *The Life of Charles F. Parham: Founder of the Apostolic Faith Movement*, Joplin: Tri-State Printing Co., pp. 148, 154-155, 160-164.

Hollenweger, Walter J. 1972, *The Pentecostals*, London: SCM Press, pp. 24, 25.

Hollenweger, *Pentecostals*, Ibid. MacRobert, *Early Pentecostalism*, pp. 63-66.

MacRobert, *Early Pentecostalism*, pp. 68-71.

Anderson, Robert Mapes, 1969, *A Social History of the Early Twentieth Century Pentecostal Movement*, Doctoral dissertation, Columbia University, pp. 319-20. Published in a revised form as *Vision of the Disinherited: The Making of American Pentecostalism*. New York: Oxford University Press.

Statistical Yearbook of Jamaica, 1974, Kingston: Department of Statistics. Wedenoja, William, 1980, "Modernisation and the Pentecostal Movement in Jamaica," Glazier, Stephen D. (ed.), *Perspectives on Pentecostalism: Case Studies from the Caribbean and Latin America*, Washington DC: University Press of America.

Barrett, Leonard, 1976, *The Sun and the Drum: African Roots in Jamaican Folk Tradition*, Kingston: Sangster's Book Stores/Heinemann. Gates, Brian, (ed.), 1980, *Afro-Caribbean Religions*, London: Ward Lock Educational. Morrish, Ivor, 1982, *Obeah, Christ and Rastaman: Jamaica and its Religion*, Cambridge: James Clark. Simpson, George Eaton, 1978, *Black Religions in the New World*, New York: Columbia University Press. Simpson, George Eaton, *Religious Cults of the Caribbean: Trinidad, Jamaica, and Haiti*, Rio Piedras: University of Puerto Rico, Institute for Caribbean Studies. Braithwaite, Edward Kamau, 1981, *The Folk Culture of the Slaves in Jamaica*, London: New Beacon Books.

Hill, Clifford, 1963, *West Indian Migrants and the London Churches*, Oxford: Oxford University Press.

Ward, Robin H., 1970, "Some Aspects of Religious Life in an Immigrant Area of Manchester," Martin and Hill, *A Sociological Year Book of Religion in Britain*, 3, London: SCM Press, pp. 18-21.

Dunn, Sydney Alexander, 1986, *First United Church of Jesus Christ (Apostolic): a Caring Christian Organisation*, West Bromwich: FUCOJC (A).

Supplement to the Minutes of the 58th General Assembly of the Church of God, 1980, Cleveland, Tennessee: Church of God Publishing House, pp. 6-9.

[27] *The 1981 Minute Book of the Pentecostal Assemblies of the World, Inc.*, Indianapolis, Indiana: PAofW, p. 17.

[28] *Minute Book*, p. 18.

[29] McFarlane, Yvonne, "42nd Annual Convention - March 28 - April 2nd, 1978," *Triumph*, January-March, 1986, p. 20.

[30] See for example Goodridge, Martin, 1984, "In Our Churches All Are Welcomed," *A Handbook of the Afro-Westindian United Council of Churches*, London: Centre for Caribbean Studies, p. 19.

[31] Lyseight, O. A., 1957, "Tidings From England," *Church of God Evangel*, 8th April 1957, p. 12. Interviews with H. D. Brown, Bishop of the First United Church of Jesus Christ (Apostolic), Wolverhampton.

[32] Statistics provided by the British headquarters offices of the New Testament Church of God and the Church of God of Prophecy, July 1986.

[33] See note 7.

[34] See note 7. All statistics on the black Pentecostal and Pentecostal-type churches in Britain can only be approximate. With the exception of the white-controlled organisations, accurate figures are not available. Two or more organisations may use the same name and it is not always possible to ascertain from the name which tradition they belong to.

[35] If we add to this 84,500 the vast numbers of irregular attenders, those on the periphery of formal membership and those who turn up for special services, "programmes" and conventions, the figure could be almost double.

[36] Dunn, *First United Church*. Gibson, Ashton (incorrectly attributed to Wood, Wilfred D.), 1984, "The Black Church Movement in Britain," *AWUCOC Handbook*, p. 9.

[37] *AWUCOC Handbook*, Ibid.

[38] Milwood, Robinson, 1984, "How Theology is Political," *AWUCOC Handbook*, p. 15.

SELECT BIBLIOGRAPHY

African Primal Region

Idowu, E. Bolaji. *African Traditional Religion: A definition*. London: SCM Press, 1973.

Mbiti, John S. *African Religions and Philosophy*. London: Heinemann, 1969.

Mbiti, John S. *Introduction to African Religion*. London: Heinemann, 1975.

Taylor, John V. *The Primal Vision: Christian Presence Amid African Religion*. London: SCM Press, 1963.

African Elements in Black American Christianity and Folk Religion

Cone, James H. *The Spirituals and the Blues: an Interpretation*. New York: Seabury Press, 1972.

Herskovits, Melville J. *The Myth of the Negro Past*. Beacon Press, 1958.

Raboteau, Albert J. *Slave Religion: The Invisible Institution in the Antebellum South*. Oxford: Oxford University Press, 1978.

Simpson, George Eaton. *Black Religions in the New World*. New York: Columbia University Press, 1978.

Wilmore, Gayroud S. *Black Religion and Black Radicalism*. New York: Doubleday, 1972.

Pentecostalism in the United States and Jamaica

Anderson, Robert Mapes. *Vision of the Disinherited: The Making of American Pentecostalism*. New York: Oxford University Press, 1979.

Gill, Jeffrey H., (ed.). *Papers presented to the first occasional symposium on aspects of the Oneness Pentecostal Movement*. Cambridge, Massachusetts: Harvard Divinity School, 5-7 July, 1984.

Hollenweger, Walter J. *The Pentecostals*. London: SCM Press, 1972.

MacRobert, Iain. *The Black Roots and White Racism of Early Pentecostalism in the USA*. London: Macmillan, 1988.

Synan, Vinson, (ed.). *Aspects of Pentecostal-Charismatic Origins*. Plainfield, New Jersey: Logos International, 1975.

Synan, Vinson. *The Holiness-Pentecostal Movement in the United States.* Grand Rapids, Michigan: William B. Eerdmans, 1971.

Wedenoja, William. "Modernisation and the Pentecostal Movement in Jamaica." Glazier, Stephen D., (ed.). *Perspectives on Pentecostalism: Case Studies from the Caribbean and Latin America.* Washington D. C. : University Press of America, 1980.

Black Pentecostalism in Britain

Brooks, Ira V. *Where do we go from here?* London: np (NTCOG), 1982.

Calley, Malcolm. *God's People: West Indian Pentecostal Sects in England.* Oxford: Oxford University Press, 1965.

Gerloff, Roswith. "Black Christian Communities in Birmingham." *Religion in the Birmingham Area.* Birmingham, England: University of Birmingham, 1975.

Gerloff, Roswith, (ed.). *Christian Action Journal: The Centre for Black and White Christian Partnership.* St Albans: Christian Action, Autumn 1982.

Gibson, Ashton. "The Black Church Movement in Britain" (incorrectly attributed to Wilfred D. Wood). *A Handbook of the Afro-Westindian United Council of Churches.* London: The Centre for Caribbean Studies, 1984.

Hill, Clifford. *Black Churches: West Indian and African Sects in Britain.* British Council of Churches, 1971.

Mixon, Roy D. *The First Twenty Years of the Church of God of Prophecy in England.* London: 27 Drewstead Road, 1973.

Pryce, Ken. *Endless Pressure: A Study of West Indian Life-styles in Bristol.* Middlesex: Penguin, 1979, chapters 17 and 18.

CHAPTER IX

THE FOLK RELIGION OF THE ENGLISH PEOPLE

EDWARD BAILEY

Its Scholarly Neglect

In 1981, at the Lincoln conference of the British Sociological Association's group for the sociology of religion, a well-supported annual meeting asked that the following year's conference should concentrate on the generality of the mainline Churches, instead of sectarian groups and sectlike activities. Unfortunately, when it came to listing possible speakers and topics, hardly a single study could be suggested. Horace Mann and Charles Booth were both part of history. The results of the Common and Conventional Religion in Leeds study, or of the European Value Systems study, were yet to be published (and still are). The discovery, that those with professional experience of the realities had both the competence and the confidence to describe them to professional students, as in the Workbook in Popular Religion, was not made until the Network for the Study of Implicit Religion began to arrange conferences for clergy and others in the following year.

146

Nor was this neglect peculiar to the social sciences: there is no article on "folk religion" in the 1918 edition of the Hastings' *Encyclopedia of Religion and Ethics*, and (as the Bibliographical Notes suggest) very little on Folk Religion in any western society since.

The reasons for this neglect indicate not only academic trends, but also the realities with which this chapter is concerned. In the first place, there has been a convenient if unconscious congruence between a certain type of attitude in the social sciences and a certain type of attitude among practitioners of religion. For the social sciences, contrary to some of the Founding Fathers, have tended to assume that a non-theological description of society demands a non-transcendentalist understanding of man. Thus, religion has been seen as erroneous, obsolete, and redundant. On the other hand, those who have equated religious reality with personal faith, have tended to assume that it is not only *sui generis*, but also incapable of objective study or rational description. Thus, whatever the generality of practitioners or of the public may have felt (or Lenski may have attempted to prove), text books, if they have acknowledged the existence of religion at all, have tended to assume it was an isolable and optional pursuit, located somewhere within the leisure industry: a dependent variable, without causal significance.

A second reason for this silence has been the traditional gulf between "the intelligentsia" (*qua* intellectuals), and "the people." (The national dislike of such phraseology by no means indicates its inappropriateness.) To some extent, clergy and teachers bridged this gulf. Yet the nineteenth century studies by missionaries of their human *Sitzimleben* abroad, seem to be almost without parallel in this country. Kilvert's Diary, and other such reminiscences, are popular; yet Atkinson's more systematic study is hardly known, and at the moment would appear to be unique. In so far as they wrote of local life at all, the clergy appear to have concentrated upon local history, and especially the history of the church buildings. This underlying tension, between their nationwide culture and their work with individuals, was revealed most clearly in the 1960's, when many of the more "intellectual" of the clergy, in the name of prophetic purity, sided with the "cultured despisers" of popular religion. Others, as "tribunes of the people" adopted a "populist" attitude towards statistics and the social sciences, possibly sensing a mismatch between current European and American models and the English realities.

A third cause of neglect is the peculiarly English understanding of religion. Canon Charles Smyth, historian and parish priest, has suggested that English religion at the Reformation passed directly from the mysticism of the late Middle Ages to the moralism of the Puritans and of today, without (it may be added) the intervening stages of Latin sacramentalism or Teutonic conceptualism. It is true that, on a wider canvas, the accustomed English disinclination to take part in Church services in no way distinguishes them from other Northern European countries, such as Scandinavia and Iceland, or, now, from most of France or Italy.

However, they may be distinguished by their insistence that they have a deeply held religion, which they are both ashamed and/or proud of practising only in secret. For they equate that religion with an inner knowledge of a God whose worship takes the form of "simple acts" of human kindness, alone. Coupled with this faith is an extreme suspicion and abhorrence of any kind of moral pretentiousness. The combination may seem paradoxical, but it is essential, according to its criteria, if such a confession is to avoid extreme sanctimoniousness. In this situation, however, an objective insistence upon the empirical importance of religion can easily be confused with special pleading, or moralistic imperialism, while an open denial of its practical significance could equally lead to suspicions of anti-social nihilism.

A fourth reason for the scholarly neglect of this whole area is the extra difficulty of defining it. Where small scale societies are concerned, it is possible to describe the social universe as a whole. The section on "religion" will describe a number of items, such as beliefs about gods, which are comparable with the reader's understanding of the term, plus a number of miscellaneous but cognate items, such as beliefs about dreams or witchcraft practices. Where historical societies are concerned, it is possible to describe the religion of the social universe in terms of those specialised institutions, such as buildings, festivals and priests, which may be seen as operating on behalf of the people as a whole. In contemporary society, it is possible to study a wide spectrum of the life of a particular religious group, such as a sect or monastic Order, or to study the individual life of a religious class. In this case, however, much of the religious aspect of the life of the bulk of the population slips through the net. For those who are self-consciously religious in some degree stand over against that for which their contemporaries stand.

Nevertheless, new light may be in the process of dawning upon this Dark Age of neglect. On the one hand, secularism is now institutionalised, especially in tertiary education, and its "new clerisy" is firmly "established," so no longer need to be defensive. On the other hand, contemporary history, even as reported in the British media, shows that religious belief can no longer be dismissed as a private matter, without public significance.

Secondly, it becomes difficult to single out the religion of the people as unoriginal or inconsequential, unauthentic or insignificant, in sole distinction from all other forms of popular life, such as the arts, the various branches of philosophy, or technology, including medicine. Indeed, not only may "folk religion" be as "real" as other "untutored" aspects of life: it, too, may have a valuable contribution to make.

Thirdly, the growing recognition of the pluralism within contemporary societies, both clarifies the distinction between religion and morality, and lessens the fear of monopolistic domination by a single form.

Finally, the development of religious studies in the last two centuries has prepared the way for the study of religion, not just as a specialised institution (as in historical societies), but as a dimension (as in small-scale societies) of ordinary life in mass society. Just as the history of religions is increasingly taking cognisance of folk or popular religion (cp. the 1987 *Encyclopedia of Religion*), so the anthropology of religion is at last becoming indigenous. Together, they can provide not only models and methods that are appropriate to this country, but also do justice to the phenomena as religious.

The power of this unacknowledged religiosity has always been apparent, in varying degree, to those who have dealt with it, not least professionally: clergy, family doctors, nurses and midwives, funeral directors, politicians, directors of broadcasting, funfair operators, the manufacturers of souvenirs and ornaments. It is only to *déraciné* theoreticians that "secular" has been like a meaningful description or an ideal. However, it is due especially to some of the clergy of the Church of England that its existence has recently been brought "home" to students of contemporary society. Yet their accustomed description of it as "folk religion" may reflect a certain ambivalence or hostility towards it.

It may be thought a peculiarly English use of the expression, which in Japan would lack the sense of *hauteur*, and in Northern Europe would have a corporate dimension. It may also be considered less than satisfactory to use an indefinite but sociological concept as the criterion of a religious phenomenon. Nor is it the only term available: a dozen years ago, over fifty terms, used by scholars to point to this area were noted. Yet the best description of the area with which this chapter is concerned remains that of the Archbishop of York, John Habgood, in his *Church and Nation in a Secular Age* (p.78). He describes "folk religion" as:

> One of a number (of terms) used to describe various aspects of something so amorphous that a single clear definition is impossible. I use it here, in an English setting and with experience of ministry in the Church of England particularly in mind, as a general term for the unexpressed, inarticulate, but often deeply felt, religion of ordinary folk who would not usually describe themselves as church-going Christians yet feel themselves to have some sort of Christian allegiance.

It is the purpose of this chapter to describe the content, and then to discern the character, of that allegiance, which, to the churchman or to the academic, may seem nebulous or self-contradictory, but to the man in the English street is the norm of both religion and life.

Its Constituents

The primary manifestation of what is known as folk religion consists in the desire for what the Church of England has traditionally known as "the Occasional Offices." Clerical understanding of the demand for such Occasional Offices has, perhaps, not been helped by the slight archaism of their collective title. For the Latinate "office," in this context, refers to "work," in the same way that the Greek "liturgy" means "a public work," not altogether divorced from such public spectacles as official games.

"Occasional" likewise refers less to their (in)frequency than to the (sense of) occasion which they mark, celebrate and engender.

The anthropological expression, "rites of passage" might have produced the necessary corrective. However, the significance of the rite, in this country, has again been seen as "momentary," rather than "momentous." (No doubt this is part of a general tendency to allow the quantitative uniformity of time, of which the bourgeoisie is now so conscious, to obscure its qualitative variability.) In this case, the tendency to minimise the meaning, both of the rite and of the request for it, has been reinforced by the habit of limiting such offices to the Baptism, Marriage and Funeral services. The dislike of including Confirmation illustrates the misunderstanding attached to the term. Indeed, properly speaking, the Occasional Offices equally include the Prayer Book services for the Visitation and Communion of the Sick, and the Commination. The "popularity" of these Offices can be seen in the proportion of the population asking for them. An increasing number of people claim no religious allegiance, or allegiance to other religions. An increasing number of Anglican clergy since the 1960's have laid down conditions and/or engaged in preparation for Baptizing or Marrying. Yet nearly half of all babies are Baptised, and over half of first marriages are solemnised, in Anglican churches alone, while even more funerals are conducted by Anglican clergy, in parish churches or local authority chapels.

Clergy, lay activists, and others, are sometimes tempted to dismiss this "popularity" as widespread, but superficial. The Baptism, it is said, is only wanted, "to keep the (grand)parents happy." It is "only" an excuse for a family gathering and a party. It is referred to as a "christening," because it is the ritual saying of the Grace to go with the "christening cake." What is really wanted would be better provided by a *thanksgiving* for the baby's existence, or by a prayer for the child's future welfare and *blessing*, or by an act of *dedication* on the part of the parents - or even by the provision of a celestial insurance policy, it is suggested.

Again it is said that the couple ask to be married in a church because it makes a better background for photographs, or because it is a nice setting for a white dress and the bridesmaids; or because the parents, or at least the mothers, insist upon it.

The funeral, it is said, is only conducted by a minister because the funeral director arranges it; because there is no easily obtainable alternative, because there is no point in upsetting the odd relation or mourner who may like it that way; because some form is necessary, and it "does not do anyone any harm."

Yet there is no reason for equating the practice of additional, social rituals, or equating the simultaneous coexistence of alternative interpretations, with superficiality of motive. Taking a positive answer to the request for granted by no means implies that either the answer or the request is unimportant. Indeed, the reaction provoked by a refusal, even to hold the Baptism and Wedding in the particular church desired, is itself sufficient proof of the seriousness with which it is made.

Although the Church holds Baptism to be a dominical sacrament, and hence an ecclesiastical occasion, and although marriage and the disposal of the deceased person's body have legal implications, the subjective aspect of such occasions is focused primarily in the family. There is, however, a second set of constituent elements in what is often called folk religion, which clearly combines the familial with the social. These occasions are catered for by special services for Remembrance Sunday, Christmas, Mothering Sunday (three weeks before Easter, in distinction from the North American Mothers' Day during May), and Harvest. At Christmas and Mothering Sunday especially, however, the cultic act in the church building is only one of numerous ways in which the festival is kept.

This social aspect extends to the national and international horizons. Thus, Remembrance Sunday includes each year the ceremony at the Cenotaph in Whitehall, and the viewing of it live on television, and the reporting of it (as "news") on the radio. Again, no Christmas would be complete, for some, without their W.I. Carol Service, or broadcast Carol Service from King's College Cambridge, or, now, a Crib or Christingle Service, or the report of "pilgrims" attending services in Bethlehem, or without the Queen's Speech. Although of more significance for Roman Catholics than others, Easter likewise includes the Papal message, and the Papal blessing *urbem et orbem*. A Royal wedding or funeral may virtually impose a public holiday upon the country, whether one has been decreed or

152

not. Similarly, national rites of passage, such as the coronation of a sovereign
or the installation of a mayor, the commencement of judicial assizes or each
day's Parliamentary business, the occurrence of a disaster or the conclusion
of a war, are often occasions that call for or allow the inclusion of specifically
religious acts and/or the presence of religious officials. The infusion of
hymn-singing into football matches, like prayers into baseball or signing with
the cross into bull-fighting, may reflect the historical origins of the institution,
but also arises from the importance attached to the particular event. In this
sense, they are all "occasional offices."

At the other extreme is a third set of constituent elements, performed
individually. Primary among these is prayer, which can be compared with the
most intimate biological functions, for the simultaneous universality and
discretion with which it is practised. A great deal of praying is done "while
washing up." Most of the "said" prayers (verbal, but silent) have probably
been taught in childhood; but almost all (including confessed atheists) will
admit that they "send up a quick one, in times of trouble." The prevalence of
prayers in the tabloid papers, and requests or references to "saying a prayer,"
in moments of crisis, at all levels of society, likewise confirm the
comprehensibility of the concept. Less invisible, but equally overlooked,
except by florists and monumental masons, is the practice of "visiting one's
(relative's) grave," at familial festivals or upon particular anniversaries, or
more often (sometimes even daily), often for many years. Likewise the
purchase and exhibition, in sitting rooms and bedrooms, of "Blessings on this
house" and such-like, in laborious poker-work, may be compared to other
countries' statuettes or icons.

Individual practices must also include consulting fortune-tellers and
reading "what the stars say"; changing a house number from 13 to 12A or, if a
choice of date is available, avoiding Friday the 13th; not wearing green; and a
host of customs regarding conception, pregnancy, childbirth, infancy,
marriage, death, and situations of crisis and danger, such as examinations or
driving. Such practices are both widespread and frequent.

Their designation as religious may be questioned. They would tend to
be justified by some expression as "Well, there may/must be something in it."
While this may not contain everything that the study of religion has shown,

regarding man's sense of the sacred, or (in historical societies) his encounter with the holy, or (in contemporary society), his commitment to the human, it points to at least one aspect of what is commonly taken to be religious: a puzzlement that smacks of the mysterious.

Its Creed

Self-conscious and avowedly missionary religions, such as Buddhism, Christianity and Islam, have spent millennia divining their own meaning. In the last two centuries scholars and participants have likewise tried to fit together and to express ("to articulate," in both senses) the meaning of other ways or philosophies of life, such as Judaism or Hinduism, and the religions of other, less influential or famous groups. As already suggested, the time is now ripe to attempt the same process for the English. So, having listed some of the activities involved, it remains to try to discern their meaning for the participants. To do this, it is necessary to take seriously their own description of that meaning, as well as bringing to bear upon that description a certain acquaintance with other religions and other aspects of human experience.

The "folk religion" of the English, although not an organised religion, does possess a creed: "I believe in Christianity." This has been said or implied to the present writer especially by parents who have wanted their baby to be Baptised: that is, by a thousand parents, of five hundred children, over twenty years. But it is also frequently stated on other occasions, ecclesiastical and otherwise, local and general. It is the kind of bedrock opinion that lies behind the desire for religious education in schools - or for government action over questions that are seen as having a moral dimension.

It is possible to dismiss it as vague and question-begging (like being "against sin"), or as a conventional statement designed to appeal to the particular audience. Yet this would be to ignore the obvious signs that the speaker is analysing himself, and despite his fears of being pretentious, is confessing what he reckons to be his faith. "This is how it is", he is saying, "I cannot pretend otherwise. *I* happen to *believe* in *Christianity*." So it is possible to use this piece of proffered data, as a primary means for

154

understanding the existential meaning of this religion. In this context, what needs to be explored is the meaning attached to "Christianity."

It is not simply a belief in Christ. It is true that he plays a part in the "Christianity" that is believed in. The verbal similarity is more than a matter of etymology, in the antiquarian sense. For it is constantly being fed and maintained by various agencies, including what (for all its diversity) is generally recognised as "the Church." Yet it is not just modesty, or embarrassment, that is responsible for their saying that they "believe in Christianity," rather than "in Christ." He represents a historical figure, and a living presence; but he is not a part of the present history, except through the influence of his spirit. He is now "Ascended," a High God, though remembered as a friend. Awareness focuses on his ministry, and his birth, rather than upon his death, or resurrection. He is an example, and he inspires those who commune with him; but he is hardly a (or the) cosmic Lord, capable of himself effecting a cure for the world's problems.

Neither is this belief in "Christianity" simply a belief in God. He too plays a part in this worldview, and in this living faith. To some, including some who have little or nothing to do with the community of those who are active in the Church, he is real, his presence is near, and his care is certain. However, they are probably a small minority, and their awareness of him may not be shared with, or known to, even their own spouse. For most of those who believe in "Christianity," God plays a part akin to the part played in the theatre by the backcloth, or the actual floor of the stage. He is the *sine qua non* of the drama, an essential part of the whole, the keystone of the proscenium arch; but he is not the centre of attention, the primary object of belief.

Just as the Christ of "Christianity" is not the same as the Christ of the New Testament, neither is the God of "Christianity" identical with that of the Old Testament, at least at its most characteristic.

Nor is the belief in Christianity simply a belief in the Church. Again, it is an important element in the "Christianity" that is believed in. It is a vehicle of "Christianity," keeping it alive; an instrument of "Christianity," supporting its adherents along the Christian way; a witness to "Christianity," teaching its message, advertising its virtues, and appealing for followers.

Indeed, sometimes it is also said to be "believed in." Yet it is never equated with "Christianity": it is "only human," that is, fallible. The belief in the Church is a derivative belief, dependent upon a prior and primary belief in "Christianity."

"Christianity," then, is a spirit. It is an important, perhaps the major, manifestation of whatever "Divinity" is. It represents "true religion." Belief in it is the "established" religion of the English: empirically, psychologically, existentially, morally, culturally. Christ, God and the Church are its three main forms, its faces, its *dramatis personae*. It is a way of life that is readily (if anachronistically) summarised as "the Ten Commandments," or "the golden rule" or (now, only occasionally) as "the Sermon on the Mount," or by the oft-repeated paradigm of "helping a little old lady across the road." Thus the second commandment of Christ is the first commandment of "Christianity." Yet this way of summarising it is sometimes chosen simply because it is quantifiable (although dominical authority could also be claimed for it): such moral behaviour is seen as a sign or sacrament of an otherwise inward and invisible grace.

The creed has other elements. These include the right of everyone to make up his own mind; the need for, and inevitably of, values; the desire for religion to be relevant to real life, and yet to keep out of politics (understood as quarrelling); the opportunity to go to Church, but the non-necessity of it; the moral duty of taking pastoral care of one's own self (for which English has no word expressing approval); the belief in "fair play," and "helping the underdog," in democracy and freedom. Yet all of these other elements are subsumed, more or less consciously or coherently, in the opening statement of the creed. They are the values that are implicit in that "Christianity" which is confessed, as being "believed in."

156

BIBLIOGRAPHICAL POINTERS

ATKINSON, J. C. *Forty Years in a Moorland Parish: Reminiscences and Researches in Danby in Cleveland*, London: Macmillan, 1892.

BAILEY, E. I. "The Religion of a 'Secular' Society," M. A. Thesis, Bristol University, 1969. *Emergent Mandalas: the Implicit Religion of Contemporary Society*, Ph. D. thesis, Bristol University, 1976 (catalogued as, The Religion of a Secular Society).

_____."The Implicit Religion of Contemporary Society: an Orientation and Plea for its Study." In *Religion: Journal of Religion and Religions*. London: Academic Press Inc., 1983: XII, pp. 69-83.

_____."The Religion of the People." In *In Search of Christianity*. London: Waterstone & Co. Ltd., 1986: 178-188.

_____.*A Workbook in Popular Religion* (edited). Dorchester, Dorset, U. K.: Partners, 1986.

_____."The British Form of the 'Civil Religion' Debate, for *Zivilreligion: Gesellschaftlicher Konsens in Mythischer und Ritueller Form*," edited Alois Muller-Herold. Munchen: Kaiser Verlag, 1986.

_____."Implicit and Civil Religion: a selection of readings and references" (in typescript).

BELLAH, R. N. "Civil Religion in America," in *Daedalus: Journal of the American Academy of Arts and Sciences*, XCVI (1) Winter, 1967.

BLUM, F. *The Ethics of Industrial Man: an Empirical Study of Religious Awareness and the Experience of Society*. London: Routledge and Kegan Paul, 1970.

BOOTH, C. *Life and Labour of the People in London*. London: Macmillan, 1903.

CLARK, D. *Between Pulpit and Pew: Folk Religion in a North Yorkshire Fishing Village*. London: Cambridge University Press, 1982.

DURKHEIM, E. *The Elementary Forms of the Religious Life*. Translated J. W. Swain. New York: The Free Press, 1947.

ELIADE, M. *The Sacred and the Profane: the Nature of Religion*. Translated W. R. Trask. New York: Harper and Row, 1961.

ELLUL, J. *The New Demons*. Translated by C. Edward Hopkin. New York: Seabury Press, 1975.

157

FOWLER, J. W. *Stages of Faith*. San Francisco: Harper and Row, 1983.

FREYTAG, J. and OZAKI, K. *Nominal Christianity: Studies of Church and People in Hamburg*. London: Lutterworth, 1970.

GEHRIG, G. *Civil Religion: An Assessment*. Connecticut: Society for the Scientific Study of Religion, Monograph, 1979.

GREELEY, A. M. *The Persistence of Religion*. London: S.C.M., 1973.

HABGOOD, J. S. *Church and Nation in a Secular Age*. London: Darton, Longman and Todd, 1983.

HARDY, Sir A. *The Divine Flame: an Essay Towards a Natural History of Religion*. Oxford: Religious Experience Research Unit, 1978.

HASTINGS, J., (ed.). *Encyclopedia of Religion and Ethics*. Edinburgh: T. and T. Clark, 1918.

HAY, D. *Exploring Inner Space: Is God Still Possible in the Twentieth Century?* Harmondsworth: Pelican, 1982.

JAHODA, G. *The Psychology of Superstition*. Harmondsworth: Penguin, 1969.

LASKI, M. *Ecstasy: a Study of Some Secular and Religious Experiences*. London: Cresset, 1961.

LENSKI, G. *The Religious Factor: A Sociological Study of Religion's Impact on Politics, Economics and Family Life*. New York: Doubleday, 1955.

LUCKMANN, T. *The Invisible Religion: the Problem of Religion in Modern Society*. London: Macmillan, 1967.

MANN, H. *Religious Census of 1851*.

MIYAKE HITOSHI. "Folk Religion." In *Japanese Religion: a Survey by the Agency for Cultural Affairs*. Edited Hori Ichiro and others. Tokyo: Kodansha International Ltd., 1972.

MOL, H. *Identity and the Sacred: a Sketch for a New Social-scientific Theory of Religion*. Oxford: Basil Blackwell, 1976.

NILSSON, M. P. *Greek Folk Religion*. Philadelphia: University of Pennsylvania, 1972. (First published as *Greek Popular Religion* by Columbia University Press, New York, 1940).

OTTO, R. *The Idea of the Holy*. (1917). Translated J. W. Harvey. London: Oxford University Press, 1923 (Harmondsworth: Pelican, 1959).

PLOMER, W., (ed.). *Kilvert's Diary 1870-1879*. Selections from the Diary of Rev'd. Francis Kilvert. Harmondsworth: Penguin, 1977.

158

REED, B. D. *The Dynamics of Religion: Process and Movement in Christian Churches.* London: Darton, Longman and Todd, 1978.

SCHOOLS COUNCIL. *Religious Education in Secondary Schools.* Schools Council Working Paper, No. 36. London: Evans Bros. & Methuen, 1971.

TAYLOR, J. V. *The Primal Vision: Christian Presence   amid   African Religion.* London: S.C.M., 1963.

TILLICH, P. *Ultimate Concern: Dialogues with Students.* London: S.C.M., 1965.

TOWLER, R. W. *Homo Religiosus: Sociological Problems in the Study of Religion.* London: Constable, 1974.

_____. *Common and Conventional Religion in Leeds.* Research Reports. University of Leeds, Department of Sociology, 1979.

VRIJHOF, P. H., (ed.). *Official and Popular Religion: Analysis of a Theme for Religious Studies.* The Hague: Mouton, 1979.

ZAEHNER, R. C., (ed.). The Concise Encyclopedia of Living Faiths. London: Hutchinson, 1964.

CHAPTER X

SECTS AND SOCIETY IN TENSION

BRYAN R. WILSON

The Character of Sectarianism

It is commonplace to refer to the cultural situation in Britain as one of religious pluralism, in which a notional and pervasive orthodoxy has been fragmented by various currents of diversified religious belief and practice. In some measure that pluralism has existed for centuries, of course, but it may be important to note that two divergent tendencies have been at work. Whilst new and exotic religions have been introduced, certain older forms of religious diversity have lost their distinctiveness. The terms in which we have become accustomed to think of religions other than orthodoxy - "nonconformity" and "dissent" - have become anachronisms, not only because we have largely abandoned the idea of religious conformity as a norm, but also because bodies once seen as radical departures from the norm have gradually come to be regarded as only marginally different. (This has occurred as a consequence of secularization, changes in social structure, amalgamations, and the general effect on Christianity of the introduction of much more markedly alien religions.) The social bases and the theological import of those old religious differences have been largely eroded as more radical departures have relativized the position of the erstwhile "dissenters," as Muslims, Sikhs and Hindus have moved into British society. What once were challenging and even dangerous rivals to orthodox faith have become more or less acceptable variants within a generalized, and perhaps increasingly colourless, Christianity. "Non-conformity" and "dissent" have virtually dropped out of the nation's (non-legal) vocabulary. The reality of such divergent "nonconformity" persists only in minority sectarian movements.

Although sociologists use the term "sect" in a completely neutral and non-pejorative sense, for the public at large, and especially for the mass media, the word remains, as for a long time it was for the Church, a term of opprobrium. Almost by definition, as commonly used, the term "sect" (or "cult") implies the likelihood of tension with society. Whereas once "sect" was seen as explicitly an opposition to "church," today, in a secularized society where the major denominations have grown closer together, the sect is seen more sharply as a challenge to society at large. The challenge is not so much to conventional religious beliefs but more a challenge to the general, secularized social mores. The sect is seen less as a combatant in religious issues than as a deviant and abnormal religious threat to conventional, generally a-religious social practice. Sects thus become an issue of social rather than of explicitly religious concern.

The sect may be broadly designated as a self-consciously and deliberately separated religious minority who espouse a faith divergent from that of other religious bodies. For present purposes, the term "sect" is not confined to minor deviations from the traditional Anglican faith, but is employed to encompass also those minority movements sometimes referred to as "cults" or as "new religious movements." Each sect is, in greater or lesser degree, unique, and although sects may be grouped as families by reference to their historical origins, or classified by doctrinal position, organizational structure or other sociological criteria, my present concern requires no such classification.[1] Rather, one may allude, on the one hand, to the general attributes of all such movements or, on the other hand, to the particular instances of tension between society and one given sect.

Within the general exclusivistic framework of Christianity, the sect challenges, usually explicitly, the adequacy of the teachings, explanations, religious practices, social mores, lifestyle and ethos of all other religious bodies, and of the public at large. Typically, the sect claims to provide better access to salvation than is elsewhere available, and does so by virtue of a monopoly of truth, commitment to, and belief in which are normally indispensable conditions. We may leave aside the variety of specific concepts of salvation, noting only that these range from bodily or mental healing to elaborate prospects of the transmigration of the soul, the resurrection of the body, or reincarnation: the common denominator is always the promise of present reassurance in the face of baleful or untoward phenomena or events. Whatever specific terms it employs, the sect is always an agency of salvation.

Salvation, although usually (and in the Christian cases, always) predicated for an afterlife, has, however, implications for present life. Two aspects of this concern for salvation are worth noting. First, that the conditions for the attainment of salvation imply a range of taboos and injunctions for everyday living; and second, that the realization of life in obedience to those strictures is also in some measure in itself seen as an at least partial achievement of salvation. The sect becomes a location for the experience of salvation as well as an agency of promise. Sects generally extol not only the virtue of their moral demands and their significance in the moral economy, but they also emphasize the joy available from fulfilling those demands. Christian sectarians readily suggest that this life may already be heavenly; that life in the sectarian community is a foretaste of God's goodness; that they have already claimed a healing experience; are building God's Kingdom; or are cultivating perfection for God, in whose service alone is perfect joy. Thus, each sect sustains an explicit culture - a repertoire of what shall not be done and what shall be done. Since many of these interdictions and injunctions run counter to the cultural assumptions of the wider society, sects are always likely to experience tension whenever their affairs impinge, as they often must, on those of the world outside.

Sectarian Alternatives

The sect is, then, canvassing either an alternative way of life or, at the least, exemptions from normal obligations of the wider society and alternatives to a specific range of its facilities. The generality or specificity of those alternative arrangements varies from one sect to another, from those which establish well-insulated communitarian settlements to others that are concerned merely to advocate a "better way" with respect to one particular element of society's operation. Some sects seek to establish a way of life and a pattern of social relations which permit the group to function as a community, or on the model of community, but the conditions for genuine communitarianism are not easily found in Britain today. The classic communitarian or near-communitarian sects exploited the free or cheap land available in the unsettled terrains of eighteenth-and nineteenth-century America and Russia: such conditions, in which vicinal isolation reinforces ideological insulation, have rarely been available in contemporary Britain. Even so, some sects in Britain have sought to recreate living communities, even if they have also recognized that not all their members could be embraced in this pattern of organization. Among groups which have experimented with such communal structures are the, originally German, Bruderhof founded by Eberhard Arnold, the Anthroposophists, the International Society for Krishna Consciousness (Hare Krishna Movement), the Unification Church (Moonies), the Emissaries of Divine Light, the Bugbrooke Community, and the Findhorn Community.[2]

Such total communities seek to reduce tension with the wider society by removal from it, but near neighbours inevitably become aware of them, and although relations are not always bad, there may be occasions for expression of disapproval or even hostility: the very fact of withdrawal into a sequestered enclave arouses suspicions of sinister practices, and may be represented as a cloak for deviant, perhaps evil practices. When the moral stance of such a community also differs significantly from that of the wider society - and this is commonly the case, and is indeed a justification for segregation - then this is easily regarded as evidence of evil intents. So it is that communitarianism, interpreted as the ideal solution to the problem of sustaining a distinctive ideology (and sometimes held as mandatory for its realization[3]), by no means ensures a sect that tension with the wider society can be avoided. Segregation is intended to limit interaction with outsiders, but periodically the very fact of segregation may in itself excite their attention, and appear almost as a challenge to investigative journalists intent on an *exposé*.

At the opposite extreme from sects which adopt communal life are those which concentrate on the provision of one specific facility for salvation - most typically, an alternative therapy. Such movements, it might be thought, might operate with very little tension within the wider society, but this is not the case in practice. Challenge to any of the institutional provisions of the wider society is likely to bring a sect into conflict with the state, or with particular entrenched cadres - in these instances, with the medical profession, psychiatrists, and the Ministry of Health.[4] The modern state, whether a corporate state or a warfare state, whether totalitarian or liberal-democratic, does not readily accept alternative agencies which claim to provide facilities superior to those of the state itself. Even the laissez-faire societies of the capitalist West, in which privatization is promoted even of vital public services (transport, telecommunications, medicare, defence supply, and education, for example) do not readily allow, much less approve, radical challenge to the established scientific, technical, generally materialist, assumptions embodied in the facilities and organization of modern institutions. Since sects always canvas more explicitly spiritual alternatives to one, some or most of the institutions of the wider society, occasions of tension between sect and society, and more explicitly, between sect and state, are almost inevitable.

Not every sect seeks to be a total alternative society. Some, certainly, see their mission as providing an interim ethic for the world until the end of this dispensation and its displacement by an apocalypse and millennium.[5] Other sects see their role as being to "build a Kingdom" on earth by instituting new ethical precepts for their followers. Yet other movements - less committed to an eschatology or to post-mortem states - concern themselves with access to only a more limited form of salvation. Yet, there is a tendency at times, for groups which stand over against society to enlarge their claims, to generalize their points of distinction, and to apply more widely the legitimating principles which they invoke.[6] Sometimes, the principles which justify one particular claim (either to exemption from state demands, or privileged access to alternative facilities) are elevated into the much more general legitimations of a separated way of life. The early Mormons illustrate this tendency in their evolution of a distinctive - at certain times, communitarian - economic organization and their (subsequently abandoned) school system.[7] The Seventh-day Adventists, in developing their educational system, their food factories, and (in America), even more conspicuously, their extensive medicare facilities, provide another example. But even where such an elaborate network of alternative facilities has not been created, the attempt to defend the sect's peculiarities, vis-à-vis the wider society, has sometimes led to an extension of contention, either by the sect widening its demands for special accommodation, or by its withdrawal from a wider area of social involvement. Thus, Sikhs, after gaining the right to wear turbans and to be exempted from the law respecting safety headgear on motorcycles and as employees on public transport, eventually succeeded, in a most curious House of Lords judgement, in winning the right to wear this religiously prescribed headwear even in a Christian school. Christadelphians who, in World War I, contested the obligation to do military service, found that their arguments for exemption also entailed that, in all logic, they must also refuse to accept special constable duty and work in armaments factories.[8] In the 1950's, pharmacists who were the Exclusive Brethren sought exemption from membership of the Pharmaceutical Society: when refused by the House of Lords, the sect extended its area of withdrawal from society by withdrawing membership from those who remained as practising pharmacists.

Institutional Exemptions

The specific foci of tension between sects and society may be broadly divided into issues on which the sect explicitly rejects the practices of the wider society, and issues on which the sect takes what might be called in contemporary vernacular "affirmative action," that is to say, matters on which the sect seeks to put into operation its own distinctive values. Some of the activities and normal social obligations to which the sect objects are rejected for symbolic, some for intrinsic, reasons. Some are rejected for both. Whatever the grounds, the very fact of exercising conscious and deliberative choice respecting social arrangements may also, for at least some sects, constitute an important symbolic indicator of protest against the assumptions unquestioningly made by the generality of the people. The items that are rejected, either on first principles, or in extension of them and in defence of the sect's separated circumstance, cover the whole range of society's institutions. We review them in sequence: defence, polity, economy, status, education, recreation, and health.

There is no consensus among Christians with respect to the obligation to bear arms for one's country, but pacifism is an ethical position that has been not infrequently asserted even among orthodox Christians. Not all Christian sects are pacifist, but clearly participation in defence of the wider society may be seen as a considerable test of the extent to which the sect pursues an ideology contrary to that of the majority. Conscientious objection to military service proved a major source of controversy for several sects in Britain in World War I and, given the liberalization of social attitudes, to a lesser extent, in World War II. When national feeling is high, the conscientious objector is likely to be an object of particular opprobrium. For the Bruderhof, in World War II, hostility was compounded by the fact of its German origins, to a point where the group decided to migrate to Paraguay. But pacifism pure and simple is not always the issue. Neither Jehovah's Witnesses nor Christadelphians are pacifists in the strict sense, although they are conscientious objectors. Their objection is to fighting the wars of what have sometimes been called "the sin powers" of this world: if a better cause were to present itself, as perhaps it might at Armageddon, then these sectarians would not hesitate to fight at Jesus' command. Here the objection is clearly symbolic and, if the cause is understood by outsiders, more likely to give rise to tension. There is, however, another function for a sect in counselling its members to object to military service: the maintenance of social distance and insulation.[9] Sectarians inducted into armies must suffer severe problems of maintaining a sense of apartness in the midst of a collectivity governed by completely alien mores, and in a system which (with even more compelling coercive power) is more emphatically totalitarian than even the most severe sect. Sects which, like the Seventh Day Adventists and some of the Brethren, reject the bearing of arms but permit non-combatant military service, may reduce the overall occasion for tension between the sect and society, but do so at the cost of increasing the experience of tension for those of their individual members who are conscripted for military service.

Bound, as are many Christian sects, by the word of the Scriptures to render unto Caesar that which is Caesar's, the interpretation of that dictum is, none the less, subject to considerable variation. Whatever general obligations of good citizenship might be accepted, and, indeed, enjoined, sectarians may also draw the line at even symbolic commitment to the support of the state. Jehovah's Witnesses make this most apparent in their refusal to sing national anthems and to salute national flags - although these interdictions have caused them greater difficulty in underdeveloped countries, and in the United States than has been the case in Britain.[10] They, the Christadelphians, and Exclusive Brethren abstain from voting in political elections, as a further indication that they hold in contempt the rights which the state confers on its citizens. Such abstention is not in itself a cause of tension, of course, whereas the symbolic distanciation of refusing respect to the monarch might well be.

Much as sectarians may hold themselves apart from the wider society in social and political activities, their attitude to economic matters is by no means so unequivocally a rejection of the practices, or even the values, of the wider society.[11] The economic orientations of sects are complex and widely variable, and we may distinguish between the economic ethic, economic associations, and economic occupations. The economic ethic espoused by each sect is by far the most complicated aspect of the response to this department of life.

Sects are by no means confined to a traditional espousal of the so-called Protestant ethic, although this may constitute a part of their dispositions. Since many sectarians eschew all contact with the wider society which is not absolutely necessary, and hold themselves apart from social activities, outside the life of the sect itself, it is work which becomes the primary focus of everyday life. Like others, the sectarian must earn his living. Unlike some others, he is often committed to high principles of integrity, to keeping his word, fulfilling his obligations, maintaining his self-esteem, and proving himself as better than the generality of men and, by extension, that his faith is better than theirs. Work, in consequence, becomes a principal arena within which to give effect to these orientations, and a circumstance in which to demonstrate to others the values embraced in the sectarian way of life. Generally speaking, sectarians are committed workers, and such dedication, whilst it may at times provoke the distaste of others, does not, in general, create any particular social tensions. On the other hand, sectarians are not materialists and, with some exceptions (among the predominantly therapeutic sects), they are not likely to endorse achievement-orientation as such. Getting on in this world, whilst it certainly occurs as a consequence of diligence in some instances, is not a primary motivation of most sectarians. That can be seen in the rejection, in many sects, of any sort of training for the highest professions, as well as by strongly expressed ideas that one must not be conformed to this world, nor lured to lay up treasure where "moth and rust doth corrupt." It must be at once evident that members of communitarian groups have explicitly rejected the most effective ways of gaining personal wealth, whilst in other sects it is often well understood that there are limits beyond which the acquisition and accumulation of personal wealth are not desirable. Thus, Jehovah's Witnesses often abandon well-paid posts and take up less rewarding part-time work in order to use their time in the work of door-to-door canvassing. Exclusive Brethren, whilst not infrequently becoming self-employed men with small businesses, none the less, do not seek to enlarge their businesses beyond the point at which personal supervision and control is possible.

Decisions of this kind, whilst exposing sectarians to curiosity and perhaps ridicule, are not in themselves sources of social tension, but where a sect affirms a more radical vision of economic organization, such tension may arise. The Unification Church is committed to a new conception of economic activity and new patterns of economic organization: work must be appropriate to the building of the Kingdom which will be a transformed social order in the world.[12] In Britain, the Church's activities have not developed sufficiently for industrial plant or financial agencies to emerge, as they have in the United States, Latin America, Japan, and Korea, but incipient sources of tension can be discerned in the public condemnation of work for long hours recompensed only by communal board and lodgings and minimal pocket money, such as is common when Moonies undertake fund-raising activities by selling literature and other small items on the streets.

Occupations are also subject to some measure of discrimination among sectarians, but less on directly economic grounds, than on the grounds of desirability in the light of the sect's own ethic. Thus, Christadelphians would not be found as policemen or lawyers; Christian Scientists could scarcely be doctors and (although cases have been known), only with difficulty, pharmacists. Entertainment, professional sport, and journalism would be seen as unsuitable areas of employment by many Pentecostal sects, among others, whilst the embargo on higher education found, for instance, among Jehovah's Witnesses, Exclusive Brethren, and the Hare Krishna movement, precludes various occupational possibilities. Although sectarians must make a living somehow, they are generally unlikely to regard making a living as a primary concern, and their choice of occupations is sometimes circumscribed by sectarian principles and in the case of communitarian sects such as the Hare Krishna movement it is even more narrowly dictated.

Economic choices of this kind are not, however, a direct source of tension with the wider society, but the restriction on economic association may be. Membership in trades unions or employers' federations is prohibited by many sects. Seventh-day Adventists, Witnesses, Brethren, Christadelphians and others eschew trades unionism, and Brethren are no less firmly opposed to employers' federations and, indeed, to any organizations in which they would be joined in association with unbelievers. Legal actions brought by sectarians have been conspicuous in testing the rules of the "closed shop," and in gaining for sectarians the right to work without being members of a trades union.[13] Such issues have been fiercely contested by trades unions, for whom the sectarian demand for liberty of conscience represents a fundamental challenge.

It follows from the general character of sectarian attitudes to work and to economic occupations, that sects deliberately stand outside both the class structure and the status system of society. Sectarian beliefs diverge fundamentally from ideologies which emphasizes class consciousness - a concern entirely alien to the sectarian *Weltanschauung*. Sects cannot be recruited for class action, and their general life circumstances and standards of comportment are themselves a radical denial of the cogency of class analysis. Sectarians consider themselves to know what their "real interests" are and they are not economic interests: their concern is salvation, whether it be envisaged as future bliss or contemporary safety and protection from evil.

Leaving aside members of agnostic or manipulationist sects which are usually preoccupied with therapeutic benefits, sectarians generally are disdainful of the status system of society. Sectarians have a different point of reference for assessing their position relative to others, and the general terms of social status are irrelevant. Indeed, they step aside from the conferment or the acceptance of social honour, and although, in a society in which many marked status distinctions have been eliminated, they can no longer make their rejection of status so pointed (as could seventeenth-century Quakers with their use of the familiar form of address and their refusal to doff hats): none the less, the search for social honour beyond the confines of the sect is disavowed. Status-striving is regarded as a threat to sectarian integrity as is indicated by the widespread practice of substituting for honorific titles the terms "Brother" and "Sister." Among Exclusive Brethren, status symbols (cars larger than strictly necessary, women's headress other than head-scarves) are specifically prohibited.

Understandably, it is in the ideational domain that sects experience perhaps most tension with the wider society. The modern liberal democratic state permits adult citizens to believe what they like, but the state is by no means so permissive with respect to the education of children. All sects have an evaluation of knowledge which diverges from that of the secular state and its institutions, and many of them reject the factual basis of some areas of the school and university curriculum. Some sects, notably Jehovah's Witnesses, Exclusive Brethren, and the Hare Krishna movement, discourage involvement in public education beyond the obligatory school age, being particularly distrustful of higher education (except perhaps in purely technical crafts and skills). Christian groups of a fundamentalist persuasion (and this accounts for many sects) disbelieve in evolution and the basic premises of all the humanities and perhaps all the social sciences. For these sects, arts subjects are often no less suspect, since literature in particular is perceived as purveying values contradictory of the moral injunctions of faith. Novels, plays, opera and ballet are often distrusted, and in some movements subject to prohibition.[14] To some extent, the natural sciences, evolutionism apart, are more acceptable than the humanities, stained as these are with the alien values of secular history, profane and immoral people and pursuits, or the traditions of a church which is seen as an agency of corruption.[15]

There are sects which challenge general educational provision on only a narrow front. Seventh-day Adventists have a relatively highly educated membership, with a very high percentage of medically educated people in their ranks. Only in the limited areas of biblical understanding and in their disapproval of arts subjects are they disposed to challenge general educational wisdom. Christian Scientists have no quarrel with education as such but, and in this respect they have a position in common with Scientologists and other New Thought movements, they necessarily regard the traditions of rational empirical enquiry as of no more than limited value. These groups organize their own teachings as alternative bodies of knowledge; they do, however, imitate the language of science, and even replicate the general higher educational system in establishing grades, patterns of instruction, and lecturing programmes. These movements are less opposed to learning than fundamentalist sects, (Pentecostal and Holiness movements, for example) which adopt an anti-intellectualist stance that contrasts sharply with the pseudo-intellectualism of sects which, in the service of their sectarian ideologies, imitate the structure and style of secular educational institutions and arrangements.

Sectarian caveats concerning the content of education have generally been resolved by the sect instilling in its young members the idea that sectarian truth is always to be accepted against secular wisdom, and by choosing to have their children exposed only for as long as was legally mandatory to those parts of general education to which the sect objected. In the optional areas of education, in religious instruction, in extra-curricular activities and recreation, sectarian scruple has more room for exercise, and in this area the distinctiveness of their religious positions becomes more obvious. Christadelphians, Jehovah's Witnesses, Exclusive Brethren, and Pentecostalists will generally seek to keep to a minimum the involvement of their children in such school activities as plays, sports, outings, holiday tours, and clubs. For sects of this kind, the time is too precious to be "wasted" on what are seen as frivolous pursuits; because the time is God's, because serious concern for religious matters is what counts, or because the advent is imminent, children are to shun voluntarily involvements in school, and are to seek their friends and to spend their time elsewhere.

These attitudes to recreative activities in school are, of course, sustained in the home and the neighbourhood. Children are to keep themselves apart from those outside, and whilst play may not in itself be prohibited, most sects have some idea of what constitutes wholesome play and direct their children to that. Not uncommonly, books, games, puzzles, general knowledge quizzes, jigsaw puzzles, and the like are produced with religious themes, so that play time may be instructional in religious facts and values. Secular entertainment is spurned for the most part, and although not all sects have firmly stated rules about such matters as watching television, or even attending the cinema and theatre, these things are carefully monitored, and overmuch indulgence is clearly perceived as being contrary to the religious ethos. Paradoxically, although recreation is in every sense an area of voluntary choice, it is precisely because sectarians do not choose what others choose, hold themselves apart - associate only with each other rather than with non-members of the sect, that sects elicit some of the strongest reactions from the general public. The child-centred society is inclined to see prohibitions respecting children's play activities as wilful deprivation. These tensions may, however, also be fired by latent feelings of guilt on the part of parents who find it easier and pleasanter to indulge their children than to exercise discipline.

Finally, the ancient association of health and religion renders healing an issue of particularly acute tension for those sects that have teachings pertaining to bodily or mental health. By no means all movements espouse a special doctrine of healing. Some, such as the various Brethren bodies, regard the healing tradition of early Christianity as having been a particular faculty available only in the apostolic dispensation. The Seventh-day Adventists, whilst not entirely ruling out the possibility of healing through God's will, gradually became so committed to medical missionary work that their ministry is, today, intimately associated with regular scientific attitudes to health as represented (marginal aspects of diet aside) by orthodox medicine. Jehovah's Witnesses, whatever biblically-based theories they may have with respect to causation of illness, normally accept medical treatment - with one important reservation, which has caused recurrent difficulties for the movement, namely, their prohibition (since 1945) of blood transfusion.[16] Particularly when babies have died, public disquiet has been evident, and today, in Britain, the children of Jehovah's Witnesses may be made wards of court if doctors consider that, despite parental refusal, they should be given blood.

Faith-healing has had its advocates and practitioners in both the mainstream churches and sects, but some sects have made faith-healing a major claim to the credence of the public. Revival campaigns have, in particular, been the occasions for demonstrations of faith-healing, but among Pentecostal sects, some of which were themselves spawned from revivalist traditions, faith healing has been canvassed as a continuing faculty bestowed by God on some spiritual people, together with the exercise of the other gifts of the Spirit as described in I Corinthians 12.[17] A similar position is taken by the Restorationist (House Church) movement.[18] Today, faith-healing is rarely pressed to the point of conflict with medical practice, even though some sects, particularly among Pentecostal groups, formally urge their members to seek divine healing before having recourse to medicine, and regularly also claim divine cures in cases which have remained unrelieved by medical treatment. Spiritualist groups take much the same sort of stance towards orthodox medicine, and there has been controversy with the medical profession, particularly when spiritual healers have sought (and sometimes gained) admission to hospitals from local health authorities.[19]

Movements which claim a special gnosis, as do Christian Science, New Thought movements and Scientology, often also claim a special faculty of healing. Although curative theories differ, these groups tend to assert that true healing occurs only under their ministry and not by *materia medica*.[20] Christian Science, in time past, has been the most vigorous exponent of such a monopolistic theory of mental healing, and there have been serious cases in which practitioners of Christian Science have been in trouble with the law when their patients have died. Children of Christian Scientists, like those of Jehovah's Witnesses, may today be made wards of court if the medical profession judges that they need medical attention which the parents are disposed to refuse. Scientology is more narrowly concerned with the improvement of mental ability by the use of a psychotherapeutic technique which dissipates mental blocks. Claims for this technique have brought the movement into dispute with the public at large, the courts, and the Ministry of Health.[21]

These then, reviewed in relation to major institutional areas, are the ways in which sects seek exemption for their votaries from the general facilities and obligations of the wider society. In some measure, they have won gradual recognition for their distinctive claims to "opt out" of a variety of activities, and in some parts of the world they have been significant contenders in establishing rights of conscience.[22] It is, however, less in those areas where sects seek exemption than in those matters in which they make an affirmative stance that tension has most markedly arisen. These issues have been outside the realm in which negotiation has had to be undertaken, and they manifest much more powerfully the sense of distinction of sectarian values. We may distinguish three general areas; public comportment, proselytizing, and family relations, all of which bring a sect into situations in which public hostility may be awakened.

The Affirmative Sectarian Ethic

Except in the relatively rare circumstances in which a sect is vicinally isolated, its members of necessity conduct their business among the general public, and their comportment may become a matter for public scrutiny. Distinctive dress, speech, diet, and behaviour may mark out adherents from others. Hare Krishna devotees often adopt Indian costume; the Salvation Army dresses in uniform for public display; Exclusive Brethren, when going to their meetings (which occur at least once daily) wear cardigans and open-necked shirts, and their womenfolk wear headscarves. Since the five-day week was instituted, the Saturday sabbath observance of Seventh-day Adventists and the Worldwide Church of God (the followers of Herbert

174

Armstrong) is no longer the same source of the friction which, for employers, once it was. None the less, these are all devices of boundary maintenance for the sect: devices which establish who is included but which also make clear who is excluded: by their use, social distance is reinforced.

It is, however, in proselytizing activity that sectarians become most obvious to the general public. Not all sects sustain a programme of the active canvass of outsiders, but those which do generally earn thereby an unfavourable reputation with the wider public. The techniques of Jehovah's Witnesses in their house-to-house "witnessing," and of Mormon missionaries have been widely experienced. Hare Krishna adherents are visible on the streets, and, in many big cities at least, many people have encountered Moonies. The obtrusiveness and the intrusiveness of all these groups is perhaps a major source of public irritation: movements which proselytize by less confrontational methods (for example by campaigns in public halls, leaflet distribution, and commercial radio evangelism) produce less tension. Even so, the very fact that sects are seeking to convert people gives rise to a vague disquiet among the public at large. People resist the idea that they ought to be changed, and attribute dubious motives to those who wish to effect such change. It is widely asserted, particularly by the relatives of converts, that those who have undergone a conversion experience have in some way been "got at," have been misled, duped, taken advantage of, or have, in contemporary parlance, even been "brainwashed." Converts who later apostacize regularly explain their conversion in terms either of diminished personal responsibility ("they came when I was depressed," "under strain," "experiencing difficulties") or of deception, exploitation, and manipulation. This is the limited repertoire of motives which allow the apostate to claim his own self-esteem and to reclaim his reputation with others.[23] The press, the anti-cult organizations, and the de-programmers virtually rehearse reclaimed converts in these reinterpretations of their earlier religious choice.

Paradoxically, it may be noted in parentheses, minority religions are likely to suffer a bad reputation whether they are active in recruitment or not. Sects which do not actively seek new members - the Exclusive Brethren are the prime example - are regarded as secretive and as having something to hide:[24] those which do seek to convert outsiders are seen as a threat to "normal" life.

Family relations might be thought to be the most secluded area of social life, in which sectarians, like others, might enjoy privacy as security from interference. In practice, it is divergence in family-life patterns and norms which appears to arouse the greatest degree of tension between sects and the wider society, including the state. Within the family, sect members are free to live in accordance with their own moral norms, yet the very fact that their moral assumptions differ from those of society at large is a source of tension. History indicates that sects, because their moral codes differ, have often been accused of licentiousness. Some sects certainly have set conventional morality aside in the name of freedom, pleasure, or by adopting antinomian positions: the Rajneesh movement is the best-known of recent cases. The children of God (later known as the Family of Love) clearly run counter to society's moral predilections, with their belief that truly to love one's fellow men the believer ought to extend to the outcast and lonely not only food, a caring disposition, but companionship, including, if need be, sexual compassion.[25] In Britain, certainly, sects of this type have been exceptional.[26] But it is not only sects which explicitly reject society's moral code which provoke tension by their unconventionality. Any institutionalized departure from the taken-for-granted values of the wider society may suffice to arouse indignation. Thus, Moonies are condemned at times - much as were Roman Catholic orders in late nineteenth-century Britain with respect to vows taken by neophytes - because converts commit themselves to a life of chastity until they marry: the ascetic sexual mores of most Christian sects are generally interpreted by journalists and media men as "repression." The inevitable conclusion is that it is not so much the actual content of their practice that causes sects to be objects of opprobrium and foci of social tension, as the fact that they choose to take up decisive moral positions which differ from the relaxed indifferentism of the wider society.

In public disputes about sectarian practice, the allegation is often made that sects "break up families." This is a particularly frequent assertion in the mass media, and one that is sometimes taken up by politicians. Such tension is most often engendered by new movements - Moonies, Krishna people, or the children of God - but the principle at issue is one known to many sects. When an individual joins a minority religious movement, he is likely to find the beliefs and the moral norms of his kinsfolk no longer acceptable. He may then choose to live more in association with his fellow religionists rather than with his kinsfolk, feeling religiously committed to a new life-style which replaces the habits and practices of his former life.[27] These are normal consequences when someone is converted to a religion that retains any of its pristine earnestness, rigour and moral obligation. If the convert cannot persuade his parents, spouse, or children to embrace his new convictions, the charge is readily made that the religion itself is responsible for "breaking up" that family. This crude interpretation of the situation meets the demand for sensationalism characteristic of the press in its reporting of minority religions. Disagreement about religion or about the morality which faith enjoins may well cause people to go their separate ways: yet, it is perhaps a measure of the secularity of contemporary British society that separation or divorce in consequence of marital infidelity, incompatibility, or cruelty occasions much less public and media indignation than separation following religious disagreement.

There are, of course, other types of case in which this same charge of breaking up families is made. Sects such as Jehovah's Witnesses and Exclusive Brethren follow the practice, long since instituted among Methodists, Mennonites and others, (which, however, with their diminishing religious rigour, they have now largely or wholly abandoned) of banning "disfellowshipping," "withdrawing from" or "putting out" the wayward member.[28] Scientologists, too, albeit not on biblical grounds, practised a not dissimilar form of "disconnecting" relations with those they deemed hostile to their beliefs. These practices are fundamentally similar to Roman Catholic excommunication. When a member is put out, those remaining in the sect withdraw normal social intercourse in pursuit of biblical prescription on the subject. In a tightly knit sect, the wayward member is, of course, cut off from friends as well as from kinsfolk, and this is, no doubt, a severe punishment. The public, led by the press, is quick to judge such action as too severe, and to regard such cases (which are, however, relatively rare) as evidence that the sect "breaks up" families, despite the self-evident fact that deliberately to break up families must be very much to the detriment of any religious body.

One other aspect of family relations in sects particularly incites attention: the upbringing of children. In a youth-orientated society, in which attitudes to children have become progressively more positive and child-rearing ideologies increasingly permissive, the maintenance by sectarian families of more stringent discipline and attitudes to children, easily labelled "Victorian," becomes a subject of vociferous complaint. Some sects - for instance, Christadelphians - inherit a hyper-Calvinist doctrine which maintains that, before the age of discretion and believer's baptism, a child has no prospect of after-life salvation, and even though, today, Christadelphians themselves might demur about this teaching, it has undoubtedly shaped Christadelphian attitudes towards child-rearing. The occasions on which sectarian attitudes to children become public are not - certainly not - cases of indictment for cruelty. More typically they occur in two instances: when, because it is seeking to take advantage of tax concessions (seeking, that is, charitable status), a sect's general polity and policy is under review; or, more generally, when parents disagree about religion and the custody of their children is at stake. It is then commonly argued by the non-sectarian or ex-sectarian parent that he or she should have custody because, it is alleged, if left in the care of the sectarian parent, the child's upbringing and education would be seriously distorted. In the case of Exclusive Brethren, the burden of complaint is that their children are kept apart from others, are not given holidays or taken to places of entertainment, and that their education is terminated at the minimum age (except for narrowly technical courses). Much the same is said against Jehovah's Witnesses, to which it is added that the children are deprived because the sect does not acknowledge Christmas and birthdays. Few issues arouse such strong sentimental concern, and although in recent years judges appear to have become less prejudiced, these items have been invoked in cases in which custody has been given to the parent leading an acknowledged immoral life simply because the other parent was of a sectarian persuasion.

Sources of Tension

The votaries of many sects do maintain standards of behaviour which excel those of both other religionists and secularists: they are generally punctilious in obeying the law, in the payment of taxes, in conscientiousness and integrity at school and at work, but they are rarely given credit by the media, the courts, or the public for their orderly comportment. Such matters are not newsworthy, and their various good works - the hostels of the Salvation army, the (much less extensive) Home Church work of the Moonies, and the reclamation of drug-addicts and wastrels by many movements - go unsung. Sects are news only when they are the objects of opprobrium. It is, of course, news reporting, with all its negativity, which forges public opinion - and at times even the opinion of judges. The pejorative language of the media in reference to sects has not, to my knowledge, been studied in Britain, but there is no reason to suppose that it differs much in character, extent, and bias from that which has been revealed by scholars to be normally used by the media in Belgium and Italy.[29] Sects and new religious movements make news only when there is supposed scandal or sensation to report; in the "human stories" of apostates or the anguish of parents about children exposed to sectarian influence (whether as converts or as offspring). Sects are a source for induced tension - of a kind unequalled even when children are drawn into or exposed to crime or drug addiction. Sectarianism is a negative issue, and news about it becomes almost serialized as what have been called "negative summary events," in which negative stereotypes are carried forward from one news item to another.[30]

No outsider, least of all the detached sociological investigator, can consider any one sect - much less all sects - to be prescribing and practising the ideal way of life. There may be movements which merely pose as religions, and others which, although genuinely spiritual, succumb to devious measures and resort to ill-advised policies. That is to be expected. Overall, however, there can be no doubt that sects sustain levels of comportment which - according to the moral prescripts of society - are generally well above the average. Yet, the negative image that has been projected recently is such that the long tide of legislation steadily, over three hundred years, extending the measure of toleration to dissenters now appears to be in danger of being stemmed or even reversed. In the 1970's, the Charity Commissioners froze the charitable trusts of the Exclusive Brethren, and refused to allow them to register any new ones - a decision which the Brethren were finally able to overthrow in the courts.[31] Subsequently, one local government authority decided to levy rates on a Brethren meeting room on the technicality that, since no invitation was issued to the public at large, the rooms were not places of public worship.[32] Recently, the Attorney General explored at length the feasibility of challenging in the courts the charitable status of the Unification Church. Yet despite all this, there can be no vestige of doubt that both the Exclusive Brethren and the Unification Church are *bona fide* religions with highly devoted followings. What then induces these occasions of confrontation of government and sects? It can only be supposed that particular sections of an "interested" public - apostates and, in the case of the Unification Church, anti-cult groups - have actively campaigned against these movements. They have been greatly aided by the press, and the hostile climate produced in the wake of the People's Temple disaster at Jonestown, Guyana. The press is not always able to distinguish one movement from another, and readily and illicitly links events in one movement with other movements to which the first is totally unrelated. Negative summary events are not always confined to accounts of one movement, they are easily transferred from one to others.

It may be noted, however, that the focus of press and public hostility is not directed towards sectarian ideology as such, and that the sect stands out against society conspicuously only on symbolic issues, and not by virtue of its total ideological rejection of the wider social order. Thus, the tension in earlier decades between such sects as Christadelphians and Jehovah's Witnesses and the public arose not because of their expectation of the end of this dispensation, but because they were (no doubt in consequence of this belief) conscientious objectors, and because the Witnesses refused blood transfusions. Seventh-day Adventists have experienced more profound misunderstanding because of their advocacy of the seventh-day sabbath than because of their expectation of the early overthrow of worldly governments.

At the general ideological level there is, perhaps, no real concern or debate: sects are perceived by their alien symbolic gestures not by their espousal of an alternative grand design in history.

Even though the media in modern Britain have created a hedonistic climate in which sexuality (the individual's own or the reported sexual activity of others) has been virtually reinterpreted as entertainment, none the less, the intrinsic content of sectarian moral practice might create little hostility were it a strictly private option. For someone to lead an ascetic life is a matter of public (and media) indifference, but when a community or a movement sponsors such a lifestyle and canvasses it, then fear is engendered. Moral panic arises not only in the well-celebrated contexts of wayward, delinquent and criminal defiance, but also even from the active example and advocacy of more rigorous conformity to traditional moral ideals than is sustained by the not-so-moral majority. For many, the sect is perceived as an affront, a godlier-than-thou commitment which they readily charge with hypocrisy, but which may awaken a latent sense of inadequate performance, guilt, and even moral envy among those who retain, as many may, half-conscious ideals of "being good." In consequence, the sect may even be seen as a more explicit threat to the young than the amorphous, unorganized sub-cultures of easy sex, drink, drugs, and petty crime, simply because the sect is overt, organized, and legitimate, and active in its canvass.

The young sect seeks to challenge comfortable and conventional moral assumptions, and demands of the general public (in a way in which mainline churches do not) that they consider radically the meaning and purpose of living. It constitutes a moral minority in the body of a society in which there is moral flux, in which social organization is less and less underwritten by moral prescriptions and in which there is increasing tolerance of dispositions once labelled "immoral." The sect emerges as a type of reassertion of community values in which moral consensus - albeit sometimes in totalist mold - is reestablished. In any but a fully laissez-faire society, tension between such a moral minority and the amoral majority is likely to recur.

181

REFERENCES

[1] For a typology of sects which has at times been used as a basis for classification, see Bryan Wilson, *Religious Sects*, London: Weidenfeld and Nicolson, 1970, pp. 36-47.

[2] On the Eberhard Arnold Bruderhof, see J. McK. Whitworth, *God's Blueprints*, London, Routledge and Kegan Paul, 1975; on Anthroposophists, Geoffrey Ahern, *Sun at Midnight: The Rudolf Steiner Movement and the Western Esoteric Tradition*, Wellingborough: Aquarian Press 1984. On the International Society for Krishna Consciousness, see Kim Knott, *My Sweet Lord: The Hare Krishna Movement*, Wellingborough: The Aquarian Press, 1986 (and, for America, see Steven J. Gelberg, (ed.), *Hare Krishna, Hare Krishna*, New York: Grove Press, 1983; and E. Burke Rochford Jr., *Hare Krishna in America*, New Brunswick, N. J.: Rutgers University Press, 1985). On the Unification Church, see Eileen Barker, *The Making of a Moonie*, Oxford: Blackwell, 1984. On the Findhorn Community, see Paul Hawken, *The Magic of Findhorn*, London: Fontana/Collins, 1975. On Bugbrooke, see Roger Curl, *Three Christian Communities : A Sociological Study*, unpublished D. Phil. thesis, University of Oxford, 1976.

[3] For the general discussion of the relation of ideology and organization in minority religious movements, see Bryan R. Wilson, (ed.), *Patterns of Sectarianism*, London : Heinemann, 1967.

[4] Thus the Church of Scientology became engaged in a running dispute with the Ministry of Health and with the National Association for Mental Health: see, C. H. Rolph, *Believe What You Like*, London: Andre Deutsch, 1973; and Roy Wallis, *The Road to Total Freedom: A Sociological Analysis of Scientology*, London: Heinemann, 1976.

[5] On the relation of eschatology and morals in Seventh-day Adventism, see Michael Pearson, *Seven-day Adventist Responses to some Contemporary Ethical Problems*, unpublished D. Phil. thesis, University of Oxford, 1986; and Malcolm Bull, "Eschatology and Manners in Seventh-day Adventism," *Archives de Sciences Sociales des Religions*, 65, 1, (1988), pp. 145-59; Malcolm Bull and Keith Lockhart, *Seeking a Sanctuary: Seventh-day Adventism and the American Dream*, San Francisco: Harper and Row, 1989.

[6] This point is made by Rodney Stark, "Must all Religions be Supernatural?" in Bryan Wilson, (ed.), *The Social Impact of New Religious Movements*, New York: Rose of Sharon Press, 1981, pp. 159-177.

[7] For a general account see, L. J. Arrington, *Great Basin Kingdom: An Economic History of the Latter-day Saints 1830-1900*, Cambridge, Mass.: Harvard University Press, 1958; and L. J. Arrington and Davis Bitton, *The Mormon Experience*, London: Allen and Unwin, 1979.

182

[8]On the House of Lords judgment in the Sikh case, see Weekly Law Reports, Mandla v. Dowell Lee (H. L. (E)) April 8, 1983, pp. 620-632. On the Christadelphians, see Bryan R. Wilson, *Sects and Society*, London : Heinemann, 1961.

[9]For a fuller discussion, specifically related to the Christadelphians, see B. R. Wilson, "Apparition et persistance des Sectes dans un milieu social en evolution," *Archives de Sociologie des Religions*, 5, Jan-June, 1958, pp. 140-150.

[10]For an account of the issue in the U.S.A., see David R. Manwaring, *Render Unto Caesar: The Flag-Salute Controversy*, Chicago: University of Chicago Press, 1962.

[11]This point was cogently, if somewhat acidly, made by Mr. Justice Walton in Holmes and others v. Attorney-General, High Court Chancery Division Group B 1979 H No 1183, 11 Feb. 1981 p.4 (see also *The Times* Law Report, 12 Feb. 1981).

[12]For a brief account of the ideological element in the running of church-related business in the Unification Church, see David Bromley, "Financing the Millenium: The Economic Structure of the Unificationist Movement," *Journal for the Scientific Study for Religion* 24, 3 (Sept., 1985), pp. 253-275.

[13]On the case in which the Christadelphians established their right in appeal to the Industrial Tribunal to work without trades union membership, see U.K. Industrial Tribunals Case No. 19377/76 and 19378/76 Folio No. 11/26/65.

[14]As examples, see the account of the attitudes of Elim Pentecostalists and Christadelphians in Bryan R. Wilson, *Sects and Society*, London: Heinemann, 1961, pp. 85-88, and 289-292.

[15]For a fuller discussion, see Bryan R. Wilson, "Sectarians and Schooling," *The School Review* 72, 1 (1964), pp. 1-21.

[16]For a succinct account of Jehovah's Witness teaching concerning blood transfusion, see M. James Penton, *Apocalypse Delayed*, Toronto: University of Toronto Press, 1985, pp. 153-154.

[17]The teaching and attitudes of the Assemblies of God, the largest Pentecostal sect in Britain, is given in Gillian Allen and Roy Wallis, "Pentecostalists as a Medical Minority," in Roy Wallis and Peter Morley, (eds.), *Marginal Medicine*, London: Peter Owen, 1976, pp. 110-137.

[18]For a general, albeit popular, account of these movements, see Andrew Walker, *Restoring the Kingdom: The Radical Christianity of the House Church Movement*, London: Hodder and Stoughton, 1985.

[19]See Geoffrey K. Nelson, *Spiritualism and Society*, London: Routledge and Kegan Paul, 1969, pp. 171-172.

[20]See on this point, Arthur E. Nudelman, "The Maintenance of Christian Science in Scientific Society," in Roy Wallis and Peter Morley, (eds.), *op. cit.* pp. 42-60.

[21]See Roy Wallis, *The Road to Total Freedom, op. cit.,* and C. H. Rolph, *op. cit.*

[22]See David R. Manwaring, *op. cit.;* and M. James Penton, *Jehovah's Witnesses in Canada,* Toronto: Macmillan, 1976, in which a large number of legal cases are cited.

[23]See Anson D. Shupe, Jr. and David G. Bromley, "Apostates and Atrocity Stories: Some Parameters in the Dynamics of Deprogramming," in Bryan Wilson, *The Social Impact...op. cit.,* pp. 179-215.

[24]This was the implication of the Court of appeal judgment in 1982, in which the Brethren lost their case against Broxtoe Borough Council which had denied the Brethren exemption from local rates for their meeting rooms on the grounds that, since no invitation was extended to the general public to participate in worship, these places did not constitute places of "public worship." The judges upheld this view, making some form of invitation to the public the decisive criterion of a place of public worship. Law Report December 7th 1983, Court of Appeal *The Times,* p. 17.

[25]On the Children of God, see Roy Wallis, *Salvation and Protest: Studies of Social and Religious Movements,* London: Frances Pinter, 1979, pp. 74-90; and D. E. Van Zandt, *Ideology and Structure in the Children of God: A Study of a New Sect,* unpublished Ph. D. thesis, University of London, 1985.

[26]A celebrated instance which no doubt to some extent lives on in folk memory (much as do Jonestown, the Charlie Manson cult, and Benjamin Purnell of the House of David in the United States) was the Agape Community at Spaxton, Somerset, led successively by Henry Prince and J. H. Smyth-Piggot. On this sect, there are only popular works: Charles Mander, *The Reverend Prince and His Abode of Love,* Wakefield, EP Publishing, 1976; Donald McCormick, *Temple of Love,* London, Jarrolds, 1962. On the House of David, see Robert S. Fogarty, *The Religious Remnant,* Kent, Ohio: Kent State University Press, 1981.

[27]For a detailed exposition, see Eileen Barker, *op. cit.*

[28]On practice among Jehovah's Witnesses, see M. James Penton, *Apocalypse Delayed, op. cit.* pp. 89-90, 299-300.

[29]K. Dobbelare, G. Voet and H. Verbeke, "Neue religiöse Bewegungen im Spiegel der belgischen Presse" and G. Ambrosio, "Neue religiöse Bewegungen in Italien," in Johannes Neumann and Michael W. Fischer (Eds.), *Toleranz und Repression: Zur Lage religiöser Minderheiten in modernen Gesellschaft,* Frankfurt: Campus Verlag, 1987, pp. 230-44; 313-35.

184

[30]This term, coined by K. E. Rosengren, P. Arvidsson and D. Sturesson in "The Barseback Panic: A Case of Media Deviance" in C. Winick, (ed.), *Deviance and the Mass Media*, has been employed effectively to characterize media coverage of many new religious movements by James A. Beckford, *Cult Controversies*, London: Tavistock, 1985, pp. 231-247.

[31]An account of this case and its background is provided in Bryan Wilson "A Sect at Law: The Case of the Exclusive Brethren," *Encounter* LX, 1. (Jan. 1983), pp. 81-87.

[32]See footnote 24 *supra*.

CHAPTER XI

TOLERANT DISCRIMINATION:
CHURCH, STATE AND THE NEW RELIGIONS[1]

EILEEN BARKER

The suggestion underlying this paper is that, although the formal institutions of Church and State in contemporary Britain have, on the whole, resisted attempts to control or discriminate against the new religions, they do, nonetheless, play a more indirect role in enabling - even promoting - both control and discrimination. This can be observed at a micro and at a macro level. First, we can observe individuals using or relying upon membership of either the Church or the State apparatus in moves to prevent the new religions from enjoying the kinds of freedom afforded to more conventional religions. Secondly, we can observe aspects of British culture, which are "carried" by the institutions of Church and State, supporting unquestioned assumptions about the "rightness" of traditional beliefs and practices that are not shared by the new religions. The result of such a situation is that there is to be found in both Church and State in Britain a rhetoric and, to a considerable degree, the practice of toleration but, *within* this rhetoric and practice, there is also an almost unnoticed rhetoric of discrimination that fosters and permits a limited, but significant, degree of discriminatory practice.

The new religions that are referred to in the paper are those which have become visible in the West since the Second World War. It should not, however, be forgotten that all religions have, at their inception, been new, and parallels in history can be found for much that is happening to the new religions (and that the new religions are doing). But there are also some crucial differences between the relations between the current wave of new religions and contemporary society and those of earlier waves - if only because contemporary society is not the same as historical society - and those who rise in righteous indignation when considering some of the religious bigotry to which the new religions are subjected by the Church, State and society in modern Britain might do well to remember, if only *en passant*, that no Moonie has been thrown to the lions, no Krishna devotee has been burnt at the stake, no Premie has been torn on the rack, no Sannyasin has been fined or imprisoned for not attending an Anglican service, no Scientologist has been committed to a mental hospital for auditing with his E-meter, and no Rastafarian has been denied entrance to Balliol because of her religion.

But questions have been asked in the House, the European Parliament has passed a motion, proposed by a British Euro-MP, that condemned the new religions; Scientologists have been refused entry to the country; Krishna devotees have been subjected to "deprogramming;" Moonies have been refused the right to speak in church halls and on British University campuses, and, having lost a libel case in which they were accused of brainwashing, they have been threatened with the loss of their charitable status.

If the research that has been conducted by social scientists into the beliefs and practices of the new religions has revealed anything over the past decade, it has revealed that to generalise about the new religions is, at best, folly. But this does not mean that Church, State and society do not generalise about the movements. In a pluralist society it is not, perhaps, surprising that men should join together those whom the gods have rent asunder; what might, however, seem unjust is the unrelieved negativity with which the conflation is contaminated. The media have had a joyous time making sweeping pronouncements, carelessly (or, perhaps, carefully) collecting the sins of any and attributing these to each and every movement that can be subsumed under the one label: "cult." This public confusion does, understandably, irritate the members of the movements, each of whom is convinced that theirs is a unique and, no doubt, uniquely true religion. One

Krishna devotee, who had written a pamphlet entitled "Please Don't Lump Us In: A Request to the Media,"[2] confessed to me recently that he felt slightly ashamed of what he had written, for he now realised that he, in his paper, had lumped all the *other* cults together. It is, perhaps, a strange irony that sociologists, usually scorned for their taxonomic excesses, comprise about the only group within modern society that has consistently endeavoured to point out the rich variety of beliefs, practices and organisations that are to be found within and between the new religions.

That said, however, I shall not be pursuing the differences between the groups, or even the variety of their reactions to society. I shall, in what follows, be concerned with the new religions as a group in so far as they are treated as a group. It is, indeed, part of sociological *data* that the new religions are frequently considered to be a single group and that they are assumed to share much more than a single label. It is also important to recognise that, in so far as the movements are treated as a group, cases that directly concern one new religion can have an indirect relevance for other movements.

Church

In 1559, the Second Act of Supremacy decreed that the Church of England was "by law established," the Church and the realm being deemed thereby to be identical. Although, throughout the centuries, the mutterings of disestablishmentarians have been and continue to be heard, and although only one in twenty of the English population is currently a *member* of the Church of England, there is little doubt in the minds of most of the Queen's subjects that the Church of England is *the* Church of England.

The story is told of the fly who warned the elephant on which it was resting to prepare for its imminent take-off. The elephant somewhat ungraciously, replied that he had not noticed the fly's landing and he was unlikely to notice its departure. It would be an exaggeration to say that the Church of England has not noticed the arrival of the new religions - Dr Donald Coggan, when he was Archbishop of Canterbury, "warned the public to be on its guard against the Unification Church," and several members of the General Synod spoke out against the movement during its 1978 meeting at York University[3] - but, generally speaking, the established Church has not paid much official attention to the movements. The Free Churches have shown some interest (the Methodist and the United Reform Churches have both looked into "the problem"), but even they have done little more than produce fairly factual leaflets about some of the movements. Individual members of the Church - both clergy and laity - have, however, made their concerns known on numerous occasions from the pulpit and in the media. This has tended to be especially the case when there has been personal involvement with someone joining one of the movements, or when one of the movements has been seen to have a local presence - when the Jesus Fellowship was set up in Bugbrooke, when the Rajneeshees threatened to control Herringswell or when the family that had owned much of Stanton Fitzwarren joined the Unification Church. This last case is of interest in that when the convert concerned gave his 600-acre estate to the movement, local clergy and parishoners objected to the diocese of Bristol and he lost the patronage that went with it and which had been held by his family since the Church of England had been constituted under Elizabeth I. In a letter to the Church Commissioners, the Bishop of Bristol is reported to have stated that the Unification Church "was something entirely other than a mere sectarian movement" and that it "has some quite sinister features associated with it."[4]

The greatest antagonism towards the movements tends to have come from certain of the more conservative sections of the Catholic Church,[5] and from Evangelical Christians. One of the main "anti-cultist" groups in Britain, Deo Gloria Outreach, is funded by an Evangelical, and its main purpose in exposing the errors of the new religions is to proclaim and preserve the truth of fundamentalist Christianity. The Swindon Youth for Christ and its affiliated inter-church organisation "Share," has distributed thousands of copies of its anti-Moon leaflet, *"Just a Family Affair?"*[6] While the Jewish community has been prominently involved in anti-cult activity in the United States, this has not been the case in Britain - possibly because, despite the fact that the Unification Church has a disproportionately large percentage of Jewish members in the States, there are practically no Moonies from a Jewish background in Britain. There was, however, an interesting *Credo* production in the late 1970s in which members of the Jewish community were complaining about evangelical Christians "brainwashing" Jewish youth in very much the same language that the evangelicals were complaining about the Moonies "brainwashing" Christian youth.

At the institutional level, the religious organisation that has paid the greatest attention to the movements has, perhaps, been the British Council of Churches. Like some of the Free Churches, the BCC has distributed literature about some of the movements,[7] but, more importantly, it has taken the new religions on board as part of its agenda in its Committee for Relations with People of Other Faiths. The Committee's secretary has continued, in the face of strong criticism from many opposed to the new religions, to keep in close contact with the movements and to take them seriously as part of the religious scene in modern Britain. Defending himself for having accepted an invitation from the Church of Scientology to speak at a London conference on religious freedom in 1985, the secretary wrote:

> ...I received a certain amount of unpleasantness from such people over this period, and various protests came into the BCC about my action. I remain quite sure that there are practically no limits to dialogue, for dialogue is personalist, about people. It is clear that however wicked or evil the systems be to which men and women have given their allegiance, they remain themselves in the image of God, and in our talking with them there is no limit to the power of the Holy Spirit.[8]

The World Congress of Faiths has also shown a willingness to inquire beyond media reports on the new religions (some of their members being more inclined than others to lend a sympathetic ear). It has arranged a series of lectures around the theme of freedom and the new religions and, although the lectures were given by non-members, Moonies and Scientologists attended the meetings and were able to contribute to the discussion and some WCF officials have recently accepted an invitation to visit a Unification centre.

While many of the movements have attacked the more mainline Churches, and the majority tend to dismiss them as apathetic, hypocritical or, most frequently, as utterly irrelevant, some of the new religions have made an effort to initiate interfaith dialogue. The Church of Scientology was responsible for the foundation of the (rather short-lived) Society for Religious Peace; the International Society for Krishna Consciousness has close ties with sections of the Hindu community in Britain; and, most persistently, the Unification Church has been devoting a considerable amount of time and energy in interfaith activities, visiting Ministers, sending out literature and videos about the movement and inviting representatives of different faiths to their centres and to some of the international conferences that the movement sponsors. These activities have certainly brought the movements a few friends. They have also aroused considerable suspicion and several of those who have responded positively to the movements' overtures have themselves been subjected to criticism.

Although it is probably only a small minority of the population which sees the new religions as a genuine threat to the more established Churches, it might be useful to try to put the numerical significance of the movements into some kind of perspective in relation to the other Churches, not least because the rise of the new religions is sometimes used in "the secularisation debate" to indicate that secularisation is (or is not) part of the modern British scene. Such an exercise is, however, fraught with difficulty: no one knows how many new religions there are - there is, indeed, no agreed definition of what constitutes a new religion; the movements, like most of the main-line Churches, have different tiers of membership, ranging from full commitment (like a nun or a priest), through associate membership (like a congregation), to loose affiliation and/or sympathy with the movement's beliefs and/or aims. To confuse matters even further, some "members" are more like "clients" who attend courses offered by the movement but have, otherwise, very little connection with the movement, and/or who might be counted as "members" by several different organisations.[9] Very few of the movements make their membership figures public, and those who do are quite likely either to overestimate or (less frequently) to underestimate their numbers; the turnover rate of most movements tends to be very high, but many of the drop-outs will continue to be counted as members long after they have terminated their association with the movement.

It is, however, clear that it would be a great mistake to believe that the new religions are "taking over" from mainline Churches. They do not even begin to take up the slack. Membership of the Unification Church may have increased by nearly 30% per annum between 1975 and 1980, but the increase was from 150 to 570. During the same period, an almost 1% fall in membership of the Church in England per annum represents a drop from 1,900,000 to 1,800,000; the Methodists lost about 60,000 members; the Baptists just over 15,000; the Presbyterians nearly 150,000 - and the Catholics, like the Church of England, lost just under 100,000. In other words, the major conventional churches lost between them about *half a million* members. The more successful of the "alien" innovative new religious movements gained a few hundred full-time members each, and, perhaps, as a generous estimate, gained between them 20,000 - 4% of the loss from the conventional religions.[10] If one adds up the total membership of *all* the Churches and the non-Christian religious organisations in the UK in 1980, and compares the result with the membership figures in 1975, there *remains* a net loss of over half a million people, despite the fact that the population as a whole had shown a slight *increase*.[11]

These are, of necessity, very rough estimates, and, of course, were casual affiliation to be included, the figures could look slightly different. But the figures of core (and serious 'congregational') membership are, I think, accurate enough to make the point that the new religious movements are hardly *responsible* for the loss of membership in the conventional movements - and that they cannot even be said to be sweeping up the dissidents. If the seeds of a new religiosity *are* embodied in secularisation, there is little in the way of convincing evidence that it has as yet manifested itself as a visible, *institutionalised* religiosity.[12]

This does not mean that the new religions have not faced the mainline religions with a challenge. The movements do seem to be offering some people, whom the mainline churches would prefer to have kept in their fold, something that they feel is not available elsewhere. As Bryan Wilson has frequently pointed out, new movements often offer a revitalisation of religious culture - and a surer, safer, swifter path to salvation than the overly institutionalised conventional Churches.[13] Although the numbers are small, listening to what the members of the new religions found lacking in the churches within which they were brought up does point to some very real discontents - discontents that are felt also by thousands of others who have *not* taken up an option offered by one of the new movements.[14]

State

The Church of England, as the established Church, enjoys certain privileges, but it is not normally a disadvantage to belong to another religion - or, indeed, to none at all - in modern Britain. "Normally" has to be stressed, however, as there are some ways in which non-established religions have to take second place to the Church of England, and, in practice, one can detect a gentle, but nonetheless clear, increase in what could be termed potential "inconvenience" as one moves away from the established Church, through the traditional nonconformist Protestant denominations, on to Catholicism, Judaism, other conventional religions such as Islam and Hinduism, and, to a lesser extent, the Sikh religion, to, finally, the new religions.[15]

Having an established Church, England obviously has no equivalent to the First Amendment of the United States Constitution: "Congress shall make no law respecting an establishment of religion, or prohibiting the free exercise thereof...." It is, perhaps, slightly more surprising that Northern Ireland is the only part of the United Kingdom in which discrimination on the basis of religion is unlawful. Although Britain is a party to the European Convention on Human Rights and Fundamental Freedoms, its domestic laws are not always in conformity with the Convention, and, although there is legislation that makes certain kinds of discrimination against a person on the grounds of sex or race illegal, there are no laws that protect the rights of religious minorities. In a case in which a headmaster was accused of discriminationg against a Sikh schoolboy, the headmaster was originally exonerated on the grounds that the Sikhs formed a religious, not a racial, group so it was not unlawful to discriminate against them. The House of Lords eventually allowed an appeal against the decision on the grounds that Sikhs could be defined as an ethnic group.[16]

So far as the new religions are concerned, the first time that their relationship with the state hit the headlines was in 1968 when the Minister of Health stated in the House of Commons that:

...Scientology is a pseudo-philosophical cult....The Government are satisfied, having reviewed all the available evidence, that Scientology is socially harmful. It alienates members of families from each other and attributes squalid and disgraceful motives to all who oppose it; its authoritarian principles and practices are a potential menace to the personality and well-being of those so deluded as to become its followers; above all, its methods can be a danger to the health of those who submit to them. There is evidence that children are now being indoctrinated.[17]

The minister proceeded to say that, although there was no power under existing law to prohibit the practice of Scientology, the Government had "concluded that it is so objectionable that it would be right to take all steps within their power to curb its growth". Foreign nationals were no longer to be admitted to the country to be students (or to work) at Scientology establishments.

In 1971, the Foster Report concluded that it seemed "wrong in principle to exclude people from this country altogether on the sole ground that they intend to carry out here 'activities which are lawful for the ordinary citizen.'"[18] In 1974, the case of a Dutch woman, who had been refused entry to Britain for the purposes of employment with the Scientologists, was taken to the European Court of Justice, which pronounced that the U.K. was entitled, for reasons of public policy, to refuse a national of another member state (of the EEC) the right of entry.[19] Despite the Foster Report, the ban stayed in force until 1980, when it was lifted on the grounds that (1) it was unenforcible as Scientologists did not need to disclose themselves as such at ports of entry; (2) it could be difficult to defend before the European Court of Human Rights; and (3) it was unfair, since Scientology was the only movement for which Britain's general religious tolerance was thus suspended.[20]

In fact, immigration difficulties have also been experienced by members of the Unification Church and, in particular, by its leader, Sun Myung Moon, when the Home Office refused to grant him a temporary stay of two months in Britain in 1978. In the event, an appeal against the refusal was allowed - by the time the appeal procedure had been gone through, Moon had already spent as much time as he wanted in the country and had returned to America. A point of interest in this case was that the Home

Office included among its reasons for refusing Moon's application inaccurate or, at least, "misleading" reports that had appeared in the British press. One allegation was that the Unification Church was planning to move its headquarters to the U.K. This was based on two articles in *The Times* that were admitted to be speculative. *"The Sun*, eschewing such delicacy, reported the proposed movement as a fact."[21] More recently, Bhagwan Shree Rajneesh was refused permission to stay in Britain after his spectacular departure from Rajneeshpuram in Oregon.

From the mid-1970s, the Unification Church was the new religion that was to find itself more frequently than any other movement the target of attacks, some of which were to lead it to try to clear its name in the courts - or, rather, the names of some of its members as the Church itself cannot sue for libel. The attacks came from two main sources: the press and the newly formed anti-cult group FAIR (Family, Action, Information and Rescue), whose founding chairman, a Labour member of Parliament, Paul Rose, had taken up the cause of worried friends and relations of the movement's members. One of the strongest outbursts from Rose took place when he had spoken at some length on the Unification Church in the House of Commons in 1975. His speech included the phrases: fraudulent fundraising...sinister political connections....slave labour....sophisticated brainwashing....masquerading under (different names)....dangerous humbug....mumbo-jumbo....indoctrination....blasphemous bogus religion....virtual prisoners....and more.[22] As Rose was protected from litigation by the privilege of the House, the Moonies were powerless to respond.[23]

One way in which the state has long helped religious organisations is by granting them a charitable status that carries with it the benefits of certain tax exemptions. Although, on 17th December 1985, a question was asked in the House of Lords about its eligibility for charitable status, the Church of Scientology has not yet succeeded in receiving official recognition that it *is* a religion;[24] in 1970, it was refused the right to register the chapel at its British headquarters as a place of worship.[25] In the House of Commons on 14th May 1984, it was, indeed, stated by the Parliamentary Under-Secretary of State for the Home Department (during a debate concerning the Exegesis Programme) that "many of the most sinister cults are not charities." Until recently, however, so long as a movement could be labelled as a religion its right to tax exemption has been all but automatic. It was Paul Rose who first questioned the charitable status of the Unification Church. In February of 1977, he complained that the Home Office had not acted on the evidence that he had previously presented to the Commons. He also accused the Charity Commissioners of "playing Pontius Pilate" while lives were wrecked and fraud prospered. Protected from the risk of libel charges, as on the earlier occasion, by Parliamentary privilege, Rose said he had amassed a file on the cult which showed that its leader was a megalomaniac degenerate - a political pimp and gangster who had built a vast commercial and political empire; the movement was based on barbaric methods and intimidation that prevented the press from doing more than "scratch at the slimy surface of what must be one of the most evil phenomena of our time."[26] Dr Shirley Summerskill, for the Home Office, replied that, since there was no Ministerial responsibility for charitable status, there was no way that the Home Secretary could intervene, short of legislation. She also added that registration did not involve a value-judgement about the desirablility of an organisation.[27] It would have appeared that the position in Britain was, in this respect, similar to that in the United States where, in a tax case in 1982, it was ruled that:

> In determining whether a particular ecclesiastical body has been organised and is considered exclusively for religious purposes, the courts may not inquire into or classify the doctrines, dogmas, and teachings held by that body to be integral to its religion but must accept that body's characterization of its own beliefs and activities and those of its adherents, so long as that characterization is made in good faith and is not a sham. On this principle it must be concluded that the Unification Church has religion as its primary purpose in as much as its doctrines, dogmas and teachings and a significant part of its activities are recognized as religious, and in good faith it classifies as religious the beliefs and activities which the Tax Commission and the Court below have described as political and economic.[28]

Again in the United States, a court in an immigration case found that the Unification Church had to be accepted as a religion.[29] However, when one of the British movement's lawyers said that it had been declared a *bona fide* religion in the U.S. courts, an Appeal Judge in the *Daily Mail* case dryly retorted that British courts did not have to accept everything that an American court ruled - after all, he added, an American court had just let some Irish gun-runners off scotfree. In fact, the jury in the case had not only found for the *Daily Mail*, but also recommended that charitable status should be removed from the movement. The Charity Commissioners said that they could find no proper grounds for making such a move. Nevertheless, in response to "public pressure," the Attorney-General, Sir Michael Havers, requested on two separate occasions, that the Charity Commissioners should set up an enquiry. When they declined to do this (possibly because they had had their fingers burned through an earlier encounter with the Exclusive Brethren),[30] Sir Michael wrote to the Chief Commissioner asking him to remove the movement from the register of charities. After some considerable delay, proceedings were started by the Attorney-General himself. In February 1988, however, Sir Michael Havers' successor, Sir Patrick Mayhew, announced that the proceedings were to be dropped due to insufficient evidence to sustain the case. Had the Unification Church lost the case, it is quite likely that a situation would have arisen, as it has in America, in which a large number of other organizations, who have little or no sympathy with the Unification Church, would become extremely worried about the implications of the right of the courts (or parliament, or "the state") to judge a particular religion according to its "merits."[31]

Following the Daily Mail case and, no doubt, frustrated by the absence of any concrete changes in the law affecting the Unification Church and other new religions, the movements' opponents in Britain joined forces with anti-cultists in other parts of Europe and turned to the European Parliament to see whether something might be done there. Two motions for a resolution were tabled. The second motion began:

The European Parliament,
- deeply concerned by the distress and family break-ups caused by Sun Myung Moon's Unification Church,
1. Welcomes the media's relentless exposure of the Moonies' activities;
2. Urges public authorities throughout the Community to ensure that the Moonies are not given special tax benefits, charity status, or other privileges;
3. Calls on its Committee on Youth, Culture, Education, Information and Sport to report on the activities of Sun Myung

Moon's followers in the Unification Church and the danger to society that they represent....[32]

In the event, a British Euro-M.P. was asked to produce a report, and in 1984 the European Parliament adopted, by 98 votes to 28 with 27 abstentions, a resolution calling for "a common approach by the Member States of the European Community towards various infringements of the law by new organizations operating under the protection afforded to religious bodies."[33] The Resolution has had no direct effect on the member states, but its passing was, at very least, a symbolic triumph for the opponents of the new religions.

But where actions are considered socially undesirable, as they undoubtedly are in certain cases such as child abuse or prostitution, there is no reason to suppose that legislation ought to be applicable to the members of new religions alone. Both Mrs. Thatcher and the Leader of the Opposition have expressed "concern," but (apart from taking away the privilege of charitable status, which, like the ban on Scientologists, involves the risk of serious disquiet about there being discrimination on grounds of belief rather than behaviour), exactly *what* a democratic state *could* do in a pluralistic society with respect to the new religions has never been made very clear.

More than one commentator has remarked that human rights in Britain are protected more by public opinion than by law. Technically, a right exists when an interest is legally protected; a liberty exists when there is no law against doing something, and if public opinion is strongly against a particular minority, liberties can be eroded more easily than rights. It is perhaps, in this negative sense, that by *not* having an influence over how the new religions are treated, the state does allow discriminatory treatment of their members. The *Daily Mail* case certainly seemed to give permission for discrimination against Moonies by the public - and, in at least one instance, by local government. The case concerned a local council's decision to refuse registration to a play-group leader purely on the grounds that, although she was not a full-time member of the Unification Church, she did accept some of the movement's teachings and was, therefore, "not a fit person to look after children." There was no evidence that she had not done her job well, in

198

fact many of the parents testified that her work had been excellent. The reasons given by the council (Hammersmith and Fulham) included the statement:

> In a recent defamation case in the High Court it was held by a Jury that a statement inferring that the Unification Church broke up families was not defamatory. Further the Jury in the case recommended that the Charity Commissioners withdrew (sic) charitable status from the Unification Church.[34]

The play-leader appealed and a magistrate over-ruled the Council's decision and the group was finally registered. But although the case had been won in law, socially the point had been made in the mind of the public that someone associating with the Unification Church might not be a fit person to have any contact with young children. Almost by accident, I came across a further repercussion. A member of the Unification Church told me that she had been an active member of a committee which organised a playgroup that one of her children attended - until the local vicar found out that she was a Moonie and said that the playgroup could no longer meet in his church hall unless the Moonie was removed from the committee. I asked a friend, who happened to be a member of the congregation in question, on what grounds the vicar had decided to make such a stipulation, and received the answer that there had been a case in Hammersmith and Fulham where the council had decided that a Moonie should not be allowed contact with children.

Before describing one more example of a case that might appear to illustrate discrimination against membership of the Unification Church in a court of law, it might be helpful, for comparative purposes, to turn once again to the United States. In November 1979, the New York University Review of Law and Social Change sponsored a colloquium on "Alternative Religions: Government Control and the First Amendment." Reading through the Proceedings, it is clear that the United States has by no means clarified all the legal issues that it has to face in respect of the new religions, but it is also clear that the problems of legislation and litigation are *recognized* as problems in a way that they tend not to be in Britain.[35] The point that leads into the British case which I wish to cite was little more than an odd "throw away" remark at the end of the final discussion. An anguished parent in the audience was berating the panel for the lack of practical help it was offering. The American Civil Liberties Union lawyer, Jeremiah Gutman, replied:

> You want some free legal advice? You think you know who is holding your son? Bring a proceeding in the nature of a writ of *habeas corpus* to make this group come in. If they do not produce your son, the judge will put them in jail until they do. How about that? In Pennsylvania, we just used this approach the other way around. Someone was kidnapped by the parents and a professional deprogrammer. The parents were brought in by a Pennsylvania Supreme Court judge and told to bring their son before the court so it could determine whether or not he wanted to be where he was. The parents refused; the judge threatened to put them in jail. The parents then produced their son.[36]

In April 1982, a 28-year-old British Moonie, Nicola Raine, received a telephone call from an old school friend suggesting that they should meet each other at Islington underground station. Miss Raine agreed, went out, but did not return. When they did not hear from her, and could not find her whereabouts, the Moonies, fearing that she was being held against her will by deprogrammers, applied for a writ of *habeas corpus*. The application was dismissed, the judge saying:

> I think that one must accept that, on the balance of probabilities, Miss Raine was, on the afternoon of 6th April, intercepted by a person or persons unknown to the court and persuaded in the first place not to return to the Church's headquarters at Lancaster Gate and, in the second place, to go to a place in the country where she met her parents. Again, on the balance of probabilities I do not think that she was physically abducted... I entirely accept that in the case of a woman of 28, parents are not entitled in any way to detain their daughter against her wishes, however much they may disapprove of the company which she is keeping. But I am satisfied, on the balance of probabilities, that this is not the situation....Parents and others are, on the other hand, perfectly entitled to advise and persuade their children, if they think necessary, with emphasis, but they are under no liability or duty to disclose to others, who have no authority to demand it, the whereabouts of a member of their family...whatever may have been the circumstances of her interception... subsequent care will have been shown by her parents. In these circumstances, and on these findings, the only conclusion to which I can come on that action is that it should be dismissed.[37]

In fact Miss Raine *had* been bundled into the back of a van and *was* held against her will for two and a half months before she managed to return to the Unification Church.[38]

It could be argued that the Nicky Raine case epitomises the general attitude of the courts towards movements like the Unification Church, and that the courts do, in a manner of speaking, reflect the attitude of the general public, which has, in turn, been both reflected and, to some extent, created by the mass media. There is a general feeling in Britain that "decent" parents (Mr Raine is a magistrate) would be extremely unlikely to resort to criminal means - but, at the same time, it would be perfectly understandable if they were to do everything within their power to rescue their daughter from a movement such as the Unification Church which has, after all, been judged by a jury to brainwash and split up families. Mr. and Mrs. Raine have since said that their decision to employ deprogrammers was largely the result of the fear that they felt about the Unification Church after having read such terrible things about it in the press.

The media will, of course, make the most of anything that will result in a "good story." The Raine case itself became, in turn, a good story of yet another family that had been split up by the Moonies, thus reinforcing a spiral of confirmation through accusation. Not surprisingly, information about the number of times that Miss Raine visited her parents after she had returned to the movement does not make the headlines. The media are rarely interested in stories which might suggest that Moonies can have a good relationship with their parents. The "atrocity tales," consequently, give the impression of being typical of the movement - and atypical of the rest of society.

One does not, of course, expect the media to refer to "control groups" in their coverage of the new religions, but an awareness of the precautions necessary in assessing characteristics that are assumed to be peculiar to a group would seem to be singularly lacking not merely among the general public but also, on occasion, among the legal profession and the law makers. The third volume of *The Crossman Diaries* contains several references to the embarrassment subsequently felt by the government as the result of imposing the ban on Scientologists before a proper inquiry had been concluded; it has already been mentioned that the Home Office relied on speculative reporting in *The Times* when refusing temporary extension of Moon's visa. Throughout the *Daily Mail* trial, reference was continually made to the "strangeness," "bizarreness," "unorthodoxy" and the "incomprehensibility" of Unification beliefs, with the suggestion that the applicability of such adjectives implied that the Unification Church must be a bogus religion. In his summing up for the jury, the judge included the comment:

> ... about those beliefs, (the appellant, Mr. Orme) has uncompromisingly stated that he believes Mr. Moon to be the Messiah. One is perfectly entitled to believe that anyone is the Messiah... and, as I have said many times, we must respect people's religious views. *But* Mr. Orme is a highly *intelligent* man....You must ask yourselves whether a *reasonable* man could believe that Mr. Moon is in fact the Messiah....Is he a dupe?....Or is he a *fraud*? (emphasis added).[39]

The Court of Appeal did say that this statement improperly invited the jury to test the quality of the plaintiff's beliefs by their reasonableness, but this was, in the opinion of the Appeal judges, a "minor deviation from relevancy (that) was not likely to have confused the jury."[40]

I do not wish to suggest that the rights of the new religions are undefended in "high places"; they are. For example, in a debate in the House of Lords on 11th July 1984, when Baroness Elliot of Harwood asked: "Do the Government realise the pernicious and wicked influence which these cults have on children and young adults in the breaking up of family life, and the sexual abuse that follows in some cults?" and Lord Denning further asked: "Is the noble Lord the Minister aware that the pernicious activities of these cults have been exposed in the courts of law from time to time and have been proved to the satisfaction of juries, especially in the Moonies case?" and Baroness Macleod of Borve spoke of "psychologically based techniques which soften the mind and very often the brain...'mental mugging' and 'assassination of the free will'," Lord Elton (the Parliamentary Under-Secretary of State, Home Office) replied:

> ... I can only say that (in the case of) people who willingly accept (leaders of the sects) or invite them then that is a matter between the individuals and the organisation in which the state cannot interfere....I believe that to argue theology in the courts with success has not been done properly since the Reformation.

202

To which Lord McNair added the question:

> My Lords, would the noble Lord the Minister not agree that there is in the House at the moment an unpleasant smell of a witch-hunt? Would he not agree that one man's cult may be another man's therapy, and that it is grossly unfair to condemn as a cult everything other than the established Church?

******

The thrust of this paper has been that both Church and State, as institutions, in their relationship to the new religions, have, by the standards of history and, indeed, other parts of western Europe,[41] been protective of the rights of new religions. Individuals who occupy positions of authority within the institutions of Church and State have, however, displayed, on occasion, a lack of insight into the problems and challenges of a pluralistic society that are underlined by the existence of the First Amendment of the Constitution of the United States of America. This does not mean that the new religions fare worse in modern Britain than they do in North America. But it does mean that the rhetoric with which they may be attacked is, sometimes, more epistemologically naïve than it is on the other side of the Atlantic.

Post Script

Both Church and state have recently become involved in a further development *vis-à-vis* the new religions in Britain.

After more than ten years' observation of "the cult scene," I found myself becoming increasingly concerned that parents often had difficulty in obtaining accurate information or help when their offspring joined a new religious movement - and that politicians and clergy were frequently beseiged with requests to "do something," yet had difficulty in knowing quite what it was that they were meant to be doing something about. Shortly after writing this paper, I approached several prominent members of the mainline churches and asked whether they felt that there was a need for a network that would be able to provide accurate information about the "cults," and whether they would be interested in contributing to a complementary network of informed people who would be prepared to help those who were experiencing problems that were related, in one way or another, to the new religions. The response was overwhelmingly positive. The Archbishop of Canterbury was particularly supportive and, along with the Moderator of the Free Church Federal Council, a Roman Catholic Bishop and Sir Ralf Dahrendorf, agreed to be a patron. After considerable consultation with an ad hoc working party, I presented a detailed proposal to the Home Office, and it was agreed that the government would provide £120,000 as set-up costs for the first three years. Further resources have come from the mainline Churches.

INFORM (Information Network Focus on Religious Movements) officially came into being in 1988; and within a few months it had responded to well over a hundred requests for information and help.

The establishment of INFORM has not been received without vocal criticism from existing "anti-cult" groups. Apart from indignation that INFORM received the support from the Home Office and the Churches that they believe ought to have been given to them a long time ago, the suspicion is voiced that INFORM condones the new religions because it condemns deprogramming and/or because it believes that, where possible, contact should be made with the movements. INFORM does indeed condemn deprogramming on moral, legal and purely practical grounds as it believes that there is plenty of evidence to show that the practice frequently makes the situation much worse than it was before. It is also true that INFORM believes that, wherever possible, contact should be made with the movements both because they can provide important (but by no means the only) sources of information, and because, in the experience of the network, it is apparent that dialogue *can* help to ameliorate some problems.

But it is also the case that INFORM is committed to a non-sectarian stance. From the beginning, it has always been clear that no money would be accepted from any of the new religions and that none of their number would be represented on the Board of Governors. It has, furthermore, when it has felt such action to be warranted, taken a strong line against some of the movements. The policy position articulated by INFORM includes the statement that all individuals have the right to believe whatever their conscience dictates, but that people do not have the indiscriminate right to perform actions (even when these arise out of their beliefs) if such actions are against the law of the land or (which is, of course, much more difficult to define) against the common good.

INFORM certainly cannot claim to represent either a Church or a government position on the new religions, but it is, perhaps, worth recording the footnote that both these institutions would seem, by their support of INFORM, to endorse a more moderate stance than that promoted by some of the groups that are virulently opposed to the new religions and their place in modern British society.[42]

REFERENCES

[1]I would like to thank both the Social Science Research Council of Great Britain and the Nuffield Foundation for the grants which enabled the research from which this paper is drawn. The disproportionate use of examples concerning the Unification Church is due to the fact that both Church and State have displayed a disproportionate interest in this particular new religion.

[2]Subhananda das, *Please Don't Lump Us In: A Request to the Media*, Los Angeles: International Society for Krishna Consciousness, 1978.

[3]*The Times*, 10 July 1978.

[4]*The Times*, 10 February 1978.

[5]After its editor had read two articles that I had written for another Catholic publication (*The Clergy Review*), I was commissioned by the Catholic Truth Society to write a pamphlet for them on the Unification Church. The manuscript for the pamphlet caused quite a *furore* because it was merely factual and had not contained an outright condemnation of the movement. I was informed that, at the heated committee meeting in which it was decided not to publish the pamphlet, it had been admitted that I had been objective in my approach but it had been objected that "we (the CTS) are not in the business of being objective."

[6]The Inter-Varsity Press, the publishing division of the Universities and Christian Fellowship, a student movement linking Christian Unions in universities and colleges throughout Britain, published, in 1980, a short book entitled *The Rising of the Moon* by John Allen, National Training Director for British Youth for Christ, in which Unification theology is critically examined in the light of a Christian interpretation of the Bible. The IVP also published, in 1981, *The Challenge of the Cults*, by Canon Maurice C. Burrell in which the beliefs and attractions of Moonies, Hare Krishna, Children of God, TM, Scientology, Divine Light Mission and the Worldwide Church of God are described, and Christians are encouraged "to meet each of them with the real good news of Jesus Christ".

[7]In June 1979, the BCC Youth Unit published an informative leaflet on the Unification Church that was distributed in churches throughout the country.

[8]British Council of Churches, Committee for Relations with People of Other Faiths, Secretary's Twentieth Informal Report, Sep-Dec 1985, p. 6. [This secretary, the Reverend Kenneth Cracknell (a Methodist minister), has since resigned in order to take up another post, but his successor, the Reverend Clinton Bennett (a Baptist minister), has confirmed the tradition of dialogue with the movements.]

[9]Rodney Stark, (ed.), *Religious Movements: Genesis, Exodus and Numbers*, Barrytown, NY: Unification Theological Seminary, 1985.

[10]Elisabeth Derrett, "Sekai Kyusei Kyo: A Japanese New Religion in Britain," in *Religion Today* 2/3, pp. 12-13.

[11]Peter Brierley, (ed.), *UK Christian Handbook: 1983 Edition*, Evangelical Alliance, Bible Society, Marc Europe, London: 1982, provides the best available source of religious statistics in Britain.

[12]Of course, if one were to look for *The Invisible Religion* posited by Thomas Luckmann (Macmillan, New York, 1967), it might, almost by definition, appear that there was as much religiosity about now as there ever had been.

[13]See, for example, Bryan Wilson, *Religion in Sociological Perspective*, Oxford University Press, 1982.

[14]See Eileen Barker, *The Making of a Moonie: Brainwashing or Choice?*, Oxford: Blackwell, 1984, for some responses by a *non-Moonie* control group to questions about the mainline Churches.

[15]See Eileen Barker, "The British Right to Discriminate," *Society*, Vol. 21, No. 4 (also in Thomas Robbins and Roland Robertson, (eds.), *Church-State Relations: Tensions and Transitions*, New Brunswick Transaction: 1986) for an elaboration of this point.

[16]*The Times* Law Report, 25 March 1983.

[17]Kenneth Robinson, Minister of Health, in the House of Commons, 25 July 1968.

[18]*Enquiry into the Practice and Effects of Scientology: Report by Sir John G. Foster, K. B. E., Q. C., M. P.*, 21 December 1971.

[19]See Paul O'Higgins, *Cases and Materials on Civil Liberties*, Oxford: Sweet and Maxwell, 1980, pp. 134-147 for details.

[20]*The Sunday Times*, 13 July 1980.

[21]J. D. Peterkin, Appeal No. TH/31554-7/1978, p. 5.

[22]Speech by Mr. Paul B. Rose, M.P., House of Commons, 22 October 1975.

[23]Earlier that year (in April 1975), however, Rose had made some remarks to the press (that were published) in which he alleged that the Unification Church "brainwashed young people, promoted sexual promiscuity, exploited its converts and deceived the public." The Moonies brought an action that resulted in Rose's public acceptance that the allegations were untrue, with an apology in open court.

[24]In October, 1983, the Church of Scientology (referred to as the Church of the New Faith) did, however, succeed in convincing the High Court in Australia, in a case filed against the Commissioner for Payroll tax, that it did qualify as a religion and that, consequently, the Church's assessment to payroll tax was to be reduced to nil.

[25]The Supreme Court of Judicature, Court of Appeal, Civil Division in the matter of an Application by Michael Segerdal and the Church of Scientology of California for leave to apply for an order of Mandamus; and in the matter of the Refusal by the Registrar General to register the Chapel at Saint Hill Manor, East Grinstead, Sussex, under the Places of Worship Registration Act, 1855, 7 July 1970.

[26]Mr Paul B. Rose, M.P., in the House of Commons, 23 February 1977.

[27]Dr. Shirley Summerskill, *ibid.*

[28]New York State Court of Appeals in *The Matter of the Holy Spirit Association for the Unification of World Christianity v. The Tax Commission of the City of New York*, 55 NY 2d 512 (1982).

[29]United States District Court of Columbia in *Unification Church v. Immigration and Naturalization Service*, 547 F Supp 623 (Dec 1982).

[30]See Bryan Wilson, "A Sect at Law," *Encounter*, vol. LX, no.1, January 1983.

[31]*New Law Journal*, 18 March 1983, pp. 241-242; *The Law Magazine*, 18 March 1988, pp. 16-18.

[32]European Parliament Working Documents 1982-1983, 9 March 1982, Document 1-2/82.

[33]European Parliament, 22 May 1984, PE 90.562.

[34]London Borough of Hammersmith and Fulham, document stating "The Reasons for the Council's Intention to Refuse an Application made by Mrs Ruth Jacobsen on 11th September 1980 for the Registration of 101 Erconwald Street, W.12. under the provisions of the Nurseries and Child Minders Regulations Act 1948 as amended by the Health Services and Public Health Act 1968," November 1981.

[35]See Thomas Robbins, "New Religious Movements, Brainwashing, and Deprogramming - the View from the Law Journals," *Religious Studies Review*, vol. 11, no. 4, October 1985:361-370 for a review essay and survey of the situation in the United States.

[36]*New York University Review of Law and Social Change*, vol. IX, no. 1, 1979/80, p. 124.

208

[37]Lord Justice May, High Court Decision, 28 April 1982.

[38]An account of Nicky Raine's deprogramming experience appears in *New Tomorrow* no. 46, February 1983.

[39]Transcript of the official tape recording of Summing-Up given in the High Court of Justice, Queen's Bench Division by Mr. Justice Comyn in the case of *Orme v. Associated Newspapers Group Ltd.*, 30 March 1981, p. 232.

[40]Official Transcript of shorthand notes in the Court of Appeal, Royal Courts of Justice in the case of *Orme v. Associated Newspapers Group Ltd.*, Judgement delivered by Lord Justice Lawton, 20 December 1982 p. 30. See Eileen Barker *The Making of a Moonie: Brainwashing or Choice?* Blackwell: Oxford, 1984 for a critical account of the evidence concerning brainwashing which was presented in the *Daily Mail* case.

[41]See James Beckford, *Cult Controversies: The Societal Response to the New Religious Movements*, London, Tavistock: 1985 for a comparative discussion about "cult problems in France and West Germany."

[42]For further information about the network, write to INFORM, 10 Portugal Street, London WC2A 2HD. See also *New Religious Movements: A Practical Introduction* HMSO: Norwich, 1989, Appendix I.

CHAPTER XII

JUDAISM IN MODERN BRITAIN: A NEW ORIENTATION

DAN COHN-SHERBOK

The structure of the Anglo-Jewish community was laid over a hundred years ago: most of the institutions had their beginnings by 1880 before Jewish immigrants vastly increased the size of the Jewish population in the United Kingdom. Today these organizations have grown, and others have been added to their ranks. Yet despite the vitality of modern Jewish life, the official organs of Anglo-Jewry are almost exclusively preoccupied with Jewish concerns - religious life, Jewish welfare, Zionism, Soviet Jewry, etc. Only rarely does the community address itself to issues which relate to society as a whole. Such a parochial attitude is regrettable since from Biblical times the Jewish people have had a universal mission; as a light to the nations, it was Israel's aim to serve all the people. The purpose of this article is to redress this balance by sketching a Jewish theology of social concern for the British Jewish community; there is an enormous contribution that Anglo-Jewry could make to ameliorating the present-day ills that afflict the community at large.

I

Anglo-Jewry Today

Prior to 1880, the Jews of the United Kingdom were divided into two major groups: Sephardic Jews of Spanish and Portuguese origin and Ashkenazi Jews of Eastern European background. After 1880 the demographic makeup of the community underwent a major transformation due to a great influx of immigrants: between 1880 and 1920 the Jewish population rose from 60,000 to 300,000. Yet despite this dramatic growth, the institutions of British Jewry remained essentially the same as before - the Board of Deputies served as the secular organization of the community; the chief Rabbinate constituted the official voice of Jewry on religious matters; and the Jewish Board of Guardians looked after the needs of recent immigrants and the Jewish poor. To these bodies were added, at the end of the century, numerous Zionist organizations as Britain became the centre of Zionist activity. Before and during the Second World War a second wave of immigrants from Germany, Austria, Czechoslovakia and Hungary, further swelled the ranks of Anglo-Jewry so that there are now about 450,000 Jews in the United Kingdom acattered among over 100 towns and cities (of which the largest are Greater London, Manchester, Leeds, Glasgow and Liverpool.)[1]

Despite this growth in population over the last hundred years, the Jewish organizations of Great Britain have not dramatically altered. As in the past, the Board of Deputies remains the largest representative body of Anglo-Jewry. Within the Board there are representatives from all branches of the Jewish faith (United Synagogue, Independent, Federation, Sephardic, Reform and Liberal) as well as welfare organizations, political Zionist groups, student bodies, and Provincial Representative Councils. These deputies are elected at Annual General Meetings of their organizations. The Board of Deputies meets once a month to receive reports from its committees. The Executive Committee is the most important of these, consisting of the President, Two Vice-Presidents, Treasurer, Appeals Treasurer as well as the Chairmen of the committees and eight other elected members. Office-holders are elected for three years but are eligible for another three year term.

The other committees of the Board cover all aspects of Jewish concern. Regarding religious matters the Board must seek the advice of Orthodox ecclesiastical authorities. To carry out its work, the Board has a Press and Public Relations Officer and a Statistical and Demographic Unit. Yet, although the Board acts as an executive body on behalf of the community, its powers are limited: it has no legislative or mandatory powers.

Recently, as a result of the findings of an investigative committee, the Board has undergone a number of modifications (including suggestions that the number of committees should be kept to a minimum, that clear terms of reference for committees be obtained, and that the standing orders should be improved). But, as some critics have remarked, more changes are needed if the Board is to continue to be an effective force in contemporary society. In particular, it has been stressed that more young people, women, academics, and intellectuals should participate in the Board's work.[2]

Turning to religious organization, approximately 80% of the affiliated Jewish community belong to one or other of the Orthodox groupings.[3] The largest of these is the United Synagogue which was established by an Act of Parliament in 1870. Today this body constitutes the Anglo-Jewish religious establishment and represents Jewry to the outside world. It maintains the Chief Rabbinate and is affiliated with Jews College (the training seminary for Orthodox rabbis and cantors). Through the London Board of Religious Education, it controls most part-time religious education and provides chaplaincies to hospitals, prisons, the military and universities. In 1976, the structure of the United Synagogue was reorganized - all member synagogues now have equal status. Though all the synagogues contribute most of their membership dues to a Central office, each synagogue has its own welfare, cultural, burial, and education committees which are financed centrally. The head of this structure is the Chief Rabbi who presides over the London Beth Din (the major rabbinical court in the country). The Chief Rabbi is appointed by the Chief Rabbinate Council which consists primarily of Representatives of the United Synagogue, of most provincial orthodox congregations, and even representatives from Australia and New Zealand. By virtue of this position, the Chief Rabbi functions as the religious head of Jewry in Britain - he is the main representative and public figure.

In addition to the United Synagogue grouping, there are several other Orthodox institutions. The Federation of Synagogues, founded in 1887, is composed of small congregations with its own religious leader (Rosh Rabbi), as well as its own Beth Din. The Union of Hebrew Congregations was founded in 1926 and consists of a large number of London-based small congregations composed of Orthodox Jews from Central and Eastern

Europe, including several Chassidic groups who follow their respective Rebbes (spiritual leaders). Other members of the Union are found in provincial areas with ultra-orthodox communities. Another wing of Orthodox Judaism is the Sephardic community with Synagogues scattered throughout London and Manchester.

The Progressive section of British Jewry comprises the remaining 20% of the affiliated population, and is divided into Reform and Liberal Judaism. The Reform movement began in Britain in the middle of the nineteenth-century and expanded during the second wave of Jewish immigration in the early part of this century. The Federation of Reform Synagogues - the Reform Synagogues of Great Britain - was established in 1942 and there are now over 30 adherent congregations. Each synagogue is autonomous, though a Reform Beth Din deals with halachic matters related to personal status. Liberal Judaism is ideologically more radical than Reform despite strong similarities between both movements. There are now over 20 synagogues which belong to the central body of Liberal Judaism - the Union of Liberal and Progressive Synagogues - over which a communal Rabbinical Board makes decisions in matters of personal status. Both movements train their rabbis at the Leo Baeck College in London located at the Sternberg Centre (which also houses the offices of the Reform movement).

Though each synagogue has its own welfare committee, there are various comprehensive voluntary agencies which deal with different types of disabilities. The largest welfare organization is the Jewish Welfare Board for London and the South East, together with the Provincial Welfare Boards, the Jewish Blind Society, and the Norwood Homes. The Welfare Boards are largely for the elderly poor, disabled and long-term sick as well as problem families and one parent families; the Blind Society is for the blind and partially sighted; and the Norwood Homes are for the orphans and other children who require day or residential care. In addition, there are other bodies providing various types of welfare service: Food for the Jewish Poor, the Jewish After-Care Association (for discharged prisoners), the Jewish Deaf Association, Nightingale House (for aged Jews), the Jews Temporary Shelter (for immigrants), the Ravenswood Foundation and the Jewish Home and Hospital at Tottenham (for the mentally and physically disabled), the

Central British Fund (for refugees), and Chevrat Bikur Cholim (for home nursing care).

Added to these welfare bodies are a number of their important communal organizations with varied objectives. B'nai Brith began in New York in the middle of the nineteenth century to provide Jewish unity and help Jews in need; today it is concerned with Israel, Soviet Jewry, and the struggle against anti-semitism. The branch in Great Britain is divided into 40 adult and youth lodges and is instrumental in establishing Hillel centres for university students. AJEX - the Association of Jewish ex-Servicemen and Women - is an ex-service group which developed from the Jewish ex-servicemen's league founded in the 1930's. Recently, concern for Soviet Jewry has been expressed by the Women's Campaign for Soviet Jewry which plans demonstrations and activities in reaction to events in the Soviet Union. There are now about 18 sub-groups which plan local functions and adopt prisoners of conscience and the families of "refuseniks." Allied with this organization is the National Council for Soviet Jewry, founded in 1976 to bring together all groups concerned with anti-semitism in the Soviet Union. More than 120 organizations are now affiliated woth the Council. The Anti-Boycott Co-ordinating Committee monitors the Arab trade boycott against Israel and prepares cases on which to base publicity and submissions to the government. The Britain/Israel Public Affairs Committee was founded in 1976 to improve the public image of Israel. This committee consists of full-time workers in the Zionist field as well as experienced professional public relations executives whose purpose is to issue literature designed to present Israel as a thriving democracy flourishing in the Middle East. In 1978 the Group Relations Educational Trust was established by individuals concerned about race relations in Britain as they affect the Jewish community. The aim of the Trust is to initiate and fund research projects and activities in the broad general field of community relations. As far as international organizations are concerned, the Institute of Jewish Affairs - affiliated with the World Jewish Congress - collects, evaluates and disseminates information of current Jewish interest. This body also arranges lectures, seminars and symposia for Jewish academics.

The final area of Jewish activity in the United Kingdom relates to Zionism. The prinicipal Zionist body is the Zionist Federation of Great Britain and Ireland; established in 1898, it now has over 600 affiliated groups and organizations. Its projects are sponsored by numerous committees: Organization, Day Schools, Public Relations, Fund-raising, Youth, Soviet Jewry, Jews in Arab Lands, Finance, etc. The Zionist Federation also runs a synagogue council which provides speakers and helps organize functions in synagogues. The Zionist Federation is a constituent member of the World Zionist Organization as well as an affiliate of the World Confederation of United Zionists. Another important Zionist group is the Mizrachi Federation which bases its Zionism on the fundamental priniciples of traditional Judaism. It envisages Israel as the spiritual centre for world Jewry and believes that only Judaism can be the common unifying link between Jewish communities throughout the world. The largest women's Zionist group is the Federation of Women Zionists of Great Britain and Ireland which raises funds for welfare projects in Israel and educational programs for Jewish women in Britain. Pioneer Women is also a significant Zionist group which supports campaigns in Israel to improve the status of women. Other important Zionist groups are the World Zionist Organization which is concerned with ideological aspects of immigration to Israel as well as educational and organizational activities in the Diaspora, and the Jewish Agency deals with the reception, settlement and absorption of new immigrants to Israel. As far as fund-raising is concerned, the Joint Israel Appeal is the central body responsible for financial revenue, and the Jewish National Fund is mainly interested in land development, reclamation and new settlements in Israel.

II

A Theological Framework for Social Concern

From this brief survey of Jewish life in modern Britain, it is clear that the community has been preoccupied with Jewish concerns. What is missing from this impressive catalogue of activities is an expression of commitment to the welfare of all those who live in the United Kingdom - Jews and non-Jews alike. Such humanitarian concern for mankind is an essential element of Jewish theology and has been at the heart of Jewish thought from Biblical times to the present day. Throughout history Jews have steadfastly adhered to the belief that God is a supreme ruler who calls all human beings to join Him in bringing about the Kingdom of God on earth. This understanding is a central aspect of Psalmist theology, and it is a basic motif of Scripture. In later rabbinic literature, this vision of man's role in bringing about God's Kingdom is elaborated further. According to the rabbis, the Kingdom of God takes place in this world; it is established by man's obedience to the Divine will. The Kingdom of God consists in a complete moral order on earth - the reign of trust, righteousness and holiness among all men and nations. The fulfillment of this conception ultimately rests with the coming of the Messiah; nevertheless, it is man's duty to participate in the creation of a better world in anticipation of the Messianic redemption.[4]

For the rabbis, man is at the centre of creation for it is only he among all created beings who can, through righteousness, make the Kingdom glorious.[5] In rabbinic midrash, the view is expressed that God's Kingship did not come into operation until man was created: "when the Holy One, blessed be He, consulted the Torah as to the creation of the world, he answered, 'Master of the world, if there be no host, over whom will the King reign, and if there be no peoples praising Him where is the glory of the King?'".[6] It is only man, then, who can make the Kingdom glorious; God wants to reign over free agents who can act as his co-partners in perfecting the world. What God requires is obedience to his ways of righteousness and justice: "you are my lovers and friends." "You walk in my ways," God declares to Israel. "As the Omnipotent is merciful and gracious, long-suffering and abundant in goodness so be ye ... feeding the hungry, giving drink to the thirsty, clothing the naked, ransoming the captives, and marrying the orphans."[7]

Throughout Biblical and rabbinic literature, Jews were encouraged to strive for the highest conception of life in which the rule of truth, righteousness and holiness would be established among mankind. Such a desire is the eternal hope of God's people - a longing for God's Kingdom as expressed in the daily liturgy of the Synagogue. For Jews, the coming of the Kingdom in which God's heavenly rule will be made manifest is a process in which all human beings have a role. It involves the struggle for the reign of justice and righteousness on earth. The Kingdom is not an internalized, spiritualized, other-worldly conception; rather it involves human activity in an historical context. Drawing on Scripture, the rabbis elaborated the teaching of the Torah about man's partnership with God in bringing God's rule. For Jews the moral life is at the centre of the unfolding of God's plan for humanity.

In presenting this message of human redemption, the Exodus experience was paradigmatic of God's power on earth. In the Biblical period, details of the Exodus were recorded in cultic sayings, in Wisdom literature, and in prophetic pronouncements - after the Exile the Exodus continued to play a fundamental role in the Jewish faith. In particular, the Festival of Passover was regarded throughout the history of the nation as crucially important in Jewish sub-consciousness. As L. Finkelstein remarks:

> The Passover celebration commemorates an event which will probably symbolize for all time the essential meaning of freedom, namely freedom devoted to a purpose. When Israel came forth from bondage, it was not simply to enjoy liberty, but to make of liberty an instrument of service ... the Israelites alone made the moment of their origin as a people one of permanent self-dedication to the principle of universal freedom as the essential prerequisite for spiritual growth. Hence the event has meaning for all living peoples.[8]

In post-Enlightenment Judaism, modern Jewish writers have emphasized the significance of the themes of liberty, redemption, and freedom as found in the Passover festival. The Jewish philosopher Franz Rosenzweig, for example, argued that there is an intrinsic connection between the Passover and the Sabbath. The Sabbath, he maintained, is a reminder of the Exodus from Egypt:

> The freedom of the man-servant and the maid-servant which it proclaims is conditioned by the deliverance of the people from the servitude of Egypt. And in every command to respect the freedom of even the man-servant, or even the alien among the people, the law of God renews the awareness of the connection holding between the freedom within the people, a freedom decreed by God, and the freeing of the people from Egyptian servitude, a liberation enacted by God.[9]

Furthermore, the Passover meal is a symbol of Israel's vocation as a people; the deliverance of the nation affords a glimpse of its destiny. It is not only today that enemies rise up against the Jews, they have arisen in every generation, and God has always taken the side of his chosen people. All this points to the ultimate redemption as prophesied by Isaiah - of the day when the wolf shall dwell with the lamb and the world shall be as full of the knowledge of the Lord as the sea is of water.[10]

The moral implications of the redemption from Egypt are emphasized in *The Ethics of Judaism* by the German Jewish scholar Moritz Lazarus. The Exodus, he writes, has a predominant place in the Biblical and rabbinic cycle of religious ideas. The most exulted moral statutes in the Torah concerning the treatment of strangers are connected with the Exodus, and are, from a psychological point of view, impressively inculcated by means of the injunction: "Ye know the heart of the stranger." The prophets and the psalmists employ this event to illustrate God's providence and grace, and the rabbis deduce from it two fundamental aspects of Jewish ethics: the notion of liberty and man's ethical task. Throughout the history of Judaism, Lazarus writes, "the notion of liberty, inner moral and spiritual liberty, cherished as a pure, exalted ideal, possible only under the Law and through the Law, was associated with the memory of the redemption from Egyptian slavery, and this memory in turn was connected with symbolic practices accompanying every act, pleasure, and celebration."[11]

Kaufman Kohler saw in the Passover a symbol of thanksgiving and hope which sustained the Jewish nation in their tribulations: "The Passover festival with its 'night of divine watching' endowed the Jew ever anew with endurance during the dark night of medieval tyranny and with faith in 'the Keeper of Israel who slumbereth not nor sleepeth'." Moreover, he believed that the feast of redemption promises a day of liberty to those who continue to struggle under oppression and exploitation: "The modern Jew is beginning to see in the reawakening of his religious and social life in Western lands the token of the future liberation of all mankind. The Passover feast brings him the clear and hopeful message of freedom for humanity from all bondage of today and of spirit."[12]

In his *Creed and Life* the English Jewish theologian, Morris Joseph, focuses on the contemporary significance of Passover. It is, he believes, the greatest of all the historical festivals in that it brings the Jew into close

218

contact with the past. No other festival, he contends, so powerfully appeals to historical sympathies. At the Passover ceremony the Jew is at one with his redeemed ancestors; he shares with them the consciousness of their freedom, their sense of nationality that is begining to stir in their hearts. "He shares," he writes, "their glowing hopes, the sweet joy of newly recovered manhood," Through God's redemption the Israelites were able to free themselves from despair, and they share in this deliverance. "We march forth," he states, "with them from the scenes of oppression in gladness and gratitude." The ideal of the rabbis fulfills itself. "In every generation it is for the Jew to think that he himself went forth from Egypt" (Pesahim 10:5).[13]

Ahad Ha-Am, essayist and philosopher, concentrates on Moses the Liberator as an ideal type of hero. Moses, he points out, was neither a warrior nor statesman. Instead he was a prophet who put justice into action. Confronted by acts of iniquity, he took the side of the victim - the early events of his life in which he struggled against injustice served as a prelude to his revolt against Egyptian oppression:

> That great moment dawned in the wilderness, far from the turmoil of life. The prophet's soul is weary of the endless struggle, and longs for peace and rest. He seeks the solitude of the shepherd's life, goes into the wilderness with his sheep, and reaches Horeb, the mountain of the Lord. But even here he finds no rest. He feels in his innermost being that he has not yet fulfilled his mission....Suddenly the prophet hears the voice of the Lord - the voice he knows so well - calling to him from some forgotten corner of his innermost being: I am the God of thy father....I have surely seen the affliction of My people that are in Egypt....Come now, therefore, and I will send thee unto Pharaoh, that thou mayest bring forth My people the children of Israel out of Egypt.[14]

In the account of the Exodus from Egypt, therefore, the faith of Israel is portrayed as a response to God's will. What is required of Israel is obedient participation in the act of liberation. For Jews this emphasis on the concrete dimension of faith is vital. The Jewish hope lies in God's rule on earth - this is the goal of the history of the world in which the Jewish people have a central role. Throughout the Bible and in rabbinic literature ethical behaviour is the predominant theme - by doing God's will the Jew can help to complete His work of creation. These themes of liberation thus provide a theological framework for social action. The Biblical narrative portrays the

Ancient Israelites as an oppressed nation redeemed by God. From the earliest times, the Jewish people have been God's suffering servant - despised and rejected of men, smitten and afflicted. Through such suffering Jews are able to gain a sympathetic awareness of the situation of others. The lesson of the Passover is at the heart of Jewish aspirations for all; in this way the message of the Passover liturgy constitutes a basis for community service in the modern world:

> May He who broke the Pharaoh's yoke for ever shatter all fetters of oppression and hasten the day when swords shall, at last, be broken and wars ended. Soon may He cause the glad tidings of redemption to be heard in all the lands so that mankind - freed from violence and from wrong, and united in an eternal covenant of brotherhood - may celebrate the universal Passover in the name of our God of freedom.

III

Spheres of Action

In the light of this religious context, Anglo-Jewry should feel impelled to add to its impressive list of activities a compassionate concern for all those who suffer in contemporary society. Having once laboured under the Egyptian yoke as slaves of Pharaoh, Jews today can sympathize with the plight of all under-privileged sectors of the community. This struggle for the emancipation of all those who are enslaved calls for the elaboration of a contemporary Jewish theology of social concern. In the account of the Exodus from Egypt, the faith of Israel is portrayed as a response to God's will. What is required of Israel is obedient participation in the act of emancipation. For a modern Jewish theology of social concern, this Biblical anchorage should led to a practical orientation of the faith in which praxis rather than theological reflection, is understood as the key dimension of the faith.

Within such a context, the poor can serve as the starting point for theological reflection - the view "from below" is essential. In Scripture God is the saviour of the enslaved; what is required of Anglo-Jewry is solidarity as a protest against the situation in which the poor today are forced to live. Such poverty is something to be fought against and destroyed. The problems and struggles of the poor thus become that of the Jewish people's - the vocation of all Jews is to opt for human love and compassion. Having endured persecution and suffering for millennia, the Jewish people should find this message of solidarity with the poor of great significance. Scripture speaks of positive action to prevent poverty from becoming widespread - in Leviticus and Deuteronomy there is detailed legislation designed to prevent the accumulation of wealth and the consequent exploitation of the unfortunate. Following this tradition, the prophets condemned every kind of abuse. Jews should thus feel an obligation to take every step to eradicate poverty and suffering from British society. In particular they should address themselves to the economic deprivation that affects various groups: the young who are frustrated by the lack of opportunity to obtain training and work; labourers who are frequently ill-paid and find difficulty in defending their rights; the unemployed who are discarded because of the harsh exigencies of economic life, and the old who are often marginalized and disregarded. In all such cases, the Jewish people - who have consistently endured hardship - should feel drawn to the downtrodden of modern society, sharing their distress.

In the United Kingdom as in other western countries, there are grave inequalities between the rich and the poor. Despite the higher general standard of living in Britain as compared with Third World Countries, there nevertheless exists for many sub-standard living conditions, poor health, concern about jobs, and constant worry about money. There are essentially two different segments in the labour market: primary sector jobs involving high wages, good working conditions, employment stability and job security, and secondary sector jobs involving low wages, poor working conditions, harsh and arbitrary discipline and little opportunity for advancement. By putting themselves in the shoes of the disadvantaged, Jews can envisage what life must be for those who are underprivileged. In this way the Anglo-Jewish community can bring to society policies of caring and sharing; this is theology "from below" from the standpoint of those who are neglected and marginalized. By bringing their past suffering to bear on these problems, the Jewish people can make a major contribution to the redemption of the poor in today's world.

In connection with this discussion of poverty, a Jewish theology of social concern should focus on life in the inner-city. Here the distinction between the powerful and the powerless is most clearly evident (as has been recently illustrated by the Report of the Archbishop of Canterbury's Commission on Urban Priority Areas, *Faith in the City*). In the cities - as opposed to the suburbs - are to be found the unemployed, families unable to cope, single-parent families, people on part-time jobs, individuals on welfare. In the city, inhabitants are divorced from the powerful forces that shape their lives: the inner-city is the place of failure and hopelessness. The graphic social divide between the rich and the poor is an everyday reality for those who live in large metropolitan centres. All too often the poverty of the inner city is the converse side of middle-class Jewish suburban life. In the elaborate hierarchy of wealth and esteem, the situation of the poor is an integral part - the existence of rich suburbs is linked to the presence of ghettos and marginal sectors.

What is needed to remedy this situation is a new Jewish consciousness, an awareness of the calamities of inner-city deprivation. By ministering to those at the bottom of society, Jews would be able to affirm through their efforts that God is concerned now - as He was in Jewish history - with the plight of those facing adversity. In pursuit of this goal, Jews should be able to embark on a task of reconstruction and restoration. Remembering their sojourn in the land of Egypt, they can identify with the impoverished; by going into the city, Jews could work alongside and for the betterment of the poor. The facts of the inner city demand such commitment to change; through urban mission Jews can affirm that hope for the modern world lies in a sympathetic response and dedication to the weak. Beginning at the bottom, it is possible to work for the creation of a community in which all people are able to regain their sense of pride and self-fulfillment.

As is frequently noted, a lack of jobs is particularly evident in the destitute parts of the inner city. Such unemployment continues to be an ever-increasing problem, and it is to this deprived group that Jews should draw attention. Jewry must labour on behalf of those who cannot find work or are dismissed because of the harsh exigencies of the present economic climate. Such individuals face particular difficulties in coping with their misfortunes.

222

With no jobs, the unemployed do not know what to do with their time, and as a consequence, they are unfulfilled in the essential areas of basic human needs - for human relationships, for financial income, for social status and identity, for satisfaction and fulfilment. Helping those with such difficulties should be a high priority within the Jewish community: ways must be sought for creating new work opportunities; labour not traditionally regarded as paid work must be accepted as valid and necessary; new manufacturing enterprises which stimulate the job market should be encouraged; apprenticeship for the young needs to be reintroduced; jobs need to be spread more through job sharing and part-time work; education must be seen as a preparation for life; voluntary activity should be stimulated and seen as a legitimate means of helping those in need. In the quest to alleviate distress and disillusionment, the numerous welfare organizations which presently exist in the Jewish community could make substantial contributions to those on the bottom of the social scale.

These, thus, are a few of the areas in which the Jews in the United Kingdom could attempt to bring about a transformation of society. In pursuit of the goal of freedom from oppression - a hallowed theme running through the Jewish tradition - committed Jews can become a saving remnant in the modern world, embodying the liberation message of the faith. Like Abraham, they can hope against hope in labouring to build a more just and humane world. Echoing the words of the Christian liberationist, Helda Camara, they can become an Abrahamic minority, attentive to the cry of oppression: "We are told," he writes,

> that Abraham and other patriarchs heard the voice of God. Can we also hear the Lord's call? We live in a world where millions of our fellow men live in inhuman conditions, practically in slavery. If we are not deaf we hear the cries of the oppressed. Their cries are the voice of God. We who live in rich countries where there are always pockets of under-development and wretchedness, hear if we want to hear, the unvoiced demands of those who have no voice and no hope. The pleas of those who have no voice and no hope are the voice of God.[15]

Throughout history the Jewish people have been God's suffering servant, yet inspired by a vision of God's reign on earth they have been able to transcend their own misfortunes in attempt to improve the lot of others. In the contemporary world, where Jews are often comfortable and affluent, this message can too easily be forgotten. As we have seen, a survey of Jewish activities in the United Kingdom reveals that the community has largely concentrated its efforts on its own spiritual and material welfare. Yet the Jewish heritage points to God's Kingdom as the goal and hope of mankind - a world in which all men and nations shall turn away from iniquity and injustice. This is not the hope of bliss in a future life, but the building up of the divine Kingdom on truth and peace among all peoples. As Isaiah declared: "I will also give thee for a light to the nations, that my salvation may be unto the end of the earth."[16] In this mission the Anglo-Jewish community can champion the cause of all the oppressed, afflicted and persecuted, thereby proclaiming the ancient message of the Jewish liturgy in the struggle to create a better society for all:

> O Lord our God, impose Thine awe upon all Thy works, and let Thy dread be upon all Thou hast created, that they may all form one single band to do Thy will with a perfect heart....Our God and God of our fathers, reveal Thyself in Thy splendour as King over all the inhabitants of the world, that every handiwork of Thine may know that Thou hast made it, and every creature may acknowledge that Thou hast created it, and whatsoever hath breath in its nostrils may say: the Lord God of Israel is King, and His dominion ruleth over all.[17]

224

REFERENCES

[1] Jane Moonman, *Anglo-Jewry* (London: Joint Israel Appeal, 1980) for a full analysis of Anglo-Jewry.

[2] *Ibid.*, p. 22.

[3] *Ibid.*, pp. 59-60.

[4] See S. Schechter, *Aspects of Rabbinic Theology* (New York, 1965).

[5] *Agadoth Shir Hashirim*, pp. 16, 61.

[6] Pirke Rabbi Eliezer, Ch. 3.

[7] See S. Schechter, *op. cit.*, p. 93.

[8] L. Finkelstein, *Haggadah of Passover* (New York, 1942).

[9] F. Rosenzweig, *The Star of Redemption*, translated by N. Glatzer in *Franz Rosenzweig: His Life and Thought* (New York, 1953), pp. 319-321.

[10] *Ibid.*

[11] M. Lazarus, *The Ethics of Judaism* (Philadelphia, 1900), pp. 28-29.

[12] K. Kohler, *Jewish Theology* (New York, 1918), p. 462.

[13] M. Joseph, *Judaism as Creed and Life* (London, 1963), pp. 213-215.

[14] Ahad Ha-Am, *Essays, Letters, Memoirs*, edited by L. Simon (Oxford, 1946), pp. 103-108.

[15] H. Camara, *The Desert is Fertile* (New York, 1974), p. 11.

[16] Is. 49.6.

[17] *Singers Prayerbook*, p. 239.

CHAPTER XIII

ISLAMIC COMMUNITIES IN BRITAIN

JORGEN S. NIELSEN

I

The presence of major, Islamic communities in the British Isles in the 1980's is to a large extent the result of a late imperial process, which is common to all of western Europe, including the Federal Republic of Germany and other smaller states.[1] It is, therefore, no coincidence that the migration into Britain of people seeking work should have come from former British colonies. This migration was of an economic nature, and it is only as the migrants became immigrants and settlers, and as their children grew up in Britain, that parts of those communities began to re-establish their Muslim identity in the new circumstances.

The main single group of Muslims in the United Kingdom originates in South Asia. Various surveys have suggested that as many as 40% of this group, consisting of people of Indian, Pakistani, and Bangladeshi origin, may be Muslim.[2] This is particularly the case with those from Pakistan and Bangladesh, at least 95% of whom are likely to be Muslim.

However, this predominantly South Asian image of the Muslim community is comparatively recent. Before the second world war the Muslim presence in Britain was very different. Certainly, there were numbers of students and businessmen from British India who made their mark in

226

London and the major provincial cities before that time. But the majority of
Muslims in the country then were people who had entered the country as
unskilled or semi-skilled workers on British ships, especially Arabs from the
hinterland of Aden. Many of the earliest Muslim groups were to be found
among such Yemeni sailors in the major ports.[3] The imperial connection
accounted for the arrival of further small groups of "colonials" of Muslim
background, when soldiers from India or the African colonies found
themselves in Britain when demobilized in 1945. Then the massive refugee
situation created by partition and independence in India in 1947 contributed
to the first noticeable Pakistani presence in the 1951 census.[4] During the
1950's this presence grew slowly but steadily, and at the same time the
troubles in Cyprus laid the foundations of a Turkish Cypriot dimension. The
core communities which had thus come into existence formed the basis of a
reception network and often also of a "travel agent" network, which came
into its own when the debate over the first Commonwealth Immigration Act
started at the end of the 1950's.[5]

It took about a year and a half to put the 1962 immigration act onto
the statute books, and during this time Pakistani immigration in particular
grew out of all recognition. The gradual restriction on the issue of entry
vouchers following the act, supplemented by another act in 1968 aimed more
specifically at British passport holders in Africa (the Kenyan and later
Ugandan Asians), served to change the nature of immigration drastically. No
longer was there a question of people entering in search of work, although
the door for professional migration remained ajar. Instead, one witnessed a
massive shift to the immigration of dependants - wives and children. In many
ways, the restrictions introduced by Britain in 1962, and their effects, thus
anticipated the similar restrictions imposed a decade later by mainland
European states at the time of the oil crisis. The transfer of, in particular,
Pakistani families commencing during the 1960's meant that the growth of
the community between the 1971 and the 1981 Censuses was mainly of such
dependants. In addition, the result has been that an increasing proportion of
the community has been born in Britain. These factors are quite clear when
one looks at the data of the last four Censuses:

	Total	-	of which UK-born	in %
1951	5,000		-	-
1961[6]	24,900		300	1.2
1971[7]	170,000		40,000	23.5
1981[8]	360,000		135,000	37.5

Using both place of birth and self-defined ethnic group definitions, later surveys suggest not only higher total figures but also a continuing steady growth in the proportion of people of Pakistani or Bangladeshi origin born in the UK.[9]

While the South Asian Muslim communities are the largest and very much dominate the public face of Islam in Britain today, many other Muslim ethnic groups have found their homes in Britain. Taking rough figures from the 1981 Census as a guide, the following table can be suggested:

Pakistanis/Bangladeshis	360,000
Indians	130,000
East Africans	27,000
Malaysians	23,000
Nigerians	15,000
Turks	5,000
Turkish Cypriots	60,000
Arabs	50,000
Iranians	20,000

Statistics are notoriously unreliable and British ethnic statistics especially so, and to attempt to translate them into religious statistics is even more dangerous. But if one takes into account the possibilities of Census underenumeration,[10] population growth, some British converts to Islam, etc. an overall total of somewhere in the region of one million Muslims in Britain in 1986 cannot be too far wrong.

The way in which the community arrived and set roots remains an important element in the development of Islam in Britain. It is clear that the community is neither ethnically integrated nor demographically "normal." The fact that the first phase was one of a search for work means that it is necessarily a young community. The General Household Surveys of 1983

228

and 1985 suggest that about 60% of the Pakistani and Bangladeshi communities are under 45 years old, compared to 35% of the white population.[11]

The kind of work sought has affected the class structure of the community as well as its place in the overall British social context. Thus, if we again take Pakistanis and Bangladeshis as an indicator, they are much more likely to be unskilled, semi-skilled and skilled manual workers than are their white neighbours. They are also more likely to be self-employed, business men or professionals.[12]

Where the work was available has determined the regions in Britain where Muslims have settled. Pakistanis have tended to settle in the West Midlands and West Yorkshire, while Bangladeshis have preferred London.[13] Of course, within these general regions the settlement has been concentrated in often very specific inner city areas of the major industrial conurbations. Similarly, specific factors in the countries of origin have determined that migration has come from very limited regions. The Muslim communities of South Asian origin in Britain are primarily from parts of the west of Punjab, southern areas of Azad Kashmir, the Sylhet area of Bangladesh, and to a lesser extent parts of the Indian Gujarat.[14]

II

Three decades of Muslim immigration into Britain have seen a deep change of perspective among Muslims themselves, although as yet only minimally in the structures of British society. This change is closely related to the movement of social and cultural focus with the family, as it moved from the country of origin to Britain.

At the social level, this transfer of the family is not complete. The traditional extended family has been fragmented. In so far as it exists in Britain it is "horizontally extended." The 1981 Census showed that 40% of Pakistani households contained three or more adults, compared to a national average of 23%.[15] But these extra adults are more likely to be uncles, aunts, brother and sisters, than the grandparents. While the pattern of chain migration has often brought several parts of an extended family to Britain, availability of employment has tended to disperse them around the country. Furthermore, the physical limitations of traditional British domestic architecture, especially in inner-city two-story terraced housing, has tended further to disperse them into several smaller households.

This geographical fragmentation of the traditional family, combined with the fact that the climate has forced it indoors, has had the most serious consequences for the women. Islamic societies have traditionally operated in separate male and female spheres, with the family as the primary area of interaction between the two. The institution of *purdah*, the rules of behaviour and dress which reinforce the separation, was not necessarily a burden in South Asian villages. Women tended to perform their household obligations collectively in the open, and large sections of villages were often, in any case, sufficiently interrelated for *purdah* to have only minimal relevance.

The partial and fragmented transfer of the family and its customary practices to Britain has created a situation in which women have been deprived of their usual context and the support this gave them. British society has given them no alternative support, which they could relate to. Their own men have seldom been able to satisfy their need for support, mainly because they had previously neither had the experience or been faced with the expectation of having to provide such support. *Purdah* has often not only been retained but even strengthened in response to the insecurities and threats perceived in the new surroundings.[16] But when it is not possible to meet female relatives or friends by going out the back door, when everybody in the neighbourhood is a stranger, then *purdah* tends to lose its traditional function of providing security and instead becomes a prison.

However, the ideals of the extended family as a prior focus of loyalty and identity have survived the immediate fragmentation of migration. Many inner-city areas witnessed a quite rapid build-up of residential concentrations of South Asians, and this soon created a situation where the immediate neighbourhood was able to reconstruct some of the institutions which could reinforce traditional ideals. The economic networks, in particular, played a role which has hardly yet been investigated.[17]

It is interesting that while much of what has been noted applies to South Asian communities generally, the Muslim sections of that population show marked differences from the Hindu and the Sikh sections. This may, in part, be because they have arrived later, especially in the case of many Bangladeshis. It may, in part, be because their background is more typically that of the smallholding peasant rather than the more mobile craftsmen and traders more characteristic of the Sikh and Hindu communities. But is also probable that the distinction is due, in part, to the continuing strong factor of Islam itself.

Several sociological surveys have noted differences between Muslim and non-Muslim Asians, when discussing the employment patterns and English fluency of women.[18] Of direct interest to the present point is a survey carried out in 1975 by Muhammad Anwar.[19] He showed that attitudes to female dress are virtually unchanged between Muslim parents and their children, while Sikh and Hindu children are significantly more flexible than their parents. Muslim children were found to be more likely to favour the traditional arranged marriage than their Sikh and Hindu counterparts. Muslim parents and children were a good deal more positive towards continuing parental control.[20]

III

Over the last decade or so, it is evident that the role of Islam in reinforcing such traditional views has gained in importance, and that mosques, and organizations working through mosques, are the focus of this development. In this, as in so many other ways, the 1960's and early 1970's were a turning point. In this regard, Stephen Barton writes in a study of Bengali Muslims in Bradford:

> When they originally migrated most Bengalis suffered an almost total lapse of religious observance; yet migration was not perceived as a threat to their heritage. It was possible to live on the margin of British society, avoiding any deeper involvement than the work necessitated. Gradually a community was formed, based on shared memories, values and goals that were all located in Bangladesh....The migrant lived and worked in Britain on behalf of his family, who, it may be surmised, prayed on his behalf. There was, therefore, at first

231

no need of any replication in Bradford of Bengali Muslim traditions which belonged and thrived elsewhere. Need arose, however, as the Bengali community rapidly grew during the 1960's. Many migrants arrived between 1962 and 1964 and towards the end of the decade the prevention of further temporary migration by the British government prompted the reunion of families here.... As the structure and character of the community thus changed, it became necessary to establish some means of support for its traditions, now located in Bradford.[21]

This process took place at roughly the same time in every part of Britain where Muslims had settled. A direct consequence has been the increasing number of mosques in use. At the end of 1960, there were in England and Wales only nine mosques registered as places of worship, and several of those (e.g. Woking, Liverpool, Regent's Park in London) had been in existence for several decades.[22] Only four more mosques were registered in the following five years, but 1966 saw a jump to what was to become a consistent level of about eight annual registrations. By the end of 1974 there were 83 registered mosques. But then the new oil wealth of several Muslim states created, if not always actual funding, at least the expectation of funding. At the same time, Muslim groups were becoming familiar with the bureaucratic processes of local government. New mosques were now being registered at an annual level of about twenty, in several recent years rising as high as thirty. By the end of 1985 there were 329 registered mosques.[23] A survey of local authorities conducted during 1985 suggests that there are more mosques which have not registered.[24]

While many such mosques are based on local initiatives, very few remain isolated from the wider Muslim community for long. The process of organizing the Muslim community on a national basis is one which is as old as its presence in Britain, but it is also a process which has been complicated by the variety of the community. Earlier organizations were often in some way related to Sufi movements, especially the "Alawiyya" with which the Yemenis tended to be associated.[25] The growth of the Muslim population from South Asia has tended to bring in Sufi orders from that area, especially the Naqshbandiyya, the Qadiriyya, and the Chistiyya, all of which continue to be influential at local levels. By the very nature of their organization and self-conception, relying as they do on informal networks and the presence of charismatic leadership, this aspect of Muslim organization in Britain is in a sense transparent - the outsider can only see it with the greatest of difficulty.

More visible and, in relation to the formal structures of British society, more important is the more recent phenomenon of theological-political movements, whose influence has increased as part of the general political resurgence of Islam in the wider world. In the British context, we are dealing primarily with movements which have arisen in South Asia, many of them in the eighteenth and nineteenth-centuries in direct response to expanding British domination. Foremost among these are the Deobandi and Barelwi movements, whose rivalry has at times contributed to open conflict, with control of individual mosques at stake.[26] Both groups retain strong links with their centres in South Asia. The Deobandis are a pietistic and politically quietist movement, as distinct from the theologically related Wahhabi movement of Saudi Arabia. In Britain they are particularly active in encouraging a return to religion among Muslims and in education. Their high school in Dewsbury, West Yorkshire, has recently achieved full registration as a private school. The Barelwis, with sympathetic links to the Sufi tradition, are particularly strong at the popular level among Punjabis.

In the worldwide context of Islam, the Jamaat-i-Islami, the movement founded and led by Abu'l-A'la Mawdudi until his death in 1980, takes on its own particular significance. The movement is far from being the most popular among Muslims in Britain and is, in fact, deeply mistrusted in some quarters. But it compensates by the quality and effectiveness of its organization and its relative efficiency in making itself known both inside and outside the community. Rather than transfer to Britain the structural models already in existence, it has instead developed separate organizations for specific identified purposes. Thus the Islamic Foundation in Leicester, founded in 1968 by one of Mawdudi's close associates, is a centre of study and publishing. The Muslim Educational Trust was established specifically to try to encourage Islamic instruction for Muslim children in state schools. By the mid-1980's it had arrangements of one kind or another with about fifty state schools around the country.[27] The third element of the Jamaat in Britain is the UK Islamic Mission. Although its head office is in London, its largest centre is in Birmingham, and important centres can be found in mosques in other British cities. It operates primarily through some twenty associated mosques in the principle areas of Muslim concentration, with an emphasis on Qur'anic teaching for children.[28]

Coming out of an Arab background, the Muslim Brotherhood has had little success in the general Muslim population in Britain. Where it has made its mark is among students in universities and colleges, primarily among foreign students. Muslim Brothers were the leading initiators in the Federation of Students Islamic Societies (FOSIS), around which has grown a group of student welfare organizations based in London.[29]

The Islamic Cultural Centre in London (the Regent's Park mosque) is a distinctive institution more akin to certain "central mosques" in other European capitals, since it is run by a trusteeship of ambassadors of Muslim countries. Its relationship to the Muslim communities in Britain and to their organizations has tended to be problematical when it has tried to play a central organizing role. The Centre has been more successful when it has sought to be a quiet facilitator of Muslim concerns on specific issues. In addition, of course, it continues to play an important part in the life of London Muslims and of the international Muslim community there.

It is probably still too early to expect the existence of an umbrella organization commanding support from all the main Muslim tendencies. The Union of Muslim Organizations in the UK (UMO), founded in 1970, experienced some initial success, but the major movements did not stay with it for long, and today its 200 or so members are mostly local mosques and associations. The last few years have seen new attempts to come together in some form of umbrella association. There are at least two such councils of mosques and associations. In both cases, there is an element of international Muslim sponsorship and a significant degree of overlapping of membership. There is clearly not one group or grouping which on its own has the strength to impress itself on the major part of the community. Equally, the community itself is too diverse for a general consensus to arise from the community. It would seem that, at least for the time being, movement towards unity is more likely to come through cooperation in the face of specific practical issues, rather than through attachment to theological ideals of communal unity.

IV

At the centre of Muslim activity are a number of common purposes and concerns. These can be considered in two main categories, namely the achievement of the best possible conditions for Muslims to live their faith, and the assurance of the survival of the faith into the next generation. The former group of issues includes a large variety of practical, and often quite technical matters covering access to facilities for worship, the status of Islamic family law, *halal* food and dress code in institutions, sensitivity to Muslim requirements in health care, etc.[30] These are issues which appear in different localities and at different times. They are often sorted out through local negotiation, and it is only seldom that a national issue arises which requires a concerted Muslim response, as happened in 1985 when the Farm Animal Welfare Council recommended legal changes which Muslims felt would have banned *halal* slaughter of animals for food.[31] Such issues are, however, often seen as a test of how serious British, and for that matter European, society is about its protestations of religious freedom and cultural openness.

The latter concern, the survival of the faith, first and foremost implies education, and the relationship between Muslim and British institutions in this area is, perhaps, a key indicator of tensions and opportunities. It should, at the outset, be emphatically stated that the *madrasa*, or Qur'an school, is not the problem. Traditional value systems governing attitudes to religion and social authority, to behaviour as between the sexes and the generations, to views of European culture and society and perceptions of education, are encouraged and preserved by the home and family environment. The *madrasa* is merely an extension and a reinforcement of this environment. No, the primary problem in the field of education is the European school.

Quite simply, the school is where, apart from the economic sphere, immigrant Muslim and native British society most deeply interact with each other. The school is central to Muslim parents' ambitions for their children's futures. But the school also represents a very deep threat. At one level, the threat is practical. Open teaching methods are at odds with the often strictly disciplined experiences of the parents' own backgrounds, and British educators have singularly failed to reassure immigrant parents as to the value of British class room methods. At a deeper level, the school is perceived as being potentially subversive of everything consciously and unconsciously considered to be of value in the traditional culture. The school environment is seen as a threat to inherited authority structures and gender roles, a threat which is viewed with the more fear because the parents' images of British society are particularly dependent on what they see on television and in the tattered remains of run-down white society in their inner city environment. The children implicitly confirm their parents' worst fears for, however attached to their own culture they may feel, they find in the school setting functional alternatives to those aspects of the tradition which seem of little relevance or value.

The tensions are not eased by the fact that the Muslim elites are increasingly articulate, both nationally and internationally, in their insistence on the centrality of education to the future of the Muslim community.[32] The mosque schools are seen as having a marginal role in this perception, and the main effort has increasingly been to try to establish Muslim schools within the state system parallel to existing Church of England, Roman Catholic and Jewish schools. In principle, this is quite possible under the still valid parts of 1944 Education Act. In practice, education authorities, community relations structures, and political parties are generally agreed that such Muslim (and Sikh and Hindu) schools are undesirable, because they would be socially divisive and retard the improvement of race relations. The debate is symptomatic of the very different ways in which the two sides look at society. The Muslim protagonists are primarily concerned with a religious framework - they are Muslims in a non-Muslim environment and they desire the best possible conditions to preserve their Islamic character. The other side has a primarily secular perspective, in which Muslims (if they are even recognized as such, rather than Pakistani or Turk or whatever) are merely one of the sections of Britain's black population.

236

V

The complex of issues around the subject of education is also indicative of challenges which arise at the very deepest level out of the presence of Muslims in Britain, challenges relating both to concepts of British society and to the Islamic character of the Muslim community in that society.

The nineteenth century produced in Britain a myth of a common culture which bound Britons together and distinguished them from other nations, the kind of national myth which found more explicit ideological expression in some other parts of Europe. The fact that this myth was closely intertwined with the self-confidence of Victorian technological and imperial supremacy contributed to its distinctive character and to the perspective through which other cultures and world views were regarded. Two world wars have disguised economic and political decline, and the waves of nostalgia regularly served up by the media have helped to preserve that myth. This concept of the "British way of life," regularly referred to by some politicians and also, with an emphasis on its "Christian character," occasionally by churchmen, is one which religious and ethnic minority communities find it very difficult to identify with.

In such a context Muslims are having to rediscover what it means to be Muslim. This is a process which they are sharing with the whole Muslim world, as it experiences urbanization and the spread of technology and communications. The oral culture of the village with its all-inclusive holistic view of life and society is fast disappearing. For those Muslims who have moved to Britain it has disappeared. The transfer immediately makes major parts of the traditional culture irrelevant. This could be ignored so long as the family stayed, but no longer when the family also moved. Choices of life-style had to be made, while at the same time structures were created which could preserve the relevance of much that was familiar. While great changes were made with little apparent difficulty, symbolic boundary markers were set up to denote the strength of continuing Islamic identity. Often, however, the particular symbols chosen would be different from the ones being chosen in the country of origin, thereby confirming the changing emphases of the new situation. At various times the emphasis has been on correct dress, on access to *halal* food, and the right to Islamic instruction.[33] Since 1975 the Union of Muslim Organizations has been seeking the introduction of Islamic family law for Muslims domiciled in Britain. At other times and in various localities Muslim burial and prayer at work have been issues.[34]

This continuing process of making choices, of selecting those areas which are necessary for Islamic identity in Britain, is taking place not only in relation to the British context. Two other sets of pressures are also involved.

Firstly, the world-wide resurgence of Islam - itself a process of rediscovery and reassertion of distinctive identity in a world dominated by the West - is presenting British Muslims with choices and perspectives developed in an international arena with little or no reference to their own experiences or needs. At the same time the resurgence is a revival calling for a purification of Islam from its many perceived illegitimate accretions. It is, thus, often a critique of the values and traditions which the Muslim villagers, migrated to Britain, hold dearest. It is an accusation against what they have considered as being their Islamic identity.

Secondly, the process of immigration has brought together in British cities Muslims from a variety of cultural traditions. Each of these traditions could be considered legitimate and absolutely Islamic within the cultural totalities of villages separated by social and physical distance. But the experience of meeting different forms of cultural expression, each with its claim to Islamic legitimacy, raises questions as to the exclusive validity of any one form. For example, the distinctive customs of weddings or funerals, which may have been regarded as an essential part of the tradition and are defended, when challenged, as being Islamic, become problematical when a neighbour from a different village is discovered to be using the same defence for different customs. In the insecure context of a minority situation, it becomes the more necessary to surmount this problem when the younger generation is increasingly applying its own critique of the validity of particular customs.

From such a variety of directions come the motivations for a reassessment of what it means to be Muslim in Britain. There is a dialogue taking place among various sections of Muslim experience in Britain and between Britain and the Muslim world generally. The aim of the dialogue is to determine what are the permanent central values of Islam and what implications they have for the daily lives of Muslims in a minority situation. The purpose is to seek to identify those aspects of Muslims' cultural heritage which may legitimately be regarded as of relative value and perhaps be discarded as a result, and to develop new and adapted cultural forms which, while functioning satisfactorily in the British environment, may at the same time be recognized as Islamically valid. This is, however, a process which is still in the initial stages and which can be expected to take one or more generations to work itself out.

REFERENCES

[1] This view is presented particularly strongly by S. Castles and G. Koszak, *Immigrant Workers and Class Structure in Western Europe* (London: Oxford University Press, 1973), an analysis recognized as representing a Marxist view. A softer view of the same basic conclusion is to be found in John Rex and Robin Moore, *Race, Community and Conflict* (London: Oxford University Press, 1964).

[2] David Smith, *The Facts of Racial Disadvantage: A National Survey* (London: Political and Economic Planning, 1976), p. 12, and Colin Brown, *Black and White Britain* (London: Heinemann, 1984), p.24; also K. Knott and R. Toon, "Muslims, Sikhs and Hindus in the UK: Problems in the Estimation of Religious Statistics," *Religious Research Papers*, no. 6. (University of Leeds, 1981). Statistical sources relating to this field are discussed in detail in J. S. Nielsen, "Other religions," *Reviews of UK Statistical Sources: Religion* (London: Pergamon Press,1987).

[3] M. M. Ally, *History of Muslims in Britain, 1850-1960,* (unpublished MA thesis, University of Birmingham 1981), pp. 26-41, 83-85.

[4] E. J. B. Rose et al, *Colour and Citizenship: A Report on British Race Relations* (London: Oxford University Press, 1969), p. 72.

[5] *Ibid.,* p. 70.

[6] *Ibid.,* p. 72.

[7] The Runnymede Trust and Radical Statistics Race Group, *Britain's Black Population* (London: Heinemann Educational Books, 1980), chapter 1.

[8] Office of Population Censuses and Surveys (OPCS), *Census 1981: Country of Birth* (London: HMSO, 1983), pp. 114f.

[9] See the General Household Survey data summarized in *OPCS Monitor*, GHS 86/1 (18th September 1986), and the Labour Force Surveys of 1983 and 1984 reported in *OPCS Monitor*, LFS 84/2 (18 December 1984) and LFS 85/1 (17th December 1985).

[10] See, for example, G. C. K. Peach and S. W. C. Winchester, "Birthplace, Ethnicity and Underenumeration of West Indians, Indians and Pakistanis in the Censuses of 1966 and 1971," *New Community* III (1974), pp. 386-393.

[11] See *OPCS Monitor*, GHS 86/1, p. 5.

[12] OPCS, *Labour Force Survey 1981* (London: HMSO, 1982), p. 22.

[13] Smith, p. 203.

240

[14]*Ibid.*, p. 202.

[15]*Census 1981: Country of Birth*, pp. 160f.

[16]Cf. Amrit Wilson, *Finding a Voice: Asian Women in Britain* (London: Virago, 1978).

[17]See, for example, P. Werbner, "From Rags to Riches: Manchester Pakistanis in the Textile Trade," *New Community*, vol. 7, no. 3 (1979), pp. 376-389.

[18]Smith, pp. 53-56.

[19]Community Relations Commission, *Between Two Cultures* (2nd ed. London: Commission for Racial Equality, 1978); the data was republished with a specifically Muslim emphasis in Muhammad Anwar, *Young Muslims in a Multicultural Society* (Leicester: The Islamic Foundation, 1981).

[20]See also D. Joly, "The opinions of Mirpuri Parents in Saltley, Birmingham, about their Children's Schooling," *Research Papers: Muslims in Europe*, no. 24 (December 1984).

[21]S. Barton, "The Bengali Muslims of Bradford," *Research Papers: Muslims in Europe*, no. 13 (March 1982), pp. 12f.

[22]cf. M. M. Ally, pp. 46ff.

[23]Figures based on The Registrar General, *The Official List*, part III (London: OPCS, 1981), and updated from the registration files in the OPCS, London.

[24]J. S. Nielsen, "A Survey of British Local Authority Response to Muslim Needs," *Research Papers : Muslims in Europe*, no. 30/31 (June/September 1986), pp. 10f.

[25]M. M. Ally, pp. 31f; cf. J. S. Trimingham, *The Sufi Orders in Islam* (London: Oxford University Press, 1971), pp.73, 121.

[26]The background to these movements is described in L. Binder, *Religion and Politics in Pakistan* (Berkeley: University of California Press, 1963), pp. 28-33, and in B. D. Metcalf, *Islamic Revival in British India: Deoband, 1860-1900* (Princeton: Princeton University Press, 1982), especially chapter 7.

[27]Prospectus issued 1981 by the Muslim Education Trust; personal enquiries by the author indicate that the prospectus is generally reliable.

[28]U. K. Islamic Mission, *Annual Report 1981*.

[29]M. M. Ally, pp. 182-187.

[30]A discussion of these issues from a Muslim perspective is to be found in N. Y. MacDermott and M. M. Ahsan, *The Muslim Guide* (Leicester: The Islamic Foundation, 1980).

[31]Farm Animal Welfare Council, *Report on the Welfare of Livestock when Slaughtered by Religious Methods* (London: HMSO, 1985), and a Muslim response available from the Islamic Cultural Centre, London.

[32]See the *Islamic Education Series* (London: Hodder and Stoughton), edited by S. A. Ashraf, which arose out of the First World Conference on Muslim Education held in Mecca, 1977; also *The Teaching of Islam in British Schools: An Agreed Statement* (Cambridge: The Islamic Academy, 1985).

[33]See H. E. R. Townsend, *Immigrant Pupils in England : The LEA Response* (Slough: NFER, 1971), pp. 61ff.

[34]J. S. Nielsen, "A survey of British Local Authority Response," pp. 22-30.

CHAPTER XIV

HINDU COMMUNITIES IN BRITAIN

KIM KNOTT

Hindus, together with Sikhs and Muslims and a lesser number of adherents of other religions, make up the South Asian population settled in Britain's major cities. The Hindus, like those from other religions, form social and religious subgroups or communities within the overall framework of their parent tradition. It is hoped that a discussion of divisions of this kind will illustrate the way in which Britain is currently experiencing not only "inter-religious" pluralism - brought about by the presence of a wide variety of different religious groups here - but also "intra-religious" pluralism, encouraged by diversity within our religions.

Owing to her history of colonialism, Britain has had a long-standing and close relationship with the Indian sub-continent. While this was largely a relationship of paternalism, there were individuals and events within it which were motivated and stimulated not solely by a sense of power and duty but by a genuine interest in the religion, society and culture of India and her people. In the eighteenth, nineteenth and early twentieth-century, this produced orientalists - most of whom were government servants, missionaries, or scholars - who, while resident in India, developed a fascination for the textual tradition of Hinduism and its contemporary social and religious manifestations. Charles Wilkins and William Jones, for example, took an early interest in the *Veda* and the *Bhagavad Gita* while William Carey and, later, Mrs Sinclair Stevenson were concerned to understand the way of life of those Hindus with whom they came into contact.[1] In the late nineteenth century this interest extended beyond its former intellectual and educational bounds to the realm of spirituality. The establishment and growth of the Theosophical Society provides the clearest illustration of this, although the influence of Vivekananda and other lesser known Indian teachers was also notable in the West.[2] Although this colonial relationship was formally brought to a close in 1947 with Indian Independence, the interest did not cease. In the late sixties and 1970's, the attraction to aspects of Indian religion and culture flowered in the rise of religious movements offering paths away from Western materialism to *samadhi, moksa* or *nirvana.*[3]

Despite this recent history of involvement and interest in India and its philosophical, cultural and social ways of being, very little is known about these matters by the British population at large. And unfortunately, except in some cases, the level of knowledge of things Indian has not been substantially raised as a result of the settlement in Britain of an Indian population from the sub-continent and from East African countries in the Commonwealth with historical ties with India. Futhermore, the serious student bent on understanding the way of life of Hindu friends or colleagues (or even a young Hindu trying to attain a fuller picture of his or her own religious and social traditions) might be more confused than helped by reading one of the several popular books available on the subject of Hinduism. While they contain information important for an understanding of this kind, the works by R. C. Zaehner and K. M. Sen, both entitled *Hinduism*, need to be decoded and explained in the context of the way of life of ordinary people who count themselves as Hindus.[4] Issues of interest such as festivals and life cycle rites, social arrangements related to caste and the family, the use of religious texts, religious duty, ethical prescriptions and so on are all discussed but in a way which seems to have little bearing on the popular religiosity of those we are seeking to understand. Neither book was written for precisely this purpose; both assuredly will be read with this in mind.[5] Those who do pursue this particular path for greater understanding may well end up very little nearer to appreciating the intricate patterns which make up the ways of life of those in Britain's Hindu community - or Hindu communities.[6]

These two books and others like them are concerned in varying ways, as the explanatory paragraph on the back of Zaehner's book suggests,

...to distinguish out of the mass of material...."the changeless ground from which the proliferating jungle that seems to be Hinduism grows." It is no longer possible to define a Hindu as one who performs his caste duties and accepts the Veda as revealed truth, for today Hinduism is in the melting-pot; what were once considered essentials are in the process of being discarded, but the hard core remains....[7]

In the face of contemporary pluralism - *within* religions as well as *of* religions - the idea of uncovering the "hard core" of a tradition seems attractive. However, this approach does not necessarily help to explain the very feature of Indian religious life with which it is designed to help us cope. A knowledge of the "hard core", if indeed such a thing exists in relation to Hinduism, may help us to ask questions in the face of the diversity of paths which together make up the Hindu tradition (e. g., What view does a particular sect hold of the concept of "karma"? How do Hindus from different regions organise according to caste divisions?). It does not help us to know why such diversity exists, or what such diversity looks like, or what happens to it when it is faced with new challenges such as transplantation from the land of its origins to different geographical and cultural contexts.[8]

While the causes of diversity within Hinduism are beyond the bounds of this discussion, the nature of this diversity as it exists in Britain and the dynamism with which it has responded in the face of transplantation are issues which need to be addressed. The Indian population settled here contains communities which hail from different geographical regions in the sub-continent, with different migration experiences, different sectarian interests and, as a result, different cultural and religious backgrounds. The fact that they exist in parallel in Britain just as diverse ways of being exist in India is indicative of the variety which underlies the overarching concept of Hinduism. "Hinduism", broadly speaking, is the name given to the religious beliefs and practices of Indians (or, at least, those who are not Muslims, Sikhs, Buddhists, Jains or Christians). Unifying features do exist. Concepts such as *dharma, karma, samsara, atman, varna, ashrama* and so on, and practices such as *puja, arti, samskara and yagna* have meaning for all "Hindus" (and for many who adhere to other religions of Indian origin). The understanding of these concepts and practices differs, however, according to situation and identity. Not all Hindus think and do the same things. This is

246

true in all religious traditions, of course, but would seem to be of particular significance in relation to Hinduism, a complex of traditions with no single founder, a variety of textual sources, and a long history of development in a large geographical area.

In addition to internal diversity, these characteristics have encouraged an interesting combination of conservatism and innovation. In the transplantation of Hinduism to countries outside the sub-continent these traits have combined in new and different ways in response to such pressures as the demands of the new location, links with India, and length of residence away from India. Tradition and change, and the ways in which individual Hindus and Hindu groups have participated in interpreting their religion in relation to these processes, are important features of religious life for Britain's Hindus. Their co-religionists in India share in this, but the particular experiences of migration and settlement have given these features a special quality.[9] It is not possible for a religious group to find itself in new surroundings, with minority status, in a situation of social and religious pluralism, as an ethnic enclave, racially and religiously different, without experiencing both the need to change and the desire to perpetuate tradition. The particular communities of which the Hindu population of Britain is comprised have responded in varying ways to this experience as will be seen later in this discussion.

First of all, what are these Hindu communities? How did they develop? Why do we need to speak of "communities" in the plural at all?

There has been a Hindu population in Britain since the 1950's, although a small number of professionals and traders were resident here before the last war. Male Hindus from North and West India began to be attracted in the fifties by the possibility of well-paid employment which might supplement the family income back home. The two regions from which these men came, the Punjab and Gujarat, contained within their histories the conditions necessary to encourage emigration: the Punjab had a close relationship with Britain owing to its part in the British army in India; Gujarat had a lengthy history of trade links and indenturing of labour in the countries of East Africa. After the war, Britain boasted a boom in employment opportunities which attracted men from the North and West:

Pakistani Muslims, Punjabi Sikhs and Hindus from the North and, to a lesser extent, Gujarati Hindus and Muslims from the West. In the 1950's and early sixties, however, the Hindus were small in number, and in 1963 an author writing on Indian immigrants in Britain commented that,

> The Muslims have mosques organised on a linguistic-regional basis...and the Sikhs have temples (Gurudwara). But Hindus do not have temples here. The elaborate rituals which are required in the temple are forbidden by custom on foreign soil. Then, too, worship at the temple is on the decline among the relatively Westernized Hindus in Gujarat and the Punjab. Much of the religion practised by the immigrant has a basis in village or caste in India; the village-kin group rather than the whole community is concerned with religious activities. This group is so small that it could not bear the cost of maintaining a temple. And even at the regional and all-India level, Hindu religious life is based on personal belief of a philosophical nature, which need not find expression in worship at a temple.[10]

As he suggested, at that time Hindus were too small in number to contemplate organising religiously in the way Muslims and Sikhs were doing. In addition, he felt there were other reasons to explain the differences. Interestingly, although most of what he wrote was true, his analysis no longer applies to the situation as we now find it. This has much to do with the tremendous growth in the Hindu population in Britain, but also suggests that those who have settled here have behaved somewhat differently from their compatriots in the sub-continent.

Since Desai wrote in 1963, the major factor which has contributed to the growth of Hinduism and Hindu communities in Britain has been the arrival in the late sixties and early seventies of East African Asian families from Tanzania, Kenya, Uganda and Malawi.[11] Encouraged or forced to leave as a result of policies of Africanisation in these countries, these migrants and refugees have swelled the Muslim, Sikh and - most particularly - Hindu populations. Although many had to leave their homes suddenly, without possessions, they brought with them their experiences of settlement outside India. In East Africa the Hindus had developed strong religious and social organisations based on caste, sect and regional differences. They had also opened places of worship designed to attract those from all the different Hindu communities.[12] Once established in Britain, the East African Hindus began to organise in the same way. In many cases, their efforts built on the existing structures which had begun to grow gradually in the early and mid-sixties as a result of the attempts of the Indian Hindus to organise for cultural and religious purposes. In some cities, small meeting groups had been set up, constitutions had been laid out, and enquiries had been made to find premises. The Bharatiya Mandala (Indian Association) had been set up in Bradford in 1959 by Gujarati Hindus, and similar cultural societies were established in the sixties in Leeds, Preston, Coventry, and so on.[13] The size, number, scope and influence of these groups grew tremendously with the addition to the population of Hindus from East Africa, and the first temples were formally opened in the early seventies in London and Leicester.

Desai was clearly incorrect in his assessment of the migrant Hindus' attitude to worship. Certainly, in the early days when the population was small, efforts to organise were centred round the homes of enthusiastic individuals and were broadly cultural rather than explicitly religious. Since then, however, Hindus in most British cities have established *mandirs* or temples, many of which contain installed *murtis*, consecrated statues of Hindu deities such as Radha and Krishna or Rama, Sita and Lakshman. Most of the 300,000 Hindus now settled or born and bred in Britain focus their temple worship - to distinguish it from worship that takes place, as Desai implied, in the home - on these *mandirs*.[14] Some attend on a daily or weekly basis; most make visits at the times of major festivals, *samskaras* or life-cycle rites, and for special occasions (*vrata, yagna* or *katha*, to make a special vow, to attend a fire-sacrifice or a talk).[15] Many groups within the population also use the temples as venues for meetings: *bhajan mandalas* or singing groups, dance groups, discussion groups, youth groups, *mahila mandalas* or women's associations, and language classes in Hindi, Gujarati or other Indian languages meet there.

This then is a general account of the way in which Hinduism became established in Britain. What it does not show clearly, although the indications are apparent even in this short summary, is the presence of important internal differences in the population which have contributed to the growth patterns of both informal association and formal organisation amongst Hindus in Britain. It has been established that Hindus from India and East Africa congregated in cities, and as such formed geographical communities. We have also seen how the early settlers came from different regions in the Indian sub-continent. A third division has obviously been between those Hindus who came direct from India and those who came from Tanzania, Kenya, Uganda and the other East African countries with experience of settlement outside the sub-continent. Added to these differences are those of caste, sect and kinship group. All these distinctions are important for an understanding, not only of the social structure of the Hindu population here, but also of attitudes and experience, cultural and religious behaviour, beliefs and practices.

One of the most common uses of the term "community" applies to a geographically defined entity. We speak of "rural community" and "the local community." When the phrase "the Hindu community" is used in a community relations context or by councils or the press, very often what is meant is "the Hindu population," either at a national level or at a local level, e. g., in Leicester, in Bradford, in North London. This boundary definition has significance in relation to local policy making, but it does not necessarily have importance for the Hindus themselves. If anything, it has a tendency to disguise the distinct social categories to which Hindus relate. For example, financial assistance is often given at the local level to a particular body which is felt to represent the Hindu community as a whole (the same occurs in relation to the Sikhs and Muslims). This is often a local temple. The result of such action may mean that only those who utilise the facilities provided by that body benefit (this may be informally restricted to one ethnic group or even one caste or sectarian group). Despite the problems which arise from defining Hindus in this way, there are considerable benefits (particularly as regards social policy) to be gained from an appreciation of their geographical dispersion in Britain. A clear example of this can be seen in relation to the Hindu community in Leicester. In that city, Hindus, and a small number of Sikhs, make up around 18.5% of the population with a total of over 50,000 people.[16] This obviously has important consequences for local policy and local provisions.

Underlying this figure for total Hindu population size in Leicester and the other major British cities are a number of significant social variables which break down the "local" community into smaller units. Perhaps the most obvious of these is that of ethnicity. Britain's Hindus have their origins in the states of Gujarat and the Punjab, and to a lesser extent in Uttar Pradesh, Bengal, South India and Sri Lanka. Of a total figure of around 300,000, 70% are of Gujarati origin, 15% of Punjabi origin, with 15% from other Indian states.[17] This is an important preliminary guide to understanding patterns of association amongst the Hindu population as it determines language spoken, cultural behaviour such as eating habits and dress, and, to a certain extent, religious practices such as which festivals one considers important, deities favoured for worship, and the procedure of life-cycle rites, fasts and regular *pujas*. Except in a few cases, Hindus of necessity use Hindi or English when speaking to co-religionists from another state. Naturally, then, the majority prefer to attend temples and cultural centres where they will meet those who speak the same language and share the same cultural background. Excluding areas where the local Hindu population is small and ethnically mixed, there is a tendency for ethnic groups to support separate organisations.[18] In Bradford, for example, the earliest temple has remained Punjabi in orientation whereas a more recent place of worship has been founded by the Gujarati population for their own purposes.[19]

Other organisations have been formed to strengthen the ties of the ethnic populations, particularly at the local level. In Leeds, the Gujaratis have joined together to participate in singing groups and dance groups, and the Punjabis have organised a "Punjabi Sabha" or society to raise funds and run religious and cultural programmes. Both communities have provided mother-tongue teaching for their children in the past.[20] In London, a recent new Trust, the London Meikandaar Adheenam Trust, has been formed to organise the work of Saiva Tamils from South India and Sri Lanka.

The other major features which distinguish Hindus from one another either divide these ethnic groups into still smaller and more specific communities or cut across the ethnic divide. It is only really settlement history which produces the latter result, although in some cases sectarianism runs counter to ethnic divisions. In the case of settlement, we find both Gujaratis and Punjabis who came direct from India, and representatives from both groups who arrived in Britain from East Africa. (The vast majority of

East African Asians, however, were Gujaratis.) Although settlement history is not responsible for overt social divisions it has been shown to have important consequences in relation to attitudes to tradition and modernisation.[21]

Of much greater importance are those features which work within ethnic enclaves further to divide them. Caste and kinship are most prominent in this regard. The word "community" is taken frequently to refer to the caste group or *jati* as it is that feature which contributes most to the identity of the majority of Britain's Hindus. This is because it is within these *jatis* that marriages are conducted and social life is organised. The strongest networks amongst Hindus in Britain are those of kinship, which, by definition, are also those of caste (although the caste groups may contain within them kinship hierarchies). Families in the *Mochi* community in Leeds, for example, maintain close, regular contact with *Mochi* relatives in Bradford, Birmingham and Greater London. Marriages are arranged within this network, or indeed within its extension in Gujarat. In addition, cultural events are organised, funds raised and help meted out within the community when required. The formal association of *Mochis* in Britain is known as the "Gujarati Arya Kshatriya Mahasabha UK", to which ten separate regional organisations belong. This association, in turn, belongs to a parent body in Gujarat, the "Surat and Bulsar District Mochi Parishad". Communication is maintained between the Parishad and its members in the UK, Fiji, Kenya, etc., by way of a journal.[22]

The other Gujarati castes organise in much the same way as this, although the larger ones, the *Patidars* and *Lohanas*, are more complex. The *Patidars*, who must number well over 50,000, have an intricate system of kinship organisation whereby they maintain their links to a series of villages in Central Gujarat.[23] Perhaps as a result of this, they have never organised themselves as the other caste groups have done, in regional and national bodies. The *Lohanas*, like the *Patidars* a trading caste, number around 35,000.[24] Their system of organisation is similar to the one described above in relation to the *Mochis*, and, like that and other groups, they have settled in particular regions. While the *Mochis* are concentrated in cities in West Yorkshire, the West Midlands and Greater London, and the *Patidars* are to be found particularly in London but also in substantial numbers in most of the areas of Hindu residence, the *Lohanas* are heavily concentrated in two places, Leicester and North London (Harrow, Edgware, etc.) where they have close-knit organisations for the perpetuation of cultural and religious traditions along caste lines.

One example of the way in which some of the *Lohanas* have maintained the traditions of their caste community is through religious practice. For several Gujarati *jatis* caste allegiance is related to sect membership. There are no regulations concerning this, and the actual situation is not as clear cut as is sometimes imagined, but adherence to certain sectarian movements can be seen to have reference to cast division in some cases. The close relationship between the Leva Kanbi Patels and a particular branch of the "Swaminarayan Movement" is an illustration of this.[25] Amongst the *Lohana* community the predominant sect is the "Pushtimarak Sampradaya", a devotional movement in the tradition of the sixteenth-century, spiritual leader, Vallabhacharya.[26]

While most of the Gujarati Hindus in Britain see their kinship and caste identity as of major significance for association, and often for cultural and religious behaviour, other Hindus organise their lives around different criteria. This is frequently a result of the nature and size of the social groups to which they belong. Punjabi Hindus and those from other parts of the sub-continent are usually in too small a number in their local area to operate strong caste organisations. In addition, they may have few relatives living in Britain, making kinship ties less relevant in the formation of their social lives here. For these people the ethnic community or religious community is often the most important. As we saw earlier, Leeds' Punjabi Hindus participate in a Punjabi society. British Maharastrians have a national organisation, the "Maharastrian Mandal," for the maintenance of strong ethnic ties.[27] In addition, some Punjabis are members of the Arya Samaj, a sect with its origins in nineteenth-century Punjab and a strong following in East Africa; many of the Bengalis in Britain have similarly made a commitment to sectarian movements with roots in East India like the Ramakrishna Mission. It would be entirely misleading to suppose, however, that these sectarian movements are restricted to particular caste communities or to ethnic communities. They are all open, and many draw their committed membership as well as their informal adherents from a wide range of different ethnic groups. The Satya Sai Baba Fellowship attracts South Indians and Gujaratis. The International Society for Krishna Consciousness has life members from all sections of the Hindu population and attracts a regular attendance of around 1,000 each Sunday to its centre in Hertfordshire. Many of these are Gujaratis from North London, but others are Punjabis, Bengalis, Hindus from Uttar Pradesh and so on.

The issue of "community" is clearly a complex one for Hindus in Britain. Individual Hindus identify with different groups according to their understanding of who they are. This assessment of personal identity depends on a range of features related both to social and religious background and to the social consequences of the migration and settlement experience. As we have seen, obvious factors such as caste and sect have an important impact on community identification but other, more general interests may also define community allegiance, especially where numbers are small. In such cases, individuals may organise according to ethnic division or may even override these and identify with the local Hindu population as a whole. This then becomes the effective "community".

It is not difficult to see that the levels of identification for the Hindu population are what we, from a Western perspective, would view as both religious and social. The same distinction does not apply within Hinduism. By "Hinduism" we mean both the religious and social ways of being of those who call themselves Hindus. The diversity which we find in the social lives of Hindus is mirrored by a diversity of beliefs and practices. Even the communities defined by ethnicity, caste, sect and kinship which were described above contain within them different views concerning social behaviour, different traditions of religious practice, allegiances to different deities, etc.

Distinctiveness and difference are not the only defining features of Hinduism in general or Hinduism in Britain in particular. The "Hindu community" in the singular is not a phrase devoid of meaning and reference. There are unifying features - though these are generally of less immediate importance to the individual - to be found in a consideration of Hinduism in

254

Britain. Some of these features, like the popular religious attitude of *bhakti* or devotion, are peculiar to the Indian religious tradition. Others are shared, incidentally, with other migrant groups. The experience of migration, and the problems of settlement, of acceptance, of growth, of alienation, of harassment, are all part of what defines the "Hindu community in Britain." There are occasions when the Hindu population experiences itself as "one": when it finds itself under pressure and in the limelight as it did in 1984 after the massacre in the Golden Temple of Amritsar and at the time of the assassination of Mrs Gandhi; or when it has occasion to celebrate as a community as it did in 1985 during the Cultural Festival of India at Alexandra Palace.

As one community, and as many communities, the Hindu population is in the process of defining its religious and social traditions in a new context. It is achieving this with reference to the past - to the concepts, practices and structures that go to make up the complex of traditions which is "Hinduism" - but also with attention to the conditions of the present and future in Britain: religious and social pluralism, minority status, and ethnic difference.

REFERENCES

[1]For an account of early Western interest in Hinduism see G. D. Bearce, *British Attitudes Towards India 1784-1858* (London: Oxford University Press, 1961); D. Kopf, *British Orientalism and the Bengal Renaissance* (Berkeley: University of California Press, 1969); P. Marshall, ed., *The British Discovery of Hinduism in the Eighteenth-Century* (Cambridge: Cambridge University Press, 1970). See also, A. M. Sinclair Stevenson, *The Rites of the Twice Born* (New Delhi: Oriental Books Reprint Co, 1971 (1920)).

[2]For further information on the nineteenth-century Hindu renaissance and its impact on the West see, D. S. Sharma, *The Renaissance of Hinduism* (Varanasi, 1944); W. Thomas, *Hinduism Invades America* (New York: Beacon Press, 1930); J. P. Rayapati, *Early American Interest in Vedanta*: (London: Asia Publishing House, 1973.)

[3]For further information concerning the rise of "new religious movements" see T. Roszak, *The Making of a Counter Culture* (London: Faber, 1969); J. Needleman, *The New Religions* (New York: (Dutton, 1970); C. Y. Glock and R. N. Bellah, eds., *The New Religious Consciousness* (Berkeley: University of California, 1976).

[4]R. C. Zaehner, *Hinduism* (London: Oxford University Press, 1962); K. M. Sen, *Hinduism* (Harmondsworth: Penguin Books, 1961). Both books are in print at the time of publication.

[5]The purpose of these books was to provide an introduction to the Hindu religious tradition as a whole rather than to the life of this faith in Britain. Both are historical in approach rather than descriptive of contemporary practice. For an appreciation of Hinduism as a living religion in Britain one would be advised to consult literature designed for use in schools by teachers and children which often is orientated towards providing an understanding of the life of Hindus settled here.

[6]The introductory books by Zaehner and Sen are not the only ones of their kind. Similar textbooks for use in the study of Hinduism are restricted in much the same way, e. g. T. J. Hopkins: *The Hindu Religious Tradition* (Encino: Dickenson, 1971): J. L. Brockington, *The Sacred Thread: Hinduism in its Continuity and Diversity* (Edinburgh: Edinburgh University Press, 1981); M. Stutley, *Hinduism: the Eternal Law* (Wellingborough: Aquarian Press, 1985).

[7]Zaehner, *op. cit.*, back cover.

[8]The issue of diversity has been discussed by anthropologists and scholars of religion alike. See, M. Marriott, *Village India: Studies in the Little Community* (Menasha: American Anthropological Association Memoir No. 83, 1955); N. C. Chaudhuri, *Hinduism: A Religion to Live By* (Oxford: Oxford University Press, 1979).

[9]For further discussion of the relationship of migration and religious change see H. Abramson, "Migrants and Cultural Diversity: On Ethnicity and Religion in Society" and H. Mol, "Theory and Data on the Religious Behaviour of Migrants," both in *Social Compass*, 26:1, 1979.

[10]R. Desai, *Indian Immigrants in Britain* (London: Oxford University Press, 1963), p. 19.

[11]For an account of the exodus of Asians from East Africa see, H. Tinker *The Banyan Tree* (Oxford: Oxford University Press, 1977).

[12]H. S. Morris, *The Indians in Uganda* (London: Weidenfeld and Nicolson, 1968). A. Bharati, *The Asians in East Africa* (Chicago: Nelsen-Hall, 1972).

[13]R. Desai, *op. cit.*, and D. Bowen, "The Evolution of Gujarati Hindu Organisations in Bradford" in R. Burghart, ed., *Hinduism in Great Britain* (London: Tavistock, 1987); K. Knott, *Hinduism in Leeds, Community Religions Project Monograph* (Department of Theology and Religious Studies, University of Leeds, 1986); S. W. Harrison, *Hinduism in Preston* (Preston: S. Harrison, 1978). R. Jackson, "The Shree Krishna Temple and the Gujarati Hindu Community in Coventry" in D. Bowen, ed., *Hinduism in England* (Bradford: Bradford College, 1981).

[14]For further information on the practice of Hinduism in the home see M. Michaelson, "Domestic Hinduism in a Gujarati Trading Caste" and M. McDonald, "Rituals of Motherhood among Gujarati Women in the East End of London" in Burghart, *op. cit.*

[15]For a detailed discussion of temple practice see Knott, *op. cit.*, and K. Knott, "Hindu Temple Rituals in Britain: The Reinterpretation of Tradition" in Burghart, *op. cit.*

[16]Commission for Racial Equality, *Ethnic Minorities in Britain: Statistical Information on the Pattern of Settlement* (London: Commission for Racial Equality, 1985).

[17]K. Knott and R. Toon, "Muslims, Sikhs and Hindus in the UK: Problems in the Estimation of Religious Statistics," *Religious Research Paper* 6 (Department of Sociology, University of Leeds, 1982).

[18]Leeds provides an example of a city where the Hindu population is comparatively small. This has resulted in members of different ethnic groups sharing facilities. See Knott, *Hinduism in Leeds*.

[19]D. Bowen, "The Evolution of Gujarati Hindu Organisations in Bradford".

[20]K. Knott, *Hinduism in Leeds*.

[21]This process has been discussed in relation to the Punjabi Sikh community in P. Bhachu, *Twice Migrants* (London: Tavistock, 1985).

[22]K. Knott, "The Mochis in Leeds: Caste and Class out of Context," unpublished paper, (Gujarati Ethnicity Symposium, School of African and Oriental Studies, 1984).

[23]D. F. Pocock, *Kanbi and Patidar* (Oxford: Clarendon Press, 1972); H. Tambs-Lyche, *London Patidars* (London: Routledge and Kegan Paul, 1980).

[24]M. Michaelson, "The Relevance of Caste among East African Gujaratis in Britain," *New Community*, 7:3, 1979; M. Michaelson, "Caste, Kinship and Marriage: A Study of Two Gujarati Trading Castes in England," PhD thesis, School of Oriental and African Studies, University of London, 1983.

[25]R. Barot, "Caste and Sect in the Swaminarayan Movement" in Burghart, *op. cit.*

[26]M. Michaelson, "Domestic Hinduism in a Gujarati Trading Caste."

[27]Asian Observer, *Asian Directory and Who's Who, 1977-8* (London: Asian Observer Publications, 1978).

CHAPTER XV

SIKHS IN BRITAIN

W. OWEN COLE

Introduction

The origins of Sikhism[1] are to be found in the life and teachings of Guru Nanak, a spiritual preceptor who was born in Punjab, a northwestern region of India, in 1469 C.E. He was, by birth, a member of one of the higher Hindu castes, a Khatri, but the message which he began to preach in about 1499 was that spiritual liberation was open to everyone regardless of caste, both men and women. He had no intention of establishing a movement, still less of giving the world yet another religion. However, his teachings emphasised mutual support and congregational worship as well as the practice of personal meditation, so it is not altogether surprising that a group of followers emerged. These became known as Sikhs from a Punjabi word meaning disciple or learner. Before the Guru died he felt obliged to designate and install a successor, and thus a line of Gurus was established which lasted until 1708, when it was deliberately ended, guruship being conferred by the scriptures, the Guru Granth Sahib, and the community, the Panth. During this period of some two hundred years, besides acquiring a scripture, Sikhism developed distinctive marriage and initiation rituals, festivals based upon birth and death anniversaries of the Gurus, Diwali, and the North Indian new year occasion of Baisakhi, and the form of appearance popularly characterised by men growing the beard and wearing the turban. The teachings of Sikhism may be summed up as belief in one formless creator God, one humanity whose divisions on lines of race, creed, class, and gender are ultimately illusory and should therefore be eradicated, and dependence upon divine Grace for salvation. The goal of Sikhism, therefore, is one humanity worshipping and serving the one God, though it is nowhere asserted that this must be achieved through the triumph of one particular religion over others. Such a notion is anathema to Sikhs.

During the second half of the twentieth-century, many members of this five-hundred-year-old movement have made their homes in Britain. They now number over three hundred thousand, the largest population of the Sikh diaspora outside Delhi. It is they who are the subject of this paper.

Sikhs and the British

The presence of Sikhs in Britain is to be explained by the Raj and especially the position of Sikhs in the Indian Empire. The Sikh kingdom of Punjab was the last sizeable area of India to be annexed by the British. This finally happened in 1849. Less than a decade later came the first armed struggle for independence against the British. During the crisis of 1857 the Sikhs, for the most part, were not involved. They did not share the grievances of the disaffected Hindus and Muslims.[2] Those Sikhs who had been recruited into the British army were allowed to retain turbans and beard and observe the practices of the Khalsa. Treated with disdain by Hindustani sepoys who regarded them as being of low caste, they had no cause to support a struggle which, if successful, would result in a Hindu India, or, even worse, a restoration of the Mughals. In Punjab there was quiet because of the wise administration of John Lawrence, chief commissioner. He encouraged the building of schools and hospitals, provided peace and just government, respected the Sikh religion and customs and channelled the well-known militaristic inclinations of the Sikhs into the army. By 1852 they had already proved their worth in the Anglo-Burmese war.

Sikh soldiers were used to recapture Delhi in September 1857. The loyalty of Sikh princes was rewarded with land grants, that of Sikhs in general by their increased numbers in the Indian army. By the 1880's they were serving overseas in various parts of Southeast Asia. They were aware of the Empire and conscious of their membership of it.

Between 1855, when the first census of Punjab was taken, and 1881, it is estimated that the population increased by nearly 20%. Pressure on land and indebtedness to moneylenders prompted the migration of Punjabis to other parts of India, but also further abroad.[3] By 1907 British Columbia was already legislating against Indian immigration. In the 1890's Indians, many of them from the Punjab, had begun to take part in the development of East Africa, especially working on the new railways.

The First Migrants

In 1854 Maharaja Dalip Singh, last Sikh ruler, the man who had surrendered the Koh-i-noor diamond as well as his kingdom, to the British, came to England with his cousin, Prince Shiv Dev Singh. A year earlier, in 1853, the Maharaja had become a Christian. However, in 1866 he was readmitted to the Sikh religion and was buried at Elvedon (1893).[4] By 1911, the first gurdwara was established in Putney, three years after the formation of the Khalsa Jatha, British Isles.[5] The gurdwara was a converted house, 79 Sinclair Road; the congregation was mainly of educated Sikhs now living in this country. It included the daughter of the Maharaja, and also traders.

The majority of Sikh migrants to Britain have become traders, and craftsmen and business people, whatever their occupations in India. Sikhs came between the two World Wars, especially members of the Bhatra pedlar class. These set up bases in such cities as London, Cardiff and Southampton, from which they sold their wares either going from house to house with heavy suitcases, or setting up stalls in open air markets. With the outbreak of war in 1939 their movements were curtailed. It was easy for them to be suspected of being enemy aliens. Many of them returned to India.[6]

The Major Migration

It was during the 1950's and sixties that most people of Asian origin came to Britain. These were years of prosperity when the British textile and engineering industries especially were eager to recruit labour. Traditional sources, the British countryside and Ireland, were almost exhausted; attention turned to the so-called new commonwealth countries. Sometimes advertising was used to attract unskilled workers. In the case of Sikhs, the prosperity of India coincided with the period of population growth and the beginnings of technological development in Punjab. The Jats, who are the traditional farmer, owner-cultivator, caste of Punjab, could not expand their holdings, could not employ all their sons, and therefore looked for other outlets. Delhi, especially, but also many other cities in India, attracted Sikh migrants. Others decided to go farther afield and answer the call of England.[7]

Those who came were not the poor, they were not well established, usually high caste brahmin or khatri businessmen, and they did not usually intend to settle in Britain. Frequently, they were younger sons, sometimes married, who intended to work overseas for some years, sending money home to develop the farm, replace kaccha houses with pukkha, or provide capital for setting up some new family business. All-male households were established in rented accommodation.

The early 1960's saw a dramatic change in the composition of Hindu and Sikh communities, less so the Muslim. New immigration legislation severely restricted, and almost prevented, new immigration from the Indo-Pakistan subcontinent and the Caribbean. However, it did permit dependants to join their husbands. Faced with the prospect of remaining in Britain without family, returning to India to the situation they had left only a few years earlier and which had not changed, or bringing their families, most Sikhs chose the last course. It would be wrong to say that all Sikh men had hitherto been lax in their religious observances. The practice of holding religious services which Ballard mentions was doubtless not confined to Leeds.[8] Bristol, Campbell Road, London and Leeds all saw the purchase of houses for use as gurdwaras in 1958-9, and the Bhatra in Cardiff was bought even earlier, in 1956. However, the growth in numbers of gurdwaras coincides with the reunion of families in the first years of the sixties.[9]

Towards the end of that decade the newly independent East African states embarked upon policies of Africanisation. Though no other country parallelled the policy of General Amin in Uganda, nevertheless many Sikhs, in common with other Asians, decided to leave Africa. They had few real ties with India. Sometimes they were third-generation settlers who had never visited India and even now had no intention of going there. Their links were with Britain and it was to Britain that they naturally turned. Sometimes they joined existing Sikh communities but they were not afraid to distance themselves geographically, setting up businesses and their homes in white areas which had no previous experience of Asians.[10] Speaking better English, often better educated, with high aspirations, they sometimes felt more akin socially to the British they had known in East Africa than the people who had come direct from the Punjab. In Africa, however, they had maintained their religious and social identity, and when they arrived in Britain they immediately set about programmes of gurdwara-building or expansion, replacing converted houses with purpose-built centres serving a social, as well as religious, purpose.[11] To apportion responsibility between the reunion of families and the presence of East African Sikhs may not be possible, but certainly the civic occasions which greeted the five hundredth anniversary of Guru Nanak's birth in 1969 bore witness to a Sikh community which no longer regarded itself as a collection of struggling migrants.

The British Sikh Community

The number of Sikhs now in Britain is uncertain. *New Society*, 20/27 December 1985, accepting figures contained in the *U.K. Christian Handbook* 1985-86, estimated that there were some 200,000 Hindus and Sikhs in Britain in 1975, and that the total in 1985 was somewhere over the 300,000 mark. However, these numbers are certainly inaccurate. According to the census of 1981 there were 855,681 people living in England whose heads of households were of East African or Indian origin. Some of them would be Christian, more would be Muslim. A number would be white, the offspring of colonial servants, doctors, missionaries, engineers, who happened to be born there! This shows the impossibility of providing reliable statistics. However, if 10% is allowed for the number of people who are neither Sikh nor Hindu, we are left with some 750,000. Of these the division is probably fairly even between

Hindus and Sikhs. It is likely that the population of Sikhs in Britain is in the region of 400,000.[12]

Jat Sikhs from India came from the rural areas of the Punjab, especially villages in the vicinity of Hoshiarpur in Punjab. The most dramatic change in their way of life was in terms of occupation. Instead of being members of land-owning farming families, they were now wage earning employees usually working in the factories. The smaller group of Indian Ramgarhias came from the towns and often found employment for the skills they already possessed in engineering or carpentry, as well as working in offices or the civil service, though some of them also had to take unskilled factory jobs. Ramgarhia numbers were considerably increased as a result of East African migration to Britain. This was the main Sikh group which had gone to Africa where the British had restricted entry to Indians with specific, usually craft, skills. They had been extremely successful in Africa, forming a major part of the managerial class, establishing business and entering the professions. Their status and aspirations fitted them better for life in Britain than in India which few younger East Africans had ever visited, but which they knew to be corrupt, dirty - generally uncongenial. These Ramgarhia Sikhs came to Britain as complete families, with money, often quite rich, with no obligations to relatives in India, and having no intention of returning to the land of their aged parents or grandparents. If Britain proved unhospitable it would be towards Canada or the U.S.A. that they would turn, and some have. Much of their wealth and skill went into developing existing gurdwaras or building new ones. The new buildings of the seventies and eighties replacing those of the sixties are often testimonies to East African enthusiasm.

An aspect of Indian religiosity is its relatedness to caste. Sometimes lower caste Hindus will outbrahmin the brahmins in their concern about purity, especially in diet, avoiding not only meat but also such things as eggs, garlic and onions. Thus, they distance themselves from other groups near them in the social hierarchy and claim an affinity with those considered to be higher. In Sikhism where, strictly speaking, the concept of purity has no place and all men and women are equal, nonetheless the Jats predominate.[13] Many of them eat meat, against which Sikhism makes no pronouncement but also drink alcohol, sometimes smoke or are sometimes clean shaven and do not wear the turban - conduct not in keeping with the Sikh code of discipline. In Britain it was frequently, but not only, the Jat migrant who considered it prudent to cut the hair, remove the beard and abandon the turban in searching for a job in the early years of post-war migration. On the other hand, Ramgarhias, regarded certainly by Jats as lower in the social scale, and Bhatras regarded by both as shudras, are extremely observant of religious tradition, taken as a group. Bhatra gurdwaras were among the earliest,[14] and many East African Ramgarhias have gurdwaras in their own houses.[15] One of the strongest revivals in Sikhism in recent years, certainly in Britain, owes its stimulus to an East African Ramgarhia Sikh, Sant Puran Singh, who died in 1983. He persuaded many Sikhs to take amrit, maintain the vows which are incumbent upon those who do, and to devote time to nam simran meditation, and akhand paths (ritual continuous readings of the Guru Granth Sahib). It was often these East African Sikhs who reformed the practices of British gurdwaras and communities and sometimes felt it necessary to establish separate ones where, it was argued, true Sikhism could be practised.[16]

The word "reformed" in the previous paragraph is used in a very broad sense to include anything from the general smartening up of the building to the proper conducting of akhand paths and the organising of amrit pahul ceremonies. It does not necessarily suggest a strict compliance with the letter or spirit of the Rahit Maryada.[17] It is, for example, possible to find a bowl of water adjacent to the Guru Granth Singh. Perhaps the main emphasis, however, has been on preserving the Sikh form (the turban and five K's) and on the strict personal regime of daily nam simran, a vegetarian diet and the rejection of alcohol and tobacco.

Adaptations of Sikh Practice

The building in which Sikhs worship, the gurdwara, usually serves only that purpose in India. Each morning, early, at dawn if not sooner, the Guru Granth Sahib will be taken from its overnight resting place and installed on a low stool (manji), covered with cushions over which is a canopy. When it is not being read the scripture will be covered over with cloths, but in major gurdwaras an attendant will read from it for much of the day and relays of musicians will sing shabads from it. People will come and go paying their respects to God as manifest through the scriptures by bowing to it, sitting for a time - listening to its teachings, receiving karah parshad, perhaps taking the food which is freely available from the gurdwara kitchen and then going on their way. Numbers of Sikhs may gather for the formal prayer, Ardas, which accompanies parkash karna in the morning and precedes the sukh asan ceremony in the evening. Often the Guru Granth Sahib is laid to rest, but otherwise the visit to the gurdwara tends to be an individual act of devotion. Weddings will be held in open spaces where marquees may have been set up specially for the occasion. (The author has even attended one which took place on the front roof of a large house!) Only at special times, such as the celebration of a Guru's birth or death anniversary, a gurpurb, is a congregational gathering likely to occur.

In Britain this situation is very different. Daily parkash karna and sukh asan may usually be observed, but some gurdwaras must be closed until the evening as no one is available to act as custodian and reader of the Guru Granth Sahib. Sunday has become a day of congregational worship, though Sikhs have no weekly holy day. Services have become somewhat formalised. A tendency may be developing to end diwan, the service, at an agreed time, perhaps 12.30, when after Ardas and seeking the guidance of the Guru by randomly opening the scriptures, karah parshad will be distributed to the congregation who will then retire to the dining hall for langar.[18] Most gurdwaras now employ a granthi and daily evening diwan is becoming more usual. The British gurdwara has also become a community centre where Sikhs from miles around come to meet relatives and friends and share news and mutual concerns as well as worship, Sunday by Sunday. It has been compelled to establish Sunday or Saturday (or occasionally evening) classes to teach children Punjabi and the tenets of the Sikh religion. There may also be youth clubs and women's associations to provide for varying needs - the loneliness of older people who cannot fit into British life easily because of linguistic and cultural difficulties, and the young who, for lack of these, are in danger of being alienated and lost to the major society with which Sikhs are surrounded. Though with young Sikhs the situation is somewhat paradoxical; their knowledge of Punjabi and the Sikh religion may be very restricted, but to an increasing extent they are adopting the turban and uncut hair, if not the five K's. A reason for this, which is often given, is encounters with racial prejudice which have prompted them to assert their Sikh identity.

Continuity

In essentials, Sikhism in Britain is the same as that in India. Continuity is also to be found at the social level. The practice of arranged marriage shows no sign of dying out, though young people often have more to say (as they do among the better educated and more sophisticated in India) and the term "assisted marriage" is sometimes preferred by Sikhs. Social activities across the sexes are still frowned on by many parents. Coeducation may have to be accepted but it is not welcomed. Single-sex youth clubs are more congenial to parents than those where boys and girls meet and mix together, but it is better still for teenage girls to remain at home in the evenings or visit known female friends. Bhatras tend to marry their daughters at the youngest legal age, Ramgarhias may encourage them to participate in higher or further education, but hope they will live at home. Jats seem more prepared to let their daughters go to college or university as residential students. The ultimate goal for all Sikh girls in the minds of their parents, however, is marriage, not a career.

Marriages are still arranged on caste lines and inter-caste marriages are discouraged. The urban Indian increase in love marriages is parallelled in Britain, but the lack of concern for caste, which is often voiced in India, seems to be matched by an increased caste awareness in this country. Jat versus non-Jat, be it Hindu in Haryana or Sikh in Punjab, is an important ingredient of North Indian life. Its significance is no less in the United Kingdom where the management of gurdwaras is frequently dominated by a particular group, that which is most influential in the local community, Bhatra, Jat or Ramgarhia.

Sikhs and the Law

The requirement to wear the turban is laid upon Khalsa Sikhs by the Rahit Maryada and upon every male member of the community by custom. Although it is breached by a considerable number of men, keeping the turban and the beard are fundamentals of normative Sikhism. It is also worn by American female converts and a few British Sikhs of Indian origin.

Wolverhampton, Manchester and Leeds have seen disputes between public transport authorities and Sikhs over the wish to wear turbans instead of the regulation peak caps. Sometimes one can sympathise with the authorities as when in Leeds two men who had hitherto made no such request, appeared for duty wearing their turbans! They had undergone initiation where the requirement to keep the turban and five K's had been emphatically laid upon them. Hence their change in appearance. These disputes were eventually ended amicably and to the satisfaction of the Sikh community, as was the issue of crash helmets.

In 1972 a Road Traffic Act was passed requiring all riders on motorcycles to wear crash helmets. Sikhs objected on religious grounds and some challenged the law by riding in groups ostentatiously without crash helmets, courting arrest. In 1976, Parliament, influenced to some extent by memories of turbanned soldier-colleagues in the Second World War, as well as by ideals of religious tolerance, passed the Motor-Cycle Crash Helmets (Religious Exemption) Act. Turban-wearing followers of the Sikh religion need not wear a crash-helmet when riding a motorcycle.

Occasionally difficulties have arisen over the right of Sikh boys to wear turbans in school. One, in 1979, ended with Kulbinder Singh Bhamra being permitted to wear the turban but with Mr. N. S. Noor being sued by the head-teacher for libel and eventually being made bankrupt when faced with a £5,000 fine and £50,000 costs. Legal history was made in 1982/83 when a case was successfully brought against Mr. Dowell-Lee, headmaster of a private Roman Catholic school, who had refused Gurinder Mandla, an East African Sikh boy, permission to wear the turban as part of his school uniform. Lord Denning upheld an appeal by Mr. Dowell-Lee stating that they were victims of racial discrimination under the Race Relations Act. The

Lords, on appeal, reversed the decision of the Lord Chief Justice (March 1983). Turbans are no longer headline news, but friction still occurs on building sites where health and safety at work regulations require the wearing of "hard hats."*

Another grievance which may be mentioned, which seems now to have been remedied, is that experienced by female Sikh nurses. If they do not use their gotra name, Sikh women should be called "Kaur." The British Nursing Council, however, demanded that on passing their S. R. N. or S. E. N. examination, they should be listed as "Singh," presumably because that was the "surname" of the father as it appeared on birth certificates! The United Kingdom Central Council for Nursing now registers nurses under their customary names (see appended letter).[19]

Khalistan and British Sikhs

Some Sikhs would not feel the inclusion of this section was warranted or desirable, but the assasination of Mr. T. S. Toor in January 1986, may have created a new situation. Time will tell.

This is not the place to tell the story of the Khalistan Movement, Operation Blue Star and the assassination of Indira Gandhi.[20] In Britain there was grief and a sense of tragedy when news of the storming of the Golden Temple was broadcast. At the death of Indira Gandhi a few Sikhs rejoiced in public and somehow television cameras were on hand to record these events outside India House and in Southall. Most Sikhs knew it boded ill for their kith and kin in India and remained silent, anxious and often disapproving. In India and in the United Kingdom, support for Sant Jarnail Singh Bhindranwale and Khalistan has come almost exclusively from Jats. Some Ramgarhias from East Africa have sided with the Indian Government. T. S. Toor was one; two Congress (Indira) M. P.s came from India to attend his funeral. For the most part, non-Jats have distanced themselves from the politics of Punjab and disputes and power-struggles related to the crisis have been confined to Jat gurdwaras. The Indian Government is annoyed at

---

* The Employment Bill now passing through Parliament contains a clause exempting Sikhs from the requirement to wear safety helmets on building sites (passed 8 Nov. 1989).

Britain permitting the so-called President of Khalistan, Mr. S. Chauhan, to mouth hostilities and stir up agitation from Slough, and probably delayed its decision to buy Westland helicopters to demonstrate its disapproval. Meanwhile, the British Government is reported to be considering how to extend the Prevention of Terrorism Act to deal with the feuding of Sikh factions.[21]

The Future

To predict developments among any migrant community may be an act of folly. To set them down in print could be said to be the action of an egotistical lunatic. However, despite the risks, a few observations might be offered.

Sikhs will remain in Britain. The myth of return still strong among those who came to these shores from India will become less of a realisable aspiration as they look at the grandchildren now being born here who could never settle in India.

Most of those children will grow up Sikhs, maintaining their sense of identity and the Sikh form, at least to the extent of keeping the turban and beard. Whether the Punjabi language will be retained is less certain. The Jews have shown that a language can survive as a relic for worship but the conduct of services in the synagogue seems to devolve upon a steadily decreasing group of men literate in Hebrew. Sikhness, like Jewishness, could become a matter of ethnicity rather than belief, but Sikhism lacks the domestic rituals and traditions which play such an important part in Jewish survival. Nevertheless, a combination of the current Sikh crisis in India together with local crises in different countries, Africanisation in that continent, racism in Britain, could result in a Sikhism being perpetuated, which is really little more than an expression of non-Hindu Punjabi nationalism.

There is another way. The gradual adoption of English by the largest Sikh community outside India. It may be too soon for this change. Only about one-third of our Sikhs were born here, and Operation Blue Star has certainly promoted a revival in an awareness of Punjabi roots. However,

Punjabi has not the status of a sacred language among Sikhs. It is even possible to meet members of the community who first read the words of their scriptures in Urdu or Hindi, not Gurmukhi, though only Gurmukhi editions are installed in gurdwaras. Sikhs will readily agree that Guru Nanak spoke to the inhabitants of Mecca in Arabic and must have used Persian or Tibetan on other journeys. Still, there is an understandable reluctance to agree that the spirit of the words of the poetry of the Guru Granth Sahib could be conveyed in English. English speaking Sikhs may eventually be responsible for asking the Panth to make the decision which Jews had to make long ago when they produced the Greek Septuagint version of the Hebrew Scriptures.[22]

Manjit Kaur (Pamela Wylam), a British convert to Sikhism, held services in English over a decade ago in the Shepherd's Bush gurdwara, and the author of this chapter came across the intention to install an English one-volume translation of the Guru Granth Sahib to hold an Akhand Path at Baisakhi, 1984. The version used would have been Ernest Trumpp's which is incomplete and in many other ways unacceptable. The proposal was dropped but the need was felt and there was a willingness to respond to it.

Sikhism's establishment in Britain in large numbers coincided with the change from Christian-based biblical studies and theology courses in schools, colleges and universities to religious studies. The influential Lancaster Religious Studies department was set up in 1967 and 1969 saw the founding of the Shap Working Party on World Religions in Education as well as the nationwide celebrations of the five hundredth anniversary of the birth of Guru Nanak. The interest of a number of non-Sikhs in Sikhism was aroused by attending the quincentenary celebrations.[23] The result has been a growth in Sikh awareness of their religion as a world religion. Western Sikhism, of which the British community is the largest component, if freed from the myth of return and all attachment to Punjabi culture may exert a strong influence upon the Sikh religion resulting in yet another of its periodic reconceptualisations and reappraisals.

For further reading:

W. O. Cole & P. S. Sambhi. *The Sikhs: Their Religious Beliefs and Practices.* Routledge & Kegan Paul, 1978, 2nd ed., 1986.

Harbans Singh. *The Heritage of the Sikhs.* Manohar, 1985.

W. H. McLeod. *Textual Sources for the Study of Sikhism.* Manchester University, 1984.

W. O. Cole. *Sikhism and its Indian Context.* Darton Longman & Todd, 1984.

P. Bhachu. *Twice Migrants.* Tavistock Publications, 1986.

Rozina Visram. *Ayahs, Lascars and Princes.* Pluto Press, 1986.

APPENDIX ONE

United Kingdom
Central Council for Nursing
Midwifery and Health Visting
23 Portland Place
London W1N 3AF

UKCC

4 March 1986

Dr. W. Owen Cole
Head of Religious Studies
West Sussex Institute of Higher Education
Bishop Otter College
College Lane, Chichester
W. Sussex, PO19 4PE

Dear Dr. Owen Cole

Thank you for your letter of 12 February which has been passed to me for reply.

Since the Council took over responsibility for registration in July 1983 our policy, under legal advice, has been to register practitioners under the names which they themselves customarily use. This we find avoids a great deal of confusion.

At the time of writing, there appear to be on the Register some four hundred female nurses having the surname "Singh". We would be willing to amend their names on the Register if they will present us with a formal written request to do so. By July this year we hope that every practising nurse, midwife and health visitor will have informed us both of their current address and the name under which they are practising, and this exercise should serve to rectify any such anomalies.

I hope the above information will meet your needs, and may we wish you every sucess with your new book.

Yours sincerely

A R Parker
Register Control

274

REFERENCES

[1]Readers seeking an extended introduction to the Sikh religion might consult Hinnells, J. R., (ed.), *A Handbook of Living Religions*, Viking Press, 1984 (Penguin paperback edition, 1985). More detailed information can be obtained from the books listed at the end of this chapter.

[2]Singh, K., *A History of the Sikhs*, O. U. P., India, 1977 edition, volume 2, page 101.

[3]*Op. cit.*, p. 153.

[4]Sikhs took part in the jubilee celebrations of Queen Victoria, 1887 and 1897, and in the coronations of Edward VII, 1902, and George V, 1911. Nobles such as the Maharaja of Kapurthala, Jagjit Singh Bahadur, and his son Hanwar Harnam Singh, also visited Britain, bringing relations and servants, some of whom never returned to India. 138,000 soldiers served in Europe during the 1914-18 war. The wounded were cared for in a hospital in Brighton. On discharge some decided to remain in England.

[5]See also Singh, N., Sikhs in Manchester, *Sikh Bulletin*, 1986, published by West Sussex Institute of Higher Education, and her unpublished B. A. thesis, Manchester University, 1984, on the same subject.Gyani Sundar Singh Saggar of Manchester informs me that the Sinclair Road Gurdwara was originally called the Bhapundra Dharamsala after Maharaja Bhapundra Singh of Patiali, who bought and donated the property. He also says that the second gurdwara in Britain was established at 15, Monton Street, Moss Side, Manchester in 1954.

[6]In Batley, Yorkshire, the first Muslim evidently arrived before the Second World War. He came from Gujarat, W. India, but was always known locally as "the Italian."

[7]Sometimes the assertion is made that some migrants were influenced by political motives in the forties and fifties, but this seems doubtful and a result of hindsight. At the time the reasons were seen to be economic.

[8]Watson, J. L., (ed.), *Between Two Cultures*, Blackwell, 1977, p.37.

[9]*Sikh Temples in U. K.*, Jan Publications, 1976.

[10]Watson, op. cit., and Knott, K., *Hinduism in England: the Hindu Population in Leeds*, Leeds University, 1981, and *Hinduism in Leeds*, Leeds University, 1986, passim.

[11]Bhachu, P., *Twice Migrants*, Tavistock Publications, 1986, passim.

[12]Knott, K. & Toon, R., *Muslims, Sikhs and Hindus in the U. K.: Problems in the Estimation of Religious Statistics*, Leeds University, 1982. These figures were computed before the 1981 census figures were available.

[13]The three main Sikh groups who have come to Britain are Bhatras, Jats and Ramgarhias. Bhatras claim brahmin origins but are regarded as shudras by other Sikhs who assert that they were a Hindu beggar caste. When they converted to Sikhism in an attempt to improve their social status they became pedlars, as begging is condemned by Sikhism. These were among the first Sikhs to come to Britain where they often earned their living as house-to-house salesmen. See DAT Thomas and PAS Ghuman, *A Survey of Social and Religious Attitudes Among Sikhs in Cardiff*, Open University in Wales, N.D.

Jats are landowning farmers, mostly of smallholdings. They are the majority group among Sikhs in Punjab and in Britain. They regard themselves as superior to Bhatras and Ramgarhias in the social hierarchy of Punjab. See J. Pettigrew, *Robber Noblemen*, London, 1975, and *New Community* 1 (5): 354-63.

Ramgarhias are not a caste group, strictly speaking. They are the descendants of men who belonged to the misl, or Sikh army group, organised and led by Jassa Singh Ramgarhia in the eighteenth century. Occupationally, they are from such skilled craft groups as carpenters and as such tend to be found predominantly in the towns of Punjab. Consequently they constituted the majority of Sikhs who went to East Africa. See Singh, C. A., *The Ramgarhias*, Sikh Bulletin, West Sussex Institute of Higher Education, 1986, and Bhachu, *op. cit.*, passim.

[14]Cardiff, 1956, Birmingham, 1961, and Manchester. In each case earlier house meetings preceded the gurdwaras.

[15]Bhachu, *op. cit.*, passim.

[16]Bhachu, *op. cit.*, chapter three,

[17]*Rahit Maryada*, printed as appendix 1, Cole and Sambhi, 1978.

[18]Langar, the free kitchen and food provision which is characteristic of every gurdwara is used of the place where food is prepared and of the food itself.

[19]Sikhism is a completely lay religion, despite the tendency of Sikhs themselves to use the word "priest." All functions may be performed by male or female members of the community.

[20]See Shackle, C., *The Sikhs*, Minority Rights Group Report, No. 65, 1984. A rather more journalistic and sensational account is given in Tully, M. and Jacob, S., *Amritsar, Mrs. Gandhi's Last Battle*, Jonathan Cape, 1985.

[21]Report on BBC Radio 4, The World This Weekend, 9th February 1986.

[22]English versions of the Guru Granth Sahib are published in multiple volume editions. The reason cannot be size as the original written in the gurmukhi script is bound in one volume. More likely it is to prevent an English version being installed in gurdwaras. About a hundred years ago, when the first printed editions were published, they were issued in five volumes with instructions that they should not be bound as one. Only slowly were printed volumes accepted for use in worship.

[23]Christopher Shackle and the present writer are two of the people who trace their interest and involvement in the Sikh studies to the quincentenary celebrations. *Guru Nanak and the Sikh Religion*, Oxford, published in the previous year and the reprint of Max Macauliffe's six volume work, *The Sikh Religion*, in 1963, were the first of many books on Sikhism to appear in England. Since then many schools and colleges of higher education have introduced courses on Sikhism into their religious studies syllabuses. Universities lag some way behind. In 1984 a Sikh studies group first met with the help of the British Association for the History of Religion. The convenor is the present writer from whom details of activities can be obtained.

CHAPTER XVI

BUDDHISM IN BRITAIN:
SKILFUL MEANS OR SELLING OUT?

DEIRDRE GREEN

Buddhists talk of the *dharma* going West, and see this event as representing the beginning of a new era in Buddhist history, comparable in importance to the earlier movement of Buddhism from India to the Far East. It has been claimed that Buddhism is the fastest growing religion in Britain at the present time; since 1969 over seventy new groups have been established (twenty-four of these having been founded since 1981)[1] so that the 1985 edition of the *International Buddhist Directory* lists 120 Buddhist centres or groups in the United Kingdom, plus a further 55 "unconfirmed" centres or groups (where current address and perhaps continued existence were in question).[2] In 1983 over twelve thousand people went on Buddhist retreats in Britain.[3]

The reasons for the widespread appeal of Buddhism in the modern West are many. Although it is certainly not true, as some have claimed, that Buddhism has "no dogmas," its *relative* lack of dogmatism and its emphasis on free enquiry, personal experience and experiment, appeal to those who have become disillusioned with the institutionalized forms of Christianity and yet still feel a need for spiritual meaning and fulfilment. Buddhism's highly developed and subtle systems of meditation and self-mastery offer practical means towards this fulfilment. Philosophically, Buddhism does not espouse any form of absolutism and therefore may appeal to intellectuals who have been brought up in the post-Wittgensteinian philosophical tradition. It is free, too, from many of the dualisms which have so racked Western thought and which so many now find impossible to accept: dualisms such as God/world, humanity/nature, mind/body, fact/value. Buddhism's nontheistic stance and its apparent compatibility with modern scientific thought are further reasons for its appeal, while a number of its outstanding values, such as a concern for peace, and care for all living things and the environment, are felt by many to be particularly relevant to our time. There is little doubt that Buddhism has a great deal to offer the West, but a central issue with regard to this, which is the subject of the present paper, concerns the adaptation of Buddhism to modern Western sociocultural conditions. We shall attempt to outline the varying options for Buddhist groups in the West in terms of their ideological stance vis-à-vis modern society, illustrating these options by reference to some of the varied types of Buddhist organisation now in existence in Britain. It is well known that Buddhism has, over the course of its history and in all the countries in which it has taken root, shown an inherent flexibility and an ability to adapt readily to new sociocultural conditions. As we shall shortly discuss in more depth, it has even been suggested (I believe with some perspicacity) by Pye that this acclimatisation of Buddhism to diverse cultural backgrounds can be understood in terms of the concept of skilful means, central to Mahāyāna Buddhism, whereby the *dharma* is expressed in formulae aligned with the karmic condition of the recipient. The question to be asked, with regard to Buddhism in Britain, is whether this inherent adaptability might on occasion result in "selling out" to the *Weltanschauung* of modern secular and "scientific" thought. It should be noted initially that this paper is concerned mainly with the options available to Westerners who have converted to Buddhism or who are contemplating doing so, rather than with the problems of immigrant Buddhists. Certainly the two groups may often be found attending the same Buddhist centres, but immigrants may be more interested in retaining their religion in a relatively traditional form, as part of their cultural identity, than in adapting it to the society in which they have settled.

As early as 1960, Christmas Humphreys, one of the pioneers of Western Buddhism, argued that Buddhism in the West must be reclothed in "...our own idiom of thought and practice,"[4] This, he held, would entail greater attention being paid to the analytical, intellectual, and scientific approaches to phenomena than was usual in Eastern Buddhist cultures. While warning against Western Buddhism's becoming over-intellectualized and thus losing its essentially Buddhist character, Humphreys saw the Eastern cultural "wrappings" that Buddhism brought with it as unimportant compared with the central *experience* of *nirvāna* which Buddhism upholds as our goal. The cultural accretions, he held, could be discarded, and replaced by ways of expression more suited to Western ways of being and thinking. Twenty-five years later, it has become apparent that it is not that simple. In order to dissociate the cultural "wrappings" from the essence of Buddhism, we need first of all to agree regarding the nature of this essence. Yet it is notoriously difficult to isolate an essence when the particulars themselves are so varied, as Buddhists themselves will admit: many Buddhists like to offer extremely broad definitions of what is to be included as representative of "Buddhism." And even supposing that we manage to reach a consensus on this point, we are still left with the problem of finding suitable ways of expression for Western Buddhism, forms which will effectively communicate Buddhism's message to a modern Western audience yet without compromising the faith's essential truths.

The question to what extent and in what ways religions should adapt to the modern world is of perennial interest. A few theoretical considerations may be helpful before looking at this question specifically with regard to Buddhism. Peter Berger, in *A Rumour of Angels*, makes a number of salient points regarding the challenges of the modern worldview to religious thought. He points out that humanity in the modern world today has, as a whole, lost contact with the religious worldview: the religious way of seeing things has become one among many possible choices in a pluralistic situation. Hence, those who hold religious beliefs are a "cognitive minority," or, in other words, "a group of people whose view of the world differs significantly from the one generally taken for granted in their society."[5] Considerable social strain is generated for the religious individual inasmuch as society at large refuses to accept his or her definitions of reality as a genuine possibility. Berger sees two options for religious thought, while pointing out that these are extreme choices and that most people will actually adopt a position between the extremes:

(1)   The first option is that of maintaining a "supernaturalist" position, i.e., one in which all the traditional affirmations of a religion are adhered to even where they may conflict with accepted scientific knowledge. Berger points out that there are extremely strong social and psychological pressures against maintaining this position, since society at large is "cognitively antagonistic" to it.   He adds that it is only in a "countercommunity," set apart from the rest of society, that this type of position is likely to be maintained, for only in such a community can the necessary "plausibility structure," i.e., the social consensus necessary to make an ongoing commitment to a set of beliefs a viable option, be upheld.

(2)   The alternative option is one in which "...the cognitive authority and superiority of whatever is taken to be 'the *Weltanschauung* of modern man' is conceded with few if any reservations...The basic intellectual task undertaken as a result of this option is one of *translation*. The traditional religious affirmations are translated into terms appropriate to the new frame of reference, the one that allegedly conforms to the *Weltanschauung* of modernity."[6] Berger points out that there are two main dangers inherent in this option: firstly, a "secularized" religion may have difficulty in showing that its newly modified doctrine has anything special to offer over and above the available secular equivalents (such as various therapies, for example); and secondly, there is the danger of what Berger calls "escalation toward the pole of cognitive surrender":[7]   the modifications may go too far, so that the religion loses ground to the modern worldview altogether, and eventually disappears in "self-liquidation."[8]

Willson, in *Rebirth and the Western Buddhist*, gives what is perhaps a rather subtler, although considerably briefer, analysis, outlining what he sees as three main approaches possible to Buddhists in the light of the confrontation between Buddhism, and modern materialistic and scientific thought.   The option which he calls "Fundamentalism" and which corresponds to Berger's "supernaturalism," he holds, is "not a live option" for Western Buddhists today.[9] His second possibility, "Retreat," entails defining separate areas of interest for science and religion, as has been done in many

Christian circles, so that science is concerned with physical facts and religion with spiritual truth. Willson's third option, "Synthesis," is his own favoured approach. This involves dismissing neither Buddhism nor science; recognizing that neither system of thought has sole and absolute validity regarding the interpretation of reality and that each is liable to error. Through this method a synthesis may be arrived at, which will involve rejecting both some elements of traditional Buddhist teaching (such as certain cosmological notions) and also certain *scientistic* "dogmas," i.e., assumptions based on the more or less unquestioning acceptance of science as an "orthodoxy." Willson adopts this synthetic and critical approach in his analysis of rebirth, pointing out that Buddhism has always assimilated and adapted itself to indigenous traditions in the various countries in which it has taken root. "It cannot be claimed that the Dharma has been established in the West," he asserts, "until it is possible for anyone to accept Buddhist teachings without feeling that they conflict with scientific truth."[10]

As has been mentioned, the adaptation of Buddhism to prevailing cultural conditions is not a phenomenon peculiar to the modern West. It has been noted already that Pye has argued that the diversity and flexibility of Buddhism can be understood in terms of "skilful means" (Skt. *upāya-kauśalya*; Ch. *fang-pien*; Jap. *hōben*). This concept is of great importance in Mahāyāna Buddhism in particular, but Pye suggests that it could also be regarded as implicit to a lesser degree in Theravāda. The concept of skilful means advances the view that the various forms of Buddhist teaching and practice are all *provisional devices* designed to lead people to enlightenment, arrived at by relating Buddhist truths to the ordinary level of understanding and cultural conditions of the recipient. None of these means or devices should be thought of as having ultimate validity: they are no more than useful constructs of our own making which serve to ferry us across the river of existence to the Beyond: to use a widespread Buddhist simile, once we have reached the Other Shore (a symbol for *nirvāna*) we leave behind on the bank the raft which enabled us to cross the stream. This notion is intimately bound up with the fact that Buddhism has not usually been concerned with the formulation of dogmas *for their own sake*, but has been a pragmatically-orientated religion, concerned to find practical answers to the problem of suffering, and with philosophy only inasmuch as it helps towards this end. The means are devised in terms of the specific problem and are not intended to have any absolute meaning beyond the attainment of the solution. In other words, skilful means entails that Buddhist teachings will be formulated in terms of the karmic conditions of the people for whom they are intended - in terms of their relative ignorance or selfishness or passionate attachments, in terms of their levels of intellectual and spiritual understanding, and (crucially for our present concern) in terms of their social and cultural situation.

Because of the inherent flexibility of Buddhism, which is given sanction by the idea of skilful means, new forms of Buddhism are to be expected when socio-cultural conditions change. Pye sees skilful means as constituting what he calls a "correlational technique" between Buddhism and other thought-systems. "The practical working out of such correlations," he says, "means that Buddhism does not reject other thought-systems but associates with them, with a view to realising the intention of the Buddhist system."[11] Thus, he says, the strength of Buddhism as a cultural force "has lain in its positionless, mediating, method. It has always thrived on control through syncretism."[12] But in spite of this, Pye considers that Buddhism has not lost ground to the various other thought-systems with which it may associate itself: Buddhism manages to maintain a grip on its own central meaning because "an apparently inadequate vehicle is accepted because latent within it is the possibility of its being transformed or resolved into a fully Buddhist meaning."[13] The Buddhist, then, can take a "relaxed view of cultural diversification" because "there could always come a day when... the skilful means arrives at its true destination of Buddhist meaning."[14] But it is important to note that skilful means, while relating Buddhist teachings to the everyday life of the recipient, should not thereby compromise the essential truths of Buddhism. Thus Pye comments that skilful means "allows enough room for creative modernists" but at the same time points out that "the normative discernment of skilful means entails an interpretative activity *within the tradition*, that is to say an activity analogous to what in the western world is known as theology."[15] One question to be asked, then, is whether some of the more extreme attempts to adapt Buddhism to the modern West to be described shortly, are to be seen as genuine skilful means, or whether on the other hand they have stepped outside the tradition altogether, so that there is little truly Buddhist meaning left in them. We are brought back to the questions: What is the essence of Buddhism and what are merely cultural accretions? What should and should not be changed in an attempt at adaption to a new culture? At what point does skilful means become selling out?

The forms of Buddhism now to be found in Britain are many and varied, and can perhaps usefully be placed along a continuum with wholesale adherence to tradition at one pole, through varying degrees of skilful means (synthesis, adaptation, accommodation) to Berger's "pole of cognitive surrender." The traditional end of the continuum would be represented, for example, by the English Sangha Association, which runs several monasteries, of which the most recently opened is Amaravatī in the Hertfordshire countryside. Here monastic discipline based on Thai Theravāda tradition is followed; the monks and nuns shave their heads and wear the saffron robe, and observe the traditional monastic rules (chastity, not possessing money, abstaining from intoxicants, only eating between dawn and midday, etc.). Most surprisingly of all, perhaps, they go on almsrounds to the local English villages. Although the total number of monks and nuns is small, many young, well-educated Westerners are attracted to this way of life.

The various schools of Tibetan Buddhism are more diverse in their outlook, but it may be noted that the popularity of some of the more traditional schools who would also be placed at this end of the continuum appears to be on the wane. Kampo Gangra Dechen Ling in Swansea, as I discovered on a recent visit, is shortly to close due to lack of committed interest. My informant told me that many students were not able to submit themselves to the discipline of two hours' meditation a day; a further problem for many people was that teaching was given along very traditional lines with no specific attempts being made to relate the *dharma* to the realities of living in modern society.

Many Buddhists feel that the attempt to preserve the forms of Buddhism traditional to another culture is inappropriate in Britain, and that there is little point in adhering to tradition for its own sake, if it is found not to be effective as a "means" to bring people in Britain to the *dharma*. The Friends of the Western Buddhist Order (FWBO) have established a specifically Western form of Buddhism which on the whole appears neither to retain tradition for its own sake nor to make concessions to the modern worldview where the latter departs from Buddhist spiritual perspectives. The Order now has over 200 ordained members and over 700 novices[16] and its overall membership runs into six figures,[17] including "Friends" and "Mitras." Many "Friends" have only a very loose affiliation with the FWBO. "Mitras" (the term is in fact simply the Sanskrit for "friend") have specifically declared their commitment to the movement and must keep up regular contact with the Order and perform various duties and practices. The Order's policy is to distinguish between "what is intrinsically the Dharma and what is merely cultural accident," looking at tradition "with a respectful but discriminating eye."[18] Claiming (with some justification) that no other Western Buddhist group has "looked in any very radical way at how the committed Buddhist is to *live* in the modern West,"[19] the FWBO emphasizes that

> for Buddhism to have any relevance in our day it must be *lived* in full awareness of the specific environment which surrounds it and which it must try to transform...Institutions, practices, and teachings which evolved within agrarian monarchies wherein Buddhism was the established religion cannot be directly transposed into the very different social and economic - even psychological - conditions of the modern West. Buddhism must express itself through the culture in the midst of which it finds itself - neither compromising with it nor ignoring it. At the same time it must remain Buddhism, faithful to the spirit of the tradition.[20]

The FWBO sees itself as creating a "New Society" through its communities and businesses. The businesses, which are run by cooperatives, include a wholefood shop, vegetarian restaurant, publishing house and others; they provide for members a means of "Right Livelihood" (a basic Buddhist precept according to which a Buddhist should earn his or her living only by means that are not at variance with Buddhist ethics). The structure of the communities varies, due to deliberate flexibility: some are made up only of ordained Order members, others include Friends and Mitras. In some most people work for an FWBO business, in others a number have outside jobs. Ordained Order members are not obliged to live in the communities, although most do; they are described as "neither monk nor lay,"[21] a paradox which seems to be reflected in the rather ambivalent position of the FWBO towards society at large. On the one hand, the Order members "are not isolated from the world in monastic surroundings"[22] and remain "in constant dialogue with the wider society."[23] On the other hand, dialogue itself implies a degree of separateness; the majority of ordained members have no family or home ties (although there are exceptions to this rule) and the FWBO asserts that "for most people, a family situation or living with a member of the opposite sex will sooner or later become a barrier to further growth...a conflict arises between their desire to grow as an individual and their marriage"[24] - an attitude for which the Order has been criticized by other Buddhists. Sexual segregation prevails in the Order's residential communities and indeed in most FWBO activities. This aspect of the movement's teachings hardly seems typical of the general policy of finding patterns of living appropriate to the modern world.

Other examples of Buddhist organisations which might be placed somewhere around the midpoint of our continuum include a number of Zen centres, such as Throssel Hole Priory which advocates "maintaining the spirit of Zen, at the same time expressing it in a British way."[25] At some of these centres, meditation techniques may be combined with psychotherapy. The Buddhist Peace Fellowship aims to bring Buddhist ways of non-violence and compassion to bear on peace and ecology issues: it is quite radical in its attunement to contemporary issues but without thereby losing its Buddhist basis. Soka Gakkai, known in Britain as Nichiren Shoshu of the United Kingdom (NSUK), aims to contribute to peace, education and culture throughout the world according to guidelines based upon the Buddhism of Nichiren Daishonin (1222-1282). This group seems to be growing quite rapidly in Britain at the present time, and certainly maintains its traditions whilst also relating wholeheartedly to the contemporary world, although some find its aggressive proselytizing attitude objectionable, and it could be argued that the movement's materialism may bring it close to what I have perhaps contentiously called "selling out" or to Berger's "pole of cognitive surrender" (as I shall argue with respect to other groups below). In NSUK, chanting, the main form of religious practice, is explicitly performed for quite worldly benefits as well as spiritual ones, e. g., to obtain money, a new car, job or house. One could, I suppose, justify this by arguing that lay Buddhists at least have always indulged in religious practices for material gain: but then one is brought back once more to the question whether this aspect of popular lay Buddhism is of the *essence* of Buddhism.

But those groups that seem to me to be coming very close to Berger's "pole of cognitive surrender" typically emphasize Buddhism's "scientific," "rational" and "nondogmatic" character and claim that their teachings have little or nothing to do with "religion" and "faith." The point I wish to make is not that Buddhism is not "rational" nor that it should not be *compatible* with science, but rather that such movements unquestioningly accept the cognitive assumptions of modern Western society, i.e., that science and rationalism are superior to religion, that a human activity must be *rationalistic* in order to be *rational* (in other words, that there is only one form of rationality - that which is judged by scientific/empirical standards), that Buddhism must be shown to be scientific and not religious if it is to be acceptable. The Scientific Buddhist Association, which I will discuss shortly, is an extreme example of this stance. It seems to me that the same viewpoint is shown to a lesser degree by Vipassana Meditation as taught by S. N. Goenka. An introductory pamphlet on the meditation retreats run by the Vipassana Association claims that:

> The entire Path (Dhamma) is a universal remedy for universal problems and has nothing to do with any organized religion or sectarianism...Although Vipassana was developed as a technique by the Buddha, its practice is not limited to Buddhists. There is absolutely no question of conversion...The rules [of the meditation retreat] are not primarily for the benefit of the Teacher or the Management nor are they negative expressions of tradition, orthodoxy or blind faith in some organized religion. Rather, they are based on the practical experience of thousands of meditators over the years and are both scientific and rational...[26]

Elsewhere Goenka states that the Buddha

"...never taught any religion, any ism. He never instructed his followers to practice any rites or rituals, any blind or empty formalities. Instead, he taught just to observe nature as it is, by observing the reality inside."[27] Certainly Goenka has a point here, and while associating himself with the teachings of the Buddha, he wisely (given his position) dissociates himself from Buddhism in the sense that he does not claim nor wish to be identified with this religion to the exclusion of others. It may be noted in passing, however, that Goenka's teachings are extremely traditional when it comes to practical discipline: Vipassana retreats are notorious for their strict, rigorous austerity which can be physically and mentally exhausting. In other ways, too, Goenka's Theravāda roots are obvious, and to some extent bely his attempt to dissociate the technique of Vipassana meditation from Buddhist tradition and culture.

Gerald du Pré, Chairperson of the Scientific Buddhist Association (which produces the magazine *The Western Buddhist*), has written at length attempting to show not only that Buddhism is compatible with science, but that it *is* a science, not a faith, having little or nothing in common with dogmatic forms of religion. He enumerates various qualities which he sees as common to both Buddhism and science (a down-to-earth attitude, a spirit of free enquiry, a combining of logical theory with acute observation and practical application); in my opinion not only giving an idealized view of scientific method, but also failing to distinguish between what the Buddha may have been like as a man, and what Buddhism has been as a religion. Du Pré's account of the similarities between Buddhism and science is far from value-free: the implication is that Buddhism is commendable *because* it is logical, empirical, based on experience, etc.; Buddhism must be found to make sense *according to the criteria of rationality of the modern West* in order for it to be acceptable. Du Pré suggests that Buddhism and psychology "cover exactly the same ground, and have exactly the same actual or potential scope"[28] and that Buddhism is actually a therapy: the experience of *dukkha* is like a neurosis, *nirvāna* is a state of mental health.[29] He argues that Mādhyamika philosophy is in reality a revolutionary philosophy of science[30] and that the *skandhas* are remarkably close to modern neurobiological theories of the nervous system.[31] "It would be possible, and quite valid," he further claims, "to translate the Buddhist theory of reincarnation [*sic*] into the language of embryology, genetics and molecular biology. The theory is not a metaphysical one, as it became in Hinduism, but is plainly biological..."[32] No doubt meditation, as du Pré says, can be *related to* modern psychotherapeutic techniques and knowledge of the nervous system, but it is significant that du Pré also claims that "This will give...Buddhist meditators an *objective criterion* against which to judge the value of this or that technique or tradition. In time, it should also give rise to such a specifically Western form of Buddhist meditation as is thoroughly at home in the modern world."[33] Du Pré, then, appears to assume that our scientific worldview is the single objective paradigm of rationality. (He does state elsewhere that science is a system of *relative* truth like all others, but adds that it is "the soundest, all inclusive [*sic*] and most successful system of relative truth mankind has yet developed"!)[34] He believes that the apparent incompatibility between traditional forms of religion, and science, can be bridged by Buddhism, emphasizing that in Buddhism there is "no divine god, saviour or authority," claiming that there are furthermore "no dogmas,"[35] and holding that a union of Buddhism and science will produce a "scientific religion" appropriate to the modern world.

It seems to me that this particular form of Buddhism is dangerously near to Berger's "pole of cognitive surrender," assuming as it does the cognitive superiority of the scientific worldview. There is, of course, a great deal of difference between du Pré's position, and that of Willson or others like him (who merely wish Buddhism and science to be seen as *compatible*). Du Pré's attempts to translate Buddhist tenets into another mode of discourse sometimes result in considerable loss of depth and significance on the part of the Buddhist teachings themselves. Du Pré imposes onto Buddhism preconceived standards of reference derived from the modern Western worldview, preconceived ideas as to what constitutes "rationality" which involve seeing this in terms of empirical verifiability and logical analysis. I would wish to argue, by way of contrast, that Buddhism should be evaluated in terms of its own criteria of rationality, its own standards of intelligibility and reality. If these standards are not always immediately comprehensible to modern Westerners, the onus is on us to try to understand Buddhist categories of thought rather than attempting to make Buddhism intelligible according to the limitations of our own cultural categories.

The crucial question, then, is whether adaptations of Buddhism such as that offered by du Pré can be considered as a skilful means - a way of relating Buddhist teachings to the modern Western sociocultural environment - or whether on the other hand they are so close to the "pole of cognitive surrender" as to be "selling out" and to be in danger of what Berger calls "self-liquidation." As previously noted, Pye, in the context of discussing "creative modernists," emphasizes that skillful means entails an interpretative activity within the tradition. Has du Pré in fact stepped outside the tradition altogether? The same salient point is raised by a statement made by an anonymous Buddhist in Campbell's survey of Buddhism in Britain, who claims that "One doesn't even have to believe that the Buddha existed, one doesn't have to believe in rebirth, one doesn't have to believe in nirvāna."36 Leaving aside the question of the Buddha's existence (which, in any case, is no longer questioned by scholars today) one could argue that a Buddhism without rebirth and nirvāna is no longer Buddhism. Indeed Willson, in his study of rebirth and Western Buddhism, argues, I believe correctly, that "...rebirth is a virtually inseparable part of Buddhist teaching. It is quite impossible to compress the richness of the Buddhist worldview...into the impoverished mental frame of those who deny it."37 Certainly many Buddhists would agree that in the end the Buddhist must transcend all particular, limited views of reality - including those put forward by Buddhism itself (and, we might add, those of science). But this letting-go of particular views, and the heightened transcendent state of insight that it implies, is reached by following the Buddhist path and committing oneself to distinctively Buddhist beliefs and attitudes; not through seeking to do away with all particular beliefs and conceptual categorizations of reality from the beginning. It is the more extreme transformations of Buddhism that make us ask when the religion's ability to adapt so readily to changing social and cultural conditions ceases to be a strength, and make us wonder whether religions should be speaking out more strongly against the problems inherent in the materialistic and logical-empirical bias of the modern world.

290

REFERENCES

[1]These figures are taken from "The Lion and the Lotus," a survey of Buddhism in Britain presented by Michael Campbell, broadcast on Radio 4, November 1985.

[2]*International Buddhist Directory 1985* (London: Wisdom Publications, 1985).

[3]Campbell, *op. cit.*

[4]Christmas Humphreys, *Zen Comes West* (London: Allen & Unwin, 1960), p. 29.

[5]P. L. Berger, *A Rumour of Angels* (London: Allen Lane, 1970), p. 18.

[6]*Ibid.*, p. 34, original emphasis.

[7]*Ibid.*, p. 36.

[8]*Ibid.*, p. 41.

[9]Martin Willson, *Rebirth and the Western Buddhist* (London: Wisdom Publications, 1984), p. 31.

[10]*Ibid.*, pp. 54-55.

[11]Michael Pye, *Skilful Means* (London: Duckworth, 1978), pp. 126-127.

[12]*Ibid.*, pp. 159-60.

[13]*Ibid.*, p. 130.

[14]*Ibid.*, p. 130.

[15]*Ibid.*, p. 160, my emphasis.

[16]Campbell, *op. cit.*

[17]1982 figure, taken from Dharmachari Subhuti (Alex Kennedy), *Buddhism for Today : A Portrait of a New Buddhist Movement* (Salisbury: Element Books in association with the Friends of the Western Buddhist Order, 1983).

[18]*Ibid.*, p. 23.

[19]*Ibid.*, p. 26, original emphasis.

[20]*Ibid.*, pp. 5-6, original emphasis.

[21]*Ibid.*, p. 140.

[22]*Ibid.*, p. 140.

[23]*Ibid.*, p. 134.

[24]*Ibid.*, p. 166.

[25]*Throssel Hole Priory Journal*, I, 1, cited in Ian P. Oliver, *Buddhism in Britain* (London: Rider, 1979), p. 181.

[26][Anon], *Introduction to Vipassana Meditation* (Llanfair Clydogau: Vipassana Association, n.d.).

[27]S.N. Goenka, *The Art of Living: Vipassana Meditation* (Llanfair Clydogau: Vipassana Association, n.d.).

[28]Gerald du Pré, "Buddhism and Science," in Buddhadasa P. Kirthisinghe (ed.), *Buddhism and Science* (Delhi: Motilal Banarsidass, 1984), pp. 95-96.

[29]Gerald du Pré, "Buddhism and Psychotherapy," in Kirthisinghe, *op. cit.*

[30]Gerald du Pré, "The Buddhist Philosophy of Science", in Kirthisinghe, *op. cit.*

[31]Gerald du Pré, "Science and the Skandhas," in Kirthisinghe, *op. cit.*

[32]Gerald du Pré, "Science and the Wheel of Life," in Kirthisinghe, *op. cit.*, p. 130.

[33]Gerald du Pré, "Science and the Way to Nirvana," in Kirthisinghe, *op. cit.*, p. 137, my emphasis.

[34]Gerald du Pré, "The Buddhist Philosophy of Science", in Kirthisinghe, *op. cit.*, p. 107.

[35]Gerald du Pré, "Scientific Buddhism," in Kirthisinge, *op. cit.*, p. 147. All du Pré's articles above have previously been published in British Buddhist journals.

[36]Campbell, op. cit. Buddhist scholars may wish to be assured that the context in which this assertion was made shows that the informant did not have in mind a Sūnyavāda-type doctrine that *ultimately* there is no rebirth, *nirvāna*, etc.

[37]Willson, *op. cit.*, p. 6.

CHAPTER XVII

"THE BEST MEN'S CLUB IN THE WORLD"[1]
ATTITUDES TO WOMEN IN THE BRITISH CHURCHES

MYRTLE S. LANGLEY

Even the most cursory glance at the depiction of woman in the
theology, history and iconography of the Christian Tradition, from the
beginning, reveals a certain ambiguity of identity and confusion of roles.
This ambivalence of the Church's teaching and practice becomes especially
apparent when we look at the two women who, it may be claimed, are
Christianity's major female saints: the Blessed Virgin Mary and Saint Mary
Magdalene.

The Blessed Virgin Mary[2]

In Christian iconography and the theology and history of the Catholic
and Orthodox Churches the Virgin Mary figures prominently, whereas she is
mentioned comparatively infrequently in the Christian Scriptures.

Her earliest mention - although not by name - is by St Paul in his
letter to the Galatians (written sometime between AD 50-55) where he
argues that Jesus is not only son of God but fully human, "made of a woman."
Yet he never refers to her again.

Mark, the earliest of the Gospels, records only two incidents in which
Mary features: in the first Jesus refuses to single out his earthly family for
special treatment, stating that anyone who does the will of God is his brother
and sister and mother; in the second Jesus visits his home town of Nazareth,

teaching and working miracles, and the local people conclude that he is "the carpenter, the son of Mary..." a prophet despised in his own country. Similarly, John, the latest of the Gospels, records only two occasions where Mary is present: at the wedding feast in Cana of Galilee where Jesus appears mildly to rebuke his mother; and at the foot of the cross where Jesus commits his mother to the care of his beloved disciple, John, and likewise John to Mary.

The only remaining fresh material is contained in Matthew's and Luke's Birth Narratives which comprise the first two chapters of their respective Gospels. It is the most substantial material in terms of quantity and mythology but the most questionable historically. Nearly all scholars believe the narratives to be later additions, albeit emanating from sources distinctively Matthean and Lucan. When we examine them we feel ourselves to be on familiar ground. In Matthew's account Joseph takes centre stage: the genealogy of Jesus is traced through Joseph's line and it is Joseph who dreams dreams. In Luke's account, as might be expected from one who has a special place for social outcasts including women, Mary plays the central role: the genealogy of Jesus is traced through Mary's line and it is Mary who is greeted by the angel and who sings the Magnificat. Matthew recounts the virginal conception of Jesus, the visit of the Magi, the flight into Egypt, the massacre of the innocents, and the settling of the family in Nazareth after Herod's death. Luke tells of the birth of John the Baptist (the prophesied forerunner of the Messiah), the annunciation, the visitation of Mary to Elizabeth, the circumcision of John, the singing of songs by Zechariah, Mary, Simeon and Anna, the visit of the shepherds to the stable in Bethlehem, the circumcision and presentation of Jesus in the temple and Jesus' desertion of his parents for the doctors of the law on a visit to Jerusalem when twelve years old. These narratives very obviously reflect the respective Evangelist's concerns and perspectives. For instance, Matthew's narrative deliberately sets out to fulfill Old Testament prophecies, made explicit at five points. Of especial significance is his quotation from the prophet Isaiah, declaring that "a virgin shall be with child and shall bring forth a son" (Isaiah 7:14). But he fails to note that the original requires only the translation "a woman of marriageable state" and not the technical term "virgin."

However, while observing that the Scriptures do not give to Mary the prominence she is accorded in Tradition we must take note that the seeds are there in the Gospels. Indeed, it must remain a probability that they already contain in themselves the first fruits of considered reflection in myth and cultus on the Blessed Virgin Mary. Based on the Hebrew story of the Fall in Genesis, nurtured in a Mediterranean milieu and formulated in hellenistic philosophical thought forms, the myth and cult of Mary - Second Eve and Virgin mother - was to develop in a highly complex but discernible manner, exalting woman to the pinnacles of a neo-platonic idealism and reducing women to humble servitude: reflecting and in turn influencing profoundly the course of western civilization. And if we were to consider here the development and content of mariology in Western Europe we should begin to perceive Mary as a "goddess," heiress to much of past religion and culture, but also as a humble and obedient maiden, at the same time virginal ideal and ideal mother. Therein lies the paradox of mariology: the figure of Mary in the Church embodying virginity and motherhood at the same time. And therein lies the destruction of femaleness. Moreover, in much Christian practice Mary may be "goddess" and healer of the human race, but in Christian dogma she is still *Second Eve*, constant reminder that through a woman sin first entered the world, and *theotokos*, meaning "godbearer," Mother of God - uniquely close to God, almost God, but significantly not God.

Saint Mary Magdalene[3]

For much of its history the Church has embodied in St Mary Magdalene its essential belief about womankind. Mary is beautiful, fallen but redeemed. Yet only by reading into the text of the New Testament, confusing the stories and compounding the images, do we get this picture of the Magdalen.

The New Testament Scriptures contain three stories which recount the anointing of Jesus by a woman. Most scholars believe all three to be variations on one theme. Yet there is one major obstacle to such a facile solution: Mark's story, probably the earliest (and duplicated by Matthew), depicts an anointing of the head and not of the feet. Hence the first stereotypical confusion: the woman is usually depicted anointing the feet of Jesus; anointing the feet indicated servility whereas anointing the head was associated in Israel with the making of priests and kings and the calling of prophets - a woman performing the role of a kingmaker, surely not! Moreover, the different accounts variously term the person who anoints: a "woman," a "sinful woman" and "Mary of Bethany," leaving it open to Tradition to compound the confusion by rolling into one in liturgy, architecture and art Mark's "woman," Luke's "sinful woman," John's "Mary of Bethany" all of whom anointed Jesus with ointment, and Luke's "Mary Magdalene, out of whom Jesus had driven seven demons."

Thus, from St Augustine (AD 354-430) onwards the anointing became the expiation for a sinful and wasted life, and on Mary Magdalene's shoulders was laid the burden of a great guilt. Yet, she who loves much is forgiven much. And so Mary Magdalene, second only to the Blessed Virgin Mary, became for Christians the typical feminine deterrent of a seduced and seductive woman, obliged to repent and be redeemed and henceforth, by way of love and gratitude, live a devout life of humble and loving service. For women in the Church and in Western civilization generally the icon of Mary Magdalene "the penitent whore" has stood alongside that of the Blessed Virgin Mary as profoundly destructive of their sexuality and personhood. Nowadays, especially since the Second Vatican Council (1962-65), this destructiveness may be increasingly acknowledged yet its pervasiveness still remains and in times of changing roles and crumbling structures in our society consciousness and practice have yet to catch up with theory.

I

Underlying, informing and reinforcing the mythology of womanhood as exemplified in the Blessed Virgin Mary and St Mary Magdalene went a theology of womanhood equally destructive. In Tertullian (c AD 160 - c 220), although the disobedience of Eve is offset by the obedience of Mary, woman is "the devil's gateway" and so women must continue to bear the shame of the first sin and seek to expiate it; for Augustine, by nature as well as on account of sin woman is man's inferior, symbol of a debasing carnality which draws the male mind down from its heavenly heights - moreover sin is to be located in the male erection thereby making woman both sin's occasion and cause; for Thomas Aquinas, following Aristotle, the male is created for the more noble pursuit of intellectual activity, whereas the female, although possessing a rational soul, is created solely for the sexual bodily activity of reproducing and preserving the species - moreover the girl child represents a defective human being, and no justification other than reproduction can be given for the existence of a "second sex." Small wonder that the only way of salvation offering hope to the female was to become as like the male as this life allowed, eschewing marriage, forsaking the hearth and pursuing the virginal ideal within the cloister.[4]

Not until the sixteenth-century Reformation did any significant winds of change begin to stir. And even then they blew in two directions. With Luther's rejection of medieval theology's distinction between Christian life lived according to "the precepts" and "the counsels of perfection," and both Luther's and Calvin's affirmation that marriage is ordained of God and therefore good, woman was taken out of the cloisters and placed firmly at the hearth. This ushered in for the Churches of the Reformed Tradition the era of good wives and in particular the role of the pastor's wife but at the same time ruled out for their women the opportunities for independence and leadership in their own sphere which existed within the religious orders. True, continental Protestants as early as the end of the sixteenth century revived the diaconate or order of deaconesses for the purposes of distributing alms and nursing, but these were subservient roles. Not until the first wave of the women's movement as we know it did women in the Churches begin to comtemplate equality and aspire to a ministerial office akin to that of their menfolk. Meanwhile, they often wielded the mighty pen, most significantly writing poems and composing hymns, from the untalented Anne Dutton (1692-1765) and the redoubtable Selina, Countess of Huntingdon (1707-91) to the princess among them all, Anne Steele (1717-78).[5]

Feminism's overriding concern is the conviction that woman is equal with man. This is not to say that man and woman do not possess distinguishing characteristics. Rather, it means that in terms of worth women are equal with men because they share a common humanity as free and responsible persons.[6]

The rise of feminism in the late eighteenth and nineteenth-centuries owes its origins to three intellectual traditions or currents of thought: 1) the egalitarian individualist tradition of the Enlightenment; 2) the evangelical revivalist tradition of the Evangelical Revival and the Great Awakenings; and 3) the socialist tradition of the English and French cooperative and communitarian movements and Marxism; or, as one writer succinctly puts it, to reason, religion and revolution. This means, not surprisingly, that in Britain, as elsewhere, the impetus for women's emancipation from within the Churches arose among the dissenting, the revivalist and socially active, while then as now the conservative, the established, the catholic and the orthodox vehemently argued for the maintenance of the status quo. Only the influence of the Oxford Movement and the challenge of the Nineteenth-century Missionary Movement dented even a little the armour of the latter.[7]

In Britain it is John Wesley who is often seen as the key innovator, so much so that one social historian goes so far as to say that "emancipation of womanhood began with John Wesley." Wesley's teaching on sin and the priesthood of all believers operated as a great leveller across all barriers of class and creed; his emphasis on religious experience contributed to a weakening of traditional religious authority as rich and poor, educated and uneducated, men and women alike testified to the work of grace in their lives; and his encouragement of new forms of ministry (for example, field preaching and class meetings) allowed for validity to be judged by results. And so as early as 1739 Wesley appointed women as "class leaders" in Bristol, in 1787 welcomed one Sarah Mallet as a preacher and, in giving approval to the preaching of Mary Bosanquet, wrote: "I think the case rests here, in *your* having an extraordinary call. So I am persuaded has every one of our lay preachers; otherwise I could not countenance his preaching at all." Thus the way is paved for the Methodist Bible commentator, Adam Clarke, in the early years of the next century, to say of women that "under the blessed spirit of Christianity, they have equal *rights*, equal *privileges*, and equal *blessings*, and, let me add, they are equally *useful*."

Others took up the torch. In 1865 William and Catherine Booth - on Catherine's insistence before their marriage - founded the Salvation Army along totally egalitarian lines, the army refusing "to make any difference between men and women as to rank, authority and duties" and opening "the highest positions to women as well as to men." From 1857, bible women began to be recruited and trained in the elements of nursing under the auspices of the British and Foreign Bible Society to distribute Bibles among the poor.

Even the Church of England witnessed two distinctive movements on the women's front. In 1845, at Regent's Park in London, under the direction of Dr Edward Pusey, the first religious community for women in England since the Reformation was opened. By 1878 it was estimated that at least 700 women had adopted the religious life. In 1861, the Rev. W. C. Pennefather founded, in partnership with his wife Catherine, a Female Missionary Training Home which later became the Mildmay Deaconess Institution. It was modelled after the continental Lutheran Kaiserswerth Institution founded in 1836 and, like Kaiserswerth, administered its own hospitals, dispensaries, rescue homes, orphanages and old people's homes. The deaconesses took responsibility also for night schools, clubs for boys and girls, district visiting and home nursing. The revival of the order of deaconesses in the Church of England soon followed in the years between 1862 and 1872.

Thus, by the mid-1860's in Britain there were at least four different patterns of women's ministry to be observed within the "home" Churches: the voluntary women engaged in pastoral and philanthropic visiting; the bible women and deaconesses of nonconformity and Pennefather; the newly established orders; and the deaconesses of institutional Anglicanism. In addition there was the recently founded Salvation Army and the much earlier instituted Methodist system of class-leaders and preachers.

At the same time the area of overseas missionary work remained largely a male preserve. It was conceded that wives could go abroad with their missionary husbands, and a few single women, often widows and daughters of missionaries, might be engaged to look after missionary children or to teach. There were also small numbers of women missionaries engaged in zenana educational work in India. But in normal recruiting the mainline denominational societies turned women away. A woman's place was in the home and in any case women sent abroad were likely to get married with an unbecoming and wasteful haste. Moreover, the preaching of the gospel in any formal manner was in the main a clerical responsibility. The only likely role for a woman was supportive and philanthropic, for example in the teaching and nursing professions.

Yet, nonetheless, by the end of the century societies such as the Anglican Church Missionary Society, the Interdenominational China Inland Mission, the Congregationalist London Missionary Society, the Baptist Church through its Baptist Zenana Mission (founded in 1867 under another name) and the Wesleyan Methodist Missionary Society were all employing women, and often on a fairly large scale. For example, up until 1887 the CMS did not formally recruit women - at most 9 per cent of its missionaries in the 1870's were women - but between 1891 and 1900, 388 women, or 56.46 per cent of its total intake, were women. Remarkably, even today, more women in proportion to men serve the Church overseas than the Church at home probably because ministry overseas provides more variety and greater responsibility: it is more fully-orbed.[8]

So too, by the end of the century, other important battles had begun to be fought: for the admission of women to read theology in the colleges and for due representation in the councils of the Churches. The Unitarian Manchester College, Oxford, in 1892 admitted two women students and invited a woman to lecture on Priscillian. The Church of England's Upper House of Convocation was the recipient of a petition, signed by 1,100 churchwomen, protesting against its ban on female candidates for election to parochial church councils.[9]

And the turn of the century saw the first ordination of women to the official ministry. It should occasion no surprise that with their strong traditions of dissent in relation to all forms of establishment, intellectual, political and religious, the Unitarians and Baptists were to be the earliest in the field. Unitarians take pride in claiming that theirs was the first denomination to open the ministry to women when Rev. Gertrud von Petzold was inducted to the ministry of Narborough Road Free Christian Church, Leicester, in 1904. But even that needs to be set in context. Almost twenty-five years earlier Caroline Soule, widow of a Universalist minister and ordained into the ministry of the Universalist Church in Glasgow, had pastoral oversight of the Dundee Unitarian Church while its minister was on leave of absence in the United States of America.[10] Then in 1922 Miss Edith Gates qualified through the Baptist Union Examination and had one pastoral charge at Little Tew and Cleveley in Oxfordshire from 1918-50. Yet, already in 1918, the same Miss Gates was the first woman minister to be given pastoral charge and in 1919 Bristol Baptist College agreed to admit women for training, although none registered until 1927.[11]

II

In the Britain of the late 1980's the Baptist, Congregationalist, Lutheran, Methodist, Moravian, Pentecostal, Presbyterian, Unitarian and United Reformed Churches ordain women to their official ministries; while for a very long time the Salvation Army and the Society of Friends have welcomed women to positions of leadership and participation on an equal footing with men. Christian bodies such as the Christian Brethren and the House Churches either do not have an official full-time ministry or have developed new, largely innovative and often experimental, forms of ministry which they claim to be biblical and relevant for the times; while a number of Christians spread across the Churches are increasingly critical of an official ministry which they believe to be bound by tradition, ridden with clericalism, shot through with anomalies, out of touch with reality and consequently irrelevant and of limited use in an increasingly post-Christian society. For example, on more than one occasion when championing the cause of women's ordination I have been met with the rejoinders - from down-to-earth Roman Catholic religious, enthusiastic House Church member to evangelical, charismatic or radical Anglican - "Why ordain women to a suspect institution?" "Why lumber women with a questionable role?" "Why not first reform the ministry itself?"

It is those Churches today which claim to lay great store by the authority of either Scripture or Tradition or both which challenge the admissibility of women to an office which until recent times has been the prerogative of males and even now remains so among seventy-five per cent of the world's Christians.

The two great branches of Christianity East and West, Orthodoxy and Roman Catholicism respectively, do not ordain women and at present have no intention of doing so, although the Roman Catholic Church worldwide contains many women's pressure groups and continues to produce the foremost among feminist theologians. In addition, many Christians from Churches across the spectrum who see their own Christian identity as primarily evangelical or catholic with a concomitant appeal to Scripture and Tradition reject the ordination of women. Catholics and evangelicals of this kind inhabit the Anglican fold, a Church which looks for guidance in matters of doctrine to Scripture, Tradition and Reason; in the last analysis, however, asserting the normative authority of Scripture.

It is no accident then that it is in the worldwide arena of the Anglican Communion that we are at present witnessing the great debate on women's ordination. Since 1944 when, due, to war-time need, Bishop R. O. Hall of Hong Kong ordained Deaconess Florence Li Tim Oi, since 1971 when his successor Bishop Gilbert Baker priested an Englishwoman, Miss Joyce Bennett of the Church Missionary Society, and Chinese-born Miss Jane Hwang, and particularly since 1976 when the irregular Philadelphia ordinations of eleven women in 1974 were regularized and the ordination of women became the official practice in the Episcopal Church of the United States of America many of the Communion's autonomous provinces have admitted women to the minsterial priesthood of the Church; but not so the Church of England, looked to as "the mother church" and therefore pivotal in the debate. In 1975 the Church of England's General Synod in actual fact expressed the view that there are "no fundamental objections to the ordination of women to the priesthood" but since then has been unable to pass the necessary enabling legislation.

In 1986 the issue became a crisis one with three matters before the July synod: the permission for women ordained abroad to exercise their ministry when on visits to England; the admission of women to the diaconate; and the scope of enabling legislation for the priesting of women (legislation necessarily made more complex by establishment). Led by certain of the small minority of bishops opposed at any cost to the admission of women to the priesthood many expressed fears of schisms and the setting up of "a continuing" or "parallel" Church of England. In the midst of the fray all the arguments pro and con were once again rehearsed, this time in both the secular and religious press.[12]

Before stating and examining those arguments, however, I wish to look at the official ministry of the Church as understood by the Church of England in the light of its appeal to Scripture, Tradition and Reason. It is widely accepted today that the New Testament itself contains no blueprint for ministry. But it is also believed by the mainline historic Churches that since early times the Church has possessed an official ministry. Churches in the Reformed tradition recognize one order: of "presbyters." Churches in the Catholic and Orthodox traditions recognize three orders: of bishops, priests (presbyters) and deacons. Anglicans recognize all three orders, although through the centuries opinion has been divided on the nature and meaning of "priesthood."

A recent report from the Faith and Order Advisory Group of the General Synod, entitled *The Priesthood of the Ordained Ministry*, traces the understanding of the idea of priesthood from the New Testament, through the patristic period to the present, paying particular attention to Anglican tradition and to the emerging ecumenical convergence on the priestly character of the ordained ministry as set out in the Lima document of the World Council of Churches, and the official reports of bilateral dialogues with Roman Catholics, Lutherans and Reformed.[13] By way of conclusion it offers a contemporary expression of priesthood. Christian tradition uses the terminology of priesthood in three distinct but related ways to refer to: the unique priesthood of Christ; the priesthood of the whole Church (the "priesthood of all believers"); and the ministerial priesthood of bishops and presbyters. Christ is unique - he is our one High Priest; the priesthood of the Church and the priesthood of its ministers are derived from the priesthood of Christ and may thus be called priestly only in a secondary sense; they are priestly only by grace and only by participation in his unique priesthood. The ordained ministry has a representative function, both in relation to Christ and in relation to the whole community of faith. It has particular relationship to Christ, which is not simply derived from the common ministry of all Christians, both in representing Christ to his people and also, in union with him, in representing the people to the Father. Bishops and presbyters represent both Christ and his people in their leadership of the Church and its mission, in the proclamation of the gospel, in the articulation of faith, and in the celebration of the sacraments. Because of their particular relationship to Christ as Lord of the Church, those who are called to this ministry receive a particular vocation to holiness and consecration of life. They are to share in the priestly ministry of Christ by lives of consecrated love and service for the sake of the whole Body.

By means of this summary it becomes possible to identify and appreciate the significance of the two major areas of argument against the admission of women to the order of priests or presbyters: leadership and priesthood respectively. Leadership is the main stumbling block for evangelicals who take literally the biblical injunction that man is head of woman, and make it normative for all time and in all cultures. Priesthood is the main stumbling-block for catholics who take as literally, historically and ontologically relevant the maleness of Christ in the Incarnation, and make the maleness of the priest who is the icon ("image") of Christ a necessary prerequisite for all time and in all cultures. This leads, as I have remarked elsewhere, to catholics protecting the altar and evangelicals the pulpit from John Knox's "monstrous regiment of women." Common to both is the view that "in the nature of things," intrinsically, it is unfitting, indeed impossible, for a woman to be a ministerial priest, that is to say either to be a leader of men or the representative of God to men. Somehow, merely being of the female sex precludes women from being able to exercise authority in the Church or from receiving the grace of orders. A woman *per se* cannot be a priest in the Church of God. To put it basically and bluntly, the female must always be subservient to or presumed to be represented by the male. Consequently, the main arguments adduced both from Scripture and Tradition against the ordination of women centre on the differences between the sexes rather than on their similarities and complementarities as created each alone and both together in the image and likeness of God.

The main arguments against the ordination of women to the ordained ministry of the Churches, all appearing in some guise in the press during the heat of the debate, are as follows:

* For almost two thousand years the ordained ministry of the Church has been male.
* Jesus chose twelve male apostles.
* The New Testament, particularly St Paul, enjoins women to keep silence in the Churches, forbids women to teach men and, on the analogy of Christ and the Church, exhorts the wife to submit to her husband.
* Nature itself teaches that man is head of woman, the female is created *from*, *for* and *after* the male.
* If the priest represents Christ to the Church, is the icon or image of Christ - an *alter Christus* (a "second Christ"), then it follows that because God became incarnate in Christ as a male, then a male and only a male can take on this priestly role.
* If a woman were allowed to be an *alter Christus* then the very concept of God himself would be threatened.
* If the two great Christian Churches of East and West, the Orthodox and Roman Communions, representing as they do the continuity of the faith throughout the ages, do not ordain women then the ongoing talks on the unity of the Churches are gravely threatened and the eventual reconciliation of all Christians seriously delayed if not altogether jeopardized.
* Moreover, for Anglicans who are at a delicate stage in negotiations with Rome on the validity of Anglican orders, the ordination of women constitutes a grave threat to eventual recognition and intercommunion between the two Churches.
* Traditionally, for instance as enunciated by Calvin, vocation alone was never considered reason enough for admitting a

person to orders, but rather personal vocation and the confirmation of the Church.

* In view of all the many evils besetting the human race, such as world hunger, war and the nuclear threat, increasing poverty, racism and many other injustices, then the ordination of women pales into insignificance: it is just not a priority.

* As a consequence of the lack of consensus and the threat to unity it is not expedient - the time is not ripe - to ordain women priests *now*.

The main counterarguments, mounted in response to the above, run somewhat as follows:

* Against the claim that the universal practice during two thousand years of Tradition militates against the admission of women to the ordained ministry it is pointed out, and justifiably so, by Anglicans that their concept of Tradition is dynamic and not static - the Holy Spirit, it is affirmed, continues to lead into all truth.

* Whether or not Jesus chose all males as apostles it is equally true that many of his most intimate followers were women, that he treated women with a dignity and integrity of personhood unusual if not unique for a Jewish man in Palestine of the time, that all four Evangelists record women as the first witnesses of the Resurrection, and that many of the prominent leaders of the New Testament Churches were women; moreover, in order to communicate the better both in relation to his person and to his mission Jesus (either historically or as interpreted by the early Church) allowed himself in many respects both to be bound by the culture of his time and to act in conscious fulfillment of Old Testament prophecy regarding the Messiah and God's New Israel, the Church.

* On the basis of New Testament evidence generally it must be said that when taken at face value two contradictory positions must be admitted: Jesus himself went out of his way to accord women a dignity and integrity of personhood which on any

reckoning recognized them as equal with men, and Paul, in his letter to the Galatians, set forth his great manifesto of Christian liberty which at baptism and therefore in the eyes of God and humankind declared there to be no difference between Jew and Greek, slave and free, male and female, thereby abolishing at a stroke inherent inequalities of race, class and sex; Paul and his disciples on other occasions - I would claim on the basis of a missionary strategy of accommodation to patriarchal structures - exhort women to play a subservient role to men in the churches.

* It is not proven that "in the nature of things" men must take the lead, always being the initiators, while women must follow; there is ample evidence to suggest that, in part at least, such reasoning is due to nurture not nature, to role stereotyping rather than to natural inclination.

* The argument deriving from the priest as icon of Christ raises interesting questions in at least two respects: the universal reference of salvation and the nature of symbolism itself. If God became incarnate in Christ so as to represent all humankind then it is his humanity and not his maleness which is operative for salvation, otherwise the female sex is excluded from the scope of redemption. If the priest represents Christ and Christ's body, the Church, then again it is not the literal historical male referent of the symbol which is significant but rather its humanness. God created man (humankind) in the image of himself, in the image of God he created him, male and female he created them (Gen. 1:27, JB). Moreover, it can be argued that for by far the greatest part of Christian history the presence of Christ in the sacrament has been seen to be located not in the person of the priest but in the elements of bread and wine.

* Similarly, if God is transcender of gender, then our concept of God can in no way suffer impoverishment but rather

enrichment when women and men respectively and equally perform the role of *alter Christus*.

* On the unity of the Churches it can be said that already not only the Churches of the great Reformed and Free Church traditions but also some provinces of the Anglican Communion ordain women and many Roman Catholics request the Church of England to give the lead and pave the way for them. And although the fact that some Anglican provinces ordain women poses a problem for Anglican-Roman Catholic dialogue, nonetheless, both sides are agreed that talks should go on, with joint study on the subject of women's ordination now firmly on the agenda.

* Undoubtedly the confirmation of the Church must be sought for even a woman's felt vocation to priesthood; all that is being requested is an opportunity to test vocation.

* The ordination of women *is* a priority: women "hold up more than half the sky"; to deny them priesthood is to oppress and diminish women and at the same time spiritually impoverish the human race. Moreover, a Church that can vote overwhelmingly for the abolition of apartheid in South Africa and deny its own women justice is deluding no one but itself.

* As for the expediency of the move to ordain women then, it can be argued that truth always has prior claim, particularly when some Churches have already made a move and others expect a lead.

The July synod rejected the measure allowing women ordained abroad to exercise their ministry when in England; the enabling legislation proved so contentious that it was passed on to the House of Bishops for consideration before February next; and the amended legislation enabling women to be admitted to the diaconate, the first rung of the clergy ladder, was accepted with an overwhelming majority.

III

In addition to ordination, the other two major items on the agenda of the Churches in relation to women is representation on the Church's councils and sexist language, especially in the liturgy.

Already the Methodist Church has published an inclusive-language edition of its hymn book and the Church of England has agreed to look again at the sexist language of its 1980 *Alternative Service Book*. But for all Churches, whether or not they ordain women, there is a long way to go in facing up to the many theological questions raised by feminism, particularly in relation to language and symbolism. This is well illustrated in the refusal of the General Assembly of the Church of Scotland to accept the report on *The Motherhood of God*, called for after the President of the Church's Women's Guild addressed God as "Dear Mother God" during the Annual Meeting in 1982. The report is a model of clarity and moderation and much was lost to the Church by its rejection.[14] Similarly, in May 1986, the General Assembly of the United Reformed Church, meeting in Blackpool, did not give the required two-thirds majority to a measure introducing inclusive language into its foundation document: the assembly was begged by a woman not to be diverting the Church from its real tasks while a male speaker "wickedly put the eighth psalm into inclusive language."

All of the Churches are in principle committed to more lay involvement in their life, most are pursuing a policy of increased representation of women on various representative bodies and many are seeing a marked increase in the number of women entering the professional ministry, both lay and ordained. The latter remains the best indicator of the role and status accorded women and will be used as the basis for the criteria and statistics listed below. However, the Church of England produced two reports in 1986 which give some idea of the involvement of women in Church structures.[15]

Servants of the Lord: Roles of Women and Men in the Church of England purports to have discovered that, in the 1980's women's activities in parish life were far less restricted than was often claimed or actually believed. In 38 per cent of parishes taking part in the survey, at least 50 per

310

cent of parochial church council members were women. Only in a minority
of councils (PCCs) was no office held by a woman. More than a third of
parishes (37 per cent) had a woman churchwarden but only one in ten had a
woman as deputy chair of the PCC. A quarter of the parishes had a woman
PCC treasurer and three quarters a woman PCC secretary. More than a
third (39 per cent) said that all parish committees were chaired by men.
None reported that all were chaired by women. Nearly half said that women
assisted with the administration of the chalice. In 35 per cent of the parishes
more women than lay men read lessons in church. Only 15 per cent of the
parishes had a woman organist who played regularly, but three out of four
churches had women in the choir.

The survey showed women to be in great demand as leaders of study,
discussion and training groups: 88 per cent mentioned women in this role.
More than half said that women assisted in preparation for baptism,
confirmation and marriage. And in the traditional "women's areas" such as
catering and flower arranging both *men* and *women* played a part in more
than half the parishes.

But the report stresses that although evidence pointed to less
restriction on women in the Church than was often supposed, it did not show
that women were enabled or encouraged to take part fully in the life of every
parish. And although at diocesan and general synod levels women often
played a significant part, nevertheless it was as a minority. Moreover, it was
found that in central Church bureaucracy qualified women did not often
apply for the jobs, and so, definite guidelines were called for "to concentrate
the minds of those responsible for appointments" and "to ensure that the
qualities, both masculine and feminine, of the true community of Christ be
represented in its central structures."

And All That is Unseen: A New Look at Women's Work (commissioned by the Industrial and Economic Affairs Committee of the Board for Social
Responsibility) traces the history of prejudice against the working woman
and the housewife, pinpointing the secondary status of women in the labour
market and demolishing the "myth" that women take jobs away from men.
But turning to the Church itself it comments, rather damningly:

The Church has been an active participant in the debate about the nature and function of work. But it cannot be an effective commentator on work without reflecting on its own position as a provider of work.... Where it employs workers, how well does it pay them? The Church should surely be the last institution to be exploiting people by capitalising on their goodwill and commitment.

Unfortunately, continues the report, the employment of women is frequently mirrored in their position as workers in the Church: "What more effective illustration of occupational segregation could there be than a Church where men preside at lectern and altar and women reside in the pews or work behind the scenes?"

ANGLICAN COMMUNION[16]

Church of England

In 1986 the Church of England: remains undecided on how to proceed with legislation enabling women to be admitted to the priesthood (although it decided in 1975 that there were "no fundamental objections to the ordination of women to the priesthood"); is proceeding with arrangements for the admission of the first women to the diaconate; is experiencing a marked rise in the numbers of deaconesses, in the number of women who wish to be readers and in those who wish to fulfill their vocation part-time.

Figures available show: 10,074 stipendiary clergy in the parochial ministry (an estimated 11,600 being needed to staff the parochial system) and approximately 700 otherwise employed ('84), about 773 in the non-stipendiary ministry ('82); 540 deaconesses (349 FT, 191 PT), 170 lay workers (102 FT, 68 PT), 65 Church Army sisters (54 FT, 11 PT) and 135 Church Army captains (133 FT, 2 PT) ('84); and 7,200 readers of whom 1,172 are women, with an increasing proportion of women to men in training ('85), men having reached their peak of 6,581 in 1963 and having declined to 6,028 in 1985.

Church in Wales

In 1980 the Church in Wales ceased to admit members to the order of deaconesses and ordained the first women to the diaconate. There are at present no plans to admit women to the priesthood.

Figures available for 1986 show a total of 755 clergy, 697 stipendiary and 58 non-stipendiary and 22 women deacons, 15 stipendiary and 7 non-stipendiary.

Church of Ireland

In 1987 the Church of Ireland will admit its first woman to the diaconate. There is currently a second in training. Otherwise, recognized women's ministry is restricted to one or two lay readers and some non-accredited women in parochial and other church appointments. The issue of the ordination of women to the priesthood has been shelved for the time being.

Scottish Episcopal Church

Figures available for 1986 show approximately 200 stipendiary and 70 non-stipendiary clergy and the first ordination of a woman to the diaconate. There will soon be about 20 women deacons but only three will be stipendiary.

BAPTIST UNION OF GREAT BRITAIN AND IRELAND

The Church has had deaconesses since 1890 and fully-ordained women ministers since 1922 (the first having been appointed in 1918). Then, in 1975, deaconesses in active ministry became fully recognized ministers of the Church.

Figures available for 1985 show a total of 2,029 ministers, of whom 61, or 3 per cent, are women. Of the 61 women 33 are in a pastorate (20 on their own, 10 as assistants, 3 in teams), 6 are in other ministerial work and the remainder are retired, out of pastorate or on leave of absence. Thus, 55 per cent of the women (as compared with 60 per cent of all ministers) are in a pastorate. Of the 61 women ministers, 10 are supplementary and 13 (including some supplementary) are probationers. Of the 157 ministerial students in Baptist colleges, 13, or 8.3 per cent, are women. Interestingly, of the 205 missionaries (including wives) serving with the Baptist Missionary Society 118, or 57.6 per cent, are women. The first woman President assumed office in 1978 and the second will take up her duties in 1987.

LUTHERAN COUNCIL OF GREAT BRITAIN

The Council comprises Estonian, Finnish, German, Hungarian, Latvian, Norwegian, Polish and Swedish congregations. In 1986 the Council had 2 Latvian women ministers and one German woman minister in pastoral charge and no sisters or deaconesses.

METHODIST CHURCH

Methodist Church (Wesleyan, Primitive and United Methodist Churches united in 1932)

The Methodist Church accepted its first women for the ordained ministry in 1973. Unofficial figures for 1985 show a total of 3,490 ministers of which 188, or 5.4 per cent, are women. The deaconess order was discontinued with the ordination of women; however, the 1986 Conference took a decision to introduce a diaconate for women and men, the matter to be discussed in the congregations and recruitment to be encouraged.

Methodist Church in Ireland

For over ten years the Methodist Church in Ireland has been ordaining women. Of 118 active ministers in 1986, 5, or 4.2 per cent, were women, and there was one female "Chairman" of District. As in Great

Britain the deaconess order was discontinued and a diaconate open to men and women subsequently instituted.

MORAVIAN CHURCH IN GREAT BRITAIN AND IRELAND

In 1986 the Church had 25 ministers of whom 3, or 12 per cent, were women. Ordinations of women began in the British Province in the early 1970s. Two more women were due to be ordained in the Autumn of 1986.

PRESBYTERIAN

Presbyterian Church in Ireland

The first woman was ordained in 1975/76 and ten years later in 1986 there were 4 women ministers out of a total of 429 serving ministers, or 0.93 per cent. A number were serving as assistants on probation. 26 deaconesses and 1 lay worker served in such varied capacities as chaplain to the deaf, chaplain in drama, community adviser, and hospital chaplain.

Church of Scotland

Women were first ordained in the Church of Scotland in 1969. In December 1983 there were 1,451 ministers in pastoral charge, of whom 50, or 3.4 per cent, were women. 39 were in parishes, 4 in some kind of Community Ministry and 1 each in Service overseas, Hospital Chaplaincy, the University of Edinburgh and the Church's Department of Education. There were 15 probationers and 23 women in training or accepted for training out of a total of 180, or 12.7 per cent. Heretofore, women have not experienced any particular difficulty in obtaining a call.

Presbyterian Church of Wales

The ordained ministry was opened to women in the 1960's, occasioning some resignations. The first woman was ordained in 1978 and in

Autumn 1986 there were 4 women ministers out of a total of about 200, and 2 more about to be ordained. All have pastoral charge. In addition the Church employs a number of women as full-time Church workers.

ROMAN CATHOLIC

England and Wales

The only figures available for England and Wales ('85) were 4,545 diocesan clergy, 2,173 regular priests and approximately 15,000 religious in the apostolic (excluding the contemplative) orders, of whom approximately 10,000 were women and 5,000 men. The viewpoint was expressed that women outnumbered men two to one in the religious orders.

Ireland

Figures available for April 1986, excluding those working abroad in the missions, are precise and as follows: 3,697 diocesan priests, 2,787 clergy in religious orders, 11,372 sisters and 1,230 brothers. The figures point up an interesting ratio of 11,372 women to 7,714 men, women making up 59.6 per cent of the total.

Scotland

For Scotland the 1985 figures are also precise: 883 secular priests, 227 regular priests, 119 male religious and 1,163 female religious. Again the percentage of women in relation to men overall on this count is significantly 48.6 per cent.

UNITED REFORMED CHURCH

The Congregational Church in England and Wales which in 1972 united with the Presbyterian Church of England to form the United Reformed Church in England and Wales had ordained women to its ministry at least since 1917. According to figures in the 1983 Directory there were

149 women ministers or 8.1 per cent out of a total of 1,838, 5 women auxiliary ministers or 31.25 per cent out of a total of 16 and 2 serving deaconesses. Serving with the Conference for World Mission were 20 women missionaries or 50 per cent out of a total of 40, although if the wives are taken into account the percentage becomes 64.28, a figure which closely reflects the overall average percentage of women serving the overseas Church.

The moderatorship is open to women, lay and ordained. A lay woman served as Moderator 1982-83, but to date no ordained woman has served as Moderator.

UNITARIAN

Unitarians have often been in the forefront of the women's movement. The ordination of women can be traced in Britain to 1904 when a woman was inducted into the ministry of a Leicester church. However, 25 years earlier, a widow of a Universalist minister was ordained into the ministry of the Universalist Church in Glasgow and had pastoral oversight of the Dundee Unitarian Church while its minister was absent in the USA.

In 1986 there were 10 fully-recognized women ministers in pastoral charge of congregations out of a total complement of approximately 83 ministers; there were also 3 female associate ministers.

ATTITUDES TO WOMEN IN MINISTRY[17]

The following findings are taken from research conducted by Edward Lehman on the reactions to women in ministry in four denominations in England.

	Anglican	Baptist	Methodist	URC
Percent willing to accept a qualified woman minister as a pastor	61	74	93	92

	Anglican	Baptist	Methodist	URC
Percent saying a woman minister can handle cross pressures of job and home	54	48	60	67
Percent saying clergy-women who are also wives and mothers are not likely to have emotional problems**	29	24	27	36
Percent saying a woman's temperament is equally well suited for pastoral ministry*	76	79	89	89
Percent saying women equally able to provide strong church leadership**	44	45	66	64
Percent *not* preferring a man for senior pastor or parish priest#	38	43	58	65
Percent *not* preferring a man for assistant pastor#	63	73	90	88
Percent *not* preferring a man for administering the Lord's Supper#	51	65	77	80
Percent *not* preferring a man for preaching a sermon#	73	71	84	86
Percent *not* preferring a man for conducting a business meeting of the church#	71	64	77	81

---
*   responding either "definitely" or "probably" true
** responding either "definitely" or "probably" so
\#   responding either "no difference" or "prefer a woman"

The analysis of the survey data to this point supports the following generalizations:

a)   Church members are highly divided in their perceptions of women in ministry.

b)   The main criterion underlying these differences in tendency to stereotype clergywomen appears to be whether women in ministry can handle the role conflicts associated with being working wives and mothers.

c)   Lay church members differ widely in the extent to which they actually prefer a man in a variety of church positions and activities.

d)   Church members' preferences for men or women in clergy roles are not monolithic.

e)   To some extent, regardless of members' tendencies to stereotype women or to prefer a man in clergy roles, nearly three-fourths of the members indicated that in an appropriate search for pastoral leadership they would accept a qualified woman as pastor if she were recommended to the congregation by the deacons.

f)   Baptist laypersons tend to resemble the Anglicans in their relatively conservative response to women in ministry, while the Methodists and URC members resemble each other in their greater willingness to accept women as ordained clergy.

By way of conclusion it remains for me to note that the secular press when reporting on the recent crisis concerning women's ordination in the Church of England did not always appreciate the churchly issues but understood only too well the issues of justice. It is neither immediately obvious nor self-evidently logical for the opponents of women's ordination to argue that theology operates on a different plane and that what applies in the world does not apply to the Church. How can the heralds of a message which is primarily a gospel of justice and peace deny to half of humanity and 70 per cent of its own membership an equal place in the sun? Moreover, the biblical message at the heart of Christianity is pervasively a message about wholeness - *shalom* - intended by the Creator for all of creation.

REFERENCES

[1] The title is taken from *Why Can't a Woman Be More Like a Man?* (London: The Laity Commission, n.d.).

[2] Cf. Marina Warner, *Alone of All Her Sex* (London: Quartet Books, 1978).

[3] See Elisabeth Moltmann-Wendel, *The Women around Jesus* (London: SCM Press, 1982); also her *A Land Flowing with Milk and Honey* (London: SCM Press, 1986).

[4] See Myrtle Langley, *Equal Woman: A Christian Feminist Perspective* (Basingstoke: Marshalls, 1983), especially ch. 4.

[5] Cf. Margaret Maison, "'Thine, Only Thine!' Women Hymn Writers in Britain, 1760-1835" in Gail Malmgreen, (ed.), *Religion in the Lives of English Women, 1760-1930'* (London: Croom Helm, 1986), pp. 11-40; and John Briggs, "She-Preachers, Widows and Other Women: The Feminine Dimension in Baptist Life since 1600" in *The Baptist Quarterly*, vol. 31, no. 7, July 1986, pp 337-52.

[6] Cf. Janet Radcliffe Richards, *The Sceptical Feminist* (Harmondsworth: Penguin, 1982 (1980)).

[7] See in particular Olive Banks, *Faces of Feminism* (Oxford: Martin Robertson, 1981); but also on the history and concerns of feminism, David Bouchier, *The Feminist Challenge* (London: Macmillan, 1983); Richard J. Evans, *The Feminists* (London: Croom Helm, 1977); John Charvet, *Feminism* (London: J. M. Dent & Sons, 1982); and my *Equal Woman*.

[8] On this and previous paragraphs see C. P. Williams, "'Powerful Arms of the Church of God': Women Missionary Candidates in the Late Nineteenth-Century (A Protestant Perspective)" in *BEFMS*, vol. 9, 1979, pp. 26-45; Janet Grierson, *The Deaconess* (London: CIO Publishing, 1981); and Catherine M. Prelinger, "The Female Diaconate in the Anglican Church : What Kind of Ministry for Women?" in Malmgreen, (ed.), *op. cit.*, pp. 161-92.

[9] See Keith Gilley, "Women and the Unitarian Ministry" in *Growing Together* (London: Essex Hall Bookshop, n.d.); Brian Heeney, "The Beginnings of Church Feminism: Women and the Councils of the Church of England, 1897-1919" in Malmgreen, (ed.), *op. cit.*; Brenda H. Fullalove, "The Ministry of Women in the Church of England 1919-70: Studies in the Debates and Reports of the Convocations and of the Assembly," M. Phil. Thesis (University of Manchester, 1986).

[10] Gilley, *loc. cit.*

[11]Briggs, *loc. cit.*

[12]For some of the arguments pro and con the ordination of women in the Church of England see, for example: Monica Furlong, (ed.), *Feminine in the Church* (London: SPCK, 1984); Peter Moore, (ed.), *Man, Woman and Priesthood* (London: SPCK, 1978).

[13]*The Priesthood of the Ordained Ministry*, GS 694 (London: Board for Mission and Unity of the General Synod, 1986); *Baptism, Eucharist and Ministry* (The Lima Text), Faith and Order Paper No. 111 (Geneva: WCC, 1982); *The Final Report* of the Anglican-Roman Catholic International Commission, Windsor, September 1981 (London: CTS/SPCK, 1982); *Anglican-Lutheran Dialogue: The Report of the Anglican-Lutheran European Regional Commission* Helsinki, August-September 1982 (London: SPCK, 1983); *God's Reign and Our Unity: The Report of the Anglican-Reformed International Commission 1981-84* (London & Edinburgh: SPCK/The Saint Andrew Press, 1984).

[14]Alan E. Lewis (ed.) *The Motherhood of God*, Edinburgh: The Saint Andrew Press, 1984.

[15]General Synod of the Church of England (Standing Committee) GS Misc 224, *"Servants of the Lord": Roles of Women and Men in the Church of England* (London: General Synod, 1986); Rosemary Dawson, *And All That is Unseen: A New Look at Women's Work* (London: Church House Publishing, 1986).

[16]I found no readily available data on the Churches and I am most grateful to a number of individuals and Church headquarters and information offices for their help. Some of this material will also appear in an edited form in *The Epworth Review*.

[17]Ted Lehman, "Reactions to Women in Ministry: A Survey of English Baptist Church Members" in *The Baptist Quarterly Review*, vol. 31, no. 7, July 1986, pp. 301-20; details of Lehman's other publications are provided in his footnotes.

CHAPTER XVIII

RELIGION, POLITICS AND
THE 'PERMISSIVE' LEGISLATION

CHRISTIE DAVIES

During the latter half of the twentieth century Britain has experienced major changes in the nature and justification of those laws that are directly concerned with individual morality. The most important of these changes occurred in the 1960s when Parliament liberalized the law relating to abortion, made it easier to obtain a divorce, decriminalized private homosexual behaviour between consenting male adults and abolished the death penalty, thus symbolically cutting back the power and willingness of the state to punish moral transgression.

Elsewhere I have suggested that there is an underlying pattern to these changes, a shift in the thinking of those who translate morality into law from "moralism" to "causalism."[1] The traditional "moralist" view held that certain acts, and activities such as abortion, divorce or homosexual behaviour were wrong in and of themselves and that the state had the right and duty to prevent or punish them. In the case of murder, the right and duty of the state to exact retribution extended to the taking of the life of the offender against morality, law and order. In such a world, justice consisted of the correct award of penalties and rewards to individual citizens on the basis of their blameworthiness or innocence. Capital punishment was just because the murderer got his or her deserts but abortion was wrong because the foetus, however inconvenient or even menacing, was innocent. Abortions and

322

divorces were wrong but they might be awarded to "innocent" parties, divorces to those who had not committed a matrimonial offence and (it was suggested) abortions to women who had been rape victims and were, therefore, innocent of causing their own pregnancy.

Those who succeeded in altering the law provided a public justification of change in terms of the moral system I have termed "causalism." The aim of the causalists was to minimize harm, pain and suffering, regardless of traditional moral prohibitions or the moral desserts of the parties involved. The causalists did not necessarily approve of abortion or divorce or homosexuality but they felt that in aggregate the amount of harm caused by the enforcement of the existing legal rules and prohibitions was greater than that which was prevented. They were not primarily concerned with (or at least did not openly press) the rights, freedoms and pleasures of women, estranged spouses or homosexuals[2] but rather stressed the *harm* suffered by them as a result of the existing laws - bodged back-street abortion, illegitimate second families, blackmailed sodomites. For the causalist, welfare not justice is the key moral concept, and a welfare society is committed to the relief of suffering regardless of individual dessert. Similarly the murderer deserved more consideration than the foetus because he or she as a sentient being with expectations, plans, relationships and a fear of death, had the greater capacity for suffering. For the causalist capital punishment could *only* be justified on the basis that it saved lives by deterring murderers. The causalist is in essence a short term *negative* utilitarian weighing up the relative consequences of legal intervention and non-intervention.

The underlying pattern to the "permissive" legislation outlined above is based on an examination of the changes in the content of English law and of the arguments employed in Parliament by those in favour of change and those against. Elsewhere I have tried to ground this shift in the nature of parliamentary moral argument in broad changes that had taken place in British society, such as bureaucratization, secularization, the growth of state welfare, insurance and complex rules of liability, all of which have eroded traditional notions of sin, blame, guilt and personal responsibility.[3] We now ask not "who is to blame?" but "who is going to have to pay when things go wrong?"

Although the change from "moralist" to "causalist" patterns of thought represented a radical break with the "deontological" or "given" character of traditional Christian teaching, the Churches in the 1960s were generally willing to endorse the causalist premises of the then debate. Thus, in the Church of England the Council for Moral Welfare, which subsequently became the Board for Social Responsibility, issued a succession of reports arguing for changes in the *laws* relating to homosexual practice, abortion and divorce which closely foreshadowed the legislation subsequently passed.[4] Similar reasoning can be seen in comparable commissions established by many Nonconformist Churches[5] and even, with regard to homosexuality, by the Roman Catholic group set up to advise the Wolfenden Committee.[6]

While these various Church reports helped to create, and were in turn influenced by the prevailing causalist ethos, it is sometimes hard to establish precise correlations between religious conviction and the patterns of voting and speech making of M.P.s and Peers. Detailed study of the speeches and voting patterns of individual members of Parliament (Lords as well as Commons) does reveal though the existence of a number of smaller, particular patterns of moral change and resistance to change within the broad general framework outlined above. These patterns were linked both to the religious affiliations and convictions of members of Parliament and to their ideological and party political commitments.

The two most interesting patterns of political-religious-moral interactions I have found concern the Roman Catholic Labour M.P.s in their response to the proposed legislation on abortion and divorce, and the Anglican Peers, both spiritual and temporal, in their response to the issues of capital punishment and of homosexuality.

The Crisis of Catholic Labourism

The clearest instance where religion has been *the* decisive factor was the strong opposition of Roman Catholic M.P.s of all parties to the liberalization of the laws relating to abortion and to divorce. Labour M.P.s were in general sympathetic to reform of the law of abortion and divorce, but on these issues the Roman Catholic Labour M.P.s were in strong opposition to their fellow socialists.   Indeed, they were the only religious group to "switch sides" so that on abortion and divorce the 20 Roman Catholic Labour M.P.s may be classed with the Conservative M.P.s of all religious backgrounds as generally opposing change in contrast to the reforming Labour and Liberal M.P.s.[7] In consequence, the Labour Roman Catholics were exposed to strong cross-pressures and often felt very bitter about their situation.

Not only in Britain but also in Australia and the United States Roman Catholics are in the main the blue-collar descendants of poor, relatively unenterprising immigrants who still constitute ethnic minorities that are tolerated but disesteemed by the dominant white Anglo-Saxon Protestants.[8] Both their class position and their sense of ethnic exclusion impel such Roman Catholics to support, enrol in and represent (and locally even to control) the Parties of the Left - the Labour Parties of Britain and Australia, the Democratic Party in America.   However, they have in consequence often found that their Roman Catholic world-view is in sharp conflict with that of the Godless Left in issues of ideology, foreign policy, and increasingly personal morality.

Conflicts between Roman Catholic and secular-leftist elements of parties with a blue-collar electoral base are not a new phenomenon.   The extreme unease with which Roman Catholics in the American Democratic Party viewed the stance of that Party's "progressive" wing towards events in Spain and in Mexico in the 1930s[9] and the split in the Australian Labour Party in the 1950's between the "Bloody Commos" and the "Bloody Groupers" (members of the Industrial Groups backed by the Catholic Social Movement)[10] were both clear instances of such conflict.   In a quieter way, individual Roman Catholic politicians and trade unionists have fought similar battles within the British labour unions and Labour Party.   However, the Roman Catholic Labour M. P.s. did not foresee the determination with which other Labour M. P.s would support the cause of abortion law reform in the 1960s nor that their own combination of economic labourism and social conservatism would soon be denounced by their comrades as reactionary. For many of them a lifetime's attempt to serve the ideals of both Church and Party seemed to be ending in an atmosphere of bitterness, hostility and rejection. Across the water in Ireland, the home of the ancestors of many of Britain's Catholics, the Roman Catholic ban on abortion was still upheld and indeed was later to be built into the very constitution of the Republic[11] but the British Catholics' failure to halt abortion law reform in Britain in practice nullified Ireland's moral stand. Unwanted Irish pregnancies are now terminated in British abortion clinics and unwanted Irish marriages in British courts.[12] By the end of the 1960s the Roman Catholics in the Parliamentary Labour Party recognised that they as a group had lost the battle against easier divorce and abortion and that the latter defeat in particular had created a crisis for old-style Catholic Labourism.

The Labour Catholics were not only defeated by their own colleagues but indeed also often subjected to personal political attacks. Simon Mahon, the R. C. Labour M. P. for Bootle, was particularly baffled when Tribune referred to him and a group of like-minded Liverpool and Merseyside M. P.s as "reactionaries." 13 He felt that it was unjust that such a label should be pinned on "Liverpool Labour Members who have spent a lifetime working among slum conditions and trying to get rid of the environment in which we were born...We have spent our adult lives in the Labour movement as did our fathers and grandfathers before us....I am not a reactionary in any way." 14

This comment made by Simon Mahon during a debate on the Sexual Offences (Homosexuality) Bill was as nothing though to the bitter public outbursts from his brother, Peter Mahon, the R. C. Labour M. P. for Preston South in the concluding stages on the Third Reading of the Medical Termination of Pregnancy (Abortion) Bill when he knew that the cause was lost:

> I have been in politics, a member of the Labour Party for 44 years and I have never had the word 'unworthy' used to me. I hope that I will go to my grave without that word ever having been said to me. I have never been an unworthy member of the Labour movement....I must calm down. I am rather over-emotional about this.....It has puzzled me that there should be so much support in Parliament for the Measure. I never anticipated that after three years in office The Labour Party would allow such a Bill to come forward. Not in my wildest imagination could I have imagined such a thing...In the whole of my public life I have never felt so badly about anything as I do about the Bill.[15]

The anger and anguish of the brothers Mahon was more than just an expression of personal feelings - it was the last cry of a petrified group crushed between the contradictory pressures of an unyielding rock-hard Church and a Party steamroller powered by class-interest-envy-and-resentment but now driven by the unco' liberated.

The Crumbling of Establishment Morality

A crude analysis of the voting patterns of members of the House of Commons by religion (i.e., simple percentaging) indicates that those in some sense affiliated to the English Established Church (Church of England, Church in Wales, Scottish Episcopalians, Church of Ireland) were the only group to provide a majority albeit slight in favour of retaining capital punishment.[16] The members of all other religious or irreligious categories were strongly against hanging and also provided large majorities in favour of the liberalization of the law in relation to homosexuality, an issue on which the Anglicans were fairly evenly divided.[17] However, at that time the bulk of the Anglicans were to be found in the Conservative Party and most of the Dissenters, Roman Catholics, Jews, and unbelievers in the Liberal and Labour Parties. If this fact is allowed for statistically then the *independent* links between M.P.s, Anglicanism and voting for hanging or for the continued criminalization of homosexuality are of negligible proportions.[18] Significantly, the strongest opposition to homosexual law reform came from the Ulster Unionists all of whom at that time described themselves as Church of Ireland or Church of England.[19] Perhaps the key question that should be asked relates to the divergence between the fierce last ditch Conservative defence of capital punishment and of legal penalties for male homosexual misdeeds and the relatively lukewarm support for these Tory shibboleths by Anglicans as such. Had the Church of England already ceased to be the Conservative Party at prayer, thus foreshadowing the more serious splits between the secular and religious wings of the Establishment that have so annoyed Mrs Thatcher? Can the roots of that deliberate absence of national triumphalism which, to the chagrin of the Tory diehards, marked the Church's celebration of the ending of the Falklands war, be located in the earlier growing reluctance of the Bishops to provide a spiritual underwriting for capital punishment and the prosecution of homosexuals? These questions can be more easily answered by a perusal of the shifting balance of the debates on these issues in the House of Lords rather than the Commons.

First, though, it should be noted that the first half of the 1980s saw the last and probably final defeat of the attempt to restore capital punishment for murder after its abolition in 1965 and the extension to Ulster of the repeal of the laws criminalizing homosexuality that had taken place in England and Wales in 1967 (and later quietly extended to Scotland). The radical changes of the 1960s had become the status quo.

The state of law and morality in the United Kingdom is thus very different from that which prevailed even in the years immediately after the Second World War when capital punishment for murder was mandatory (though not always applied since reprieves were often granted) and private homosexual acts between male adults were rigorously punished by law in the small but increasing number of cases where they were detected and prosecuted.

Capital punishment and the legal and moral condemnation of homosexuality were each key aspects of an establishment morality that punished offences against social order. Murder was a crime not merely against an individual victim as was, say, causing death by dangerous driving but against God, King and country. A foul murder so disturbed the sacred moral order, so polluted society, that only the infliction of capital punishment on the offender could bring redress through retribution. Homosexual acts between consenting adults lacked any victim at all but they were degrading and disorderly, abominable and unnatural forms of behaviour that were the antithesis of the natural moral order designed by God and upheld by Church and State for centuries.

It is not surprising that the most vigorous defenders of capital punishment and condemners of homosexuality were those most attached to the traditional and organic view of state and society outlined above - those who belonged to the disciplined interlocking hierarchies that made up the Establishment viz the Conservative Party, the established Churches of England and of Scotland, the judiciary, the senior officers of the armed forces, those who governed the then still vast colonial empire. The opponents of capital punishment and the defenders of the homosexuals though drawn from all Parties and classes, tended most often to be found among those radical middle-class critics of the Establishment who joined the Labour and Liberal parties. For most of the twentieth century the clash between the parties has been based on economic issues - the conflicts between economic classes, planning versus the market, socialism versus capitalism - which are quite irrelevant to the moral issues discussed here. In a society such as the Soviet Union it is the upholders of the socialist order who have defended capital punishment even for crimes against (state) property and introduced heavy penalties for homosexuals.[20] The British relationship between socialism and radical abolitionism is a purely contingent one rooted in the fact that socialists, though strong believers in central state power, have felt alienated from and in opposition to the particular state in which they live and its distinctive hierarchies and associated moral order. Homosexuality poses no threat to free enterprise and the abolition of capital punishment is not the abolition of capital, nor have those who opposed these moral changes done so openly or covertly in defence of an economic interest.

The key to the willingness of middle-class socialists in Britain to oppose capital punishment and defend homosexuals is that they had inherited the earlier radical anti-Establishment views of the left-wing Liberals and shared with the surviving radical Liberals an ideology of "underdoggery" which enabled them to leap to the defence of any groups (including even murderers and sodomites) who could be plausibly represented as the victims of those who had traditionally exercised power in Britain and its Empire. Even today muggers and buggers, Rastafarians and foxes are all grist to their mill. Only Muslims and rapists defy the simple dichotomies of the progressive mind.

Traditionally, the Conservative groups most committed to capital punishment and to the severe treatment of homosexuals have not been those in charge of production but the members of the sacred hierarchies of the state who on the one hand were concerned with the maintenance of traditional symbols, rituals and values and on the other with the disciplined, regulated use of force on behalf of the Crown. In the House of Lords, the leading defenders of capital punishment and upholders of criminal sanctions against homosexuality when these were assailed in post-war Britain proved to be those who had enjoyed a career in the military, the colonial service or the judiciary. They saw any relaxation in retribution as a threat to the nation's moral fibre and sense of discipline. Military leaders, colonial rulers and judges alike had had to order the taking of life in the name of the state and within a very strict framework of rules. As such they were likely to see the act of murder as an anarchic slaying motivated by undisciplined passions or as a direct attack on the established legal order, and thus an infringement of their just monopoly of force, a defiance and contradiction of the impersonal discipline and obedience to regulation that had been the centre of their own lives. The abolition of capital punishment would have indirectly cast doubt on the validity of their own past actions as men who had ordered the infliction of death in defence of their society through legal executions or just wars. In a quite different way male homosexuality also threatened their orderly world of isolated male hierarchies in which strong group loyalty co-existed with carefully maintained social distance and formal relations governed by impersonal rules. There was a threatening anarchic promiscuity about male homosexuality which could have led to the improper involvement of officer and private, soldier and civilian, colonial administrator and native ruler, High Court Judge and questionable kerb-side loafer, the loyal and the alien.[21] Male homosexuality threatened to break down the vital internal and external boundaries of their professional hierarchies and to introduce passions and jealousies that would destroy order and discipline and upset the balanced unity of impersonal rule and comradely loyalty upon which their institutions depended.[22]

It might reasonably be expected that the senior official spokesmen of the Church of England, those Bishops who sat in the House of Lords would also be keen upholders of the moral order outlined above. They were after all a traditional part of the political as well as the religious order and represented the established Church of the dominant country of the United Kingdom. However, a systematic examination of the votes and speeches of the Bishops in the House of Lords on the subjects of capital punishment and homosexuality since the Second World War indicates a gradual growth of distance between these religious leaders and the substantial body of Peers who opposed any change in the law on moral issues.

The first post-war challenge to capital punishment came in 1948 when a large group of backbench M.P.s passed an amendment to the Criminal Justice Bill suspending the death penalty for murder.[23] The House of Lords voted against the amendment by 181 votes to 28. Of the 28 abolitionist Peers, only 3 were Conservatives.[24] Only two bishops voted, the Bishop of Chichester (Bell) in favour of the suspension of capital punishment and the Bishop of Winchester (Haigh) against but it was estimated that the Bishops in general were 3 to 1 against abolition.[25] The Bishop of Winchester (Haigh) stressed that:

> ...it has never been a characteristic of Christian belief to say there is nothing sufficiently sacred to allow of life being surrendered or taken for its sake. If anyone is interested in the *official* view of the Church of England on this subject, I may recall the modest language of the Thirty-Seventh Article of Religion which says that for sufficiently heinous offences Christian men may be put to death....[26] The death penalty has about it a vertical dimension and, therefore, in my view is capable of arousing and does, in fact, arouse among an immense number of people, what I can only describe as a quasi-religious sense of awe[27] ...the question to be considered is not simply whether there will be a few more murders or a few less but the whole attitude of the British people to what I have described as the criminality of crime and to the majesty of the whole system of law from the top to bottom.[28]

The Bishop of Truro (Hunkin) was even more emphatically in favour of retributive justice and felt that -

> ...certainly modern science could make it such that the final act of the hangman was clearly to him an act of duty comparable to that of an artilleryman bombarding the enemy in battle.[29]

This explicit comparison between the civil executioner and the soldier in a just war is a particularly striking one. The Bishop of Truro knew from direct experience the nature of artillery for he had been a gifted mathematician (twelfth wrangler) who as an army chaplain during the First World War had been awarded the M.C. (1917) and Bar (1918).

The Archbishop of Canterbury (Fisher), as he was to do many times later, sought a compromise solution but his moderation was not endorsed by many other Peers. In particular the judges stressed the wickedness of the murders committed by those they had tried and condemned,[30] and the measured ex-colonial rulers spoke now, and indeed again in 1956, of the curbing of terrorists in Bengal and witch doctors in West Africa by means of capital punishment. Whatever might be said of the progress of civilization in England, the leopard-men of Nigeria would never change their spots and examples must be made and set in the heart of the empire.[31] Suspension, let alone abolition, was overwhelmingly defeated.

The next major debates on capital punishment occurred in 1956 when the House of Commons again voted to abolish capital punishment only to have the Bill defeated in the House of Lords by a large majority (238 to 95).[32] This time, however, only the Bishop of Rochester, Christopher Chavasse [a First World War chaplain (M. C., Croix de Guerre) a former Deputy Assistant Chaplain General (1918-19), a chaplain for the Territorial Army (1921-49, OBE (Milit) T. D.)] voted against abolition. The two Archbishops and eight of the Bishops voted in favour of abolition, though when they spoke in favour they did so with qualifications and reservations.

The Archbishop of Canterbury now urged the division of murder into capital and non-capital categories *not* on the basis of greater retribution for the more heinous crimes but such that premeditated murder or the murder of the guardians of the social order (such as the police and prison officers) could be properly deterred and society and the moral law defended with accuracy. He argued that:

> Within these given categories the deterrent power of the death sentence obviously would have its maximum possible effect for a murderer would have to put himself into the reach of the death penalty by deliberate act.[33].... It is true that some murders, some of the most abominable murders, would fall outside the categories and would escape the death penalty. They would be murders of a specially beastly and passionate kind.[34]

Whether the Archbishop's views encouraged the Government to introduce the 1957 Homicide Act which made a distinction between capital and non-capital murder, may be doubted, but he certainly became one of its most enthusiastic supporters[35] and the Lord Chancellor, in introducing the Homicide Bill, quoted in support Dr. Fisher's speech of 1956,[36] adding:

332

> The death penalty is to be retained for those cases where murder is most dangerous to the preservation of law and order and where the death penalty is likely to be a particularly effective deterrent.[37]

The Archbishop of Canterbury strongly welcomed the new Bill and declared:

> that the State has a right in the name of God and of society to impose the death penalty whether as an act of justice or for the protection of its own citizens from violence....There is no immorality in it at all. It may be wise or unwise, expedient or inexpedient; but it is not against the laws of God or the doctrine of the Christian Church.[38]

Although the supporters of the Homicide Act of 1957 had hoped that a measure so consistent with the emerging causalist morality of the time would endure, it proved to be only a half-way house to complete abolition of the death penalty. By resting their case so heavily on the factual assumption that capital punishment had a unique deterrent effect in relation to certain types of murder they had given a hostage to fortune. In the years that followed there seemed to be little difference in the trends of capital and non-capital murder and in 1965 the findings of their own experiment were turned against them.

In 1965 the House of Lords voted by 204 votes to 104 to give the murder (Abolition of the death penalty) Bill a second reading. Seventeen bishops including both Archbishops voted with the abolitionist majority on either the second or the third reading (or both) and none voted against abolition.[39] Between 1948 and 1965 the Bishops as a group (it was one with a fairly rapid turnover of members) had in the main moved in line with the shifting opinions of all but the most die-hard members of the House of Lords, neither strikingly leading the way nor following in the wake of a trend but the traditionalists nonetheless felt betrayed. The Church now seemed to be merely echoing the moral divisions and uncertainties of the contemporary world. Even death itself had changed for the Bishops no longer spoke of the just repentance of the person in the condemned cell about to go before yet another tribunal[40] but of the wrongness of imposing on the convicted murderer a suffering rooted in "the fear of the unknown, the agony of apprehension."[41]

The anger of the Conservative traditionalists in the House of Lords at what they saw as moral betrayal by the leaders of their very own Church was even greater in the case of homosexuality. The first severely critical mention of the subject by a traditionalist was in a speech denouncing homosexual crime by the Earl Winterton in May 1954 when he attacked a pamphlet issued by the Church of England Moral Welfare Council[42] supporting the legalization of "homosexualism between adults"[43] which expressed the causalist view that: "As a social problem (Homosexualism) is not, as a rule, so far reaching and devastating in its third-party consequences as ordinary pre-marital or extra-marital sexual relations."[44] Earl Winterton, by contrast, took the moralist view that the "filthy, disgusting, unnatural vice of homosexuality was more evil and more harmful to the individual and community." The causalist view quoted above he regarded as "an astonishing doctrine to emanate from an organization of the Church of England."[45]

The Bishop of Southwell (Frank Russell Barry D.S.O., an army chaplain in World War I) in responding to Earl Winterton's comments carefully avoided pre-empting the Church's response to the report of the Committee of Inquiry (concerning *inter alia* homosexuality) that had just been set up,[46] but he did roundly condemn the homosexual practices that were "injecting poison into the bloodstream"[47] of society in the strong language of Christian and national tradition:

> Public opinion at the present is deeply stirred about the whole matter, and well it may be, because the increase in unnatural offences is an ominous warning of something going radically wrong in the moral foundations of the social order. And historically, as Earl Winterton pointed out in his opening speech, this always seems to be a sign of a demoralized or decadent culture. Where people cease to believe effectively in what has hitherto been the communal religion, and when there is scepticism and cynicism about the meaning and value of life itself, people get driven back upon themselves, and introversion very easily brings perversion with it. It is a warning which cannot be ignored, and it is one more bit of evidence to show that once a people lets its ultimate convictions go, then there can be no stopping halfway and the whole moral bottom is in danger of falling out of a society. As St. Paul said about this very point a long time ago, once the creature is confused with the Creator, once people cease to believe in God and, therefore, in ultimate moral obligations,

334

everything begins to go bad on us, and natural instincts and affections become unnatural and perverted.[48]

The next major explosion occurred in 1957 when the Report of the Committee of Inquiry had been published and was debated in the House of Lords.

The Bishops were divided on the recommendations of the Wolfenden Report. The Bishop of St. Albans (Jones), the Chairman of the Church of England Moral Welfare Council, noted with pleasure that the recommendations of the report proposing the decriminalization of homosexuality were very similar to those of his own council in 1954[49] but the Bishop of Carlisle (Bloomer) did not agree. The Bishop of Rochester (Christopher Chavasse M. C.), who had held out against his fellow bishops for the retention of capital punishment the year before, was strongly opposed to the legalization of male homosexuality; he, and he spoke for many others in the Church, could not:

...agree that natural vice - heterosexual vice - and unnatural vice - homosexual vice - are to be equated together as equally heinous.[50]

He felt that:

There is no more baneful or contagious an influence in the world than that which emanates from homosexual practice. It makes a life of leprosy[51]...the emotion and moral indignation and horror which are aroused in the human heart by the thought and contemplation of unnatural vice, and which find expression in the Holy Scriptures, both in the Old and in the New Testaments, are probably more right in teaching us our attitude toward unnatural vice than academic discussion divorced from reality.[52]

The Archbishop of Canterbury (Fisher), as in the case of capital punishment, sought to find a stable moral point in the centre of the warring moral factions:

....if it proved legally possible - I do not know whether it is - to separate what the noble Lord, Lord Pakenham, called the extreme offence (sodomy), and to leave that still a crime, I should wish to leave it as a crime still....I believe that this crime does stand in a class by itself and is almost different in kind from other homosexual offences. I believe personally that that opinion can be upheld on moral grounds.[53]

No major changes in legislation in regard to homosexuality were made immediately following the Wolfenden Report for the then Conservative

Government declined to act on its controversial suggestions regarding homosexuality. The government did not, as it had done in the case of hanging, take up the "wise and expedient" suggestions of Dr. Fisher, but in 1965 when it became clear that there would probably soon be a complete decriminalization of all male adult homosexual acts Viscount Dilhorne, no doubt speaking for other conservative traditionalists among the lawyers, tried to revive the former Archbishop of Canterbury (Fisher)'s distinction between the extreme offence of sodomy and less flagrant homosexual crimes.[54] However, they failed to gain any support from the Bishops, none of whom was willing to support the judicial traditionalists in making a sharp moral and legal distinction between different types of homosexual acts. Dilhorne's attempt to retain the law of sodomy was defeated by 86 to 52 with the Archbishop of Canterbury (Ramsey) and the Bishops of Chichester, Lincoln and Manchester voting against.[55]

Indeed the Archbishop of Canterbury (Ramsey) went so far as to say:

...it is impossible to distinguish between the abominableness of various kinds of homosexual actions, and I do not really think it makes for morality when there is embodied in the criminal law a distinction that is not really a rational moral distinction.[56]

The Bishop of Worcester (Charles-Edwards) was even more tolerant and speaking of his pastoral work among homosexuals said of them:

I must put completely on one side any feelings of repulsion at conduct which I personally find disgusting. I must indeed beware of assuming that I am normal and he is abnormal for in the artificial life we live today it is extremely difficult to define what actually is the normal and what is the abnormal.[57]

The willingness of some Bishops to see merit in arguments that ignored the social basis of the moral doctrine that homosexual acts were abominable and a threat to the social and moral order of a people, or a nation, and reduced it to a mere expression of irrational personal disgust is a measure of how far they had departed from the traditional Establishment morality of Church and state.

The Bishop of Chichester (Wilson) was not well received by the traditionalists when he said:

We should be inclined to say that the moral fibre of the nation may be just as much undermined by heterosexual misconduct as by homosexual misconduct -

Noble Lords : 'Nonsense!'[58]

Viscount Dilhorne, a leader of traditionalist opposition to a change in the law was particularly shocked at the reluctance of the Archbishop of Canterbury (Ramsey) to condemn homosexuality as a specially and peculiarly vile sin:

> Some of his (the Archbishop's) observations ...seem to draw little distinction and to suggest quite emphatically that little distinction can be made between an act of sodomy and an act of adultery[59] ....I was surprised again today to hear it rather suggested by the most revered Primate that sodomy was really not such abominable conduct after all.[60]

Although the Bishops were by no means unanimously in favour of reform none of them voted against any of the Bills to decriminalize homosexuality before the House of Lords in the period 1965-7 (those who disagreed either abstained, stayed away or were not senior enough to be members of the Lords) and only one, the Bishop of Leicester (Williams) spoke out strongly to the contrary.[61]

From 1964 onwards the traditionalists felt thoroughly betrayed by those very Church leaders whom they thought should have automatically supported them. As Lord Rathcavan, an Ulsterman, put it:

> ...they could not believe that the attitude which (the Bishops) are adopting will be adopted by the great mass of the decent, honest, clean-living members of the Church of England (and wondered) what is going to become of the Church when we see the attitude of the Bishops on this Bill.[62]

The damage that the traditionalists feared would be inflicted was not damage to the family but to the discipline, order and moral fibre of the nation as a whole and particularly to the all-male hierarchies of the services (and the uniformed character-building youth movements these had inspired) and of the merchant navy. These views were expressed again by the judges and former Conservative law-officers, by Lord Rowallan of the Boy Scouts and by the military men. Viscount Montgomery's speech characteristically knitted together religion, patriotism, discipline and war in his opposition to reform:

> I cannot reconcile with my own beliefs what was said in their speeches by the most reverend Primates. To condone unnatural offences in male persons over 21 or, indeed, in male

persons of any age seems to me utterly wrong. One may as well condone the Devil and all his works.....a weakening of the law will strike a blow at all those devoted people who are working to improve the moral fibre of the youth of this country. And heaven knows! it wants improving....[63]

Homosexual conduct has in fact remained an offence against service regulations for members of the armed forces, but the military men in the House of Lords and indeed the House of Commons were no longer able to impose their world view of "order-discipline-moral fibre" on the civilian population. Today the military, like the Church, are still valued and respected, but pushed to the periphery. The hierarchies of service, sacrifice, and sacred duty are no longer central to a society devoted to individual consumption and impersonal welfare. As the traditional establishment declined in authority, influence and confidence, so too it split and divided. Also, by the 1960s, the very boundaries and identity of the *nation* were becoming less clear. Anglicanism too was not only ceasing to be the dominant religion of England but also through change and consolidation abroad, was ceasing to be a predominantly English community of Churches. Many found such changes threatening but progressive middle-class opinion in general tended to view the slow dissolution of the nation's boundaries with complacency and even enthusiasm. Even when later in the 1980s a belligerent and seditious political minority declared that the new deadly sins were racism, sexism and heterosexism and proclaimed their belief in a formless, multi-cultural, androgynous, and unboundedly ecumenical colloid of a nation, no one among the English influentials felt sufficiently concerned to offer effective resistance.

The one place where a national and religious frontier remained sharp and was fervently defended in the face of a perceived threat was Northern Ireland and it was from Northern Ireland that the most stalwart defenders of capital punishment and especially of stern laws against homosexuality came. In the 1960s and 1970s no one dared to suggest that the legal toleration of homosexuality should be extended to Ulster. Despite this the Ulster Unionist M. P.s who in the 1960s were all active members of the Church of Ireland/Church of England were even more strongly opposed to the liberalization of the law on homosexuality relating to England and Wales than their Conservative allies or their co-religionists in England (the Church of Ireland itself formally opposed any change in the law). The new permissive British legislation was only extended to Northern Ireland in 1980-1983 at the insistence of an international body, the European Court of Human Rights [64] and against the wishes of Ulster's M.P.s who now included Paisleyite Presbyterians. The Protestant Ulstermen's concern with preserving intact all boundaries that could be seen as a metaphor of the one crucial national and religious boundary was displayed in their fierce campaign to "Save Ulster from sodomy" and had its mirror image in the continued prosecution and persecution of male adult homosexuals in the Republic of Ireland. The educated English felt emancipated and superior. In the past they had been unable to understand why their neighbour sought to assert a different and separate identity from theirs. Now they could not understand why anyone ever asserted a separate identity at all.

REFERENCES

All references to Hansard are to Parliamentary Papers 5th series.

[1]See Christie Davies, *Permissive Britain, Social Change in the Sixties and Seventies* (London: Pitman, 1975) and Christie Davies, "How our Rulers argue about Censorship," in Rajeev Dhavan and Christie Davies, (eds.), *Censorship and Obscenity* (London: Martin Robertson, 1978).

[2]See Christie Davies, "Moralists, Causalists, Sex, Law and Morality," in W. H. G. Armytage, R. Chester and John Peel, (eds.), *Changing Patterns of Sexual Behaviour* (London: Academic Press, 1980), pp. 13-43.

[3]See Davies (1975 and 1980) and Christie Davies, "Crime, Bureaucracy and Equality," *Policy Review* 23, (Winter 1983), pp. 89-105. See also Bryan Wilson "Morality and the Modern Social System," in *"Religion, Values and Daily Life,"* Acts 16, International Conference for the Sociology of Religion, C. I. S. R., Paris, 1981 and Bryan Wilson, "Morality in the Evolution of the Modern Social System," *British Journal of Sociology*, vol. 36, no. 3, Sept. 1985.

[4]*The Problem of Homosexuality* (Church Information Board 1954) foreshadowed the decriminalisation of homosexual activity between consenting adults in the Sexual Offences Act of 1967; *Abortion: An Ethical Discussion* (Church Information Office 1965) foreshadowed the Abortion Act of 1965; and *Putting Asunder* (London: SPCK, 1966) recommended a Divorce Law for Contemporary Society almost identical to that instantiated in the subsequent Divorce Reform Act of 1969.

[5]For useful surveys of such commissions see Peter Coleman, *Christian Attitudes to Homosexuality* (London: SPCK, 1980) chapters 9 and 10; R. F. R. Gardner, *Abortion: The Personal Dilemma* (Exeter: The Paternoster Press, 1972) chapter 10; and A. R. Winnett, *The Church and Divorce* (London: Mowbrays, 1968) chapter 4.

[6]*The Dublin Review*, Summer 1956, volume 230, no. 471, pp. 57-65.

[7]On this point I am indebted to George Moyser of the Department of Government, University of Manchester for allowing me to read his unpublished paper "Voting patterns on 'moral' issues in the British House of Commons 1964-9." I am also grateful to Rex Walford for letting me examine his research information on the religious affiliations of British M. P.s. They are of course not responsible for any use I have made of their data. See also P. G. Richards, *Parliament and Conscience* (London Allen and Unwin, 1970), p. 183 and M. R. Fuller, "Parliamentary voting patterns on non-party issues," M. Phil Thesis, University of Southampton, 1970.

[8]See Will Herberg, *Protestant, Catholic, Jew* (Garden City, New York: Doubleday, 1960); Thomas Sowell, *Ethnic America: a History* (New York: Basic, 1981).

340

[9]See Ronald H. Bayor, *Neighbors in Conflict, The Irish, Germans, Jews and Italians of New York 1929-41* (Baltimore: John Hopkins, 1978).

[10]See John Douglas Pringle, *Australian Accent* (London: Chatto and Windus, 1958), pp. 73-95.

[11]See Andrew Rynne, *Abortion, the Irish Question* (Dublin: Ward River, 1982) and see H. Butler, *Escape from the Ant-Hill* (Mullingar: Lilliput, 1985) regarding the Eighth Amendment to the (Irish) Constitution Act 1983.

[12]See Rynne, p. 19 and pp. 22-25.

[13]Hansard, Commons vol. 738, col. 1083.

[14]Hansard, Commons vol. 738, col. 1083-4.

[15]Hansard, Commons vol. 750, col. 1354.

[16]See Richards, p. 183 and Fuller.

[17]See Richards, p. 183 and Fuller.

[18]See note 7, Moyser.

[19]See note 7, Moyser and Walford.

[20]See Y. Brokhin, *Hustling on Gorki Street* (London: W. H. Allen, 1971), Albert Parry, *The New Class Divided: Russian Science and Technology versus Communism* (New York: Macmillan, 1966) p. 198 and the relevant Amnesty reports. On homosexuality see H. Mannheim, *Criminal Justice and Social Reconstruction* (London: Kegan Paul, 1946); Kate Millet, *Sexual Politics* (London: Hart-Davies, 1971); Mikhail and August Stern, *Sex in the Soviet Union*, Times, New York, 1980; and D. J. West, *Homosexuality Re-examined* (London: Duckworth, 1977).

[21]See Christie Davies, "Sexual Taboos and Social Boundaries," *American Journal of Sociology*, volume 87, number 5, March 1982, pp. 1032-63. See also Kenneth Ballhatchet, *Race, Sex and Class under the Raj* (London: Weidenfeld and Nicholson, 1980).

[22]See Davies, 1975.

[23]Hansard, Commons vol. 449, cols. 1093-98.

[24]See Elizabeth Orman Tuttle, *The Crusade against Capital Punishment in Great Britain* (London: Stevens, 1961), p. 73.

[25]See Hansard, Lords vol. 198, cols. 835-36 and also col. 694.

[26]Hansard, Lords vol. 155, cols. 424-25. Emphasis added.

[27]Hansard, Lords vol. 155, col. 427.

[28]Hansard, Lords vol. 155, col. 428.

[29]Hansard, Lords vol. 155, col. 483. See also Tuttle, p. 69.

[30]See Hansard, Lords vol. 155, col. 492.

[31]See Hansard, Lords vol. 156, cols. 23-24, and 28-30 and cols. 148-51 and vol. 198, cols. 592-93, 644, 672-73 and 726-77.

[32]Hansard, Lords vol. 198, cols. 839-42. See also in the meantime the "Royal Commission on Capital Punishment 1949-53 Report," Command 8932 (London: HMSO, 1953).

[33]Hansard, Lords vol. 198, col. 751.

[34]Hansard, Lords vol. 198, col. 751.

[35]See Hansard, Lords vol. 201, cols. 1191-94.

[36]See Hansard, Lords vol. 201, col. 1169.

[37]Hansard, Lords vol. 201, cols. 1168-69.

[38]Hansard, Lords vol. 201, col. 1190.

[39]Hansard, Lords vol. 268, cols. 711-14.

[40]See Hansard, Lords vol. 198, col. 597, and cols. 695-98.

[41]Bishop of Chester (Ellison), Hansard, Lords vol. 268, col. 610.

[42]See Hansard, Lords vol. 187, col. 738 and Church of England Moral Welfare Council, *The Problem of Homosexuality* (London: Church Information Board, 1954).

[43]Hansard, Lords vol. 187, col. 738.

[44]Hansard, Lords vol. 187, col. 738.

[45]Hansard, Lords vol. 187, col. 739.

[46]Hansard, Lords vol. 187, col. 754.

[47]Hansard, Lords vol. 187, col. 752.

[48]Hansard, Lords vol. 187, col. 752.

[49]See Hansard, Lords vol. 206, col. 766.

342

[50]Hansard, Lords vol. 206, col. 796.

[51]Hansard, Lords vol. 206, col. 797.

[52]Hansard, Lords vol. 206, col. 798.

[53]Hansard, Lords vol. 206, col. 757.

[54]Hansard, Lords vol. 266, cols. 702-03, vol. 267, col. 291, and vol., 269, col. 719.

[55]Hansard, Lords vol. 267, cols. 315-18.

[56]Hansard, Lords vol. 267, col. 302-23.

[57]Hansard, Lords vol. 266, col. 134.

[58]Hansard, Lords vol. 266, col. 660.

[59]Hansard, Lords vol. 269, col. 719. See also vol. 267, cols. 291-92 and 293 and vol. 268, col. 435.

[60]Hansard, Lords vol. 269, col. 720.

[61]Hansard, Lords vol. 284, cols. 1307-08.

[62]Hansard, Lords vol. 267, col,. 309. See also vol. 266, col. 688-89, vol. 267, col. 291 and vol. 268, col. 411.

[63]Hansard, Lords vol. 266, col. 645.

[64]For details see European Court H. R. Dudgeon judgement, 24 February, 1983 (Article 50), Series A, No. 59. Registry of the Court, Council of Europe, Strasbourg, Carl Heymans, Koln 1983 (Series A = Judgements and decisions). The Dudgeon case was funded and presumably brought by the Nigras of Northern Ireland.

CHAPTER XIX

IN CAESAR'S SERVICE? RELIGION AND POLITICAL INVOLVEMENT IN BRITAIN

GEORGE MOYSER

INTRODUCTION:

The relationship between religion, state and society in modern Britain has been undergoing considerable change. So far as religion and society are concerned, there is the continued unfolding of religious pluralism and secularization as well as the conscious attempts of particular institutions to reassess the manner of their engagement with that society (see *Faith in the City*, 1985). Equally, one can point to major changes in the way religious bodies relate to the state - or the polity. Above all, this concerns the Church of England as the established church of the largest constituent nation within the United Kingdom. Here, the constitutional linkages have been undergoing considerable change to give the Church greater autonomy (see Welsby, 1984, esp Ch. 12). Finally, society and state have also experienced great changes. For example, there has been a partial collapse of so-called "consensus politics" (Kavanagh, 1985) and the introduction, through legislation, of substantial changes to contemporary governmental institutions.

344

Given all this, it is indeed appropriate that some assessment, or re-assessment, be made of the contemporary picture. This involves many different levels and types of analysis: normative and empirical; institutional and cultural; national and local. Inevitably, therefore, this essay can only focus on a part of the totality. However, one very important component concerns the way religion, state and society overlap amongst the grass-roots population (see Preston, 1983, p. 135). The pattern of religious adherence in contemporary Britain, and the associations this may have with political outlooks, must constitute an important context within which more particular or prominent events can be interpreted.

It is to this subject, therefore, that the present essay is addressed: What does the map of religious adherence in the mid-1980's look like? Have such attachments any significance for political attitudes and action? Is it the case, for example, that committed Christians see their political role as one of service to Caesar or of challenge? And finally, what does this imply for the future, not least for the leadership of religious bodies as they seek a new social relevance for their institutions in what is now a largely post-Christian society?

RELIGION AND POLITICS - A Framework for Analysis:

The study of the empirical relationship between religion and politics in Britain has mainly been undertaken by historians who were, naturally enough, concerned principally with the previous three centuries when the two spheres had a particularly intense and conflict-ridden relationship. (See, for example, Sykes, 1934; Dickens, 1964; Bosher, 1951; Machin, 1977.) So far as the modern era is concerned, studies have continued to focus on national considerations, leaving the grass-roots relatively untouched. Where the latter have been considered, interest has focussed largely on the voting habits of particular religious categories (Miller and Raab, 1977; Bochel and Denver,

1970; Wald, 1983) reflecting a seemingly wide-held view amongst political scientists that it is in elections alone that religion has retained an at best marginal political significance.

On such a judgement two observations seem apposite. First, it is at the very least a conclusion that should only be drawn after the relevant evidence has been carefully weighed. On the one hand, it is clear that religious bodies are not the major source of politically-relevant cues for their mass membership that possibly once they were. Britain's political agenda, in other words, is one in which explicitly religious interests or issues are nowadays largely missing.[1] They have been substantially replaced by secular conflicts and concerns based principally on class cleavages and economic interest. On the other hand, secularization has not gone so far as totally to eradicate the practical relevance of religion to politics. Apart from some recent questioning of the assumption that secularization is a permanent and irreversible trend in British society (Gilbert, 1980, Ch. 6), the religious bodies themselves still retain a very considerable following; a following indeed that rivals or exceeds that of any other mass organisation in the country. Furthermore, it is also a following that, through the efforts of some religious leaders (for example, Sheppard, 1983; Habgood, 1983), and through a greater emphasis upon lay participation and "outreach" (see *All Are Called*, 1985; *Servants of the Lord*, 1986), may well once more take religious cues more seriously in shaping their social outlooks. At least this may be so amongst those most attached to the religious institutions concerned. Finally, the major economic and political issues now at stake (as exemplified, for example, in the Miners' Strike of 1984-5) may themselves provoke a broader and more critical reflection upon the moral framework in which they arise and are debated.

Secondly, although the findings have considerable interest, one should be very careful not to draw too much significance from observations based on patterns of voting. As a mechanism of political engagement, voting is but one way in which individuals can try to make themselves heard. Indeed, evidence is rapidly accumulating that voting is a rather poor guide to what may be going on in these other channels and arenas (Verba and Nie, 1972; Moyser, Parry and Day, 1986). Similarly, in terms of posing questions about the way religious values feed into political perspectives, voting for one party or another is somewhat unsatisfactory. The question of whether people of particular religious persuasions vote for the Conservatives, or some other party, does not directly address the more fundamental issue of their stance towards the basic political arrangements of British society. What are their attitudes towards Britain's form of "liberal democracy" and the political leadership which it throws up? It is in these areas, surely, that the basic associations between "the religious" and "the political" need to be established. Only then can religious linkages with partisan commitments be set in an adequate political and normative framework.

In pursuit of these general arguments, it is appropriate to map out a basic analytic framework for examining the contribution of the ordinary citizen to political life in these more fundamental terms. This can be constructed, albeit with some over-simplification, from two basic dimensions. First, there is the pattern and level of personal engagement, or activity, in the polity. Ultimately, (and at some risk to the complexities involved), this is a question of being active or inactive, a participant or a spectator. It is also a question of the particular profile of that engagement - not just in voting turnout but in all the major ways through which citizens can stand up and be counted.

The second dimension relates more to the content of the message the citizen delivers, than if he bothers to deliver a message at all. Again, at its simplest, it is ultimately a matter of acceptance or rejection of existing political arrangements. In short, is the citizen for Caesar or against him? Of course, as with participation, the reality is far more complex. there are many aspects of Britain's public life about which individual opinion could and should be separately weighed. Nevertheless, it seems sufficient, if taken as a first approximation, in helping briefly to sketch the alternative stances on offer.

Relating these two axes establishes a somewhat crude but useful typology as set out in Figure 1. This identifies four basic modes or patterns of political engagement. The first, the "support mode" is a matter of active commitment both to the regime and to its leadership. Like all of them, it is an ideal type which cannot do sufficient justice to the complex and possibly contradictory nature of the real world.

Figure 1: Basic Patterns of Political Engagement

		Attitude to Regime	
		COMPLIANT	**CRITICAL**
Level of	**ACTIVE**	SUPPORT	DISSENTIENT
Participation	**INACTIVE**	SUBJECT	EXIT

Nevertheless, one can certainly point to contemporary and historical examplars of this category both in Britain and in other countries. Indeed, in so far as it is linked historically to the idea of a "sacrilized polity" (Medhurst, 1981, pp. 117-18) it is a very ubiquitous phenomenon. Perhaps its clearest expression is to be found in those arrangements where religious and political offices were united in one person - the Pharaoh of Ancient Egypt or the Islamic Caliphate (Medhurst, p. 119). In the case of Christianity, which is obviously more pertinent to the British experience, there has never been such a complete merging of the two domains. The Judeo-Christian tradition has always sustained, at least in principle, the "sacred" and the "profane" as distinct if interrelated spheres. (See Gilbert, 1980; Pannikar, 1983.) However, from Constantine to the Reformation, and above all in Byzantium, mediaeval Christianity approximated an "integrated religio-political system" (Medhurst, p. 117) in which ecclesial and civil loyalties were, in effect, taken as one and the same thing. Of course, in an era long before the dawn of mass politics, the practical contribution of the ordinary populace was very limited.

It was by and large a matter of mutually supportive compacts between princes and bishops or, above all, between Pope and Emperor.

This tradition has had a considerable effect upon the British experience, not least in the creation of churches established by law in England, Scotland and Wales.[2] This was intended to give institutional expression to the idea that the role of the religious adherent was simultaneously to give loyalty to the state. As Hooker put it (as quoted in Cornwell, 1985, p. 42) "there is not any man of the Church of England but the same is also a member of the commonwealth, nor any man a member of the commonwealth, which is not also of the Church of England." But, in post-Reformation Britain, such a view became increasingly unsustainable: the existence of so many "non-conformists" could not in the long run be denied. Nevertheless, this association between the established Churches and established secular authority has remained as something of a guiding principle well into the modern era.

In doing so, it reinforces an underlying tendency, seen by some sociologists and theologians, for religion to act as an instrument of social integration and control. It is a means of providing social and political cohesion in face of an increasingly intolerant and centripetal pluralism. A key empirical question is, of course, the extent to which this is still the case. To what extent is adherence to religious groups (above all to established churches) linked with an active and largely compliant political posture? To Habgood, for example, it is clear that, whilst an active political commitment on the part of Christians is essential, it is not the case that "accommodation," in Niebuhr's (1952, Ch. 3) terms, is the only practical or desirable alternative. For him, a prophetic or critical "resistance" to present arrangements is also a proper task for some individual adherents (although not for religious bodies acting corporately). This introduces the second basic posture in the typology - that of active challenge to political, economic and social arrangements.

This "dissentient" mode also has a lengthy history. The Old Testament is replete with examples of religious leaders calling Israel back to the "straight and narrow" (Preston, 1983, pp. 94-98). In the Christian experience, this type of intervention was most spectacularly represented in the Reformation, although in that case it was much more a call to the Church to mend its ways than to the nation or the state. In Britain, religious commitments have historically played their part in the active antagonism of particular individuals and groups towards the state through, as latter saw it, the destabilizing implications of non-conformity. This extended even to armed rebellion and alleged "plots." From such experiences, something of a continued cultural legacy, lasting well into modern times, can be detected, buttressed by various civil disabilities and discriminations that in some small but notable instances still exist (Robilliard, 1984, p. 89 and Appendix). As with the "establishment connection," however, it is interesting to examine how much of this legacy, if any still exists in the mid-1980's.

In fact, modern dissentient claims are not based so much on the religious partiality of the state as on its potential for sinfulness. A vivid non-European example is the case of the Presbyterian Reformed Church in Cuba, cited by Preston (1983, p. 108), which saw its public role in the following terms:

> The Church lives 'prophetically' in its members when they become committed participants in the depth of the capitalist society and the dehumanizing and decrepit values it represents.

In the British context, this is obviously an extreme position probably advocated by no significant group of Christians (but see Preston, 1983, Ch. 1). And yet, there clearly is a theological tradition, drawing upon Jesus's sayings and the activities of the Early Church, which emphasizes the need for Christians to speak out against the short-comings of the established political and economic order (Reckitt, 1948). Indeed, there is evidence that such a critique, historically neglected by the European Church, is now coming back into vogue. Preston, for example, speaks of an international and ecumenical "trend to the left in Twentieth Century social theology" (1983, p. 75). Certainly, one can find major figures amongst Britain's religious leadership who have very firmly confronted the inequity, injustice and discrimination of the present day. Temple (1942) is, perhaps, the most influential figure of recent times, but one can also point to such individuals as David Sheppard, David Jenkins, John Collins, Bruce Kent and Lord Soper to indicate the extent to which this general posture has now established at least a toe-hold

350

within different religious groups (see also Medhurst and Moyser, 1982, and 1988, Ch. 6).

Again, however, there remains the question of whether and to what extent such cues have percolated down to the grass-roots? In certain localized circumstances, such as Britain's inner cities, where injustice and oppression is most visible, the conditions are ripe (Wheale, 1985). But has it achieved significance on a national scale, or is it the case that, so far as political commitments are concerned, those with an avowed religious adherence still tend to line up on the side of order and stability rather than of change?

Those who adopt the dissentient mode towards state and society seem to imply, by their active participation in secular affairs, that the world is in the long run redeemable. To that extent their "resistance" is probably contingent and limited. There are, however, situations and perspectives where hostility runs much deeper, where state and society are seen as so intractably sinful that an active crusade is misplaced. At best it will leave the problems unresolved, at worst it will contaminate and subvert pure Christian commitments.

It is out of such orientations that the third "exit" mode is conceived (see Hirschmann, 1970). As a tradition, it has been well identified by Niebuhr (1952, p. 54) when he wrote that:

> ...the new faith was accompanied by Christian flight from...Graeco-Roman civilization. In mediaeval times monastic orders and sectarian movements called on believers...to abandon the 'world' and to 'come out from among them and be separate.'

In the modern era, he speaks of "little groups of withdrawing Christians," holy huddles of people who are deeply antagonistic towards contemporary society and whose response is to exit from it, as best they can.

As Niebuhr suggests, such a response, whilst possibly infrequent and certainly exceptional within the major Christian denominations, is not unknown historically. The separatist and dissenting Pilgrims who went, via Holland, to America, and the Boers who decamped to what is now South Africa, withdrew physically. Others, like Soviet Jews and some American Black Muslims would if circumstances allowed. Yet others, principally extreme fundamentalist sects, in effect form inward-looking communities of true believers within the host society (see also Preston, pp. 133-34).

Even in Britain's more "mainstream" religious traditions, however, this exit posture is not entirely absent. Towler (1969), for example, has noted amongst Anglican ordinands an evangelical puritan type whose hallmark is a "withdrawal from the world and aversion to the cultural values of secular society." Equally, Gilbert (1980), notes the same disposition amongst Catholics and Baptists. So far as the latter are concerned, he says (p. 148):

> Never as deeply involved as Congregationalism in the great nineteenth century struggles for equality, respectability and worldly acceptance, the Baptist denomination has largely retained its historic commitment to a concept of the church as a fellowship 'gathered' out of the 'world.' It has remained loyal to the idea of Christian 'separation' from dangerous or unnecessary worldly involvements...

For this orientation, however, it is again important to see the extent to which it still persists in particular religious groupings. In short, is there a significant exit mode present within modern Britain?

One of the criticisms of theological liberals is that to exit is to leave the world unchanged. For them this is unacceptable, which is of course why they tend to espouse active dissent. And yet there is another religious persuasion which is entirely happy with leaving the world as it is. It is this persuasion which underpins the fourth orientation under review, that of the "subject." Theologically, it seems closest to Niebuhr's fourth "answer" to the problem of Christ's relation to culture. In this syndrome, he speaks of both of them as having their legitimate scope of authority and claims to obedience. This, however, entails a certain internal tension in the overall position. On the one hand, the claims of Christ must not be accommodated to those of an essentially sinful culture. Hence there is a sharp difference between this very sceptical stance and that of the support mode which sees in active social and political participation the fulfilment of the Christian message. And yet, on the other hand, there is also the "conviction that obedience to God requires obedience to the institutions of society and loyalty to its members" (Niebuhr, 1952, p. 56). It is this quality of loyalty to the state combined with an unwillingness to become actively involved that is the distinctive hallmark of the subject mode.[3]

352

Kee (1986) has found its modern expression in "right doctrine protestantism," a term originally coined in Alves's (1985) analysis of religion and politics in Brazil. As with those who exit, the world is seen as essentially sinful. But salvation is not to be found by action but by right understanding, the secular order is sacrilized; whatever its sins and ills, it represents and expresses the Divine Will, it is God's order and not to be interfered with. Thus, present arrangements are given a transcendent status: whatever Caesar is doing, he is performing God's Will and should therefore be given due obedience.

Another relevant strand of conservative thought also exists, although in this case the linkage to the subject mode is not so explicit. One suspects, however, that it propels individuals in the same direction. This is the position of Powell (1977), Norman (1979) and others who deny that religion can have, or ought to have, any specific political linkages. For them, Christ's message is wholly supernatural - a concern solely for the "sacred" rather than the "profane." No specific political or social prescriptions can be drawn; no one action in that realm is any more, or any less, imitative of Christ than any other. Furthermore, for Norman, the historical record of Christian political involvement is proof that there is no such thing as a specifically Christian programme of political action. Those interventions in fact merely take up (in his view) the changing fads and fancies of the secular intelligentsia rather than express eternal and distinctive Christian verities.

From such views one might well deduce that no association should exist between religious commitments and political engagement. Certainly, the proponents' overt position is to leave the latter entirely to the private judgement of the individual. At the same time, however, one cannot but suspect that, in practice, they are decrying above all the active, critical and liberal interventions most characteristic of the dissentient mode and to which they represent something of a polar opposite inclination. To that extent, it may be that what they are underwriting, in the British context, is the uncritical passive acceptance of traditional erastianism and established social and political arrangements. It is for this reason that, more as a matter of praxis than of theory, their position would seem to lead toward the subject style.

353

In this instance, as with the other three, what is important now is to examine its practical manifestation in contemporary Britain. That it has a considerable popular following, at least for the view that the Churches should keep out of politics, is undeniable.[4] But to what extent does the more general tendency manifest itself? Is it only a vocal minority, or perhaps a majority amongst the most committed, who shun overt political action? It is to these and the other empirical questions raised in this section that I now turn.

RELIGIOUS ATTACHMENTS:

The empirical analysis centres above all around the nature of religious adherence in Britain. Information about this is set out in Table 1. The figures represent responses to a question about religious attachments asked, with slight variations of wording, in national surveys conducted in 1974, 1979 and 1985. It therefore provides a basic map covering the last decade and illustrates the continuities and changes which seem to have taken place over that period.

Amidst the relatively familiar contours, one interesting aspect concerns the variations in the Anglican and "no religion" figures. There seems to be no obvious differences of wording that would suggest why, in 1985, the percentage of Church of England adherents should have risen by 12.6% over 1979, whereas those seeing themselves as outside any religious fold should have reduced by 17%.[5] As these two movements would seem to be related, they may indicate that, for those concerned, the difference between the two responses can psychologically be very slight: that claiming membership of the National Church is, for many, tantamount to having no real religious commitment at all.[6] Of course, a similar effect may also operate with respect to the established Church of Scotland. But, being so relatively small on a British scale, it is not so apparent. However, it should be noted that, amongst Scottish residents, fully 52.8% claim an attachment to that Church which is slightly more than the 48.1% in England who adhere to the Anglican persuasion. Thus, overall, the evidence of continued

354

secularization so far as these basic attachments are concerned cannot be readily established. All Churches seem to have increased slightly their support base between the two time-points though this, in itself, is little indication of any substantial turning of the tide.

Table 1: Religious Attachment in Britain, 1974-85

	1974[1]	1979[2]	1985[3]
	%	%	%
Anglican	41.6	31.2	43.8
Church of Scotland	4.5	4.4	5.9
Methodist	4.5	4.7	5.0
Baptist	1.8	1.5	1.9
Roman Catholic	9.0	9.9	10.8
Other Christian]	4.8	3.9	3.6
Non-Christian]		2.0	1.6
Christian No Denomination	-	-	2.2
No Religion	33.8	42.3	25.3
N	2349	1859	1571

[1]Do you belong to any religious denomination?
[2]Do you belong to any church or religious group?
[3]Do you regard yourself as belonging to any particular religion?

What is required is a mapping of religious commitments more elaborate than mere nominal attachment, an indicator which makes no distinction between those who have solely a residual link and those who see themselves as being very much a part of the institutions concerned. To provide this more nuanced perspective, two additional criteria were employed: measures of attendance, and of the strength of attachment. The former taps a behavioural or ritualistic sense of religious engagement whereas the latter seeks to measure the extent of adherence at a more psychological level.

That both give somewhat different readings of religious commitments (in 1985) can be seen in Table 2 which provides the relevant figures for both aspects. The pattern for the traditional attendance dimension is set out in Part A. The original coding scheme has, for purposes of presentation, been simplified so that the "very active" are taken to be those who attend at least "several times a month"; the "semi-active" are those attending less than that, but at least "several times a year"; and the "inactive" are all the rest - those who claim to belong to a denomination but in fact attend religious services no more than annually. In addition, an "attendance score" has been calculated from the original, very refined number of categories which provides an illuminating summary measure of the differences that exist between the religious groups.

The variations are indeed quite striking. Although the overall proportion of "very active" adherents is just under a quarter, the rates of particular groups vary between the 13% of the Church of England or the 12% of those "Christians" who espouse no particular denominational connection, at one end, and the 61% recorded by the Baptists at the other. It might also be noted that Roman Catholics, who place a strong emphasis on ritualistic activity, have nearly half their membership in this category - a figure roughly similar to that achieved by "non-Christians" (an aggregated category of Jews, Hindus, Moslems and Sikhs) and by "other" Christians (a heterogeneous collection of Salvationists, Quakers, Pentecostalists, Moravians, Orthodox and Jehovah's Witnesses etc).

The "inactives," at the other end of the attendance spectrum, comprise just over half the total number of adherents. This points clearly to the necessity of such a distinction, as well as to the fact that religious disengagement may well have proceeded further in this quarter, than in basic allegiances.

Within particular religious categories, not surprisingly, the highest "inactive" figures are recorded first amongst those lacking any particular denominational attachment (71%) and secondly in the Church of England, 60% of whose membership seems nowadays to be largely inert. Conversely,

Table 2: **Level of Attendance and Strength of Attachment, by Religious Group Affiliation, 1985**

A: Level of Attendance

	% Very active	% Semi-active	% In-active	Average Attendance Score[1] (RANK)		N
Anglican	13.3	27.1	59.6	10.7	(7)	686
Church of Scotland	19.6	38.0	43.5	15.1	(6)	92
Methodist	28.2	21.8	50.0	22.2	(5)	78
Baptist	60.7	10.7	28.6	41.8	(1)	30
Roman Catholic	48.2	23.8	28.0	35.8	(4)	169
Other Christian	51.9	16.7	31.5	37.8	(2)	56
Christian - No Denomination	11.8	17.6	70.6	10.0	(8)	33
Non-Christian	52.0	8.0	40.0	36.6	(3)	25
Average	23.4	25.5	51.1	17.9	-	1170

B: Strength of Attachment [2]

	% Very Strongly	% Fairly Strongly	% Not Very Strongly	% Not at all	Average Attachment Score[3](RANK)		N
Anglican	19.7	42.5	26.3	11.5	1.70	(6)	19
Church of Scotland	14.4	40.2	31.7	13.8	1.57	(7)	87
Methodist	34.4	35.4	18.9	11.3	1.91	(4)	68
Baptist	60.6	35.1	2.9	1.4	2.48	(2)	29
Roman Catholic	26.3	39.4	29.4	4.9	1.85	(5)	158
Other Christian	38.9	31.5	25.9	3.7	2.06	(3)	54

B: Strength of Attachment [2] (Cont'd.)

	% Very Strongly	% Fairly Strongly	% Not Very Strongly	% Not at all	Average Attachment Score[3](RANK)		N
Christian - No Denomination	14.4	38.2	35.4	12.0	1.52	(8)	29
Non-Christian	62.5	29.2	4.2	4.2	2.50	(1)	24
No Religion	6.2	27.0	38.2	28.6	1.10	(9)	297
Average	20.2	37.4	28.5	14.0	1.64	-	1367

[1]Estimated average annual attendance rate: "once a week or more" = 75;
"practically never" = .25
[2]Excluding "Does not apply"
[3]Very=3; Not at all=0

only just over a quarter of Baptists and Catholics are in this same position.

Finally, as noted above, the overall level of involvement across the denominations is set out in the attendance score. On average, religious adherents by this estimate turn out to attend religious services some eighteen times a year. Within the two state Churches, however, the rate is distinctly lower - fifteen for the Church of Scotland and a mere eleven occasions for Anglicans. The latter figure is, indeed, only marginally above that of the non-institutionalized "Christians." In sharp contrast, the *average* Baptist attends chapel neearly forty-two times a year - almost once a week - and Roman Catholics and "other Christians" are not far behind. Clearly, therefore, attendance is a powerful and important discriminator.

However, it is not adequate by itself. As previously mentioned, some religious groups place more emphasis on attendance than others. Equally, so far as being open to corporate religious influence and cues is concerned, the strength of an individual's denominational self-image might be just as significant as the number of times he attends a religious meeting. For these reasons, therefore, the inclusion of a further measure of religiosity seems appropriate, a measure based on the strength of attachment felt towards "people of the same religious belief or background." Here, the alternative responses are exactly those set out in Part B of Table 2, although the 11% of the sample who thought the question "did not apply to them" (presumably because they felt that they themselves had no such beliefs, etc.) have been excluded.

Amongst the remainder (c 89%) who could think of themselves in these terms, attachments to co-religionists again varied considerably. About one-fifth felt "very strongly," and a further third "fairly strongly," attached - together, just over half of those classified. This is reflected in the "average attachment score" which is about half way (1.64) between the minimum of zero and the maximum of three. Altogether, therefore, the picture is one in which religious criteria still seem to play an important role in the self-images of perhaps half the present day adult population. This is yet another element in helping to map the current spread of secularization, although, without data from earlier time-points, no assessment of the pace or direction of change can be made.

Across the denominations, differences in strengths of attachment seem by and large to follow those revealed by the church attendance measure. Indeed, as might be expected, there is a modest association between the two; enough to suggest that they are tapping a common underlying syndrome of adherence, but sufficiently weak as to underline the need for this sort of multi-indicator approach. Not surprisingly, therefore, the same religious categories seem to appear at the bottom and top of this psychological scale. Bringing up the rear are the two established Churches together with those who claim to be Christian but have no denominational affiliation, and those of no religious persuasion at all. The last is a particularly interesting, and perhaps unsurprising, finding, not least because they were excluded from the attendance measure. However, this evidence makes clear where they generally stand in religious matters: agnosticism or atheism as a belief system does *not* produce much fellow feeling or group solidarity.[7] At the top of the scale, one finds the same three groups as previously - non-Christians, Baptists and "other Christians." The only slight but possibly significant discrepancy is that the Jews, Hindus and Sikhs, etc. collectively reveal themselves as having a very high level of attachment, somewhat belied by their relatively less spectacular attendance record. This may possibly be the product of ethnicity reinforcing religious identity (or vice versa).

All these patterns strongly support the use of a measure of the strength of religious adherence that combines both the behavioural and psychological components. Using a simple additive scoring procedure that gives each element roughly equal weight,[8] a single six point scale can be devised defining a "core" of adherents at one end and a "periphery" at the other. The distribution for Britain as a whole, together with those for each particular religious grouping, is set out in Table 3.

Table 3: Level of Adherence by Religious Attachment

Attachment	CORE 0	1	2	3	4	5	PERIPHERY TOTAL %	N	AVG ADH Score	Rank
Overall	11.5	12.7	19.8	26.7	18.4	10.9	100.0	1143	2.61	-
Anglican	6.1	9.4	21.9	28.8	20.0	13.8	100.0	677	2.89	7
Church of Scotland	5.0	12.4	21.0	34.5	18.0	9.1	100.0	91	2.75	6
Methodist	19.3	12.3	10.2	30.5	19.3	8.4	100.0	74	2.43	5
Baptist	45.5	19.9	7.6	18.7	2.8	5.5	100.0	30	1.30	1
Roman Catholic	16.9	26.0	19.6	19.2	13.0	5.3	100.0	166	2.01	4
Other Christian	32.7	16.4	14.5	16.4	18.2	1.8	100.0	56	1.76	3
Christian - No Denomination	7.5	4.5	13.8	22.4	31.2	20.6	100.0	33	3.27	8
Non-Christian	45.8	8.3	20.8	16.7	8.3	0.0	99.9	24	1.33	2

This table shows that as many as, or as few as, one in ten of the British population are in the most central, core religious stratum - those that are both "very active" attenders and feel "very strongly" attached to their co-religionists. A further 13% is in the next most central position. These are roughly balanced, at the other end of the spectrum, by 11% in the outermost religious periphery ("inactive" and "not at all attached") and a further 18% who are in these respects close to them. This rough balance between the two extremes is reflected in an average "adherence score" of 2.61 - half way between the core (at zero) and the periphery (at five).

Amongst the religious groupings, the differences follow familiar lines, or even perhaps accentuate them. Thus, the Baptists and non-Christians have by far the most adherent followings. In both cases, nearly half fall into the most central "core" category, a circumstance reflected in their average scores of around 1.30. Not far behind come the "other Christians" (a score of 1.76) and the Roman Catholic Church (2.01). The two groups with the weakest adherence are, by now very unsurprisingly, the Anglicans (2.89) and the Church of Scotland (2.75) although those Christians who lack any denominational focus for their religious commitments are very definitely bottom of the pile.

Perhaps, in this discussion, it is appropriate to make one final point. Although the Anglicans are as a whole a very weakly adherent group, and with a proportionately very small core membership, their sheer size within the population gives them a relatively large part of the total set of very committed religionists. In fact, amongst that inner core, well over one third are Anglicans, a figure only distantly approached by the quarter who are of the Roman Catholic persuasion. In other words, though Baptists and non-Christians may have very closely-bound flocks, their very small numerical base in the population at large weakens the social and political importance of this circumstance very considerably. In fact, only 7% of the core are Baptists and less than 5% are non-Christian. In this sense, the big episcopally-based denominations, though with a looser fraternity of the faithful (no doubt in part because of their size), still dominate the active grass-roots presence of religion both in society and in the political field.

RELIGION AND POLITICAL PARTICIPATION:

With the measures of religious attachment in place, it is now possible to address the first of the central questions raised in this chapter, the association of those measures with political participation - one of the two axes in the analytic typology. As the measures used to operationalize political participation have been thoroughly reviewed elsewhere (Moyser, Parry and Day, 1986), they will be outlined only briefly here.

In the 1985 national survey, information about some twenty-three different types of political activity was obtained, ranging from voting in General Elections, through canvassing for a party and contacting one's Member of Parliament, to attending a protest meeting or using physical force against political opponents. It was, in short, a very comprehensive exercise. Responses revealed the British adult population to be generally non-participatory. Outside of voting, or signing petitions, never more than a fifth, and usually well under a tenth, claimed to have engaged in these activities even once over the previous five year period. This context provides a key baseline for understanding the effect of religion: most citizens do little, few do a lot so far as British politics is concerned.

Further statistical analysis of these twenty three activities showed that they organized themselves into six broad clusters which, judging from the groupings they formed, could be readily identified as voting; party campaigning; group activity; contacting; protesting; and, finally, political violence. All of these are self-explanatory, except that the group activity syndrome included not only actions such as working in an organized group to raise an issue, but also attending a protest meeting and gaining support for a petition. It should also be noted that the political violence dimension consisted principally of only one item - the aforementioned use of physical force. As, not surprisingly, not more than a mere handful said that they themselves had indulged in it, its action content is consequently negligible and so has been deleted from the subsequent analysis reported here. Finally, yet further investigation of the relationships between these six broad types of political participation revealed that they could, in turn, be represented in terms of a single overall scale. The central element of this was, above all, group action and party campaigning; the most peripheral, or idiosyncratic, being voting and political violence. In so far as this provides a powerful summarizer of political participation in Britain, it is at this particular variable that we first look.

The nature of its relationship with level of religious adherence and religious attachment (denomination) is set out in Table 4. This provides estimated scores on the overall political participation scale (a scale which runs from -1.10 for the most totally inert respondent, through the average score of zero, to +10.21 for the most politically active individual) representing the unique effect on the individual of being in the particular religious category. That is, the collective impact of a number of other potentially confounding "background" factors, such as age, social status, educational achievement, political interest, etc., has been allowed for and statistically eliminated.

The general effect, thus established, of progressively stronger levels of religious adherence (ie moving from "periphery" to "core") is to increase, or stimulate, political participation. The effect is not large (the range of -0.15 to +0.21 is only 0.36 in the context of a total range of 11.31) but it is clear, relatively linear, and statistically significant. Thus, religious participants, and above all "core" adherents, tend also to be political participants. This finding, incidentally, contradicts that of Barnes and Kaase (1979, p. 119) who argued that, on their evidence, "church attendance and participation in the spiritual life of the community is in some sense an alternative, even exclusive activity compared with political participation."

Table 4: Overall Political Participation by Level of Adherence [1] and Religious Attachment

Adherence	Score[2]		Attachment	Score[3]
CORE	0	+0.21	Anglican	-0.01
	1	0.00	Church of Scotland	-0.13
	2	+0.02	Methodist	+0.05
	3	-0.08	Baptist	-0.22
	4	-0.11	Roman Catholic	-0.01
PERIPHERY	5	-0.15	Other Christian	+0.05

Table 4 (Cont'd.)

Adherence	Score[2]	Attachment	Score[3]
		Christian - No Denomination	-0.15
Overall	-0.03	Non-Christian	-0.46
Beta	.12	No Religion	+0.07
		Overall	-0.01
		Beta	.10
		N	1514

[1]Excluding "no religion"
[2]Controlling for effect of Attachment and other factors
[3]Controlling for effect of Adherence and other factors

Here it is not an alternative but a complementary pastime which mildly reinforces engagement in the nation's secular life. However, as noted above, this does not mean religious activists are "political activists," merely that they are somewhat more active than the generality of Britain's largely non-participatory population.

In some contrast to all this, the net effect of attachment to a particular religious grouping (having removed differences due to denominational variations in adherence) is either to leave political participation unchanged,[9] or to depress it. Thus, the strongest positive effect is amongst those with "no religion," although at +0.07 it is barely worth noting. The more deviant scores are, in fact, in the opposite, low participatory, direction and present a more interesting story. One at least of the established churches has such a negative score (that for the Church of England being exactly the same as the national average[10]). More importantly, those associated with the Baptists and the non-Christians are -0.22 and -0.46 respectively. In these two cases, we see clear evidence of an effect opposite to that of adherence. As these are precisely the two with the most strongly adherent memberships, the net result must be that their political participation rates are substantially below the levels that such a situation would initially suggest. For these two, therefore, the apparent political norms or cues of the group would seem to

364

be anti-participatory; such secular engagement as exists in this quarter derives from their propensity to be religiously active, not from the particular corporate religious belief system or institutional ethos. This, of course, supports earlier comments made about the Baptist Church.

Having established the overall picture, we can now look at some of the more detailed findings concerning particular forms of participation. Scores for the two dimensions of religious engagement on each of the five modes of participation previously identified are set out in Table 5. So far as the adherents are concerned, the patterns are broadly the same as in Table 4, with the notable exception of protesting. This particular form of political action has no discernible relationship, other than all categories being slightly lower than the national average. Such a situation reflects the fact that it is those of "no religion", and who are excluded from the adherence scale, that provide the major contrast.

Table 5: Particular forms of Political Participation by
Level of Adherence[1] and Religious Attachment[2]

A: Adherence

		Group Activity	Campaign-ing	Contact-ing	Protest-ing	Voting
Core	0	+0.21	+0.18	+0.18	-0.07	+0.29
	1	+0.18	-0.08	-0.05	-0.01	+0.10
	2	+0.01	-0.01	+0.02	+0.03	+0.17
	3	-0.09	+0.03	-0.08	-0.08	+0.05
	4	-0.13	-0.06	-0.03	-0.10	+0.10
Periphery	5	-0.20	-0.14	-0.01	-0.07	-0.08
Overall		-0.04	-0.01	-0.01	-0.06	+0.10
Beta		.12	.09	.08	.04	.10

B: Attachment

	Group Activity	Campaign-ing	Contact-ing	Protest-ing	Voting
Anglican	-0.04	0.00	+0.01	-0.06	+0.15
Church of Scotland	-0.21	+0.08	-0.15	-0.05	+0.07
Methodist	+0.10	-0.02	+0.07	-0.09	0.00
Baptist	+0.15	-0.30	-0.23	-0.14	-0.25
Roman Catholic	-0.04	-0.04	+0.05	-0.03	+0.22
Other Christian	+0.14	+0.01	-0.06	+0.11	-0.08

B: Attachment (Cont'd.)

	Group Activity	Campaign-ing	Contact-ing	Protest-ing	Voting
Christian No Denomination	-0.16	+0.03	0.00	-0.26	-0.13
Non-Christian	-0.27	-0.22	-0.32	-0.33	-0.54
No Religion	+0.10	+0.04	+0.03	+0.09	-0.10
Overall	+0.01	0.00	+0.01	-0.01	+0.02
Beta	.10	.07	.09	.08	.15
N	1514	1514	1514	1514	1514

[1]Excluding "no religion"
[2]Scores are the net effect of each category controlling for the other religious factor and background variables.

Any positive religious adherence, in other words, no matter how minimal, has the effect of slightly lowering engagement in political protest. In so far as such activity implies a critical posture towards the state, this finding provides us with some initial clues about the general role of religion in the second dimension of our analytic typology.

With this important exception, "core adherents," relative to those in the periphery, are more likely to be active in all the modes of participation. The stimulus is, for the former, most pronounced in voting (+0.29), but is strongest across *all* the religious strata in group action, where the beta (which measures the strength of statistical relationship) is .12. This is perhaps, not surprising. After all, adherence is itself a measure of institutional or group participation and self-attachment. It is, therefore, understandable that this propensity amongst individuals in the religious domain should be most clearly generalized to group action in the political arena. Indeed, the active role of individuals in the former may well provide an organizational basis for engagement in the latter (see also Verba and Nie, 1972, Ch. 11; Verba, Nie and Kim, 1978, Chs. 5-7; Nie, Powell and Prewitt, 1969).

The effect of denominational cues, as distinct from questions of religiosity, also tends to reinforce the earlier conclusions. Most striking is the quite marked and consistent tendency for non-Christians to opt out of participation in any form of political activity, above all voting (-0.54). Here we have the strongest apparent association between a particular form of religious attachment and secular passivity, although in this instance cultural factors associated with immigrant status may have a bearing. The Baptists too exhibit a similar profile, with the exception of group action. Particularly in party campaigning and voting, both electoral and therefore conflictual-partisan activities, the norm seems to be withdrawal or non-involvement. Apart from these, however, the other relationships are generally weak or inconsistent. However, lacking a religious attachment certainly seems to encourage both group activity (which includes a protest component) and protesting itself, but not voting. Conversely, Roman Catholics and Anglicans do seem to derive some inspiration from their denominations to turn out at election times. But such stimulation apparently occurs in no other domain.

RELIGION AND POLITICAL SUPPORT:

I turn now to the second dimension of the analytic framework - that relating to the level of support for Britain's political institutions and leadership. Again, the relevant measures and associated conceptual issues have been discussed in detail elsewhere (Moyser, Parry and Day, 1985). It is, therefore, sufficient here to summarize briefly what will be examined.

Two different, but not unrelated, aspects of an individual's propensity to look favourably or unfavourably on Britain's political arrangements, have been included. Together they give a relatively comprehensive picture of such judgements and how these may be influenced by religious commitments. The first, and arguably most central, concerns the regime itself. The scale in this instance (as with political participation) comprises a number of items all tapping somewhat different and particular features of the nation's political institutions and norms. Under the former heading, for example, there is a question concerning the "marks out of ten" individuals would give to "Britain's overall form of parliamentary government." With an average score of 6.4 on this item, the bulk of respondents gave relatively favourable ratings. At the same time, they were far from unqualified - 17% gave less than five marks out of ten. Thus, the baseline may be generally supportive, but there certainly is scope here for critical or dissentient voices. The same might be said about one of the more normative measures included - whether or not one has a "duty to vote in General Elections." Fully 87% agreed, but 13% did not.

This regime scale can, in turn, be distinguished from another fundamental political judgement - support for the authorities or leadership. In practice, the two obviously influence each other, although with a correlation of a modest .31, they clearly are empirically distinct. The items in this second scale comprised assessments of levels of cynicism and trust present in the population with respect to Members of Parliament and Local Councillors, collectively the two most salient elements, perhaps, of Britain's national and local political elite. Again, responses showed there to be plenty of scope for critical outlooks: 42% of respondents, for example, thought that "most Members of Parliament are out for themselves rather than the public good." Equally 44% felt that one could not "generally trust MPs to do what's right." If anything, therefore, Caesar, in these terms, evokes less supportive reactions than when construed in a more structural or normative sense. In both cases, however, the scales have been arranged so that zero is the average response and positive (or negative) scores represent relatively favourable (or critical) postures.

The empirical relationships between regime attitudes and religion are set out in Table 6. So far as religious adherence is concerned, a strong commitment is clearly associated with a supportive political orientation. Indeed if anything, the association is slightly stronger than with participation: the range here is 0.53 (compared with 0.36) and the beta .15 (.12). The overall effect, therefore, is to put all categories except the most peripheral into the positive range. The major counter-balance, however, is not so much the latter as those (listed under the attachment heading) with "no religion" who, though having a slightly less negative score, are a much larger category. But both serve merely to underline the basic effect: religious engagement is clearly associated with generally supportive regime attitudes; religious disengagement is linked to a mildly critical stance.

This basic linkage is given further weight when the rest of the attachment dimension is taken into account. Apart from the avowed atheists and agnostics, already mentioned, the only other negative score is that recorded by non-institutionalised Christians. Generally speaking, therefore,

368

the corporate norms of all specific religious groupings, as manifested amongst their grass-roots membership, seem to be of a somewhat politically uncritical variety. Above all, this is the case with the "non-Christians." Rather surprisingly, perhaps, given their marginal and generally disadvantaged position in British society (excepting the Jews), they are the most uncritical of all, once class and educational, etc. factors are taken into account.[11] After them, the Methodists and members of the Church of Scotland are the only other two denominations who have more than a very modest supportive effect associated with them. The latter, as an established Church, is not surprising: the former, as a bastion of "non-conformity" perhaps more so. Finally, in this context, the position of the Roman Catholics might be mentioned. Though their stance is barely more favourable than the overall average, clearly any historical associations with anti-regime outlooks (both recusant and Irish-based anti-British sentiments) seem to have evaporated. They have taken their place alongside the other major Christian grouping, the Church of England, as a body of individuals somewhat more likely to render favourable judgements on Caesar than the average Briton.[12]

Table 6: Regime Support[1] by Level of Adherence[2] and Religious Attachment.

Adherence		Score[2]	Attachment	Score[3]
CORE	0	+0.38	Anglican	+0.13
	1	+0.22	Church of Scotland	+0.31
	2	+0.24	Methodist	+0.36
	3	+0.11	Baptist	+0.14
	4	+0.17	Roman Catholic	+0.11
PERIPHERY	5	-0.15	Other Christian	+0.21
			Christian - No Denomination	-0.01
Overall		+0.16	Non-Christian	+0.48
Beta		.15	No Religion	-0.09

Table 6: (Cont'd.)

Adherence	Score[2]	Attachment	Score[3]
		Overall	+0.07
		Beta	.10
		N	1023

[1]For measurement see text
[2]Excluding "no religion"
[3]Scores are the net effect of each variable controlling for the other, and background factors

**Table 7: Support for Political Authorities[1] by Level of Adherence[2]
and Religious Attachment**

Adherence		Score[3]	Attachment	Score[3]
CORE	0	+0.56	Anglican	+0.17
	1	+0.33	Church of Scotland	+0.31
	2	+0.08	Methodist	+0.20
	3	+0.13	Baptist	+0.03
	4	+0.12	Roman Catholic	+0.13
PERIPHERY	5	-0.13	Other Christian	-0.16
			Christian -	
			No Denomination	+0.13
Overall		+0.16	Non-Christian	+0.05
Beta		.19	No Religion	-0.19
			Overall	+0.07
			Beta	.09
			N	1023

[1]For measurement see text
[2]Excluding "no religion"
[3]Scores are the net effect of each variable controlling for the other, and background factors.

The patterns associated with the second measure, support for political authorities, are set out in Table 7. Its relationship with adherence is the same as for the regime, only slightly more so. Once again, the "core" adherents are the strongest source of uncritical opinions; the periphery being the only category where the balance is tilted the other way. Furthermore, as can be seen under the "attachment" section of the table, it is again the atheists/agnostics who are, in religious terms, the most hostile. Only the "other Christians" approach them, a circumstance which puts that small catch-all group into a particularly ambivalent position when their regime orientations are taken into account. A similarly discrepant profile also seems to be associated with the non-Christians who, in contrast to their position in Table 6, have only average attitudes towards political incumbents. For these two categories at least, the distinction between the two aspects of political support clearly needs to be drawn to do justice to their opinions. Finally, at the positive end of the spectrum, no one group is markedly enthusiastic about the political authorities. Denominational norms seem to support Caesar more as a set of institutional arrangements than in terms of the general run of political leadership. However, the Church of Scotland, Methodists and Anglicans (in that order) lead such support as exists.

DISCUSSION:

I move, finally, to a synthesized assessment of the linkage between religion and politics among Britain's grass-roots population. Perhaps the first observation to be made is that it appears not to be a very strong one. The lack of any overt or sustained religious content to political life over at least the last half century together, no doubt, with the general effects of secularization, have eroded the association. In that sense, Britain does not provide a context where the potent interactions between religion and politics seen in many other nation-states can readily be found. And yet the pundits who write off any relevance of religion for politics are clearly not justified in their views either. The evidence does not point to random and nonexistent associations but forms a reasonably coherent picture, albeit in relatively minor relief. As at the level of elites, therefore, religious commitments still make some contribution to the understanding of mass political behaviour and outlooks in fundamental and varied ways.

A framework for highlighting the nature of that contribution was provided in the early part of this chapter. We must now examine what the evidence suggests about how different religious groupings fit into that four-fold typology. To do so, it seemed appropriate to summarize the tendencies at work by representing the two political dimensions in Figure 1 graphically and then to plot on it the scores appropriate to the various religious categories. For the sake of simplicity, the two axes are represented by overall participation scores, on the one hand, a simple average of the regime and authority scales on the other. The results, for both types of religious commitments, are set out in Figure 2.

It should first be emphasized, perhaps, that the location of each religious category as indicated in the Figure represents merely its overall centre of gravity. Each group, no doubt, has some spread even across more than the one quadrant in which that central point is to be found. This spread merely restates that the relationship in question is not a very strong one. However, by plotting solely the category averages, the underlying tendencies can be more readily appreciated.

The categories comprising the religious adherence measure are located in three of the four sections of the graph. Most striking, not surprisingly, are the two most extreme strata. Being a "core" adherent strongly disposes one, irrespective of denominational attachment, to an active-support posture. Indeed, as can be seen, this is the clearest example of all of this particular type of political involvement. Conversely, the most peripheral of adherents are almost as decisively to be found in the opposite camp - that of exit. They are relatively alienated from regime and authorities, but they are also inert. In short, the hallmark of a withdrawing posture. In so far as no other category is to be found in this quarter, it is perhaps somewhat ironic that it should be occupied by such a relatively irreligious grouping. Thus, if the theological syndrome associated with this political perspective is to be found in Britain, it must not exist as a dominant tendency within any denominational group separately distinguished in this analysis.

The middle categories of adherence are to be found in or near the "subject" quadrant. This is most clearly the case with those next to the outer

372

Figure 2: Political Engagement by Religious Adherence and Attachment

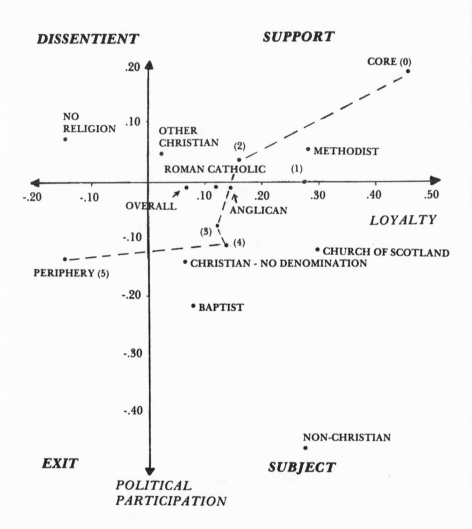

periphery (ie a score of 4 on the adherence scale). Thus, at no point on the religious adherence scale does it cross into the dissentient zone.

So far as grass-roots religious engagement is concerned, that particular political posture is not one that generates any noticeable sympathy. Indeed, there is only one religious grouping to be found clearly in that area - those lacking any religious commitments at all! It seems that only agnostics and atheists display, as a general trait, this particular style of gladitorial criticism. Only they, it will be remembered (apart from "other Christians" who are also the nearest of the "religious" camps to this quadrant), also espoused above average levels of protest. It is, therefore, noteworthy that theologically inspired political dissent, with its illustrious line of ecclesiastical exponents, should in fact be most typically associated at the mass level with those most unsympathetic to traditional religious values. For those religious prophets, indeed, it perhaps indicates the educative task that lies ahead of them in achieving some greater and more broadly-based resonance for their cause amongst the ranks of the faithful. To those whose outlooks are of the conservative variety, on the other hand, it may provide some grist to their mill that such leaders are linked, albeit tenuously, with this sort of constituency. And for ecclesiastical leaders it indicates something of the potential splits and gaps that exist, and the dangers to institutional coherence of a too-critical official posture. In that sense, those who, like Habgood, counsel caution, and prefer to leave public dissent to particular individuals rather than making it a corporate task, certainly have, in the British context at least, the weight of "real-politik" on their side.

In fact, if there is any one general direction in which denominational cues (as opposed to adherence) tend to lead, it is towards a subject political stance. This is particularly true of non-Christians. They are relatively uncritical (especially of the regime) but are also generally very inert. Apart from them, the two relatively homogeneous groupings that most manifest this syndrome are the Baptists and the Church of Scotland, although, as can be seen, the precise combination on the two political axes are not quite the same. That this should be so is not, from my earlier discussion, surprising. Both are evangelical in character. Furthermore, the conservative strand in the Baptists' outlook has been specifically commented on. Equally, the

Church of Scotland, as an established Church, has its own, if different, inbuilt allegiance to the status quo. Clearly, therefore, the latter's particular emphasis on loyalty, and the former's on passivity, can well be understood.

Finally, we turn to the two major Christian Churches in Britain - the Anglicans and the Catholics. As can be seen, they are both extremely close together in Figure 2, being only mildly on the uncritical side, but no different from the population average in terms of political activism. To that extent, their denominational signals in terms of the typology are rather ambiguous or indistinct, at least as they are manifested as a single net tendency amongst their very large and diverse followings. These signals are not clearly of the "support" not of the "subject" variety. If they are anything, they are to be found somewhere between the two; but certainly there is little of the "dissentient" or "exit" quality to be found in either of them.

In so far as over half the population in Britain is either nominally Anglican or Catholic, it is perhaps not too surprising that such conclusions in these two cases should be rather muted, not least in that religion is nowadays at best a minor basis for overt political cleavages. However, having said that, it is significant to point to the relatively clear disjuncture between the critical orientation of Britain's most secularized parts of the population and the compliant tendencies of all the rest. To some, above all those of a conservative political and theological persuasion, this may be a cause for satisfaction if not complacency. But for those who wish to see religious groups staking out a more radical ground and who seek a new relevance for such institutions in society it must at the very least give them pause for thought about the magnitude of the task that lies ahead.

375

REFERENCES

[1]Here, as at most points in the discussion, Northern Ireland is excluded. That part of the UK, perhaps uniquely in Western Europe, places religion right in the middle of the political system, although its effects are compounded by those of nationalism, class and culture. (See, for example, Hickey, 1984; McAllister, 1983; Moxon-Browne, 1983.)

[2]The Church was disestablished in Wales by the Welsh Church Acts, 1914 and 1919, which came fully into force in 1920.

[3]A small number of individuals whose attendance rate "varies or depends" are also included amongst the "semi-active."

[4]Amongst lay members of the Church of England, for example, when asked in a Gallup survey in 1984 whether "the Church should or should not take sides in political issues," 73% said "no." For Roman Catholics and Non-Conformists, the figures were 61% and 72% respectively. Amongst clergymen, however, only 34% took that view. It is interesting to note that the survey was sponsored by the conservative evangelical Church Society, precisely that theological current most allied to the "subject" mode. (See Gallup 1984.)

[5]One might, however, speculate that belonging to a church or religious group (1979) requires a degree of organizational commitment less apparent certainly than in the formula used in 1985.

[6]Of course, as both "readings" involve different sets of respondents, one cannot be sure that they are linked. No doubt the turnover is more complex, but it seems plausible, given the relative stability of all the other figures, that this particular connection is the biggest element.

[7]This finding may yield a clue as to why humanist or atheist societies have been so spectacularly unsuccessful in Britain, despite the size of their potential constituency.

[8]The scale was calculated as the sum of attendance and attachment using the following numerical values: attachment: 0 = very strong; 1 = fairly; 2 = not very; 3 = not at all; attendance: active = 0; semi-active = 1; inactive = 2. Hence, the scale varies between 0 (very strong/active) and 5 (not at all/inactive).

[9]Barnes and Kaase (1979, p 118) found no differences as between "Protestants" and "Catholics." On the other hand, this dichotomy seems to be too crude to capture the nuances across the various religious categories revealed here.

[10]When all respondents are included, the participation scales have a mean of zero. However, missing data on some variables eliminates 5-10% in any

one table and that sometimes slightly affects the apparent overall average. In Table 4, for example, it has drifted to -0.01.

[11]This is one case where, given the internal diversity of the group, the average effect may be misleading. Thus, Orthodox Jews, it has been suggested, are much more supportive of political institutions than the non-orthodox. No normal-sized national survey of Britain, however, could distinguish such categories and hence solve the problem.

[12]There is a view (not pursued here) that the position might vary as between English, Scottish and Welsh Catholics: that the former, especially, might be particularly allegiant, particularly keen to demonstrate their loyalty as a reaction to perceptions of their co-religionists in Northern Ireland.

BIBLIOGRAPHY:

All are Called: Toward a Theology of the Laity. (1985), London: Church House Publishing.

Alves, R. (1985). *Protestantism and Repression: A Brazilian Case Study.* London: Orbis Books.

Barnes, S. and Kaase, M. (1979). *Political Action: Mass Participation in Five Western Democracies.* London: Sage.

Beer, S. (1982). *Britain Against Itself: The Political Contradictions of Collectivism.* London: Faber and Faber.

Bochel, J. M. and Denver, D. T. (1970). "Religion and Voting: A Critical Review and a New Analysis." *Political Studies.* Vol 18. No 2. Pp. 205-219.

Bosher, R. S. (1951). *The Making of the Restoration Settlement: The Influence of the Laudians, 1649-1662.* London: Dacre Press.

Cornwell, P. (1985). "The Church of England and the State: Changing Constitutional Links in Historical Perspective." In G. Moyser, (ed.), *Church and Politics Today.* Edinburgh: T. & T. Clark.

Dickens, A. G. (1964). *The English Reformation.* London: Batsford.

Faith in the City. (1985). The Report of the Archbishop of Canterbury's Commission on Urban Priority Areas. London: Church House Publishing.

Gallup Poll. (1984). *Attitudes of the Laity, Clergy and Bishops Towards the Church of England.* London: Social Surveys.

Gilbert, A. D. (1980). *The Making of Post-Christian Britain.* London: Longman.

Habgood, J. (1983). *Church and Nation in a Secular Age.* London: Darton, Longman and Todd.

Hickey, J. (1984). *Religion and the Northern Ireland Problem.* Dublin: Gill and Macmillan.

Hirschmann, A. O. (1979). *Exit, Voice and Loyalty.* Cambridge: Harvard University Press.

Inglehart, R. (1977). *The Silent Revolution: Changing Values and Political Styles Among Western Publics.* Princeton: Princeton University Press.

378

Kavanagh, D. (1980). "Political Culture in Great Britain: The Decline of the Civic Culture." In G. Almond and S. Verba, *The Civic Culture Revisited* (Boston: Little, Brown and Co.

Kavanagh, D. (1985). "Whatever Happened to Consensus Politics?" *Political Studies*, Vol 33. No 4. Pp. 529-546.

Kee, A. (1986). "The New Religious Right." Fourth Ferguson Lecture in Series "Domination or Liberation: The Place of Religion in Social Conflict." University of Manchester.

Machin, G. I. T. (1977). *Politics and the Churches in Great Britain: 1832 to 1868*. Oxford: Clarendon Press.

McAllister, I. (1983). "Class, Region, Denomination and Protestant Politics in Ulster." *Political Studies*. Vol 31. No 2. Pp. 275-283.

Medhurst, K. N. (1981). "Religion and Politics: A Typology." *Scottish Journal of Religious Studies*. Vol 2. Pp. 115-134.

Medhurst, K. N. and Moyser, G. (1982). "From Princes to Pastors: The Changing Position of the Anglican Episcopate in English Society and Politics." *West European Politics*. Vol 5. No 2. Pp. 172-191.

Medhurst, K. N. and Moyser, G. (1988). *Church and Politics in a Secular Age*. Oxford: Clarendon Press.

Miller, W. T. and Raab, G. (1977). "The Religious Alignment at English Elections Between 1918 and 1970." *Political Studies*, Vol 25. No 2. Pp. 227-251.

Moxon-Browne, E. P. (1983). *Nation, Class and Creed in Northern Ireland*. Aldershot: Gower.

Moyser, G. Parry, G. and Day, N. (1985). "Regime Support in Great Britain: A Cross-Sectional and Dynamic Analysis." American Political Science Association Annual General Meeting, New Orleans.

Moyser, G. Parry, G. and Day, N. (1986). "Political Participation in Britain: Images, Structures and Characteristics." Political Studies Association Annual Conference, Nottingham, April, 1986.

Nie, N,. Powell, G. B. and Prewitt, K. "Social Structure and Political Participation." *American Political Science Review*. Vol 63. Nos 2, 3, Pp. 351-78, 808-32.

Niebuhr, H. R. (1952). *Christ and Culture*. London: Faber.

Norman, E. (1979). *Christianity and World Order*. London: Oxford University Press.

379

Panikkar, R. (1983). "Religion or Politics: The Western Dilemma." In P. Merkl and N. Smart, *Religion and Politics in the Modern World*. New York: New York University Press.

Powell, E. (1977). *Christianity and World Order*. London: Social Surveys.

Preston, R. (1983). *Church and Society in the Late Twentieth Century: The Economic and Political Task*. London: SCM Press.

Reckitt, M. B. (1947). *Maurice to Temple: A Century of Social Movement in the Church of England*. London: Faber.

Robilliard, St. J. A. (1984). *Religion and the Law*. Manchester: Manchester University Press.

Servants of the Lord. (1986). London: Church House Publishing.

Sheppard, D. (1980). *Bias to the Poor*. London: Hodder and Stoughton.

Sykes, N. (1934). *Church and State in England in the 18th Century*. Cambridge: Cambridge University Press.

Verba, S. and Nie, N. (1972). *Participation in America: Political Democracy and Social Equality* New York: Harper and Row.

Verba, S. Nie, N. and Kim, J.-O. (1978). *Participation and Political Equality*. Cambridge: Cambridge University Press.

Wald, K. D. (1983). *Crosses on the Ballot: Patterns of British Voter Alignment Since 1885*. Princeton: Princeton University Press.

Welsby, P. (1984). *A History of the Church of England, 1945-1980*. Oxford: Oxford University Press.

Wheale, G. (1985). "The Parish and the Politics" in G. Moyser, (ed.). *Church and Politics Today*. Edinburgh: T. & T. Clark.

CHAPTER XX

CHURCH, PARTY AND STATE

The decline of Britain in the last forty years is due in part to bad government; and behind that lie attitudes that are ill adapted to the modern world. Behind these attitudes in turn are certain social facts, among which is the existence, in a very loose sense, of an establishment, which is largely uncritical of the values and concepts which are brought to bear in the running of the country.[1] One corner of the arrangements of British society is Establishment in the Church sense. It is one of the obstacles to a freshly conceived society, and one of the regrettable features of British life.[2] But first let us place our discussion in a wider perspective, and look to a broader analysis of some of the key ideas involved in religious establishment.

It is of course obvious that if we seek to separate the State and religion, much turns on the definition of religion. In recent times the impinging of Buddhism and some other religious traditions on Western consciousness has called into question some older conceptions of religion (as involving belief in God, for instance). Moreover, some modern students of religion are inclined to stretch the notion to include what Tillich called quasi-religions, that is, secular ideologies. It makes a lot of sense to do so, for when it comes to the crunch about the best way of differentiating religions from quasi-religions is a rather philosophical one, turning on whether a system of belief involves reference to the Transcendent. But obviously it may well be that non-Transcendent entities may attract, phenomenologically, as much loyalty and self-sacrifice as do Transcendent ones. The North

Vietnamese soldier dying in a tunnel West of Saigon displays as much determination and commitment as a Christian martyr; and the pain of the Spanish Catholic and that of the Anarchist both dying in the Battle of Irun were directed at achieving what each considered was an ultimate goal. The stretching, then, of the definition of religion, or at least the extension of our targets of exploration to include both religious and non-religious (traditionally defined) worldviews has empirical merit. Incidentally, had the comparative study of religions started in China rather than in the West, it would no doubt have been unnecessary even to make this move. Such a view of our subject matter, to include ultimate belief-systems in general, and not just religions as more traditionally defined, has dynamic consequences in the debate about Church and State. It is a matter of more than mere words. The proposal to treat all ultimate worldviews together involves a conceptual revolution which some may find hard to make. It has, however, fruitful consequences in other directions too: we can see certain modern religious developments as blends of traditional religious and modern "secular" themes - a kind of syncretism of worldviews. For instance, much liberal Protestantism can be represented as a blend between Biblically-orientated Christianity and democratic liberalism (into which typically various nationalisms are blended). Catholicism blended with social democracy accounts for much of the spirit of Solidarity. Sinhalese Buddhist modernism combines motifs from Theravada Buddhism and modern scientific humanism: and so on.

Another terminological issue of some importance is to do with the concept "secular." Unfortunately this word has two quite different senses, but this is not always noticed. In one sense "secular" contrasts with "religious." It means (roughly) non-religious. People sometimes, in this sense, contrast the sacred and the secular, and it was in this sense that Harvey Cox celebrated the secular city.[3] But in a second sense, when we speak of a secular constitution, such as that of the United States or of India, we mean, roughly, "pluralist." It means that citizens are free to hold varied beliefs and worship according to differing modes. The two sense are quite different. Thus in Sense 1, India is not at all secular; but in Sense 2 it incorporates a secular system. Conversely, East Germany is secular in Sense 1, but is not at all secular in Sense 2, since citizens are notoriously disadvantaged if they do not hold the official Marxist position.

It happens that often in the West the proponents of liberal constitutions, such as were fashionable during the European nationalist period, were also anticlerical, as often in Italy, Spain, and France. So there was an actual tendency for the two senses of secular to go together.

But the equation of the two meanings is dangerous. It confuses people. Thus through much of Europe the principle of *cuius regio eius religio* was applied, as a consequence of the Reformation and its aftermath: an Englishman was supposed to be Anglican, a Swede Lutheran, a Spaniard Catholic. The true heirs to this system today (since England, Sweden and Spain have got more or less pluralist constitutions, albeit with some establishmentarian hangovers) are the Eastern bloc countries - Poland, Romania, the U.S.S.R., etc. There the principle is the same, but with different metaphysics - *cuius regio eius ideologia.* "Of whom the government, of them the ideology." Of course, the ideology is secular in the sense of non-religious, but the systems are in no serious way pluralistic. Because of this ambiguity, I shall henceforth use "non-religious" and "pluralistic," and abandon the use of *secular.* So I shall refer to the "pluralistic university," "non-religious humanism" and so on.

Another general point which needs making by way of setting the scene for our discussion concerns the nature and role of nationalism. In many ways a given nationalism (for instance French nationalism or Russian nationalism) is like a religion. In its modern form it is organized through the State, which is, as it were, its Church. It has myths, namely national history, highlighting glorious events and people - statesmen, poets, sportspersons, and so on, such as Henry VIII, Shakespeare, Churchill, W. G. Grace, Nelson, Wellington, and so on. It has its ethics, namely that you have to be a good and effective citizen, raising a family of good citizens.

It has its feelings, of patriotism, stimulated by songs such as "Rule Britannia" and "God Save the Queen," music such as "Pomp and Circumstance." It has its rituals, such as Remembrance Day, the Opening of Parliament, royal weddings, Cup Finals, standing to attention during the national anthem, marchpasts, and so forth. It has its institutions, such as schools, where history teachers and others are priests of loyalty and the telling of the group myths. It has its works of art and sacred territory - the land, its war memorials, its great buildings and palaces, and so on. In brief, a country generates loyalty in a manner not unlike a traditional religion. The modern period has seen the elevation of this swarm of religions to the first rank. Many more people die for their country than for anything else, and patriotism is often looked on as the highest form of behavior and feeling.[4]

The notion of the sovereign people with its State is of profound importance in understanding modern history. Ultimately religions and worldviews tend to be subordinated to it, partly because the modern State makes such strong demands on its citizens that it needs a deeper justification than the mythic history of the people, and so tends to underpin its authority with a worldview, religious or otherwise, or by a blended worldview. So Vietnamese nationalism was underpinned by Marxism, Italian nationalism by militant Catholicism, and so on. National wars are thus dignified on both sides by the thought that they are conducted for some ultimate cause as well as patriotism. But this itself generates a tension since worldviews are typically universalist, and can thus come into conflict with the particularities of patriotism. Theories such as Stalin's "Socialism in one Country" can attempt to smooth over the conflicts, and the idea that a nation has a special Christian or Buddhist or Islamic destiny. But the groupism implicit in nationalism does collide with the universal calls to love or compassion or brotherhood found in the ethics of such faiths. We could put the tensions in another way by saying that in so far as the State, representing the nation, claims ultimate loyalty (operationally, this means that it may legitimately claim that you should die on its behalf), it is potentially in conflict with worldviews which also claim ultimacy and so unlimited loyalty.

We have now set the scene for the discussion of the relation between Church (Mosque, Sangha, etc.) and the State. We may pose an important question by asking what happens if the ultimate doctrine which so to speak underpins the State is that of pluralistic democracy. What is interesting is that the United States had, in its constitution, an explicitly democratic ideology which was in a sense constitutive of its citizenry. Other nations had their citizenship defined quite independently of their later constitutional arrangements - mainly through sharing what came to be perceived as a common history, often based on a common language (or what came to be constructed in the nineteenth century as a common language). Also, even in the United States the case of the Blacks was ignored, virtually and as came to be perceived more and more clearly, inconsistently. The imposition on the population of some religious test, without fulfilling which a citizen has less than the rights accorded to others, or without fulfilling which a person cannot be counted a citizen, seems to run contrary to the application of democratic rights. There is then it seems a conflict between religious or more generally worldview establishment and pluralism. Even if minority groups may not be hindered from worship or the propagation of their faith, they may still sense their political disadvantage in having less access to the levers of political power. It may be that nationalism as a religion includes rituals from which they are emotionally or actually excluded. This is especially obvious in Britain, with the Monarch's status as head of the Church in England. As is well known, this was part of a situation in which Catholics, Non-Conformists and Jews were long denied civil rights. Though the legal situation has been remedied, the symbolic aspect remains important: for although "Anglican" establishment might see to be giving way to "Christian" establishment in that it is now commonplace for the Cardinal of Westminster and the Moderator of the Free Church Council to share by invitation in Royal rituals, this still does not do justice to the pluralism of modern society; such rituals still lead people into vague thinking about England as a "Christian" country, and it symbolically rates Jews, Muslims, atheists, Buddhists and others as not fully English (or British). What the situation presents, albeit in rather a muddled way, is the identification of official religion with the supreme symbol of national identity and loyalty. In events such as Coronations, Royal Weddings we see celebrated traditional English or British nationalism, which has no explicit place for the "new British", that is for people who are citizens but historically have connections to religious and cultural traditions outside of the British Isles.[5]

These arrangements have ramifications, of course, in education, in society, in politics and in the media. To these I shall turn shortly. In the meantime let us turn briefly to address the question of the limits of freedom of non-religious worldviews. The most influential worldview in the ruling echelons of British life is scientific humanism, which lives unreflectively together with various forms of more or less liberal Christianity. Since scientific humanism typically involves an individualistic and democratic standpoint, it implies both senses of "secular," i.e., it is both non-religious and pluralistic. Traditionally, various non-humanist worldviews have been tolerated; forms of Marxism, including modern militant Trotskyism, Fascism (within limits before World War II), as well as various kinds of religion. But does a pluralistic or open society have to set limits to the worldviews tolerated, because they threaten pluralism? And does this itself not imply a kind of "official" worldview, no different in principle from the older official religions of the post-Reformation period?

There are, however, differences. First, we may note that worldviews come in varying forms and have a certain flexibility in their modes of belief and practice. So it is quite possible to have forms of Christianity, Islam, even Marxism, which can absorb into themselves the pluralistic attitude (or perhaps one should say "find within themselves the materials for" a pluralistic attitude - for there are tolerant and outward-looking elements in all traditions). Consequently, it is only some "hardened" forms of religious and non-religious worldviews which are incompatible with pluralism. This being so, a pluralistic framework provides possibilities for persons of any belief-tradition to exist freely within a given society. By contrast with a totalitarian or intolerant society the possibilities of worldview-practice are very much greater.

Moreover, a pluralistic society may allow the intolerant kinds of belief-system to exist within its fabric. It is true that it cannot ultimately survive if there is a majority of people in the society who favor some intolerant worldview. But this merely affirms what pluralism requires to stay true to its principles, namely that people be allowed freely to express their views. It is the faith of the liberal that people will prefer a tolerant society. But if the intolerant stage an attempt at a coup d'etat, then of course it is legitimate to do something forceful about it. So we go further than Popper, whose slogan was "Tolerate the tolerant." We would argue for tolerating them anyway, and using force only when illegitimate means of seizing power are attempted (but this is a right which every sort of government holds to, and is not per se a case of being intolerant).

Now obviously, the existence of a pluralistic system affording equal rights to all citizens irrespective of their worldviews does impose limitations on traditions, in the sense that some older attitudes have to be abandoned (the Catholic Church of the Inquisition, the traditional Islamic attitude to "polytheistic" religions, etc.). But these are light limitations compared with those that an overbearing worldview might seek to impose.

The extension of our notion of separation to include the separation of all worldview-expressing bodies and the State has important consequences. It implies the separation of political worldviews and the State. From this angle it would be inadmissible to build into the constitution any substantive worldview-values, such as Socialism. This would rule out, for instance, the present Sri Lanka Constitution, which explicitly incorporates "Socialism" into the official name of the country (a name more honored these days in the breach than in the observance, be it said). It may be noted that the narrow definition given to religion in the United States constitution made McCarthyism possible: to accuse his opponents of being Communists was dangerous to them precisely because (irrespective of the veracity of his charges) no protection was afforded as such to belonging to a movement espousing an ultimate worldview which was not merely not religious but also anti-religious.

But what if the Communist Party is actively conspiring to overthrow the State? Clearly a pluralistic State has the right to defend itself. However, individuals should still have the right to advocate Marxist principles, even if one of the organizations which does so is involved in dangerous illegalities.

The doctrinal basis of pluralism is among other things epistemological. We cannot establish for sure that one worldview is true over against others, by any conclusive argument. It is the nature of worldviews to go, so to speak, to the edge of the cosmos, beyond which lies obscurity. It has the appeal that if we are to settle disputes about ultimate values by argument, and this is the peaceful way, then we cannot expect decisive conclusions to the argument: partly because in any case the quest for truth always involves criticism and openness, so that theories and ideas can be continuously subjected to test. It may be said, of course, that by the same argument pluralism cannot be proved: indeed it cannot, and so we must have faith in it, and fight for it, if we believe in it. Because it stresses the variety of views which is consonant with an open society it is I believe the presupposition both of modern science and of the modern university. But even about that there will be some disputation. It is at this point that we can begin to explore the imperfections of British pluralism and their bearing on various aspects of society - education, social relations, politics and the media.

First, the Establishment situation has set the scene for a still powerful educational view that religious education's chief function is to hand on Christian values. The change from the use of "instruction" to "education" is largely cosmetic. For those who espouse this model, we assume Christian premisses. Those who do not like this may have their children withdrawn. The alternative model introduces children to the values of Christianity, and Judaism, and Islam, and scientific humanism, etc., partly because these are the genuine constituents of our religious scene in Britain; and partly because we are educating children who willy-nilly will be citizens of the world.

Because many teachers are hostile to official religion, often R.E. has two pernicious results: it does not give tender tolerance to our minority religions, and it damages R.E. by alienating non-religious teachers. Similar remarks may be made about higher education.

Here, in some ways, the situation is even more scandalous. The norm (reinforced by recent government policies) is the Faculty or Department of Theology (or Divinity, as in Scotland). Public monies are disbursed for studies which entrench a particular kind of Christianity. In some cases there are still denominational credal tests, in that occupants of some chairs have to be clergypersons. In the early 1960's there was only one Roman Catholic teaching in a Theology Department, and he part-time. Since then things have gone more ecumenical, but ecumenical Christianity is itself a quasi-denomination, and in any case in a pluralistic educational system credal or denominational tests should not be applied. My own chair at Lancaster was advertised, amid controversy, as being open to someone "of any faith or none." Since then the example has been followed here and there. Nevertheless the overwhelming proportion of posts remain in areas of study that ecumenical Christianity sees as normative. The first post to be created in modern Judaism as a living religion had to wait till 1971, despite the long and important history of Judaism in the UK. There are very few posts teaching non-Christian religions in our Universities, less than the number employed to teach Old Testament from a Christian perspective. Conversely, fearing establishmentarianism, many universities do not teach religion at all. This means that the greatest part of worldview analysis is neglected.

One consequence of comparative religion's attempts to disentangle itself from Christian theology has been the evolution of a careful doctrine of informed empathy as a means of "getting inside" other people's beliefs, practices and values: this gears in with similar work, e.g., that of Geertz, in anthropology. This attitude is educationally of great importance, and one which is greatly neglected in all sorts of ways in our schools and universities (e.g., in education about other sex). Now it is true that the U.S. Constitution has in recent times been seen (incorrectly interpreted, however) as banning any teaching about religion and religions. But the logical consequence of a separation of Church (etc.) and State should be the application of a thoroughly pluralist education, in which all varieties of worldview are brought to the attention of students. There are of course various more or less disingenuous objections - "The teachers can't be found" (answer: train them), "It can't be done" (answer: there are lots of good studies of world religions, a few of them on Christianity), "You need to share a faith to understand it" (answer: Heaven help us - but it is not true, for there are lots of good books, dialogues and films where the condition does not apply), "It would be confusing for students" (answer: the alternative is even more confusing: and in any case ours is a complex world - do we want to conceal that fact?), and so on.

Regarding the effects of Establishment on social relations, we tread on delicate ground, for here we treat of the social effects of the Monarchy. It is not necessary here to enter into the damage to the critical mind caused by the system of feudal titles which flows from the Monarchy. More important, from our viewpoint, are the symbolic effects of the soft Christianity in the rituals surrounding the Head of State. Here it is necessary for a moment to digress and say something about the democratic theory underlying some

British thinking and the myth of Britain which we can construct to convey the national essence. For, after all, the idea of the Monarch as Head of the Church once expressed something important about retaining a relatively plural set-up in the post-Reformation period over against the more conformist and authoritarian Catholic alternative. So we need to look at our myth again. Let me depict that myth now in a way which attempts to reconcile our real situation in the modern world with aspects of our history.

We need to tell our story as laying the foundations for a pluralistic democracy - Magna Carta, the Civil War, the toleration (relatively) of the Church of England, the successive struggles for reform and enfranchisement during the nineteenth and twenthieth centuries, the establishment of democracy in parts of the Empire, the battle against the Slave Trade, the welcoming of Marx and other political exiles, the war against the Nazis. All these phases of our history are relevant to the theme. The importance too in our thought of several radical thinkers, such as Locke, Hume, Adam Smith, J. S. Mill, Paine and Russell can be underlined. The transformation of the Empire into a Commonwealth can help to give new shape to our thinking about Asian and Black migrants and their children. We need to stress the older pluralism of ethnic groups in Britain - Scots, English, Welsh, Irish, Manx, Jewish, Huguenot: now West Indian, Pakistani, Indian, and so forth. But this plurality of populations is not served by the present symbols of Monarchy. And the present system is wide open to tokenism, through the elevation of one or two brown or black people to the peerage and the like.

The symbolism of the Queen as Head of the Church means that other religions, even if more vigorous, have the appearance of being second class - Catholicism, Judaism, Methodism, Nonconformist varieties, Sikhism, Islam, Hinduism, and so forth. Also devalued is Scientific Humanism, which is a greatly important segment among the British intelligentsia and is also important in expressing a strong element in working class agnosticism. The undervaluing of some of these religions has led subtly to the less than equal social status afforded to many of their adherents - such as the Irish, the Indians and others. It has contributed to British antisemitism, especially important among the echelons of the civil service and the political establishment in times gone by. As Head of State, the Monarch (or

President) should be able to symbolize the aspirations of all groups. There is no reason why, in Britain, we should not have some Council of Religions which the Monarch could preside over, as she does over the Commonwealth. The Church of England could revert to a more realistic status, as one denomination in the realm. Likewise the Church of Scotland could revert to a denominational status. However, is should also be noted that ecumenical Christianity has a property lacking in the Church of England as such: namely it is necessarily transnational in character[6] and the same applies to the other major traditions. So there is inherently the chance of a clash between a religion and the national State (similarly with other crossnational entities and ideas, such as transnational corporations and the ideal of democracy). The advantage in having the Monarch preside over a Council of Religions is to link the ideal of pluralism to the potent symbolism of the monarchy. The alternative is for the Head of State to be disengaged entirely from any spiritual values other than the virtues of pluralism.

The fact that the Church of England (and by parity of reasoning the Church of Scotland) has played a vital role in the history of our nation does not mean that its problematic status should be continued. We should stress its relative toleration in the past, but this should not blind us to aspects of soft intolerance which it still enfolds.

It may be that some will react against so tender a concern for minorities: does the Asian and Jewish tail have to wag the British dog? But it is not as if there have not already been severe problems in Britain with minority ethnic groups (the Welsh, Irish and Scots, for starters), of a longstanding nature. A more aggressively pluralistic philosophy would do much good if it were translated into social action and education in all its varieties. It is a philosophy that needs inculcating into the police, the judiciary, in education and in many branches of our public life. But this is at the moment smothered by the woolly blanket of an Establishment tradition.

At the political level, the present arrangement causes confusion and embarrassment. It is easy for the Government to consider that an Established Church should keep out of politics except in the politest way, since it has to cater for all shades of opinion. Moreover, though the Church of England politically seems to have moved from being the Conservative

Party at prayer to the S.D.P. at communion, the official place of the Church invites conflicts with the Conservatives especially. The extra weight provided by the trappings of Establishment does not compensate for the inhibitions of the position. The Churches need to have political views, for they offer a critique of this world from the perspective of the Transcendent. They have a point from which to offer criticism which goes beyond non-religious criticism.

There is in this connection a tendency to treat religion as simply a private matter (partly because of a special way of interpreting Church-State separation) and to suppose that political and social issues are not the province of religious institutions. This is reinforced by the tax law, which gives a favored place to religion; but on the supposition that the primary thrust of religious institutions is not political. it seems to me more logical to open up the scene to the free and open exercise of lobbies and movements, but not to give them tax exemption. In any event the "privatization" of religion and ultimate worldviews is natural enough as a means of ensuring social harmony, but neglects nevertheless the importance of social groups in the formation of policies. Surely, voluntary associations, of which the Churches and mosques, etc., are a subclass, should have as much right as individual citizens to offer political and other advice, to try to win support for such advice.

Finally, the media exercise their own version of establishment: namely the privileged segregation (a kind of kiss of death) of religion to particular slots. This has been modified in recent years by the trend towards a more documentary approach to religion on TV. But again, there would seem to be promise in a conceptual revolution, of the treatment of worldviews not only as exercising some purchase on the world, looked at empirically, but also as being human alternatives which can be openly discussed.

Perhaps one of the reasons for the persistence of Establishment in Britain is that in pulling the teeth of the Christian religion (and of others secondarily) it is favorable to the outlook of scientific humanists, who are the chief force perhaps among influential members of the British elite. The very blandness of British religion is a virtue from the point of view of humanists. I am not suggesting of course that we need intolerant fire-eating faiths - but where the Church has somehow to represent the mind of the majority (who do not darken its doors, for the most part), its image and pronouncements are bound to be bland, and where they are not, as with the Bishop of Durham, there is a certain outrage.

This is finally where there is a mule-kick in our notion of pluralism. I have long striven for genuine pluralism in the teaching of religion. It ill benefits a university in particular to favour the blinkered teaching of one sub-tradition of one religion. But by the same token it ill befits a university to entrench in sociology or philosophy departments, as sometimes happens, one particular worldview. Pluralism applies in the secular as well as in the religious world. There has sometimes been a scandalous degree of conformism in our public institutions.

It seems to me then that we can do much more to make ours into an open and critical society, and one in which the different ethnic and religious groups may feel much more at home. We can also try to spread our democratic ideals across the world, in coordination with our democratic European partners and Commonwealth and American associates. We should not be ashamed of our European heritage, which incorporated the Enlightenment. It is because the present Church-State relationship reflects an earlier and less worthy ideal that it would be desirable to modify it or abolish it. But politically is there much hope of this? First, we have to bring home to our citizens that Britain's rather mean and second rate performance in the last forty years stems from insufficiently critical attitudes towards our conceptual heritage and social stratification, resulting in our being led by a rather incompetent elite.

POSTSCRIPT ON THEOLOGICAL REASONS FOR
DISESTABLISHMENT

I have argued in this essay from premises which can be shared by many. My arguments have not been directly Christian-theological. But it is useful briefly to see how pluralism and Christian faith should live together. First, Christ's service is perfect freedom, and requires a personal response which is not brought about by coercion or worldly rewards. Second, Christian faith is *faith*, and if there were proof we would have it here now. Faith cannot be proved, and as unprovable it can have no privileged epistemological status over alternative faiths (though of course one can have reasons, not amounting to proof, for faith). Third, the Church is transnational and should not be bribed by privilege into subserving merely national interests. Fourth, the appearance of privilege arouses moral indignation amongst outsiders, and Church faith is seen as somehow cheating. This is a disastrous face with which the faith looks out on the world. Fifth, the most fruitful reassessments of Christian self-expression arise from situations where pluralism is recognized and dialogue is entered into.

REFERENCES

[1]See the rather depressing statistics about Anglican and Roman Catholic attitudes in George Moyser's chapter.

[2]I happen to be an Anglican and a Christian: I think the toleration displayed by the Anglican tradition well described, in its modern forms, in Gerald Parsons' chapter.

[3]It is this sense which is displayed by Paul Badham in his treatment of secular trends in the Church of England.

[4]See Christie Davies' chapter on the reasons for traditionalists' fear of homosexual permissiveness as undermining national moral fibre: and the nationalist ramifications of the Northern Irish conflict are alluded to in Bill McSweeney's contribution.

[5]Even Wales long had the problem of a Minority Established Church: see the chapter by William Price for its present slightly muddled situation. Also ecumenical establishmentarianism bears unkindly on sects and "new religions" as Bryan Wilson and Eileen Barker indicate.

[6]So also was Catholicism overtly transnational, hence suspicion of it in times gone by. But now Catholics are more "tamed" as M. Hornsby Smith points out.

A NOTE TO THE CONTRIBUTORS

Gerald Parsons is Lecturer in Religious Studies at The Open University, Milton Keynes, England.

Rev. Dr. Paul Badham is Chairman of Religion and Ethics, and Reader in Theology and Religious Studies at Saint David's University College, Lampeter, Wales.

Rev. William Price is Chairman of Church History and Senior Lecturer in History, Saint David's University College, Lampeter, Wales.

Rev. Peter Bisset is Warden of St. Ninian's Center, Crieff, Scotland.

Dr. Michael Hornsby-Smith is Senior Lecturer in Sociology at the University of Surrey.

Dr. Bill McSweeney is Head of the Department of Peace Studies at the Irish School of Ecumenics, Dublin, Northern Ireland.

Dr. David Thompson is a Fellow of Fitzwilliam College, and Lecturer in Modern Church History at the University of Cambridge, England.

Rev. Iain MacRobert is Principal Lecturer at Sandwell College of Further and Higher Education, England and Secretary General of the Centre for Black and White Christian Partnership, Selly Oak, Birmingham, England.

Canon Dr. Edward Bailey is Rector of Winterbourne, Bristol, England, and Governor of the Network for the Study of Implicit Religion.

Dr. Bryan Wilson, Fellow of All Souls, and Reader in Sociology at the University of Oxford, England.

Dr. Eileen Barker is Senior Lecturer in Sociology and Dean of Undergraduate Studies at the London School of Economics and Political Science, London, England.

Rabbi Dan Cohn-Sherbok is Director of the Centre for the Study of Religion and Society based at the University of Kent at Canterbury, England.

Dr. Jorgen S. Nielsen is Director of Islamic Studies at the Centre for the study of Islam and Christian-Muslim Relations, Selly Oak Colleges, Birmingham, England.

Dr. Kim Knott is Research Fellow in Theology and Religious Studies at the University of Leeds, England.

Dr. W. Owen Cole is Principal Lecturer and Head of Religious Studies at the West Sussex Institute of Higher Education, England.

Rev. Dr. Deidre Green is Lecturer in Religious Studies at Saint David's University College, Lampeter, Wales.

Rev. Dr. Myrtle Langley is Diocesan Missioner, Liverpool, and Honorary Lecturer in the Department of Theological Studies, University of Manchester, England.

Professor Christie Davies is Professor of Sociology at the University of Reading, England.

Dr. George Moyser is Professor of Political Science at the University of Vermont, U.S.A.

Professor Ninian Smart is Professor of Religious Studies at the University of Lancaster, England, and the University of California, Santa Barbara, U.S.A.; and is Honorary Professor of Religious Studies at Saint David's University College, Lampeter, Wales.

TEXTS AND STUDIES IN RELIGION

35. André Séguenny, **The Christology of Caspar Schwenckfeld: Spirit and Flesh in the Process of Life Transformation**, Peter C. Erb and Simone S. Nieuwolt (trans.)

36. Donald E. Demaray, **The Innovation of John Newton (1725-1807): Synergism of Word and Music in Eighteenth Century Evangelism**

37. Thomas Chase, **The English Religious Lexis**

38. R.G. Moyles, **A Bibliography of Salvation Army Literature in English 1865-1987**

39. Vincent A. Lapomarda, **The Jesuits and the Third Reich**

40. Susan Drain, **The Anglican Church in the 19th Century Britain: Hymns Ancient and Modern (1860-1875)**

41. Aegidius of Rome, **On Ecclesiastical Power: De Ecclesiastica Potestate**, Arthur P. Monahan (trans.)

42. John R. Eastman, **Papal Abdication in Later Medieval Thought**

43. Paul Badham (ed.), **Religion, State, and Society in Modern Britain**

44. Hans Denck, **Selected Writings of Hans Denck, 1500-1527**, E. J. Furcha (trans.)

45. Dietmar Lage, **Martin Luther on the *Imitatio Christi* and *Conformitas Christi* and Their Relationship To Good Works**

46. Jean Calvin, *Sermons on Jeremiah by Jean Calvin*, Blair Reynolds (trans.)

47. Jean Calvin, *Sermons on Micah by Jean Calvin*, Blair Reynolds (trans.)

48. Alexander Sándor Unghváry, **The Hungarian Protestant Reformation in the Sixteenth Century Under the Ottoman Impact: Essays and Profiles**

49. Daniel B. Clendenin & W. David Buschart (ed.), **Scholarship, Sacraments and Service: Historical Studies in Protestant Tradition** *Essays in Honor of Bard Thompson*